SACRA S0-AUI-462
828 "I" Street
Sacramento, CA 95814
02/16

TIMEWALKER FOREVER
IN SEARCH OF A WOMAN'S LOVE

Roy Allan Kellosalmi

 www.trafford.com

North America & international
toll-free: 1 888 232 4444 (USA & Canada)
fax: 812 355 4082

The following is dedicated
to every loving mother.

Thanks go to the patient, dedicated research staff at the Kelowna branch of Okanagan Regional Library (downtown), whose many hours spent in lending valued assistance I could not have done without. Also, the kind people at the Vernon branch of ORL were quite helpful in researching some last-minute facts for the final draft of this book. Thanks go to them as well.

This book is also a tribute to every other poor soul who has suffered torture or lasting injury at the hands of any department, agency, or institution of government—and consequently, had his or her life severely and irrevocably impacted, then—in an effort to obtain truth and rightful compensation for pain, psychological trauma, or bodily injury incurred, experienced the same public entity stonewall the victim and lie to the victim in the government body's members' bid to conceal the truth, truth—in place of which they've provided to the victim documentation where some telling fabrications they've later failed to account for have been rendered. And for what little it may be worth to each victim who has been tortured by government and by government blinded of its sense been driven to attempt suicide (as I was once), and as a result undergone a near-death experience—I extend my deepest sympathy. As for those unfortunates who've encountered torture, and owing to that torture died at the hands of government—I hope their souls rest in peace, away from harm forever.

That declaration issues from my horrific, twice almost fatal experiences in Canada with the British Columbia Government's Interior Health Authority (IHA)—the regional bureaucracy of the southern interior in this province's Ministry of Health Services. Bearing on my body the ugly scarring from an old wound and in my mind the eternal psychological scars relating to that injury and its aftermath and the circumstances that led to the injury, regarding that last near-demise, it is my firm belief that owing to an action of a certain member of the IHA and the immediately prior action of the member's directing, independent medical practitioner (providing services to the public through that organization) I've suffered a permanent physical disability and undergone an incalculable amount of needless suffering, lost property and finances—and submitted to me under the province's Freedom of Information legislation is the documentation containing those notably untrue statements I refer to above. Yet I plod onward, my quest for truth, and compensation, *fair* compensation, from the IHA through the British Columbia Government, and from all involved in this matter, will continue. At a fundamental level my quest is a drive for both transparency and justice.

This page-long addition to the existing text was entered here April 3, 2013.

"TRUTH"

Truth be a silver sparrow

Whose wings beat steady in the night

Braving through thick and narrow

Never gone come daylight

— the author

Author's Note

My preference in having adopted simplicity of language wherever I reasonably could in this work, is representative of speech I used as the small boy I once was. It is plain writing unadorned by the artificialness derived of age and sophistication, a use of language unaffected by the choking halter of convention which really has made it essential for my purpose—a lifelike narrative of my childhood years. It was precisely because of this intent to keep my writing age-related, that in many instances throughout this book I've not conformed to a practice writers are taught to adhere to, that of elimination of unnecessary words in writing. You will, in good measure, see the word *of* (or *that*) used where the sentences do not require it; *the* appears rarely in like fashion and *which* regularly. (In the pages ensuing, the aforesaid are also used to lend emphasis.) Many would question the writer who writes in this way, but young children are first taught to speak and write in complete sentences, only later are they taught to do away with excess. In "voluntary" applications herein, these words, *of, that, the* and *which* slow the pace of the script, allowing the reader to *sense* this writer as though I were often still a young child, enthusiastically intent upon telling the world my life story, employing the manner that my teachers had taught me—"Write *clearly* as though you are *speaking.*"

However, my teachers had further cautioned me: "Write only in complete sentences, not in fragments of sentences."

But the ideals of the young are prone to decline tradition—although that realization is likely to be in regard to solely this book. As with the other component of proper language use deviated from in the passages soon to follow, in telling the story with a child's simple mind the rules sometimes have to be broken to achieve a realistic effect. After all, the script is oft being conveyed to the readers as though a child *is* telling the story through the veil of a grown-up's understanding.

The frequent utilization of fragments, which virtually anyone who has ever written a book has sought to avoid, create dramatic presence via sudden impact. *Timewalker Forever* contains more than a few such entries, else I would not have cause to mention it.

In closing here, I must apprise you that in possessive use the *'s* or *s'* normally occurring at the end of the first word of a pair I've sometimes opted to forgo in order to impart to my writing a feel of informality, for, it is through the free flow of words that this is best expressed.

I rest my case. In your hands now, dear readers, is the power to judge what I've written.

FOREWORD

I have had the privilege and pleasure to read the works of some of the greatest fiction-writers of all time who'd ever put pen to paper. These works have enriched and inspired me to at last become a writer myself. Classics and old favorites such as Jack London's *The Call of the Wild* and *White Fang*, Ernest Seton's *The Biography of a Grizzly*, Howard Pyle's *Men of Iron*, Erich Remarque's *All Quiet on the Western Front*, and twenty-six magnificent novels of one Edgar Rice Burroughs' creation—the *Tarzan of the Apes* series—are but some of the very best literary works I have come across. In particular, *Tarzan, Lord of the Jungle* and *Tarzan and the City of Gold* struck a deep emotional chord in me. To my boy's mind long ago, both of these books were filled with high adventure and romance as was every Tarzan novel written by Burroughs. But these two works of his were unmistakably superb in quality. The writing in them possessed kind of a poetic grace, a silky-smooth rhythm linking each word to the next. As he always did, Burroughs displayed impeccable skill in choosing his words with the utmost care. Words which conveyed his intended meaning precisely—words, mere words, which leapt into vibrant being at the magical touch of his accomplished pen. Now, having so praised the artistic wizardry of Edgar Burroughs, it may surprise you to learn that my favorite work of all was not written by him. No, the best book of all, I thought, was *Shane*, written by Jack Schaeffer. However, every one of these aged publications, the bulk of which are available exclusively by special order, is very good, and some, like *Shane*, are literary masterpieces. In my view, *Shane* shall stand alone for all time—unequaled in the language of emotion. *Timewalker Forever* is my first book, and, as an autobiography, when understood in its entirety, it is an accurate account of my boyhood experiences. And I sincerely hope you all shall enjoy it.

R.A. Kellosalmi

Chapter One

FROM EARLY IN MY EXISTENCE when the world seemed a younger place, I remember the harsh reality of my life in Campbell River, British Columbia. I remember the smooth well-worn gray and brown rocks hugging the seashore and the sound of lapping waves against the rock-and-sand beach. I remember, too, the raucous noise that the gulls would make as they swept by shore in search of fish in the ocean. The pungent smell of rotting kelp lingered in the air and would have delighted any true sailor.

Then a man of six years in age, my analysis of personal events has not changed much through time. But my perspective of life in general has. I relate to you something of my boyhood, and the events that helped make me what I am today.

Our family lived in a single-story building of gray brick; our rented quarters were almost next door to the main thoroughfare now known as the Old Island Highway. It was a commercial complex with just three businesses. A television-repair shop was situated beside my father's motor-rewinding enterprise, with a car wash on our other side. Our building was drab. And slightly run-down, due to age and the elements. It wasn't so bad as to be called a dump. It was a few shades above that. There were five of us living in this cramped, dreary, spartan abode of gray. There was: my father, Arvo Kellosalmi; my dear mother, Lempi, who father always called Lena; big brother, Raimo; older sister, Helen, and of course—me.

1

Mother worked at the Beehive, a small restaurant whose back alley faced the Pacific Ocean. The Beehive stood one short city block away from us. Just a skip and a holler as any seafaring man would tell you. Or a nice man by the name of Skip McDonald, who was the proprietor and head cook.

The Beehive was a popular, and thus, busy eatery owing to its many local patrons. And during summer tourist season, sport fishermen from the U.S. frequented the establishment. The atmosphere between Skip and his employees, as with his customers, was more relaxed and friendlier than that at the always bustling Discovery Inn, further down main street from us, where mother had worked briefly a short while before.

And now, please take a big breath. You are entering the memory of my perilous past. When I was three, mother called me by a nickname. "Happy." She also called me by another pet name. "Oje." Oje, pronounced oy-ye, doesn't mean a single thing. This was but a name, which, as a baby, I'd invented for myself. In time, both of these names were lost along with the changing seasons.

Now, I have no doubt that I was quite content at the age of three. Since I was called Happy by my very own mother, I must have been. Anyhow, I shall not disagree with mother upon this point.

I only know that in 1965 at Campbell River, which was then just a small town located midway up the scenic east coast of Vancouver Island, I was, at the age of six and later seven, blissfully engaged in an activity of pure profit. My motivation was sincere. I simply wished to be fabulously rich. To achieve this end bit-by-bit someday, or so I hoped then, me and Helen, she—five years my senior at eleven years of age, would conduct forays onto the restricted premises of the local supermarket. Canada Safeway Limited.

This meant the fenced outdoor enclosure containing all the empty pop bottles that had been returned by customers to the store. Me and Helen would always raid the pen and scoop out the bottle cases by the half-dozen. Then we would immediately return them to the store and pocket the deposit money, that had just been cheerfully "refunded" to us.

I was, naturally, totally innocent. I maintain that my free will to decide between right and wrong was distorted by my tender age and my partner's influence and motivation. You may disagree.

Helen was anxious to remain free of prosecution, in the event that we were caught. She'd always make sure that if our daring operation did go awry, she would be able to make a quick getaway. Being eleven years old, Helen was wily enough to delegate the riskiest task to me, whose job it was to hand her the bottle cases from inside the open pen.

My given duty necessitated my climbing five feet over the fence, which was chainlink, and then, back over it to freedom. Had we ever been discovered, matters could have taken a very unfortunate turn for me; in an emergency then, there is no slightest shred of doubt in my mind now, as to who would have been left behind to face the music.

Helen justified the act of theft, by reason that her pet feline, Tiger, had to be provided for. My parents were working hard to make ends meet. They could not afford the extra expense of feeding another body, even though it was just a small house-cat.

Being no quick study in most things, I nevertheless mastered quickly the ins and outs of stealing pop bottles. But, in the absence of my sister, the supermarket was a long way for a little boy to travel from home. Vehicle traffic on main street in town was brisk. And I hadn't quite enough nerve to cross the street without my sister being present. Nor was I yet allowed to do so by my parents. It was especially mother who worried about my safety whilst she remained oblivious of my less than honorable intention.

So I did what my entrepreneurial spirit told me to do. I shifted my pop bottle operations—legitimate in the case of bottles I happened to find on the ground or buried amidst trash in a Dumpster, and the bottles that I stole, to the immediate neighborhood.

One day, midmorning in late August, the roof on the sporting goods store, Lavers, where Raimo worked part-time, was undergoing total renovation. Lavers' near side fronted on AC/DC Electric, my father's shop. The young roofer, who was probably a decent hardworking fellow, had only one careless habit. He liked to drink pop and in turn would leave each successive bottle, half full of beverage, *on* the sidewalk. He would leave each new bottle at the base of a ladder propped up against Lavers, on the side of that same building which faced main street.

And, in so doing, he made a mistake that cost him. I'd spotted an opportunity and had moved in. Every time I would empty the half full bottle on the sidewalk, and walk off with the treasure.

The supermarket paid a good price for pop bottles. The staff there never asked questions, either. Two cents for the smaller bottles and five cents for the large. I was well on my way to getting rich.

I sincerely hope that the poor roofer, an unwilling participant in my grand plan for future wealth then, did not die of thirst in the summer heat.

One noon hour, I walked into the boat-repair shop behind our place. The men who worked in the shop were seated atop stools, enjoying their lunch break. They were a rough-looking lot. All four of them. And I had to dig deep within me to find the nerve to ask them this. I inquired about three two-cent pop bottles, that lay empty on a counter.

It was then that one of the men, a kind sort he seemed to me, smiled. He got up from his seat and bent down, kneeling in front of me. We were eye to eye. I could see that he was almost as old as my father. "Son," he said. "You sing us a song and we'll give you the pop bottles for free."

I obliged. I sang "Ten Little Indians" to them. My voice was strained a little from embarrassment, yet I managed to finish the song. The men responded with an eager round of applause, and I walked off with the bottles. The bottle business was easy for me to manage. A smooth swim all the way.

THE GREAT DIFFICULTY OF MY LIFE was learning how to fish. On one calm sunny morning, a Saturday it was at summer's end, father outfitted me with a bamboo rod, complete with a reel, fishline, and an artificial lure. And as father was too busy tending to his motors, he dispatched me on my mission—to catch a fish—solo. I assumed that any fish would do. Big and smelly, teeny or . . . It didn't matter. Just so long as I caught the fish all by myself, as father wished. By trial and error.

I walked out to the shoreline behind the boat-repair shop and wetted my line, having cast the line as far as I could. But the rod had not been made for a small boy to wield, and my cast had fallen into the salty sea only a dozen feet from shore. Not to be denied a fish, I reeled my line in and cast again. Over and over again, I did. And always, my cast fell short of deep water.

Positively, this was disturbing for me as I could clearly see some tiny fish, each of these about the size of a goldfish, darting in and out from the nearshore to the deep water. Right in front of my eyes. I could appreciate the obvious reluctance of the fish to bite. Put in the proper perspective, who, in his right mind, would try to swallow bait his own size? These fish were not total idiots. Perhaps they all had gone to fish school and thereby learned about fishermen, I thought: that fishermen who catch fish—eat fish. Almost everyone had to go to school. Maybe even fish.

As my child's mind mulled over that matter, I decided to try my luck for one last time. As I had before, I reeled my line in and moved my rod behind me for leverage, in the motion of a fisherman, a motion that I'd seen my father assume when he had been fishing. To be fair to the fish, who were proving worthy opponents, I admit that I was quite frustrated and I'd verily hurled my fishline up and behind me.

It was then, in trying to cast, that I became aware of something. I realized that I could not move my line forward. And I knew that I could not move my line forward because my hook was stuck hard—in what?

As I further tugged on my line, I knew that whatever it was that I had caught, it was of considerable size and weight. More than just a fair catch—it was huge. And when I tried turning about in an attempt to find out more, whatever it was, moved even as I moved. Perplexing! It was only when I attempted to cast again that I became aware, from the telltale tug on the seat of my pants, that I had fallen far short of father's expectation and hooked my own behind!

Many a father would have laughed himself silly over such incompetence. Not father. Always stern of face, he did so not a whit as he removed the sharp point of the fishhook from my pants. In the end, the only thing that was damaged was my pride.

A major problem in my life was school. The other major problem in my life was learning to tie my shoelaces so that I could get there. I and Helen attended Cedar Elementary, which was about a mile-long walk from our shop. Now, I'd like to think that I am not retarded. Yet, learning how to tie my shoelaces took much time to figure out. V-E-R-Y much. "After you cross your laces, make two loops and cross them again," mother told me. But I have never been much good at following directions (see? I'm not dumb?). I prefer to experiment by myself. And at last, my persistence paid off. I learned.

Too, the color of my running shoes, a stunning bright red, nearly got me into a fight at school. Not only that, but for some inexplicable reason, it seemed to me way back then, mother had bought me girl's running shoes. At least, being bright red, they sure looked to me like girl's running shoes. If these shoes were meant to be gender-neutral, I didn't know it. That's right, because they were, as I say, a girl's color—red. As such, I reasoned that these shoes were suitable for only girls to wear. Not boys.

This was exactly what one young lad in my class at school, a kid who wished to bring me trouble, thought also. And it was fortunate for him, a bespectacled seven-year-old, that he withdrew his loud public complaint to my classmates after I stood up to him. A wise choice for him. The unruly fellow had claimed that my wearing "girl's" running shoes, which, incidentally, mother had purchased at a department store sale, and, which were the best value that she'd found for her money, demeaned his fledgling manhood. How? I knew not; but the young fellow made the right decision in having shut his yap before it would've landed him in trouble. Had he not done so, I would have had no choice but to see whether I could shut it for him. I knew how to fight.

School was another matter. I could not adapt to the necessities of survival. Reading, writing, and arithmetic were a major headache. Because my performance in school was dismal, with grade failure likely if intervention was not swift, my parents sought out the help of my older siblings. Originally immigrants from Finland, mother and father were not fluent in the English language. Therefore, mother and father never tried to tutor me. Very unfortunate and fortunate for me this was then, because after my scalp hair was yanked a couple times with considerable force by my older brother—I strove mightily to learn the basics of civilized culture.

And though my progress was very slow at first, ponderously I began to acquire a rudimentary knowledge of spelling words in English, and along with it, the ability to read and pronounce words correctly. However, not before I had lost more than a few strands of hair.

I still remember those early English lessons as though it were but yesterday. I still remember reading about a peppy little boy called Dick, and a peppy little girl named Jane, and a peppy little dog, christened Spot, and a peppy little cat, Puff, happily run. All of my peppy friends. Peppy.

As for the unfortunate loss of hair that I suffered so young, I have this to say. Maybe this is why I now have a terrible fear of aging, and, of slowly becoming as bald, someday, as the lunar landscape. And if I ever do, I shall blame and curse my brother first. Then I will check the yellow pages of my phone book to find myself a good hair-transplant surgeon. Or get myself a glue-on hairpiece and affix it to my scalp with Zany Gloo.

Also, I received Raimo's worst regards for a then obscure reason. But fifteen-or-so years after 1965, Raimo recalled the curious manner in which I had behaved at the ages of six and seven on those rare days when I did not receive some unpleasantness at his hands. Raimo said of this time that I had, "always run around confused, in a state of nervous being all day". I, seemingly expectful of corporal punishment to be levied upon me, I behaving as though I knew not at all what course of activity to pursue during the unoccupied hours of my day. According to Raimo, my odd behavior at this early age in life would never remit until the morrow then—when I was sure to garner a licking from him. I suppose that for my brother, his observation serves as his slick attempt to belatedly justify to me his physical and emotional abuse of myself during my raw years of childhood.

Back in grade one and part of grade two, numbers confused me more than the English language did. Reading, writing and arithmetic. All three were doggoned difficult for me to learn. But arithmetic. This subject was the worst.

I did not like to think about numbers in school. Nor at home. Nor anywhere between school and home. I did not like to think about numbers at all. Well—almost. I did not like to think about numbers except when I cashed in the deposit from the odd pop bottle that I'd found along the beach or in a back alley, or that I'd stolen. And, when I happened to find a loose coin lying about somewhere.

With this being the case then, it should be very strange and inexplicable that I would then be the least bit fascinated by the most intimidating number in the world of numbers then. An imposing number, yes. A quantity called googol. We've all heard of googol, I'm sure. I often

8

called this number, "The Great Google". Yes, my interest in google then, should be very strange and inexplicable—but it's not.

My brother had wetted my interest by way of a contrivance. A challenge, or so I figured. A challenge that I simply could not resist contesting. My brother, you see, is a foxy fellow. After telling me about googol, how this number is bigger than any number that I could imagine, I am sure that you will understand why it was literally impossible for me, not to challenge my brother.

In my long life I had stood up to a kid who had peed my pants wet from behind. I shall tell you about that shortly. I had yet to stand up to mean-spirited dogs, bent upon tearing my leg off. Aye, that was to come. And it is true that I had not attempted to steal another man's wife. That was still to come too. But my point is this. What was a mere number to me?

My hands did not tremble at all as I tore a sheet of unlined paper loose from mother's writing pad. I then sat down at the kitchen table and proceeded to draw. I drew as many zeroes as I could fit on the face of the sheet. I then turned the sheet over and covered the back side with zeroes as well. Having finished my task, I promptly queried of my wise older brother: "Is this a googol?"

I showed Raimo both sides of my sheet of paper. For a moment my brother stared at the sheet. Seemingly, blankly. Then his coconut-powered brain appeared to kick itself into gear. "No," my brother said. "That is not a googol."

I tore twenty sheets of paper from mother's writing block and sat down at the kitchen table a second time. I ground my elbows into the tabletop for another try to unseat my nemesis, googol. This time, I figured I'd succeed. And all of that day, which happened to be a Sunday, I labored in silence. I would not eat. I would not speak. Googol was my enemy.

From the morning onward, into the evening, I drew untold numbers of zeroes, and I drew them as small as I could make them. I drew them tiny, so that I could fit them all onto both sides of my sheets of paper. Darkness was coming on and I was finished. Now I was a hundred percent sure that I had cornered the mysterious number called googol, by the scruff of its neck. I was sure that I had beaten googol.

I had worn out my pencil by repeatedly sharpening it with my pocketknife. Capturing the elusive quantity googol was a very time-consuming and expensive pursuit. But I was a hunter. And—googol—was the hunted. Now, with my work finished, I was ready to pounce on googol. Now—I would own victory. A small victory, many folks might say. Yet a victory. An accomplishment that I could be proud of in my ripe old age when I would turn eight years old. And I could tell all of my classmates at school about my deed.

My brother was sitting atop a stool in one corner of our shop, he engrossed in reading the comics in *The Vancouver Sun*. Tapping him lightly on one shoulder, I asked him the all-important question. Is this a googol? As I showed Raimo the fruit of my hard, daylong labor, I smiled confidently, self-assured of my victory.

"No," said Raimo. This, with level voice. Not the barest trace of interest in his tone. "It is not a googol."

The air in my chest came rushing out, and I must have looked like I was stifling a sob. "It's not a googol?" I stared out into space in disbelief, nearly thinking that I had heard my brother announce his verdict wrong.

"No," said Raimo again. Mechanically. As disinterestedly this time it seemed as he had the first. "It is not a googol."

"Well," said I. "How big is this googol anyway?"

"Oh," my brother replied as his calm gaze reverted to the newspaper's comic section. "It's big." He was probably reading the comic strip *Archie*, which, along with *Tarzan*, was a favorite of his. And if he was reading *Archie*, he was, I bet myself, probably looking at Veronica or Betty in a swimsuit. I couldn't be sure that he was because I couldn't fully see over the newspaper with its upturned pages.

My brother harbored at school no girlfriend I knew about. And I knew that there was no one hiding beneath his bed at home. I knew this because I had looked there before. There was, however, one blonde cutie from his high school (I never knew the name of the school that Raimo attended), who worked at the Beehive, alongside mother who worked there as a waitress and cook.

This girl's name was Christy. And it was from mother I had learned that Christy had apparently taken a shine to my brother. Why? Search me. Girls! Who can understand their preferences? I couldn't, back then. Now me. I, on the other hand, was a full-grown and able-bodied man. Back to uh, numbers.

Seeing that my brother was likely engrossed in the matter of love, I left him. Much to his liking, I'm sure. You have to understand. He was at that strange age. An age where absolute secrecy is a must when reading the newspaper. Big. The word stuck in my small mind. What could possibly be bigger than big?

There were only two possible answers. I was beginning to grasp the concept of googol just now. Googol was either a very, very large number, or it was infinity—something that no number could ever rival. But I didn't know which of these possibilities googol was.

Outdoors, I looked at the blinking light of the stars that night when the clouds drifted apart enough to permit my inspection of them. My sharp eyes, seldom still when I was awake, saw numbers and numbers of stars. Pinpoints of light against a backdrop of cosmic blackness. A sea of stars. I knew not much about stars. I only knew that like our local star the sun, which I did not think of as being a star at all back then, stars could pretty much be counted on to have been sitting where they sit in the night sky for almost forever. I knew that forever was a long time.

Forever, like googol, was too large for me to fit into my life. My life was made of little things. Like dimes and nickels and pennies. And seashells. And little rocks. And my prized collection of postage stamps. I was starting to get sleepy just thinking about it all.

The clouds rolled under the blanket of stars as I went back inside our shop, brushed my teeth, undressed, and put on my pajamas. I was fast asleep. Snuggled peacefully beneath my own warm blanket. In my own bed. And I was already dreaming when mother kissed my forehead, as she did every night when she bid me a goodnight. And the dreams I dreamed were warm pleasant dreams. Dreams that were meant only for me to dream.

I THOUGHT THAT MY SCHOOLING, both in the classroom and at home, was hard, but let me tell you non-classroom time at school was not always a walk in the park, either. Having too much free time on my hands then, and not knowing what to do with it, could have meant serious trouble.

Unwisely, I once took it upon myself to eradicate a nest of wasps living out in the brush beside my school. This incident happened on a frosty morning in early fall. Right before the start of class.

Perhaps I fancied myself to be a hands-on, pest-management sort of guy. With no concern for my safety, I brazenly attacked the wasp homeworld, a hive attached to a low bush growing at the base of a large rotting tree stump, with a short, but stout, tree branch. It was just like me to be like this. I oft neglected to think much ahead. I only did. And with this weapon, the tree branch, a tool possibly quite formidable for a singular purpose like digging the chocolate-colored crap out of one's behind in an emergency (yes, I never did try this poopy experiment, and thus I am unable to rate the effectiveness of a stick for such purpose), events could easily have proven disastrous for yours truly.

After I had hacked at the hive for but seconds with my stick then, the wasps, still groggy from the unwelcome early morning arousal—came swarming out of the strewn wreckage that now remained of their home. In all fairness to my stuporous small foes, those poor buggers had no choice except to greet me with open hostility. Those of them that survived my rude surprise, that is. Being abruptly evicted from one's home is one thing. Having one's home demolished, right in front of one's eyes, is quite another.

Oh, the wasps did get to me. I ended up taking a dozen stings in all. And the only thing that had saved me from worse was a swift pair of feet.

My hands, which had borne the brunt of the wasps' fury, were soon swelling and red at each bite-site. This, while my face and neck had attracted just a few bites between them. I had, however, also suffered grievous misfortune about the lower extremities, where some of the more adventurous and, in fact, flagrantly kamikaze personalities amongst the wasp fraternity, not one of which had been notably shy in expressing its feelings when roused to self-defense of its home, had seen fit to execute a strategic and often suicidal course in their venturing up each of my trousers' legs.

For myself, the inescapable result was that the area from where the protective cover of my socks ended, up to where my thin cotton brief began, I'd not been spared their hatred of me. Even so, I would yet consider myself lucky in one regard. This was that my second-grade teacher, Mrs. Case, didn't know of this and my other extracurricular activities about the schoolyard.

I spoke of crap. Excrement is actually the proper word. I have had daunting experiences with urine too, implying in that that I've had bad luck with muck. I am going to describe for you the incident I referred to earlier.

I remember one day in the fall of 1965. This happened about the same time in my life that my altercation with the wasp enclave took place. It was midmorning and recess time at school. Feeling heavy, I proceeded to the boys' lavatory and selected a urinal. I unzipped my fly.

The relief of the yellow stream exiting my body fairly lulled me into a false feeling of security. I thought that I was alone in the boys' washroom. I was not. It was only when I heard a rude laugh behind me and simultaneously felt a warm presence on my buttocks that I realized just what was occurring.

One of the fellows in my class, a joker named Larry—and he was a boy whose surname I'd never know, was using my rear end as his urinal! Realizing this, I instantly zipped up and, in the same motion I turned about and gave chase to the fleeing culprit. Please make no mistake. I fully intended to kill the boy.

Larry must have had a pretty good idea as to what he could expect from me in retribution. Much to my chagrin then, although I pursued Larry all over the school grounds the fleet-footed imp ran with the desperation of a boy condemned to death—and Larry, as much as I still hate to admit it today, outdistanced me. My-oh-my, what rampant fear will do to the wicked!

For the rest of that day in class I had to endure a soggy, smelly behind. From that day onward Larry did his utmost to stay out of the lethal grasp of my clutches. And, mortified as I was, I could not bring myself to tell Mrs. Case about Larry.

Wherever he may be today, I certainly hope that Larry does not rest easy for his ill deed of long ago. I still keep one eye peeled about me whenever I visit a public restroom. I, knowing that Larry, or someone like Larry, might be there, lurking, waiting.

LIVING INSIDE A COMMERCIAL BUILDING has its drawbacks. One of these is hygiene. To each member of our family, personal hygiene was a luxury which had to be sacrificed.

Of course, hygiene didn't really matter to father, who willingly cleansed himself from head to toe just once each week. And though hygiene mattered a lot to mother—her sentiment was not considered by father. Yes, our family bathed once per week. But not in our tiny washroom, which had only a sink with cold and hot running water. And a toilet.

Unable to rid ourselves of body grease and odor in our premises, we Kellosalmis did the only thing that we could under father's wanting leadership. We washed in a Finnish sauna. Just outside of town. In a spacious though somewhat crude structure which had been built by our friends, the Lokren family.

I shall have you folks know that the Lokrens were a family that we hardly knew. But amongst themselves Finnish people are known for their hospitality. That openness was fortunate for our family's bathing needs. Being that we scarcely knew these folks, my description of them is predictably lacking. I will say that our hosts were a happy couple of my parents' generation, who, like mother and father, were not childless. This is all that I know of them.

As I said before, there were three business operations in our building block. My family's relations with the Dewhursts were excellent. An elderly man and his wife, the Dewhursts ran the TV-repair shop I told you about, next to us and right next to main street.

Very friendly folks the Dewhursts were. The couple even invited all of us over to their house for dinner once. Nice folks.

The owners of the other enterprise, the car wash on our other flank, were far less amiable. For sure. I am unable to recollect the name of the car wash. Nor do I remember the names of the folks who ran the place.

What I do remember, is that on one weekend morning while I was playing with sis on the gravel parking lot in front of our building, the car wash neighbors' two boys came by, spoiling for a fight. They were, without question, looking for trouble. Only trouble.

The scrawny, sandy-haired, self-proclaimed elder of the pair, who I took to be about my age because his weasellike eyeballs stood at the same height as my eyes, wanted to fight me. And in hurling insults at me and Helen he'd wasted no time. (Back then, I referred to this odious practice of insulting one's foe as name-calling, and of course that is what it is.) Too—true to his challenge he was quick to make his attack.

With his (so-called) younger (and slightly bigger) brother looking on, the punk came at me, spitting in my face and intent on shoving me back—in an attempt to get me off balance. I heard Helen's shrill war-whoop ring in the air, and my sister's words of encouragement as she urged me onward.

However, my attention was by then almost entirely riveted on my adversary. In fact, from this point onward 'twould sure seem to me for a while that my sister had become just a passive onlooker. With no immediate help from that quarter forthcoming, I'd already dug my heels into the gravel—and let loose with my fists in what was the first real fight of my young life.

And it was Fate, a debatable quantity some folks believe, which smiled on me that day as I swiftly repelled my assailant with a flurry of bone-hard punches to his face. After less than a minute of being under siege, the boy decided that he had experienced enough. He then tried to withdraw from the fight. But I was angry at him because he'd attacked me. I pressed forward, relentless, sensing victory, and determined to teach the rascal a lesson he'd never forget.

I punched in his nose. And now, as the frustration of defeat played in his eyes, the bigger boy jumped in, no doubt fully intending, from his scowling demeanor I judged, to beat my brains out. Like his brother, he was a bloodthirsty sucker—I'll give him that much. And the two would surely have overpowered me. But. It was not to be.

Pricked by her conscience perhaps or for some other reason (I may never know which), seeing that the two were about to hand me a shellacking, it was then that Helen decided to step into the fight and, well, basically, save my hide. Helen simply pushed both of my attackers back. An easy feat for sis, considering that she outstripped these boys in height by a good foot and a half.

The day was done. Those buggers would never dare to bother us again. Us, being the key word.

Their sudden change of heart did nothing to dissuade Helen and me from doing the unstoppable. And dump we did their cherished, stinky, old inflatable rubber dinghy, which sat above the timber breakwater overlooking the ocean, straight into the sea. Then we heaped a great many rocks from shore onto the raft until it sank. After, of course, we (sis) had pulled the plug on their boat to ensure that the air ran out of it. After all, in both love and battle, all be right. Right?

Unfortunately, as Fate, also known as chance, decided to have it, their pappy espied our mischievous act and began jumping up and down in the parking lot, twenty feet above us. We skedaddled.

Yet the poor guy. He had himself quite the tantrum. Raving his intense dislike for us, we feared not at all that his suspenders would give way and, that his pants would fall off.

Like his name, I have forgotten most of what the man said in the heat of his anger. But I still remember three choice words: "You cursed kids!" Given the sincerity of his impassioned performance then, nothing short of a brief tirade, I am inclined to think that if anyone had checked inside of his trousers that one might well have discovered that the fearsome fellow had crapped in his undershorts. Oh well. That's life. You just can't please everybody.

I later found the rubber dinghy airless on the beach, about a mile from home. And yes, I am sure that it was the same sorry boat that me and Helen had sent to its briny grave at the bottom of the ocean. How it had risen sphinxlike from the shallow depths and managed to travel such a distance sure beats me. Especially because of the large heavy stones that me and sis had piled on it.

Back then: Within myself, for a while I'd debate the question of whether the sins I shared with my sister had finally *caught up* to us. Did supernatural forces exist to account for the unexpected? I thought, if so, the only trouble is that the only person who I've *told* of my find, sis, does not believe in the occult.

What's wrong with an overly active imagination? All little boys have one.

Chapter Two

BACK IN THE DARK AGES I had meager experience of the world. Beyond the range of my limited experiences, I had, at seven years of age, no set philosophy to do with life. I knew not much about unemployment and its relationship to capitalism. I knew nothing about communism, that archenemy of the free market.

Because of my then complete lack of expertise regarding these two politically and economically competing systems, I really do not know how it was that I arrived at the intriguing conclusion that an unusual rock which I had discovered while walking along the beach, was a communist rock. It is true that I had heard father use the word communism to describe news events of the time. But I had no clue as to what the heck he'd been talking about. Ignorant I was. And for this reason, it is implausible that father's views influenced my mind.

The rock, you see, bore a striking resemblance to my father's head. In fact, father's exact facial features were cut into the stone, worn down by the elements over the ages. The ocean, a vast reservoir of timeless change, had worked its magic into the piece. Sand from the seabed had combined with water and tidal forces to manufacture this result. Looking at the rock, I dubbed it communist.

My family soon became aware of my newfound keepsake and, much to my amusement, they jokingly slipped the label on myself. I did not mind. As I say, I didn't even know what a communist was.

Some keepsakes are valuable. Real treasure always is. Speaking of treasure—I haven't told you of the time that I discovered Blackbeard's Grave. This is a title I now bestow on a trash bin then. Or precisely, the holy ground that surrounded it.

One day, while I was looking for pop bottles behind Lavers, I became tired and sat down atop a large flat rock. This rock lay right beside the Lavers' bin.

I had already checked the garbage for any articles with defects in them, articles that would have been discarded by the store's staff. Nothing. Looking down in the late afternoon sun, the gleam of reflected sunlight caught my eyes. Peering into the green carpet of tall, thick grass that grew like a miniature jungle all about my rock, I bent down further, and my keen eyes made out the round shape of a dime. Then, as I looked a short step beyond it I saw another dime. Then a nickel. A penny. A quarter! More pennies, nickels, and dimes. More quarters too.

Eagerly I scooped up the coins, as many as I could find. And pocketed them. I bent down on my knees in the grass, as my delighted eyes searched for more coins. But I could find no more. Even so, I had struck it rich. I could not contain my joy.

Immense joy. I jumped up, shouting "Treasure, treasure, treasure!" Then, as an afterthought, as I became aware that shouting my discovery to the whole wide world wasn't wise, I stopped.

I had to do something though. My energy level, fed by exuberance, would have registered a reading that was right off of any known chart. I began to run. I was running with a purpose. For home. And home was less than two hundred feet away.

I bounced in by our front door. Our only door. A rickety door that slammed shut as I tore into our shop.

My siblings were on hand. Seeing my beaming countenance, curious they were to be apprised of the reason for it. The story came spilling out of me. I dug my right hand into my pants' right side pocket, the front pocket, extracted my fist and opened it, showing my brother and sister the coins. A trove of wealth lay in the palm of my hand.

I counted the coins in no time. My find included thirty-nine pennies, twelve nickels, five dimes, and four quarters. Two dollars and forty-nine cents, in all. So many coins there were that they just barely fit into my palm.

Had I been wise, I would have kept my secret to myself. But this would have been asking too much of a small boy who was, at the time, very—very—very excited. In my enthusiasm to impart the good news to my brother and sister I was anything but wise.

Driven by the lust for instant wealth common to so many of us, plus her consuming need to provide for Tiger, the wretched, starving cat, Helen seized the opportunity and was soon hightailing her rear end toward the site of my find. Helen returned fifteen minutes later; she'd found fifty cents after she'd conducted a thorough inspection of the ground surrounding the Lavers' trash bin.

Alas for Helen and her hungry cat. When my brother became aware of her discovery, he made her fork her gain over to me. Much to my sister's dismay, Helen realized for the first time in her life that a crime of greed doesn't always pay. Finders jeepers. Losers—well?

I added my newfound wealth to my existing collection. This money, coins exclusively, I kept inside an M.J.B. coffee tin that father had modified.

Father had soldered the open end of the empty old coffee tin shut. An unconventional piggy bank, I'd received it complete with the slot at the top center that allowed coins of any size to be easily inserted. And unconventional it was, not only because my piggy bank did not resemble a pig, but because there was no way to extract coins from the tin except by using a flat-tip screwdriver or a coin or even a nail or sliver of wood to pry two underlying, flexible jaws of sheet metal apart at the spot that marked the slot.

The only other way, the legal way into the bank, was to let father have his way. He would open one end of the tin once my bank had amassed its share of hard currency and was full. I guess that father wished me to save my money for necessities later in life.

Still, father's ingenuity and wish were only an annoyance for me. It is true that father had altered into being the ultimate bank. The Alcatraz of piggy banks. Impenetrable to my devices, he thought. How wrong he was. The bank's design and solid construction did not deter me from robbing the bank.

I simply shoved any of the mentioned illicit means of entry between one end of the jaws. Then I turned the can upside down and shook it. As a coin would drop out of the can now and then, my patient efforts were always rewarded. I just had to make damn sure that no one, especially father, ever heard me shaking the can.

I used this money, stolen by myself from my own bank, to buy candy with. This was whenever my sweet tooth needed sustenance. And I would resort to this theft whenever I suffered a dry run of luck because there were no pop bottles to be found anywhere, to be cashed in for the deposit. Except, of course, those pop bottles which lay within the high-risk stockade at Safeway, usually in abundant supply.

I suppose that I could have made life much easier for myself had I not put all of the proceeds of my bottle operations into my piggy bank. But keeping a few loose coins in my pants' pocket, for a rainy day, would have deprived me of the immense satisfaction of breaking into my own bank.

ALMOST EVERY DAY I WOULD WANDER all over the shoreline after climbing down from the breakwater to the rocky beach. The breakwater, a structure built to withstand the ravages of the tide, was made of massive three-foot-thick logs, likely Douglas fir. A preservative had been applied to the logs, which lay horizontally, on one another. The wall of wood kept the tide at bay and thereby protected the parking lot above from erosion by the sea.

There were a variety of crabs inhabiting the countless crevices between the rocks. Crabs disgusted me. More so then than now. Because they are ugly, I still find crabs repugnant. But I used to be a little bit afraid of them. Or more accurately, their sharp, serrated pincers.

Resting at anchor, less than a hundred feet from shore, were both commercial fishboats and pleasure craft. These vessels were tied to wharves just a couple hundred feet from our shop. I largely ignored their existence. I have never had the slightest fascination for boats, be it any type of boat.

I was, and still am, a true sailorman. However, my preferred size and style of vessel is best exemplified when I splash about in water with a pumped-up car inner tube. And there ain't too many old-style seaworthy tubes like this in existence any more. Except in Henry Ford's museum. Nevertheless, I assure you that I am a real seaman. One worth his salt. A real pro.

You may gather from earlier in this narrative that I can ill afford to make the same boast about my ability to hook a fish. Even one the size of a goldfish. But my shortcoming to catch a fish will not deter me from telling you about the monster fish I once ran into, behind the boat-repair shop. A dogfish shark no less.

The dead shark, about four feet in length, had been left to decay on some oil drums. A shortened railway tie had been placed between the shark's upper and lower jaws, holding them apart and exposing two rows of giant saber-sharp teeth. The odor that rose from the carcass was horrible. And I didn't care to prod the corpse with a stick. The expired shark still looked quite menacing.

I knew that dogfish sharks were plentiful in the open water of the Strait of Georgia. Like all big fish, dogfish eat smaller fish. And they have an especial appetite for salmon, salmon—for which Campbell River is famous to sport fishing enthusiasts all over the world. Yet I, never a mighty fisherman as a kid, have later in life come to consider the so-called sport of killing, be it fishing or hunting, a cruel expression of our inner, primeval, instinct.

So much the sea fascinated me that, whenever there was a lull in the frequent rains and whenever I was not immersed in my after-school studies I would bide my time about the waterfront. And sometimes I would just daydream. On each outing I would survey the gray and brown colored rocks, discerning these from the strings of brown, bulbous kelp that washed up on shore, partly covering sand and rocks where they lay. Deep-green algae often hid blue mussel and clam shells. As a rule, if the shell was occupied I let it be. If it was open and empty, I collected it.

Visible, I took it to be—a couple of miles down the shoreline, was the steel hulk of a ship that had run aground years before. Half buried beneath the waves, only the top of the rusting giant wreck remained for human eyes to witness. A monument to the past that was slowly, inexorably, being claimed by the sea.

On this clear morning with the sunlight shimmering upon the water I could easily make out what I took to be a tugboat in the distance. About a mile offshore. As is customary with tugboats, this one appeared to be towing something in its wake. I did not even care to guess at what the likely object might be. With my naked eyes, I could not clearly make the suspect object out at this distance. I was walking, on this morn to the Beehive, while I kept my eyes riveted on the tug and the mystery object that seemed to break above the surface of the water for an instant, then disappear beneath the chop of water generated by the boat.

At the Beehive there was news awaiting me. This being a Saturday then, mother was there. And mother told me that the whole town was buzzing with excitement. The word was out that a killer whale had been captured at sea, and was now being escorted by boat to an unknown destination.

Many years later I learned that this whale had been bought by the Seattle Marine Aquarium to which it had been transported in a floating pen. Dubbed Namu—for the tiny central-coast B.C. community nearest to where it was captured in a salmon net, the whale, a male, was later killed (on July 9, 1966) when it had made an attempt to ram its way, headfirst, out of that holding pen on Seattle's waterfront.

This is an update as of April 3, 2013:

An Internet info source on killer whales, at http://www.rockisland.com/~orcasurv/changing.htm, does not specify whether Namu, at the time of his death, was still suffering from a "bacterial infection" that the account states "damaged his nervous system", the inference in the account, I suppose, being that this damage may have been responsible for the whale's destructive behavior.

So, was nerve damage arising from an infection the actual cause of the whale's action, or—did Namu make a desperate attempt to escape?

Accounts vary as to how Namu died. The account cited indicates that the orca died when he thrust himself with maximum force into the "wire mesh" of his pen and soon succumbed to injuries sustained in the impact. A book source from the late 1960s, a book on marine life entitled *The Life of the Ocean*, by N.J. Berrill, gives a somewhat different version of events: After smashing into the side of his pen the whale became trapped underwater, "entangled in" ruptured "cables" encircling its enclosure, and drowned.

Regardless of the discrepancy (death via impact vs. death through drowning) between the accounts I deduce that, had nerve damage resulting from a bacterial infection caused Namu to launch himself at full thrust into the wall of his pen this action would have been preceded by his involuntary repetitive movement in the pen. I note that the literature I have read about Namu makes no mention of any such action of the whale in his pen; there is no movement by Namu prior to him striking the pen at top speed. Further, had an infection all but paralyzed the whale's nervous system, Namu would have been incapable of attaining considerable speed—the literature available does not address this point. And consider this: Namu had rammed a colossal hole (that hole exceeded his length of twenty-four feet) into his pen—his action clearly portending a resolve to escape.

In the wild, typically swimming at a varying rate that is the equivalent of a slow-to-brisk walking speed for a human, killer whales cover significant distances in the hunt for food each day. It is therefore difficult for myself to imagine that a creature Namu's size would be content in a "sixty-foot-by-forty-foot" confine with a depth of "sixteen" feet—the dimensions of his pen.

For the reasons given I conclude that Namu's action was a deliberate and desperate attempt to gain his freedom.

I should mention here that another killer whale, subsequently given the name Shamu, was captured in Puget Sound in October of 1965. That young female orca ended up at the Sea World aquarium in San Diego, California and became a performing exhibit. In 1998, I learned that this orca had died in captivity in 1971, well short of the remarkable eighty to ninety year lifespan some female killer whales in their natural element are thought to reach. In the wild it is common for female orcas to live approximately fifty years; feral males do poorly in comparison; on average, males attain about thirty years of age (these longevity figures are mentioned in *The World Book Encyclopedia*—2013 edition).

The average longevity of orcas in confinement that would be derived from info on all killer whales that died in captivity and from whales that yet survive is not mentioned in 'World Book', but average life expectancy for killer whales in an aquarium, I construe from info at http://www.orcanetwork.org/nathist/releasability/survival.htm, is, based on deceased killer whales at Seaworld since 1987, less than seventeen years, and based on info at http://www.orcahome.de/lifeexpectancy.htm, is—what? Answer: Eight years, four months—inclusive of all whales (197) that have died in aquariums worldwide and captive orcas still alive. Whatever.

Since the original Shamu, Sea World has featured a number of killer whales named after the first, though other orcas there carry various names.

Killer whales, whom belong to the same order of marine life that dolphins and porpoises do, are highly intelligent mammals. I have always felt that it is a real pity mankind ever undertook the practice of imprisoning such magnificent animals. In recent memory, some aquatic parks have moved forward with the changing times and adopted the policy that they will no longer use killer whales captured in the wild as exhibits. This does nothing to change the cruel reality that a prison-bred population of orcas continue to exist in captivity worldwide (update ends).

WHILE HANGING OUT BEHIND THE BEEHIVE I would occasionally find articles of value lying in the dirt of the alley. One day I found a starter's gun. I had no idea whether it was a toy or a real weapon. So, I took it home and asked my brother.

My brother examined the sleek black pistol carefully before he said anything to me. Then he said: "So you found this in the back alley did you?"

"Yep." I was not the least bit surprised by Raimo's question. "Is it a real gun?" I was hopeful.

"Nope. It's a starter's gun. But it's still too dangerous for you to have. I'll tell you what. I'll give you fifty cents for it."

I could tell by the way that Raimo said this that he would not take no for an answer. I realized then that my brother intended to expropriate my new toy. And I had no choice other than to agree to his inflexible terms. To have refused would have meant having my hair yanked. I didn't want that. Beside' the physical pain and the fact that any objection I made meant nothing to my brother, I knew that he would confiscate the gun.

Even so, I decided to make one final pitch. "How about a dollar?" I ventured bravely whilst my feet shook in their running shoes. I was a businessman and, I was in the business of making a profit for myself whenever I could.

"Are you kidding?" retorted Raimo, a degree of amused annoyance in his tone. "This thing isn't worth a dollar. Fifty cents and you're lucky to get that. The gun's mine." And that was that.

Folks, I tell you this. Trying to negotiate with someone who towered more than 2.5 feet above my head, and who possessed a bad temper, definitely didn't make good business sense. For me, it was case over. And my brother has kept the gun to this day.

The starter's gun was not the only item of value that turned up behind the Beehive. On another day, I came upon a two-foot-long machete. The haft was not worn, and the knife was in good condition overall. Which meant that it was not too old. And with no rust on the blade, which meant that it could not have lain alfresco in the dirt for long.

At first, I took it to be a cook's knife. But to be sure, I took it home and asked father for his experienced, worldly opinion. My candidness has always been my undoing.

Perhaps I should have hid the weapon, although this course would surely have proven unwise in the long run. To have concealed such a large object and to have it remain undetected for long would've been not only improbable, it would've been impossible.

As had the starter's pistol, this fine article was quickly removed from my possession. Still, in hindsight, it was just as well: had I been unwise enough to have hidden the blade and been found out later, I would, no doubt, have found my arse subjected to severe discomfort. This always meant no less than being whipped with a leather belt. Ouch! My poor fanny.

Along the rocky beach at low tide I always found some kind of treasure. Frequently small change. Usually a red cent or two. And so often did I chance on these, that I now guess the coins had been abandoned there intentionally. I did not reason this in my simple child's mind then.

I knew at the time nothing of the common practice of throwing money into a wishing well.

Too, I know that some people just like to throw things. Some throw rocks. Others prefer to throw their spare change away.

Mayhap my finds were on account of a continuing sporting match of a sort then, designed to see which competitor could propel these little missiles the furthest from land.

Or, at high tide the result of attempts to make the coins skip off the surface of the water before they succumbed to the tireless force of gravity and slipped beneath the waves.

The last two of those three highlighted possibilities make no sense, because what were the coins doing sitting right beneath the breakwater?

Just a penny here and a penny there. Sometimes even a lucky dime. Not enough to have made me rich in a single lifetime of beachcombing. Not enough. But you know, I, who now write from my heart, never tired for long then of the search for the vast wealth that I just knew lay hidden about me. The pennies that I came across were, with rare exception, Canadian mint too.

Queen Elizabeth would not like knowing that her distinguished image has been sitting idly in the deep, defiled by the saltiness of the water until a bluish-green layer of corrosion has blotted out the fine features of Her Royal Highness's face, I thought.

Occasionally, I found not money lying on the exposed seabed at low tide, but plastic slugs shaped like dimes. Exactly the same size and thickness, excepting weight, as dimes. Because these had been manufactured of plastic, the light-green slugs were much lighter than dimes. The slugs came in quite handy.

The nearest automotive service station and gas bar, and, of course, the chewing-gum machines, two of them to be specific, were only a block from our shop, in the opposite direction from the Beehive, along main street. The service station sat on the waterfront, behind the boat-repair shop just back of us.

Miracles sometimes happen in life. Most other times, one has to make them happen. Whatever. I've always classified getting something for nothing as a bona fide miracle. And my little plastic gems, with few exceptions, worked quite nicely.

On the infrequent, I must add—unhappy, occasion when my slugs did not produce gum, I would attribute the malfunction of the gum machines to the fact that, for some reason my precious slugs got stuck midway in them—jamming the machines. Just imagine the headache that the poor proprietor must have experienced at each of those times in trying to unplug the devices.

I never knew where the slugs came from. Nor how they wound up along shore.

Which was very fortunate for the proprietor. And for me: had I discovered a substantial cache of these slugs, my teeth would all have begun to rot, and mother would have seen no end of taking me to the dentist.

In view of this, I can now humoredly chastise the proprietor for his unswerving generosity. He never moved his machines indoors where I would have been less likely to interfere with his certain wish to operate a viable business.

All things that came my way by way of fortune or dishonest means seemed to have a special flavor to them in my early days. I know this for sure: Of the gum that I stole, I of course had no regrets then. Indeed, those blue marbles of pure delight had me chewing contentedly for many an afternoon.

My pilfering escapades then, were kept confined to land by necessity. Since I commanded no ship of war, I could not be expected to engage in a lawless activity whilst riding high on the seven seas, blithely chanting something as luridly absurd as this:

Skull and dirk I sail by.
Cross my sharp and you'll bleed dry.
Curse my grit—in the briny you'll lie.
Rest in hell, your soul will fry!!!

And so, as sad as it may seem to you, I was a pirate who swore that I loved the sea. Yet, a lack of means (a vessel which would not sink the moment that it would taste the drink) *and* my liking for convenience, manifested then by my hearty desire to stay safe, dry, and warm by keeping my two feet planted on solid ground—in case my ship sank under heavy enemy fire (I now argue) would largely prevent me from then realizing my true potential in life as a pillaging maritime ruffian of the lowest moral caliber.

With my love for land always foremost in my mind then, some folks might have easily argued that I was not a real pirate at all. Only a fruity fake. This criticism, which I now fully expect to receive once my experiences become public knowledge, is completely unfounded. I always was a true pirate at heart. Still am. Right down to my smelly, unwashed socks. Okay-okay. Maybe I am laying it on a bit thick with the dirty socks. But, I was a pirate long ago. Such, always shall I be.

I HAVE MENTIONED TIGER the cat. Distinctly catlike in his preferences, this gray cat of Helen's had a not unusual hankering to curl up wherever a soft, warm spot could be found. A hankering quite common to any feline. Less common to a lonely pair of hard-shelled, little, green Martians that sis contained to a bowl then. I pitied the latter. I still do.

About the cat. I awoke to an intrusive odor one night. A rudely foul smell, a smell like a rabbit's fart, had impinged upon my semiconscious mind and jolted it wide awake.

Of course, I had to open my eyes. I was immediately half-sorry that I did: there, stuck right in my face, was a bushy tail. Yow! I ejaculated—as I leaped from my bunk—with my shocked mind plumb scared, scared out of its wits.

Accidents happen. In my hasty departure from bed I accidently dislodged my table lamp, which fell to the hard concrete floor and shattered into no less than fourteen pieces. This being the glass base of the lamp I speak of. I'd count the shards of glass in the morning.

Believe me when I say this now. I am usually good at explaining things. Usually. I can fully explain my cowardly, and certainly less than manly, reaction then. I knew not what manner of peril I faced. Besides this, I *used* to subscribe to the philosophy that when mortal danger strikes, I will, given the opportunity, try to run away as speedily as my feet will carry me. Yep, not any more. I've matured. I no longer run. I walk. Judge me not; you folks have to admit that it really is of strategic advantage to be *walking* on earth—not buried beneath it.

That is, I hope, a diplomatic explanation for the all-out terror that had seized my soul in an icy grip then. And as I picked myself off of the floor and my eyes centered upon the small mass of greater darkness still nestled right beside my pillow, I swore more than a few profanities. Some, loud. I accidently bit my tongue too.

The commotion had sent a large figure scurrying to see what manner of burglar it was that dared to invade our humble dwelling. Even before the lights went on I knew that figure was father.

Illumination came instantly. It was father. And he actually looked more surprised than angry. I thought that too soon.

"What the hell is going on?" father jabbered in Finnish, in his most threatening tone. A tone that made me quake like an aspen leaf, in my pajamas and bare feet. Helen, who slept above me in the other bunk, was awake now. So was everyone else.

Helen climbed down and joined father, mother, and brother, who were all now crowded about me. Everyone was looking at the busted lamp, and at me. Tiger, the mischievous cat, had split from the scene and was now, I could see, happily hiding his burden of guilt in safety beneath our kitchen table. That left myself to be the fall guy.

With every eye on me, I felt very little and insignificant. It occurred to me then. This would have been an excellent time for me to have followed Tiger's example and promptly sought refuge myself. Beneath my bed. I wondered if there were any large, black, scary-looking spiders beneath it.

While I was wondering, father spoke for the second time. All had seen that I was in no way injured. With his eyes shut, Tiger now looked either bored or fast asleep beneath the table. I'd solemnly have sworn that Helen's cat could have slept peacefully right on through a tornado.

Father wanted me to tell him what had happened. So, with a cherry-sized lump stuck midway up my throat, or so it felt, I explained to all that Helen's no-good cat had wished to share my bed, rather than sleep in his own designated place. Which was an open corrugated box on the floor. I explained that the cat had frightened me and that I had leapt from my bunk—upsetting the lamp. Here I stopped. There was no need to explain further. I was trying to look as innocent and cute as possible, hoping that I would not suffer a spanking on account of Helen's troublesome cat.

Father made a decision. The climax to this incident was that Tiger wound up back in his box while father ordered that Helen and I swap bunks.

As a kid, I didn't worry too much about hygiene. And I knew that my sister never worried about it. How times have changed. Today, wild oxen could not drag me into any vacant berth that Helen ever once occupied. Nope. Not in a million years. That goes for Tiger the cat too. I am very picky about my bedfellows.

I would rather share my bed with a colony of man-eating lice than get stoned on dirty, smelly gas erupting from the rear end of a single small cat. I was born into this world under the star of Leo the lion, but I share no common blood with lions, tigers, or cats of any size. Where any of those be concerned, my bed is strictly private territory. No cats, cat burglars, dogs, and alligators allowed. Private territory.

Although my sentiment may appear less than sociable to the many pet lovers sure to exist amongst those of you who read this book, the fact is that I never possessed any fondness for animals as a kid, and never have I as an adult. Respect most animals and the rights of animals I do, but like them, no. As such, today, I respect nice dogs that refrain from biting one of my legs off, for say, lunch. Yet there is nothing more than that respect. Why? I don't know.

When I speak of the past in relation to this regard, in aged and experienced hindsight, maybe I had everything I really needed in mother. I had no overpowering emotional need for more love. Like an electric current, love flowed to me straight from mother's heart, coursed through my body and ran into my soul, energizing it. In a life of hardship, her great love for me balanced and sustained my emotional existence.

With no further unwelcome interruption to disturb my slumber I slept peacefully on through the wee hours of morning when darkness rules half of Earth. And as I slept the darkness slowly gave way to the gray dawn of a new day. And the new day found me carrying out my routine search for bottles.

Finding none about my usual haunts this morning, I wearied of the search in little time, and laid my butt to rest on my favorite sitting place behind Lavers. On my flat rock beside Blackbeard's Grave.

Looking out from shore into the distance, I saw that the ocean was choppier than it ordinarily was on an overcast day. This, while the somber, leaden sky appeared threatening of rain. Other than the fact that the small boats tied to the wharves were dancing about a tad livelier than usual, I didn't notice anything interesting transpiring in the scene before me.

I like to believe that I am a man of action. And at times like this, when there was no action happening anywhere about me so far as I could see—I would sit and think. I would sit and think about anything that came to mind. With nothing of real interest occurring about me, this was an ideal day to do just that.

CHAPTER THREE

I BEGAN MY MEDITATION this day by considering the journey of my life to the present day. From what mother had told me, my life, it seemed as I sat on my rock, had begun in a black hole. I knew, from what mother had said, that I had come into this world from inside of her. Born on August 12, 1958, I had whimpered helplessly like a small lion cub.

I didn't have whiskers back then and never would, but I had to have been nearly bald as any new arrival will be. Terrified, I must have been, that I had been thrust from my warm cocoon of happiness, expelled I, into a surreal, colorless void. No doubt, I would have been quite content to have pulled down the shutters, stayed indoors, and not made the harrowing journey into the unknown.

Following my compulsory debut, I'd found myself bathed. And cradled in the comfort and safety of mother's arms. I must have felt nice and warm in mommy's arms. And more than a bit tired. Being born is a nerve-racking experience and I must have been plainly pooped. Not long thereafter, I must have fallen asleep to mommy's lullabies.

At first, I'd be entirely oblivious to the truth that I had plenty of instant company. I had not only a mother, but as well, I had a father, a sister, and a brother.

Like everybody else, or most folks anyway, I'd been delivered into existence within the usual setting. This having been a hospital of course. Born I'd been in the sleepy, small, but beautiful orchard town of Penticton, in

35

British Columbia. With a fine sand beach touching the azure breadth of Okanagan Lake at its doorstep. In the south of Canada. The far south.

Of the world immediately beyond the four confining walls of my room at the hospital I remember nothing from my first year of life. However, old black-and-white snapshots from this era, the (late) fifties, reveal that we lived in a little, white house. And of our time spent in Penticton, I have been told that money was the sole concern then. Specifically, where father would receive his next paycheck from.

This was the only time, after their journey from Finland to Canada, in 1951, that my parents lived in Penticton. In the interim, they had spent a short time in Toronto before their departure for Edmonton, which they, in turn, had left after one year of residency, bound for Vancouver on the west coast.

Facts are hard to come by. But I know that at some point in time father had managed to obtain temporary summer employment of just two weeks duration in Penticton, as a relief worker at an automobile dealership, he performing the duties of a car mechanic then. Later, father tried operating his own electrical-motor-repair shop in town and, for a while, father's business worked.

However, his fledgling enterprise had run up against stiff competition from the established businesses in the same field of work as father. And father's competitors had, so to speak, greased-the-ground beneath his feet.

No longer able to procure the copper wire necessary to rebuild his clientele's motors with, wire from the sole supplier of the product that his competitors in town were buying the wire from, father was forced out of business. It was, as father recalled years later, a conspiracy between the supplier and father's competitors, designed to drive him out of the service market.

I don't know whether we as a family were any more financially strapped at this earlier time than would be usual. I do know that mother had once worked in town as a waitress, at the Elite cafe on Main Street. And I know that she had given up her employment to look after me. Mother also told me, years ago, that a nice neighbor lady (whose name I do not recall) sometimes baby-sat me while mother worked.

I know too—that whenever father tired of life in one locale, it always meant that a change of scenery was not far in the offing. And instead of lounging comfortably in a rocking chair for the livelong day in small-town civilization with a lit cigarette resting between his fingers, jobless, and with his mind dwelling on the downside of capitalism, father had figured out that he could accomplish the same thing in privacy elsewhere. So it would have seemed to any adult bystander who might have known something of father, and chanced to be watching events then, day by day. Any such bystander would have been inclined to agree with mother, who would always maintain that father's intention then was transparent enough.

Yes, in the end of his good long sit then, father, who was always the boss in our family, and, who always made decisions which mother ultimately would be forced to agree with, always against her better judgement, had decided that another move was in order.

Whatever else one might say about father, he had an appreciative eye for nature's unrefined beauty. So it is not at all strange to me that father had picked a location near the village of Hedley, which stands 46 miles to the west from Penticton, along Highway 3.

Details can often be sketchy when an effort is made to compile a family's history from long ago. Exactly when in time my parents had gone forth and purchased a wooded two-acre parcel of land overlooking the Similkameen River is of no real importance in my story. Of significance in this narrative is the fact that this site came to be my home as an infant.

Time, as we all so well know, never stands still for even a moment. And it is here in the now long-dead echo of the past, here—in the decade of the fifties as that old guard almost faced the new—here—at a time not so long ago for some of you perhaps—yet a time so very long ago for me—here—in this secluded spot next to the Stemwinder Provincial Campground, that I and my family lived. In grinding poverty. Not abject poverty for me, as I was happy to be near mother. But poverty nonetheless.

Certainly, it was not an existence that mother liked. Gosh no, our life was a pioneer type of existence. My brother and sister, but children, didn't mind the outdoor lifestyle. And father, the author of our predicament (as mother made clear to me when I had grown to manhood), didn't mind at all.

Looking back, to be fair to father, at the beginning of our wilderness tenure he did try his entrepreneurial hand at rebuilding electric motors in Princeton (which lies twenty miles west of the Stemwinder precinct), thereby earning money. But Princeton was a small community in the fabulous fifties, just as it is this day. And with little heavy industry in this town to carry his business then, it was but a matter of time before father's enterprise would bite the dust. Bite the dust, regardless of the fact that father had received his vocational training for electrician in Europe, which made him highly competent as a tradesman, though one without sufficient motivation, patience, and plain business savvy to ever succeed as a businessman in the often cutthroat, competition-driven market in North America.

BEING JUST A BABY AT THE TIME, I could have no inkling of father's pending second failure in the world of business. Nor did I yet know that my family was poor. Not in land of course, but in the necessities of modern living. We had no running water within the cabin that father had built for us all. And living without electricity for quite a long while here we would be, with never a TV, radio, or even a telephone. I did not know, as I peered upwards from my highchair, that the awe-inspiring reflection of the kerosene lamp on the ceiling shone so bright from the aluminum foil that papa had attached to the ceiling. Nor did I know that the foil was there to help keep me and everyone else in my family warm. To shield us from the howling cold of our first winter, and what would come to be our only winter, in the Similkameen Valley.

With my two eyes of bright blue, I could only observe. Though I don't remember it, I know that I saw that our tiny home rested on a short, steep incline that overlooked the emerald waters of a large, fast-flowing river.

I had not yet learned to speak. As such, what else I saw, I was forced to keep it to myself.

Truth be told, I know now that I didn't know much then. And I crawled. I could not yet walk because my legs were too young in life and too weak. What I now knew was the feeling of mother's loving caress as she held me in her lap. I knew warmth and security. I knew father as a tower of strength. It was high atop his strong shoulders that I received my first real tour of the campground next door to us. I was beginning to make use of shapes and facial features, in association with colors, to identify people.

According to what my parents later told me, I now knew that I had a brother. A sister too. Too bad that I don't recall it, but I now knew of my sister's existence for a certainty then. And should there be any amongst you of my readers, any at all, who deign to doubt my good word, let me tell you how it was that I came to know this.

I CAME TO KNOW of my six-year-old sister's existence in dramatic fashion eight months after my birth, when I choked, almost half to death, on a full bottle of formula.

I had been left into Helen's care by mother, who was absent. This was a big mistake on mother's part. Oh, Helen *was* quite enthusiastic about me at first, being that I was her baby brother. Stirred by an older sister's instinct, Helen wished to play mom, herself. Accordingly, I found the whole bottle of nourishment shoved into my mouth.

After a short while when mother, my real mother, returned home, she was, naturally, astounded and quite alarmed by what she saw: my small face, from mouth to jaw, was stained dark-yellow. Thanks to the drubbing with vitamins I received on this day, I began to grow in leaps and bounds—as the saying goes.

Fortunately for me, my sister's reckless infatuation for the new baby cooled swiftly. It must have—because I am still here today. Alive and well.

I suppose that with each passing hour Helen had found it increasingly difficult to adjust to the unabashed attention that mother bestowed on me as the new arrival then. To have the spotlight shift suddenly from her, as the heretofore youngest child, over to me, this, my sister at age six, could not accept.

And, as mother had later told me chuckling, the day came when she again asked Helen to look after me for a brief spell, as mother had an errand to run then. But mother's plea for help met with an icy glare.

"Hoira ite—kun olet ite ottanyt." Thus came Helen's reply. These formidable fighting words, exceptional from one so young as my sister then, were spoken in Helen's very own broken version of Finnish. And when translated word-for-word they mean, with perfect clarity: "Take care of him yourself—since you have taken him yourself."

The jealousy bug had bitten my sister hard. In time, Helen's sense of rejection by the world would slowly rescind itself. For the most part, anyway.

As mother told it, and as Helen herself later recalled with a grin, before the troublesome bug bit her, Helen had made a circuit of the immediate neighborhood, this being the few homesteads in our vicinity then, and had told the good-natured country folk here, as well as anyone out on a morning, afternoon, or early evening stroll in the campground beside us—anyone who had stopped to listen to her enthusiastic speech—anyone at all, about her wonderful "new" baby brother until she'd been out of breath. In a child's exuberance Helen must have cut a big circle around our humble Hedley homestead a dozen times that day, looking for anyone to spill the joyous tidings to.

Whatever attention my sister felt cheated of from mother, who had to look after me then, father strove to make up to Helen. And with his business in Princeton failing due to a lack of customers, being essentially unemployed—father had lots of time. Helen was his favorite child amongst we three kids because she was his only little girl. Most fathers who have both girls and boys, seem to favor girls over boys.

Myself then too young to remember, I have been related the true story of how father used to fool Helen into believing that Santa's elves had paid us a visit. Each time events began like this. Mother would give Helen a couple of cookies that mother had baked, and Helen would lay them out on a plate on our wood porch. Helen would then depart, leaving this token offering for Santa's little helpers to enjoy.

Well, my sister figured that these elves of Santa's must be incredibly fast of feet, because the cookies would always disappear within a matter of a few minutes. And on one occasion, the cookies vanished in a couple of seconds from the moment that Helen turned her back on them!

Father said that, on this occasion he hid beneath our porch and, with his left arm he managed to pilfer the cookies just as Helen turned her back. And when Helen turned about a few moments later, the cookie dish was still there. But the cookies had disappeared into thin air.

Having seen the irrefutable evidence herself, Helen was convinced that Santa's elves had swiped the cookies in a flash and that they had then hurried back to the North Pole where Santa lives—to enjoy Helen's treats in the comfort of Santa's heated den. Helen speculated that these elves of Santa's were careful diners too. Careful, because if they usually lingered long enough to finish the cookies on site when my sister was not about, they never left a single crumb behind for the jays of blue or gray to salvage, and the crows.

But what troubled Helen was the mysterious fact that Santa's helpers never lingered on for a good chat once they had snatched the cookies. Rarely, my sister would find a brief printed note done speedily in father's hand, which gave thanks for the tasty treats Helen had provided. For my sister, at least this provided some recognition that what she did in her life each day actually mattered to Santa's elves, and therefore, that it mattered to Santa also. Afore long, I shall tell you more about our simple Christmas in the wilderness.

THE FIRST VERY SHORT, DELICATE, EBONY FOLLICLES of baby hair that I'd sported upon birth were still as black as midnight. I would have been well satisfied with a crown of black hair in life, and why my hair color would later see fit to change to medium-brown I can now only guess. And I guess that the answer is hidden in the mystery of one's genes. Very light of hair that mother was in her years of youth, likely it was mother's genetic influence which overcame my inheritance from father. I suppose that this is the reason.

I learned long since that mysteries abound in life for those who must always seek the truth. But my first spoken words were no mystery. Even though they shot out of my mouth like a thunderbolt crashing to earth, from out of a clear sky. "Pap auto!" I exclaimed in infant glee one day as the sudden roar of a car engine died in the midafternoon silence of the forest.

To mother, who heard the words, it was clear that I had spotted my papa from our window as he returned from a trip to Vancouver, in search of work. The word *papa* has become a term for father in several languages, and I would not care to venture a guess as to its ethnic origin. The Finnish equivalent of mother is *äiti*, with these two dots resting just above the first letter which is pronounced soft, like the letter *a* in the word *bat*. In comparison to papa, äiti is an unknown term outside of the Finnish language.

It was later, but not many awakenings later, that "Pap auto!" was eclipsed when I espied an item that father had just mounted on the wall of our cabin. It was the long steel barrel which intrigued me the most. It was a carbine. My curious mind, through my hand, wanted to feel. Seeing my interest in the rifle, father lifted me from where I lay in my crib. Taking me into his embrace, he casually strolled over to the rifle—whereon I grabbed the barrel of the weapon with both hands!

To a child's touch, the steel must have felt cold and displeasing. I don't know how I sensed what it was intended for, but I had to have known instinctively. "Kylmä pyssy," meaning "cold gun," I said softly. Cold. And deadly. Deadly cold. So very cold. I had never witnessed a gun being fired in my short life. Yet I felt, rather than *really* knew, the dormant power hidden within this quiet, inanimate piece of metal. And—I felt—whatever the iron was, it was meant to protect us.

When the sun shone and it usually does in the Similkameen, I would say "Owkio paistaa". Meaning: "The sun is shining." I must have liked the warmth of the northern sun. Warm, but not usually too hot to bear.

Like all babies, I was fond of food. And except for a distinct dislike to broccoli and spinach, an aversion common to every infant, I was not a discriminating diner. Usually, whether it happened to be an enticing fruit cocktail that mommy had so lovingly prepared for me, *or* an unappetizing vegetable broth, I voiced no disenchantment about the food by wailing my head off.

And according to mother, when the last remnants of food were gone from my plate—I seldom failed to show my gratitude. I would then turn to mother, smiling, and say "Opoti kai". This was my very own baby language for "Kaikki loppu, ei ole ennä". The last is proper Finnish, which I learned to articulate later. I know just how unintelligible these expressions must be to anyone not versed in Finnish. Let me help. What I said was: "All finished—it (the food) is all gone".

In my world of happiness, the very best place for me was in mother's arms. And when I had learned to say as much, I did. "Äitin sylin luona on niin hyvä olla ja äitin kaulan

43

luona niin lämmin." Translation: "In mother's lap it is so good to be and by mother's neck it is so warm."

Another day and another line. Another day and another time. "Peppe ooga vauvalle." Not having invented those particular words myself, I cannot take credit for them. Those words were uttered in true baby dialect by my sister, or so she claims, much before my birth. Those words meant: "Food for the baby". Or quite possibly: "Peppy food for the baby". And regardless of whether it was my sister or brother who spoke those words as an infant, now, at mealtimes, mother repeated the same words to myself as she spoon-fed me.

In the event that you would otherwise choose to wonder about it (I don't any more, because I am no longer a baby), my rotten drown-me-dead-with-a-vitamin-bottle-while-momma-was-away attention-seeking sister's middle name is, Sinikka. Sinikka, which because of my inability then, as a baby, to pronounce every adult word I heard spoken, I quickly condensed to become, "Kika". As a name, Kika is much shorter than Sinikka, and thus, Kika was easy for me to pronounce and remember. Plain, pragmatic solutions are always easy to remember. That is why I like them best.

From mother, I would like to say that I had acquired a loving nickname. In reality, as I told you at the outset of this book, I was the author of my own nickname. Unable, then, to pronounce my proper first name Roy, I instead called myself Oje. This was just baby language of course. But the nickname stuck.

Soon, mother added her special touch. This was what mother said to me every day: "Oje poika Oje, pikku poika joje. Pikku poika, hyvä poika, kilti poika, empotasta joje." Translated from Finnish to this language and somewhat modified, or unbabyfied, from beginning to end, that sentence can be interpreted as follows. It says that I was in mother's fond estimation: "A sweet, darling little boy". That everyone in my family adored me, there was no question.

Yet, from mother it was primarily, that I learned the full meaning of love. And it was mother, that unfailing bastion of warmth and complete security, who was especially instrumental in helping me to learn about my surroundings. Mothers are always helpful in this regard.

For instance, it was from mother I learned that my brother and sister disappeared, five days out of seven, to an unknown place called, "koilo". Now, in proper Finnish, koilo doesn't mean a hill of beans. Koilo was a word of my sister's invention a few years earlier, when Helen had been told that one day in the future she would follow her brother's path to school. Koilo was kid talk for school.

What the heck—my sister must have thought, reckoning that her pronunciation was close enough to the actual Finnish word for school. In Finnish, *koulu* is the word for school.

No matter. Since I was by now, a few years later, no doubt already confused as to where exactly my siblings disappeared to on each school day morning, my current preoccupation with my sister's adaptation of a word more than four decades ago would have been of no importance to me then, had I foreseen it.

From our window on each school day, I must have seen a yellow school bus arrive early in the morning. My brother and sister would stand together, waiting at the roadside a short distance from our cabin, up the steep embankment. A small, skinny, eleven-year-old boy, red of hair and freckled of face. And a blonde-haired, six-year-old little girl. Standing in each other's company, beside a lonely gravel road, so very long ago.

The loud, gruff sound of the idling engine on the bus would reverberate down the incline in the morning's broken silence, ripping asunder its pristine fragility. The door of the bus would open wide and my familial companions would disappear in its cavernous belly. The gaping maw of the yellow dragon would close, and the bus would leave for the small primary school in Hedley, three miles east.

The familiar silence of the pine forest would return, leaving only the steady, muffled roar of the emerald river next to our cabin, and the interrupted chatter of squirrels and chipmunks as they scampered between the many pine cones that littered the ground about our home. They, wisely foraging for food in the face of the lean winter months ahead.

AS YOU KNOW, HERE IN THE DARK SHADOW OF THE FOREST our lifestyle was anything but luxurious. A shanty that father had built from planks, passed for a sauna. For anyone older than me, anyone who could understand, the necessity of proper hygiene was important. On the exterior, tarpaper covered the thin plywood shell of our cabin; the interior of our cabin boasted a second layer of plywood sheathing; the space between the exterior and interior panels was taken up by sawdust that father had used as insulation when he'd built our home.

Though we in our cabin could stand winter's cold, the rigor of frontier life placed a burden upon mother. With no place other than the river in which to wash our family's wearables, mother was forced by circumstance to do just that. Thick rubber gloves covering her hands, her washboard perched on the rocky bank of the Similkameen, she labored in her chore until the first snowflakes began to fly in the cold, pure, valley air. Mother resumed this onerous task in early spring of the following year. And she later developed osteoarthritis in her hands, which she attributed to the cold-water washing.

On the far bank of the Similkameen, across the swift-flowing current, a steep face of gray rock rose majestically. In the spring that would grow into being from the frigid depths of the coming winter, part of this wall would give way, and a huge section of the cliff would hurtle downward, spilling over the bank into the river channel. Recollecting the event, mother described the sound as a deafening roar. Mother was easily upset by most anything. Such an occurrence was enough to upset her nerves terribly. But it would have upset anyone's nerves, anyone who might have been in the vicinity when the wall gave way.

On another occasion, likely in the fall, mother sighted on the far bank a large black bear trying its luck at catching fish in the channel. Mother was keenly aware of the wilderness about our home; she respected the dangers that could lurk, crouching behind the trees, or high above her head—hidden from her sight in the camouflaging fold of pine branches.

Having no flush toilet handy in our cabin, the necessity of going to the nearby outhouse in the Stemwinder campground at night was a frightening experience for mother, who carried a flashlight each time. Especially scary it was for her when the wind whistled through the forest and all manner of strange, rustling noises could be heard during darkness. Mother's concern was perfectly understandable to the community: a full-grown tom cougar had been sighted by one of our neighbors. The large cat had been hanging about the campground which was now empty of people, the grounds closed for the fall and winter seasons.

Except for me, everyone in our family made use of the campground outhouse. Being but a babe then, I was oblivious of any danger. But, being a baby—has its perks. Right? Mother had reserved a plastic poop-pot, with just enough of a flange to act as a seat, for my sole use inside our cabin, and this fine piece of now near-ancient ingenuity was always ready for my intestinal emergencies. In this way, mother saw to it that I was never placed into any situation that might have posed a danger to me. Thank-you mother.

The chill of winter was surely in the air now. And the days were short, as the sun took long to ascend from below the eastern horizon to its zenith in the sky, and once it had, it quickly dropped from sight below the western horizon in late afternoon.

Then one morning a six-inch blanket of white lay over the pine forest and the frozen riverbank. And it lay over the tarpaper roof of our cabin. But not about the steel chimney pipe: there, heated wood smoke rose slowly into the frosty air. Mother's busy stove.

Snow, ice, and cold. These are synonymous with winter in northern latitudes. Yet these three components are fundamental to the merriest time of year. Just ask Santa.

Despite the hardship of wilderness life, much accentuated by our extreme poverty as a family then, I have been told that Christmas of 1959 was a happy occasion for our close clan of five. As I imagine it, the nicely decorated Douglas fir tree, that stood in one corner of our cabin, will have smelled sweet, spilling its wild-bred fragrance into our small abode.

Santa's elves, always on the move, must have been noseying about too. To see who was being good. And who was being naughty. At least in Helen's mind. Whether Raimo still believed in elves, he at the old age of eleven, I can only speculate. Probably not.

The cute and colorful hand-knitted elves of mother's making, which hung from the branches of our Christmas tree, provided, no doubt, a rustic ambience to our home. Not unlike maple syrup when it runs free and hot from a boiling cauldron that has been tapped, so that the sweet liquid can spread itself over the smiling face of a pancake.

Every one of the miniature characters, none of which were more than three inches from head to toe and even less than that wide, wore a bright red, pointed hat, shaped like a witch's hat. And these adorable little guys and gals, impressive with their baby-blue and dark-green torsos, and wide red belts of the very same thickness of yarn as that comprising their bodies—about their midsections, looked mighty content and lively with their short arms and legs outstretched as though they had all been caught in the act of performing jumping jacks.

But the joyous Yule scene with the tree and the golden star at its top—besides the nicely set dinner table and mother's great cooking, would not have been complete without the four smiling faces of my companions. I could not tell if I smiled on this dark Christmas Eve at our candlelit table, like I did on every other day—I could not see my own face. Without a mirror, who can? Right?

And the food? Like I said, mother made great food. Her preparation of a meal was always of the highest caliber and, my just thinking about mother's cooking makes me drool. Our Christmas entree featured potatoes with gravy, turnip casserole, macaroni casserole, and thick cuts of both dark and light rye bread.

With myself being strictly a vegan now, as much as I disdain to admit it there was meat too. At the very least, even in such a poor household that we lived in, there had to have been cut, roasted wieners and probably a trout or two that father had caught by rod and reel while standing on the thick ice of the Similkameen River.

I do not happen to know what gifts we three children received this Yule, except for one which made the front page of the *Penticton Herald*. A photographer from the paper just happened to be in our vicinity on Christmas Day then, and he spotted Helen slowly pedaling a red tricycle, which our parents had somehow managed to scrounge up enough cash to have bought for her as a present.

The photographer had a practiced artist's eyes. And seeing that my sister, at six years of age, looked undeniably cute with her long, blonde hair having been nicely worked into curls by a mother's deft touch, this man could not resist his first impulse. He wished to snap a picture of Helen on the instant, but he had forgotten to bring his camera when he'd left home.

And, with this being Christmas Day then, the photographer had the day off from work. Engaging mother in a brief conversation, he asked her for permission so that he could take a photo of Helen. To which mother agreed. So the man waved mother good-bye, promising to return the next day with his camera and film. Of course, he did.

However, the unforeseen had transpired in the course of one day passing on to the next. A windstorm had hit Hedley just as Helen was slowly pedaling around the Stemwinder campground on her trike. And guess what had happened to my sister's wonderful head of hair?

Well, with Helen seated, smiling, atop her three wheels, the large black-and-white photograph in the *Herald* said it all. I think that most folks know the windswept look. But my sister felt good. She'd made it onto the front page of a newspaper, and thus she received lots of attention.

Here, in the privacy of the woods, we did have four-legged company too. There was Tessu. And Missu. Tessu was a dog. A small black dog. A cocker spaniel cross. And Missu was a gray house-cat. Exactly how each of these poor creatures met its tragic end in life does not make for a pretty manuscript. Indeed no.

Missu, father killed somewhere along the riverbank. With an ax blow to the head, apparently. And this gruesome act, inhumane in its gory brutality, shows the sadist father was. A senseless and uncivilized act by a man who stooped to the level of a barbarian. An evil man yes. Sometimes yes. At other times—no. Yet, even in this tiny, rural community with its backwoods' customs, so far from the comforts of real civilization, what father did to Missu—was an act of a monster. Had father killed a snake on our porch, or elsewhere about our home, it would have been quite different than him having killed a domesticated creature, a house-cat, a family pet. This was an act not possible for anyone to have committed, anyone other than a person without a human heart. An indescribably cruel and ugly act.

Tessu, father let loose from our Studebaker along a local country road. And as my brother and sister watched as passengers, with silent tears streaming from their eyes, father stepped back into the car. And father, with his foot on the gas pedal, drove speedily away as Tessu the dog, always the loyal family pet, receded into the distance. Abandoned and left to fend for himself. Or die.

Tessu was later shot dead by a neighbor, after the dog made a meal for himself in the man's chicken coop. Or in his stockyard. Particulars such as this I know not. Nor do I care to.

The last time that I laid my eyes on our former home in the wilderness was back in 1985. At that time, graffiti painted on the wall facing Highway 3—paid our previous residence its proper respect. This told me that the artist, whomsoever he or she was, was endowed with a keen sense of market value in affordable housing. The message read, "little dump".

On the opposite side of the highway, across from the Stemwinder campground and our place, there used to be an old, long-since deserted apple orchard, up the side of a hill. Left to the wild for decades, I don't know whether the orchard exists today. In later years a small, privately-run grocery store was situated beside the campground. I don't know whether the store still exists.

It is my understanding that our family left our Hedley home for Vancouver in early spring of 1960. Our basis for having left then had been simple. Father had needed to find work to earn money. And we'd needed money to buy food and live. Further, mother had become tired of having to cleanse our dirty clothes on a washboard by the river. Mother had wanted hot running water—tap-tamed water, that is, and a flush toilet. Not a bad idea each of those conveniences is, huh?

Further, mother knew not how to drive a car back then and she'd hated the feeling of being powerless, dependent on father for transportation to the grocery store in Princeton, this well beyond reasonable walking distance. And so, the stage had been set then—for dramatic change in our standard of living.

Chapter Four

SOMEHOW, MY PARENTS MANAGED to acquire an old, white, one-story house with a roomy attic on Lanark Street, in the east end of Vancouver. 6152 Lanark Street, to be exact. As I understand, they didn't pay much for it, either. How much? I don't have the faintest idea. Sorry.

I took my first, halting steps on our lawn out front. Let me tell you, learning to walk was a big improvement over having to crawl where everyone else walked. Although this time frame is too far in the distant past for me to recollect from such an early age then, still, I know instinctively, by my nature, that I could not have been a big fan of such a slow and cumbersome means of covering even the shortest distances. Crawling is for snails. Not for me. I do not remember taking my first steps any more than I remember my second Christmas in life, my very first at Lanark Street. But you know—big deal.

And though the memory eludes me, what I must have known that had to have been important at the age of one was that every man worth his salt, must know how to spit properly. To some men of dubious repute, spitting is an art form as essential to their self-image as cussing. I don't like to swear. And I never spit now. Spitting is not a habit that will make the mother of any grown man or woman who engages in this pursuit, proud of her offspring. And generally speaking, girls find the habit downright gruesome.

Certainly, if a young man plans to spend the rest of his life sunk deep in lonely reflection, I advise him to take up the habit at once. A habit that so many people seem to regard as hideous, and therefore, they despise it.

However, early in my life spitting must have held a powerful fascination for me. Apart from its other virtues, whatever those are, I had to have realized that spitting involved time and effort. And any activity that involved time and effort then is certain to have kept me preoccupied in my very own world of happiness. Further, since spitting is completely independent of any strenuous exertion of mind, I know that I was, at age one, perfectly suited for it.

Toh-toh-toh-toh. Having barely realized the ability to walk then, and garbed by mommy in the finest attire that any gentleman could hope for, this being a suit of teal and shorts to match, I splattered the sidewalk with small, usually round, droppings of saliva. And to speed my boring day along, I then felt obligated to inspect my handiwork more closely. So I bent over into a squat and did just that, only to discover that I soon lost my balance on these weak, developing legs of mine—and fell on my behind!

And there on the edge of the sidewalk, under the bright morning sun, I would sit as mother watched protectively over me, while the world leisurely spun a little more on its axis in space. Spitting is man-sized work and mother later told me that it mirrored my burgeoning sense of self-importance then.

If I disinclude my prior admission of the rare wail when dining as an infant in Hedley, I had never been a squaller as a baby. As a toddler now, I would usually spend my day playing contentedly on the living room rug, for the most part by myself, while mother attended to her domestic chores. Father was at work. My siblings were at school. I had lots of time to play with my toys. Play, until mother decided that it was mealtime. Or time for my daily afternoon nap. "Kaikki, kaikki, kaikki," I would say, looking innocently from laughing eyes at mother whenever she would tell me to gather my toys off of the carpet, and put them away into my toy-box. "Everything, everything, everything." Earnestly, in Finnish, I repeated mother's directions.

Still very young, I showed my potential to be a beaver. "Kikeri ja kekeri," I said, as I played about on our rug, whilst I chewed, rodent-like with my sharp teeth, on the tasteless paws of my two six-inch-long plastic tigers. In proper Finnish, only a single letter, an *i*, is attached to the end of its English equivalent, tiger, becoming *tigeri*. But kikeri, and kekeri, in my mind, sound much more cute than tigeri. Even today, I prefer my own vocabulary.

Just like I did at Lanark Street when I came up with two similar names to describe the same striped animal. I have always felt that baby talk has its advantages. Whatever those advantages might be? Time moves forward. Always it does.

CHAPTER FIVE

AT THIS POINT IN MY DISSERTATION, I find it incumbent upon me to fill you in on the family history of each of my parents. This of course being where in Finland they came from specifically, and, the early days of their lives before they met each other.

Mother's maiden name was Hämäläinen. Lempi Hellin Hämäläinen. Aside from this fact, of mother's early life I know only the following. I know that mother lived on a farm. I know, too, that her homestead lay quite a long walk from the village of Rantasalmi, which is located in southeast Finland, about sixty air miles from the Finnish-Russian border. I know that mother's home was at least five miles from the village. The name Rantasalmi, incidentally, stands for either shore of a strait.

Of the Hämäläinen children, of which there were seven— five girls and two boys, mother was the second youngest. Her little brother, Urjo, who was two years mother's junior, was the very youngest of a large family.

I remember what mother told me. As seen through her eyes long ago, I can imagine the biting cold of the northern winter she faced as she slogged on cross-country skis to elementary school in Rantasalmi.

I remember her recollection of the hot, dry summers when viper snakes were frequently to be found hiding in tall grass on the ground, between loosely stacked bales of hay that her father, a veteran farmer, had harvested from the land. Or basking to soak up the sun's heat, on any one of numerous large boulders that lay about the woods.

I remember mother telling me that the viper snake, when roused to fury by taunting stick-and-stone-throwing children, would throw itself end over end in pursuit of them.

The European common viper, whose size in length and girth mother likely recalled with a child's frightened eyes— which can be somewhat misleading, is a venomous snake much like another viper—the rattlesnake that is native to the Americas. The E. common viper's poisonous bite is comparable to that of a rattler of the same size. Getting bitten by either viper snake is in no one's interest.

The single strategic difference between the snakes is that the E. common viper gives no warning before it strikes. The rattlesnake, and there are many species of this snake, possesses loosely connected bead-like growths in its tail; it rapidly vibrates these before it strikes, creating a buzz that's audible to most people. It *usually* does, that is, and this may be whenever the rattlesnake has time to issue this warning. I remember mother's image of her father bearing down with a pitchfork on a viper's neck, while stomping its head in with the heel of his knee-high leather work-boot.

I remember that there were a couple of draft horses that her father used to ferry supplies to their homestead with, from Rantasalmi. Through mother's eyes, eyes that had seen much in their lifetime, I remember her small, half-frozen feet on one winter morn. Feet, which she had thrust near the flames of their fireplace, to deliver them from the icy grip of a plunge she'd received in a nearby river channel. On her way to school. As usual, on cross-country skis. A shortcut which did not pay off that day.

I imagine mother as a little girl, blonde of locks. Running, as she told me, in a threesome. Running with her sister, Kerttu ("Kepa"), and Urjo about their small home. Each endeavoring to fart in unison with the others, directly before dear old dad, as they circled their home, much to the chagrin of their stern-faced father who sat, smoking a pipe on the front porch.

And I remember, through mother's words, her father's almost comical reaction then. "Ja hah! Nyt te saat." Translated from Finnish, this means, "Okay! Now you're all going to get it".

The kids knew that whenever their papa resorted to using that kind of language, it generally meant a whipping. And knowing this, the swift young legs of the not-so-intrepid three skedaddled their mischievous little bodies from sight—before their befuddled father could even move his butt off the porch.

I remember mother telling me of her having hid from her own mother at the age of five or six. Beneath their front porch. Oh! What a terrible place mother had picked to hide then. Especially when one's bare toes were then cleverly placed to stick out from beyond the porch—a fact which would ensure discovery. The only requirement in mother's early thinking then, now being that the intended discoverer, her mother, display sympathy, if not outright affection, once a sufficient number of hours had passed from the crime that mother, as a young girl, remember, had committed on this day.

On this day, mother must have known that her mother would evince sympathy toward her, now that the hour had grown late with darkness soon to set in. And mother—was not wrong. No punishment was levied. I've no idea what mother's crime was.

I remember, too—mother's excellent account of the dismay that the rash two, mother and Urjo, would soon feel as mother clambered up a tree to fetch some unfortunate bird's eggs from its nest, high in the tree. Then finding on her return that her precious cargo, a nice meal in itself for two little ones, had been crushed in her dress pocket as she'd slid down the tree trunk towards her younger brother, waiting on the ground. Minor details are so often overlooked, it seems.

Through leaden eyes I remember these things. And whatever minor details these true tales may have lost in my telling them I cannot know. But I do know this. My eyes are mother's eyes.

I knew mother as a very warm and sensitive lady whose entire world revolved around us—her children and father. Mother had been marked and molded by the rigors of her life early on, when, as a youngster, she had been thrust into the world at the age of fourteen, following the death of her mother. Her father had taken a new wife; there had been no place for a growing teenager in the cottage that had been her home since her birth in 1921. Forsaken and heartbroken, she had packed her bags and gone to live with her older sisters for a while.

For an unknown length of time, mother resided with Kepa in an apartment in Helsinki. Kepa was two years mother's senior. Just so that you know, Helsinki is situated a good two hundred miles southwest of Rantasalmi—by road.

From this point in her life, from what was really the first chapter of her early adulthood, mother went on to work at a string of menial jobs. Eventually, mother took a short course in waitressing and learned how to carry a full tray of food in each hand, supporting the trays from the underside as she walked to the dinner tables of clientele. On first consideration, this may not seem much of a feat to write about, yet, try it for yourself when you are in a hurry and you'll see that the task requires good physical balance, steady hands, and calm nerves.

Mother no longer lived with Kepa when mother met father. Mother now shared with a girlfriend a small space at a rooming house in Helsinki. A girlfriend—who was so strong that she could easily heft and carry a full-bodied drunken man, who happened to be her estranged husband, on her back. Yes, this really happened; though, I know not the particulars of the incident.

Father, born in 1915, came from the fishing village of Kotka (Finnish for eagle), in southeast Finland. Unlike mother's town of Rantasalmi to the north, but like Helsinki—83 road miles southwest, Kotka lies upon the shore of the Baltic Sea.

Father's father had been a man who father could barely recall. A mysterious figure of a man. A man named Peterskoff.

Peterskoff, as father told it to me, had been a general in the imperial army of Czar Nicholas II, the last Russian Czar. Peterskoff apparently, had been a trusted ally of the emperor.

I know little else about this man and I am assuming, as father did before me, that General Peterskoff was pop's father. Indeed, I know not for certain whether father, who had five siblings, three girls—only one of which was younger than he—and two older boys, was Peterskoff's progeny.

I do know that this man Peterskoff had liked to spend his summer holidays in Kotka, where the emperor had maintained a villa as a summer retreat. And, I am assuming it was here that he had met father's mother, who worked as a maid at the Czar's estate then.

Honestly, I don't know what to make of Peterskoff. I know that he was almost always absent from the scene. This may well have been the reason that his wife had to work to support a big family. Yet, I cannot judge a man without knowing more about him.

Peterskoff's absence means little to me now. And whether he financially supported his wife and family (and if so, how long?), I know not either. What I know is that there are reasons, sometimes for years undisclosed to the world, where precautionary measures can be necessary to safeguard life. This, in part, may serve to explain Peterskoff's absence. Beside' this, I gather that the general's final disappearance took place during either the October revolt of the Russian Revolution of 1917—or during the civil war spawned in its aftermath—in 1918. Given the heavy demands of war, the then-existing war campaign probably made it impossible for Peterskoff to periodically visit his family in Kotka. That, or the general may have already met his fate in the Revolution itself, well before hostilities in Russia reached an end.

WITH PETERSKOFF'S CONTINUED ABSENCE, father had found much time to amuse himself alone, by doing amusing things alone. Father once told me that he had, at five years of age, let go a stone the size of a football from the top of a tall fence of brick separating the Kellosalmi family from their neighbor's yard. And the neighbor, a man whom father's mother had disagreed with on some matter a bit earlier, had received this token of father's dislike for him—square on the top of his head.

The man had grunted when the stone had hit him. And apparently so dazed by the impact had he been, or, so drunken on vodka, that he'd given no other sign to acknowledge he'd been hit. Kneeling in his dormant veggie garden on his side of the fence he'd been, and he had not even looked up to see who the stone's thrower was.

And what about father? I suppose that this kind of behavior might have been expected from a young boy who lived in a cold, dirt-wall dugout, with his brothers and sisters crowded into the same pit. From he who lived in a small cabin then, sheltered from the fierce autumn winds flowing inland from the Baltic.

Father had, as a youngster, gone on to work for a flower shop, pedaling bouquets to clients, on a bicycle. This was a service for which he was usually rewarded with the gratuity of a markka or two then, the U.S. equivalent of twenty-five or fifty cents. Back in the mid-to-late 1920s this was excellent remuneration for a lad.

Following his schooling, father became an electrician. And by the time that World War II hit Europe and Adolf Hitler was busy spreading death, mayhem, hatred and fear across the European landscape, father was a mechanic in the service section of the Finnish army.

On the day that father met mother, and father had been married once before by then, mother was stricken with sudden shyness and had taken refuge below the sill of an open second-floor window after she'd spotted father standing in the street below. But she was too late.

Curious, father queried mother's live-in girlfriend who I mentioned earlier, as to who the young lady crouched— hiding beneath the window ledge—would be. Father had captured a glimpse of mom before she took the dive. Mother's girlfriend, whose first name was Nanni (nun-nee), now convinced mother to show herself. And the rest, as they would say, is history.

For some inexplicable reason—short, blonde-haired young ladies, natural blondes, that is, always seem to prefer handsome men who are dark of hair, men who are taller than these ladies are. I guess that mother must have thought father handsome enough. And father, who stood five feet eleven inches tall, was tall enough to please mother, who stood five feet even—when standing perfectly straight and minus her shoes.

And father's hair, so dark a brown that it appeared almost black, was dark enough. And—father's eyes were blue. From mother's perspective, everything worked.

I am a fairly shrewd judge of both physical and inner beauty. Judging from my parents' wedding photograph, what father saw before him was a blonde-haired girl, somewhat chubby of face, with very beautiful, laughing blue eyes. Eyes with wondrous soul to them, eyes that revealed a kind heart.

Eyes, which mother said she had inherited from her own mother, who I judge from a black-and-white photograph nearly one hundred years old now, to have been a very beautiful woman. Both inside and out.

Unfortunately in life, things which seem too good to be true, generally aren't. Having once been essentially forced out of her childhood home by her own father, had created in mother a sense of abandonment and insecurity, and throughout her life mother could never quite find enough love to satisfy her emotional need for unconditional love— true love. You see, my father's interest in mother had never been unconditional.

In her final years mother had certainly seen enough to have known that separation would end up being the result. Yes, notwithstanding the six-year difference in age between them, father did as men often do. He lost interest in mother as she grew older with age, and in their senior years father and mother split.

As I find nothing positive to say about my father's conduct, I shall not dwell on the preceding further. To that particular regard, I simply have no wish to further belabor his behind. I shall instead remain true to my founding purpose and stick to matters of substance.

Chapter Six

I WILL NOW NARRATE to you the events that came to pass after my parents' introduction to Canada. You'll recall that they'd arrived from Finnish soil in 1951.

Er-excuse me! I forgot, this is first: From father's perspective, the question of why my parents had ever left Finland would have been easy to answer: economics had been foremost—and there'd been the opportunity to travel, to witness change. And, there's no doubt the oft frigid northern weather had had an influence on he and mother. But that's not all. Father, as I said before, always made every important decision in the family. For mother too. To father, who had operated his own successful electrical-motor-repair shop in Helsinki, the continental move had, I put it this way now, mostly been a case of the grass having looked greener on the other side of the fence, and father's mind—fiddle-footed, had sealed the deal. Only, in this case the grass on the other side of the fence had lain over seven thousand miles away, on the opposite side of the broad Atlantic Ocean, and across Canada.

From Helsinki, my parents, *and* my brother Raimo—then three years of age, our half brother, Reijo—who was thirteen years old at the time, dad's mom, Hilma Kellosalmi, *and* dad's youngest sister, Sirkku, had flown to Montreal after their plane had made a stop in Gander, Newfoundland, to refuel.

I know what you're thinking. Why didn't I mention earlier that I have a half brother? The answer is simple. Reijo

63

is my half brother, not brother. Thus, for the whole of my life I have seen very little of him.

Reijo is ten years Raimo's senior. And Raimo, born in August as was I, is very near to being ten years older than I.

Reijo's path in life led first to the seven seas—as a sailor on a merchant vessel. From thereon, his working life was that of an all-purpose range hand on a cattle ranch in the southern interior of British Columbia. Taller than father by an inch, Reijo was, at six-feet-even in his prime, a blond-haired, lean, handsome man. Rugged. And well suited for a life to be spent on the range. Reijo later married a nice girl and became the father of a trio of boys. I know very little else about him. Heck, back to my parents and company—in 1951.

In Montreal, father purchased a used automobile. (I am no fan of early transportation methods and I know next to nothing about antique cars but that car, I've been told by someone who should know, looks much like a classic Packard or Chevrolet sedan in one photograph of our family album.) Father then drove everyone to Toronto.

I remember mother telling me, light-years in the future, that at the time of their being in Toronto it was summertime, and very hot outdoors. I believe that my parents and the merry troop with them stayed in Toronto almost one summer, and that the group of six departed for Alberta, and Edmonton, in late August of 1951.

There are a few memories of incidents along the highway to the west that mother spoke of. Such as their having encountered some type of mechanical trouble with their relic auto while crossing the parched prairie land of Saskatchewan. Of the drinking water in some of the small communities which somehow clung to life by the roadside, mother said that the water hereabouts was the color of dark tea. And she said that the corpses of locusts covered their windshield as they drove through the prairie heat. Arriving in Edmonton after one week spent on the road from Toronto, the six were a weary bunch of travelers.

Father was soon accosted by an officer of the Edmonton Police Department. A traffic cop, who stopped father for a pending violation.

Father could see that the man wore a uniform and father knew that he was a policeman. Yet father, who had learned very little English during the stay in Toronto, could not understand what the well-intentioned officer was excitedly jabbering about. And when the cop at last finished his sermon and bade father free to go, father smiled appreciatively and thanked him. Father then drove right on past a no-entering sign. The good officer shrugged his shoulders in defeat.

And yet, the roof of father's old sedan had been strung over with heavy rope to hold down a load of suitcases that stretched from just above the windshield to the back bumper, covering the rear window entirely. Since these suitcases obstructed father's view of traffic behind him, maybe this also, not just a traffic violation of that other kind, was what the poor policeman had been so worked up about. Oh well. You can't win them all, chubby. Just go with the flow. The policeman had done exactly that.

In Edmonton, my parents decided to stay on. While mother worked as a seamstress assembling denim jeans in a factory, father worked at a service garage as a car mechanic. As I said before, I know that my parents (and I now include Raimo, Reijo, father's mom and his sister) lived in Edmonton for only one year.

Their decision to depart town had had much to do with the winter weather common to northern Alberta. In one word—frightful. Frigid temperatures down to minus-forty degrees Fahrenheit, and a fair bit of snow during their winter there. Edmonton, my parents had figured, is no better than Finland. Too far north. Too cold.

So, my parents had left town for the major port city of Vancouver on Canada's wet west coast. Dad's mother had then made a decision also. And rooty-tooty-too—she'd gone back to Finland. While I know that my brother and half brother were dragged along with my parents to Vancouver then, I am uncertain whether Sirkku accompanied my folks when they left Edmonton.

Whatever the case, I know that Sirkku came to be present in Vancouver. And I know that my aunt was not alone in Canada for long, because somewhere along the line of destiny, either back in Finland or in Canada, she had picked up a husband by the name of Reino Rauhala, a Finnish fellow years younger than herself. He—a cabinetmaker.

Sirkku, would work as a barber and hairdresser for some years in her adopted country, but she would later return to Finland with Reino, and their one young son, Pekka. Grown to manhood, Pekka returned to Canada to reside.

Details of these events are sketchy because today I have virtually no association with any surviving figures from my past, none with the Rauhala family, or what remains of it, and there is no one besides the Rauhalas who could be more specific than I. As time has a way of doing, the trail of truth is often lost when people who do know, pass on.

CHAPTER SEVEN

ENOUGH ABOUT MY TRIBE'S OLD HISTORY. I am back at our house at 6152 Lanark Street. It is Halloween night of 1960. I am in the escort of mother and sister.

Of course, All Hallow E'en as we all are perfectly aware, is synonymous with various nefarious creatures that go bump in the night. Out of kilter with the essence of the strangely garbed dark spirits roving about our neighborhood then, and out of kilter with the connotation of Halloween that most children old enough to understand possess, mother had cast me in a robe of the purest white—as an angel.

In lieu of a halo, which would have been impossible for mother to manufacture, she had placed a silver hair-band of, er-uh, unknown origin about my forehead to make the look complete. As for my magnificent gown, mother had taken a narrow white bedsheet and folded it several times over to make it just the right length and width so that it fit loosely about me. Mother had joined the two ends of the sheet at my backside with a couple of safety pins.

Years later, I'd recall strolling from door to door in our neighborhood and being given candy by strangers. All that I had to say now, was trick-or-treat. The experience wasn't turning out to be fun for me because I was finding all the walking I was having to do to be tiring work.

And by whatever late hour it was that mother, Helen, and me, bent our steps toward home, Helen (who was dressed appropriately in black as a witch, minus the pointed hat) and I had each amassed a large shopping bag full of candy and other edible treats; although, by the time that we three got home, I was dead beat.

Still dressed in my costume, I sat on the tile floor of our kitchen with my short legs stretched before me, and began to tear away at the candy wrappers. With mother's blessing of course. I was especially enamored with the chocolate bars of Hershey. And this. Oh Henry! This was the first time in my life that I had been granted the latitude to feast with more than my hungry eyes. So I did. I gorged my tummy on chocolate. Given the least opportunity, any hungry child will do the same. I kind of overdid it though.

With my appetite for chocolate and sweets more than satiated, I sat on the floor, with a sagging back like an old man, literally stuffed to the point of exhaustion. Mother had seen my unhappy face and she approached me.

Repulsed by the very thought of sweets, I had abandoned my candy bag, nearly full, on the floor beside me. "Roy? Would you like some more chocolate?" mother asked me good-naturedly.

My answer was swift and resounding. Baaa! I didn't want any more candy. Baaa! Baaa! Baaa! Tears streamed down my face. Mother had her answer.

Bending down before me, mother hugged me and kissed my forehead. Then she rose and took the candy bag off the floor, and put the undevoured sweets in the kitchen cupboard.

Mother put her arms around me and lifted me from the floor. And she carried her tired little angel up the stairs and to my room.

Mother took my costume off, which I had badly stained with dark chocolate, and slipped me into my pajamas. She laid me down in my own bed and pulled the sheets up to my chin. Mother kissed my forehead again. "S-l-e-e-p, my little angel," she murmured in Finnish. Soon, I had drifted off to sleep and the world of little boy's dreams. Pleasant dreams.

The morning following, when I awakened and looked out from my bedroom window at the brilliant rays of sunshine in our backyard, I did not stop to ponder the question of why, on the evening before, mother had offered me more sweet treats when I had been plumb full. I didn't because I knew, I always knew, that whatever goodies mother gave me, she did so from the goodness of her heart. Mothers are just not meant to be confusing.

Not so are cousins. I speak of my first cousin Pekka Rauhala.

You see, Pekka's antics were the stuff of big-screen Hollywood. As a kid, Pekka was a shrewd character who often sought to mislead others. Including mother. But, with the way that matters would turn out on this day for Pekka, the result may well have blunted any future ambition of Pekka's for a career in theater.

And the only problem for Pekka on this day, was that mother was always a cautious sort of lady—wise in the ways of Pekka. This episode of Pekka, starring who else but Pekka of course, began when Pekka and myself were seated on the living room floor.

Mother was busy skinning carrots in the adjoining room, our kitchen. And when my cousin, who is three years older than I, began wailing his fool head off, screaming at the very top of his lungs, alleging that I was attacking him and pleading for help, mother, who—without any doubt— could hear Pekka's ear-numbing frantic plea then (at the time, everyone else was outside, lounging in the comfort of lawn chairs in our backyard, and oblivious of Pekka's siren song), decided to have a peek from behind a friendly corner. And moving stealthily, what mother saw when she poked her head around the entrance of the kitchen wall, brought an instant smile to her face.

On the floor of the living room I sat, minding my own business, utterly dumbfounded, staring at Pekka. Mother could see that Pekka, who was still seated on the floor of our living room and with his back to mother, was a good ten feet from where I sat on the other side of the room. And mother saw that I, instead of doing to Pekka what Pekka claimed I was doing to him that very moment, was, in truth, being held spellbound by Pekka's solid-gold performance. Pekka always did give me the creeps. Especially the time that he had wrapped his bony hands about my throat and squeezed, squeezed hard.

We were under the stairwell then, inside of my playhouse which father had built for me and Helen to amuse ourselves with. And it was pitch-black in there with the door closed. My sister was outside the pen and knew nothing of the deed Pekka was in the process of committing. Had she, I am sure that she would have beaten the stuffing out of him. Almost.

For several long seconds, Pekka had squeezed so hard that I had been unable to breathe. I remember the sheer terror I felt that day. I truly had thought that I was going to die. For Pekka, I now am fairly sure that it was a prank. But for me, a two-year-old child then, it was anything but that.

Pekka, you know, he used to revel about blood-soaked bones every time that his folks came for a visit and brought him along with them. And I truly believe that Pekka, who fancied himself as a bloodthirsty buccaneer, would indeed have made an excellent pirate. I have no slightest doubt of that because I am sure that his diabolical personality as a kid would have served him very well.

LIKE I SAID, father was a fiddle-footed fellow. Never was he satisfied to linger long in one place if he could, by *any* means, avoid doing so. And his never-ending search for better employment opportunities supplied him with the perfect excuse to uproot our family's quiet life at Lanark.

The doors of our home on Lanark Street were locked, and we all left to go to Finland. Follow the leader. I had to. I had to, inasmuch as mother and my older siblings were being dragged along too. Father's order had to be obeyed. And I was only into my third year of life.

So, from our comfortable home on Lanark Street, in late May of 1961, we all stepped into our Buick. Then father drove our family across the Canadian landscape to

Montreal, where we boarded a Polish-registered passenger liner, named the *TSS Batory*.

From Montreal, our group journeyed up the St. Lawrence Seaway and would now cross the broad, green, and often turbulent Atlantic Ocean to that other shore. Continental Europe. To Finland, or Suomi as the Finns call it. With the Atlantic beneath us now, we were already encountering considerable waves in the stormy sea.

Not surprisingly, by this time, on the way to Suomi, we were all experiencing some degree of seasickness. Raimo threw up on deck and a strong gust of wind suspended his vomit in air, carrying this aloft to sea and back over deck in a circular path. Raimo's finest regards landed on the exposed neck of one unfortunate fellow who stood, fighting for his balance, against the rolling motion of our vessel in the high sea.

After ten days of voyage the *Batory* finally steamed into the port of Stockholm. From here, in Sweden, our party boarded a smaller vessel of unknown name, which took us to Helsinki. Now at the finale of our voyage, all in our family were bone-tired of travel.

CHAPTER EIGHT

IN HELSINKI, WE IMMEDIATELY TOOK UP RESIDENCE at my Aunt Kepa's place. In an upper floor apartment, in a concrete high-rise in Roihuvuori—this being a district in the city of Helsinki, this was. We were soon made to feel at home.

Kepa lived in this apartment with her husband, Eika, and Pirkko, Kepa's daughter from an earlier marriage. Blonde-haired Pirkko was just a teenager at the time. Eika, a policeman, was tall and black of hair. As for mother's father, he, like mother's mother who was long deceased by now, was not amongst the living on earth.

One of the first things I discovered about my parents' homeland was that there were many rules to take heed of here. Particularly in Helsinki, which is the capital of Finland, and the country's largest city.

Too many rules. Especially in the capital's parks. Rules like—"Don't trample the lawn."—for instance. As if anyone, 'specially a child, would set about to wear the life out of the turf with his running shoes. But I guess that kids do possess a lot of concentrated energy. Just like Eveready batteries. An active kid might run on one small spot of grass all day. Go home. Return the next day and follow the exact same routine, if he—or she—were thus inclined to do. In so little time a lawn could wear out.

I can't say that I ever tried this, though. In action, a whirlwind I was, but I never got the opportunity to wear any of Helsinki's fine lawns out by repeatedly trudging on them. I was seldom let out of Aunt Kepa's apartment for a substantial period of time then, and *always* was I subject to supervision, indoors and out.

And believe-you-me, the confinement of our apartment weighed heavily on me—mother, the only unboring person in my world, was busy in her day job. Too, father was absent from home in his employer's electrical-motor-repair facility. Though I don't know what kind of work it was mother did then, I do know that mother usually sought work in restaurants, bakeries, and hotels. In other words, the service sector of the job market. You know, whoever devised work was a real idiot. It is much better to play. All day.

When my keen ears first heard of mommy's departure on a workday morning, I did not, at all, wish to accept this reality of work. To me then, the emotionally painful reality of being separated from mother for any length of time. And, with that torturous reality confronting me, I proceeded to attempt an escape from my brother's custody as we stood at the bus stop in front of our building.

The city bus lay in front of me, the front exit wide open. Mother had already said good-bye to us and she had already stepped onto the bus. I saw that the door of the bus was about to close.

But there was an instant in which time seemed to freeze for me. As quick as lightning, I bolted from my brother's side onto the bottom step of the bus. My right foot was already rising to plant itself on the second step, my mind intent on only one goal. That I be reunited with mother. At once. Rules, I felt, exist to be broken.

Now, mother as I said, was already on the bus. But she had turned back when she'd heard the frantic pitter-patter of little shoes on the first step. Mother caught me at the top of the second. "Mother," I begged. "Please don't leave me behind." I spoke in Finnish while I tugged on mother's coat sleeve as though to drag her off of the bus.

Mother comforted me. Smiling, she peered into my distraught face and assured me that she would come back home in the evening. It was then that my infinitely dense older brother caught up to me, Raimo having been shaken awake by the rapidity of my elopement.

Saying good-bye to momma for the second time on this miserable morning was every bit as hard as the first had been. Tears came from my eyes. Yet, even crying in open misery did not help. I'd be escorted back into our apartment by the firm hand of Raimo, who, seeing my plight, was himself near tears. Dragged along I was, by the arm. Spoilsport!

Oh, I was let out of our apartment sometimes, so that I could play in the small sandbox in the yard. Here I met a fellow by the first name of Tappu, who was my age. Like me, Tappu liked to play in the sandbox. Thus it was that we became fast friends.

Tappu likely had a close relative who was a seaman. Though I never saw either of Tappu's parents about, I believe that the little boy's father was a seaman who was often absent from home.

"Hullu jätkä," Tappu would say whenever some big dude had attracted his annoyance. His phrase means, "Crazy chap". Tappu also taught me about the ways of the men who ride the waves of the sea to earn their livelihood. My friend often sang a single line, an old creation by this time, a seaman's companion which Tappu always performed in perfect key. I recall the words well enough, though I shall not disclose them as copyright law may still apply after all this while. As for the content of this short piece that may be part of a larger, I will say that the tune gave one no reason to question the message in the lyrics, which describe the allure that a bottle of whiskey holds for many an addicted seaman.

So long as our ears are clean of wax and we can hear, we never know what interesting things a little boy can teach us. We grown-ups can only wonder at the amazing phrases that can pop from a little boy's mouth.

I tell you this. Being a very good boy can be exasperatingly hard work for a little boy. Being a truly good boy, to me at least, required a commitment to be perpetually bored. A commitment that I never subscribed to. I remember one incident that was prompted by my complete boredom. An incident yes, that transpired during the four months that my family and I spent in Finland.

I remember it this way. My brother and sister were seated at the dining room table then, after lunch, pleasantly engaged in a game of cards between just them. They were playing rummy, a game in which the players try to collect the right set and sequence of cards.

But I was then too young to fully understand how the game was played. Not surprisingly, I often watched in boredom as a match wore on.

And the spoil of victory (this being the right to brag) I saw, would go to my brother on this day. Helen was losing badly. This much I could gather.

Other than that, there was nothing at all happening. I yawned at my seat at the table. I was close to being hypnotized by boredom and I knew that I would soon fall asleep, unless something stimulating occurred soon. I did not wish to fall asleep. Nothing terribly exciting ever happened when I fell asleep while watching a card game. Even in my dreams. Since I wish to stay awake, I need to make some merriment for myself, I thought.

With that in mind, I rose from my chair and walked around the circular wood table to a position behind my brother's back. Here, from my vantage point, I looked at the spread of playing cards that Raimo held in his hand. Now was the time.

I blurted out what I could discern of my brother's deck of cards. Being almost three years old now, I could understand just enough about playing cards so that I could readily identify, for instance, a queen-of-hearts from a queen-of-diamonds.

I knew, full well, what a dastardly thing it was I had done, the instant after, when my brother half-turned in his seat to grab me. But I evaded him. The card game continued.

Shortly thereafter, just to even things between the players insofar as my involvement with them was concerned and to make matters hopelessly messy so far as their match went, I ventured behind my sister's back and pulled the same stunt on her. By doing thus, I am sure that I gained her enmity then as I had my brother's.

I thought I was safe. Alas for me, Sir Eika had been watching me from his recliner in the adjoining room, this being the living room. And being a policeman, he had this peculiar, ingrained sense of fair play that perplexed me as a young one.

Without uttering so much as a word, Eika put aside the newspaper he had been reading, and began to walk slowly toward me, all the while loosening the narrow black leather belt he wore about his waist.

I think that Eika had not a thing more sinister on his mind that day than the wish to scare me for being disobedient. This is what I think now.

Yet, Eika looked real stern of face to me then. If his appearance was an act—I didn't know it. And I didn't bother to hang around to find out if he was bluffing. I shot into the kitchen where mother stood, she stirring a pot of stew. I was lucky. This was a Sunday and mother was not at work in the big world that lay beyond our apartment home. My desperate flight ended beside mother.

Looking back and forth between mother and the gradually advancing Eika—I caught mother's attention. I am sure that what I did next was highly entertaining, not only for mother who recalled the incident with a laugh many years later, but for Eika as well.

Lacking an impressive-looking belt like Eika, I began to tear frantically at my suspenders, and, whilst looking mother in the face, I blustered, "Nyt minä annan sinulle remmiä". The English equivalent of my fearless Finnish diatribe means—"Now I am going to belt you".

During these last hectic moments it hadn't mattered to me that I had no belt about me. And how, on Earth, I yet designed to use my suspenders to do the deed with then, I don't know. And why—did I wish to belt my mother, you ask? Patience. Patience.

I remember enough of that gray day, to know this for a fact. Always calculating, I'd reasoned on the instant that if mommy, my eternal protector, wouldn't ensure my immunity from being dished a licking at the rough-and-ready hands of Eika, mommy would be, in such case, terribly failing in her parental duty to shield me. As a mommy should not be.

Back then, given the menacing visage of Eika (or so it appeared to me) and his towering height, I figured that I was in deep trouble. I felt that if mother could not be relied on to afford me protection—then—she needed to be reminded of the reality that I was, after all, just a little boy who would *always* belong to mommy, and who, at that moment, was *very* much in need of mommy's protection.

So. Faced with this stark situation and lacking any other means of credible defense, I did the only thing that made sense. I hugged one of mother's pants' legs as tightly as I could, while I peered out from beneath the comparative safety of her kitchen coat. And I hoped like tarnation that the apparent danger would pass me by. It would.

Mother laughed hard that day when she saw (and felt) my little arms glued about her, besides the look of absolute terror on my face. Yes, and from that day onward I would be entirely convinced that I had barely escaped a licking. And, in my memory—mother will forever remain the only true friend that I ever had in family life.

Father had decided again then. Our residence in Helsinki would soon become just a memory, as would our stay in Finland. But instead of our setting foot on a ship with which to ride the rolling waves of the Atlantic back to Canada and home, on one weekend we boarded a twin-engine airplane in Helsinki.

And as the light of the evening sun caught her hand, my Aunt Kepa stood on the tarmac, waving good-bye to us. Then the roar of the engines deafened ears as the plane lifted us into the air. To high in the sky we soared as our transport flew all of the long way back to Canada. And Vancouver.

We came back home to Lanark Street and the beginning of a West Coast autumn. Now, with our globe trotting over with for the time being, life would soon return to normal for our family. I guess that getting back home does that.

Chapter Nine

TINY TYKES ARE PRONE TO MOUTH many amusing things. Just ask a chubby fellow called Van Norden. His impressive degree in medicine sat on a wall. He sat in a chair. And I wanted to know where in the world it was that the good man put his garbage.

Dr. Van Norden, I figured, is supposed to be an intelligent man. And if the middle-aged doctor is indeed intelligent, I reasoned, then he really should have expected me to ask him this, to me, very perplexing question. You see, I had already asked the doctor my question—a question to which I had received no reply. Only a barren stare.

The man's office trash can was empty. Right down to its metal bottom. Devoid of even a used Band-Aid, which I had rather expected to see when I had craned my neck over for a look as I sat in my chair.

An important man such as the doctor, I knew, must generate a lot of trash. All important people do. And since I believed this to be undeniably true, it became abundantly clear to me that the man stashed his garbage elsewhere. Where, I didn't know. The clean trash can was merely a ruse. A ploy designed to get me to believe that the good doctor lived a sanitary, exemplary life.

But even though my consuming desire for knowledge about the man's garbage-disposal habits had met a dead end, all was not lost. It wasn't, because mother—the sunshine of my day, was here too. Mother, who sat in a chair next to me, smiled, as the good doctor finished examining my hands which were in a sorry state from eczema. Dr. Van Norden penned a prescription for cortisone and handed it to mother. And without me finding out where the man hid his garbage, mother took me by the hand and dragged me from the premises.

Sitting on the city bus on our way home, I thought about that hidden garbage. This turned out to be the consuming topic in my mind for the rest of the day. As you might expect, I was getting awfully tired of guys like Van Norden, guys who refused to cooperate with me by their refusal to reveal their garbage secrets.

Today, garbage holds no fascination for me. So, please do not send me a letter asking me to inspect the contents of your trash can.

AS I ILLUSTRATED earlier on, wasps annoy me. So do bees. I know that bees make honey. And I do like honey. I just don't like bees and any who wear the black "yellowjacket" stripe, meaning wasps and hornets. I have no affection—whatsoever—for any of these.

In my view, these guys are all a major nuisance. All that they ever really much do is to go around and sting nice people. Because this activity is what they would rather do. If they all got psychiatric help, which they are in dire need of, and landed themselves real jobs where they would experience pride in being gainfully employed in the work force, odds are, they wouldn't have the energy and inclination to be so rude as to sting anybody. In my optimistic scenario, they would all be so awfully tired, and so well brainwashed, that they would not wish to sting anybody.

None of this bunch of irrational rejects, then, would wish to impale our tender flesh with their incisors—if I had my way. This is how I look at it.

These buggers have no appreciation for we humans. Bees are the worst. Being the biggest amongst the named predators here, they must be. And outside of the honey that bees work so hard to make, *we* humans don't have any appreciation for bees. Nor do *we* have any appreciation for their kin. To any of us who have even once been inoculated by their sharp prong—the bee, or the wasp, or the lowly hornet are the epitome of evil. They are the incarnation of evil.

Bees and cars, I know, are not related by blood. And bees and cars are usually considered two distinctly separate subjects. But lost under the spell of the bright sun on a warm summer morning, in our backyard at Lanark Street, they became one subject to me.

I was standing on a carpet of green grass, fresh cut by father. Father was not at work today because this was a weekend morning, either Saturday or Sunday. I was keeping father company as he repaired our old 1948 Studebaker sedan.

On our lawn to the left of the Studebaker, facing us, was parked another car. Father's pride and joy. A 1957 Buick sedan. The same car that had carried us to Montreal on our trip to Finland. Returned safe and sound. How? Don't ask me.

This was one of the fastest cars of its time to roll off of a production line and become a popular means of transport for those with a family, those who were in a big hurry. Folks older than me say this. A generation of folks that began before baby boomers like me hit the surface of the Earth, running and squealing as we hopped about on the baking pavement on sunny summer days, each of us with a Popsicle stuck to the mouth.

Just why anyone would want to be in such a confounded hurry, I do not know. I don't know everything. Even on this day in time, I don't know everything. Nor much of anything—my detractors will be pleased to tell you.

But about this Buick of dad's then. With its bullet speed and aerodynamic, once agreeable pale-blue body, at one time this car would have been adored by any teenager of the day on his or her way to a good time. Lackluster from constant exposure to the outdoor scene, in its current state it sat, like the Studebaker, somewhat faded and badly rusted, dejectedly minding its own business like a has-been.

Anyhow, I need to get back to the story I wish to tell you. The closed hood of this car was a perfect trap. The closed hood of any car can be a trap under the wrong circumstances. Father had completed his work on the Studebaker. Father now turned his attention to the Buick. Like the Studebaker, the Buick required maintenance, despite the fact that it was, notwithstanding its weathered appearance on the outside, a newer car. Father lifted the hood of the Buick. As he did so, and I was standing to the left of father, a small, fuzzy ball of yellow, about the size of a dime, shot out from beneath the hood with the speed of a projectile fired from the muzzle of a cannon. I was squarely in its path.

The blurred ball of energy struck me just above the middle of my mouth. Between my nose and mouth. And the instant that this miniature meteor hit me I felt the sting of something. This hurt. In the next moment I realized that it was a bee. A bee that had bumped into me with a storm cloud of fury in its tiny heart.

I knew, too, that this bee had bitten me real good. I knew this because this greeting, as I prefer to call it, hurt pretty bad. It hurt awfully bad. It hurt baaaaad! Baaaaad! Baaaaad! Without screaming from the pain, and without telling father, I ran across our backyard and along the cement walk skirting the edge of our house, and entered our front. I ran up the steps of our house, opened our front door and shut it. I ran for the kitchen, where I knew that mother would be. I ran to tell mother.

Mother was the one person in my world to tell things to whenever something was terribly wrong in my life. Mother, I knew, could be counted on for everything. "Äiti! Äiti!" I shouted. I then let mother in on the all-important news of my day thus far. "A bee kissed me mommy!" I said this with bated breath.

Mother bent over and examined the puncture wound. Telling me to stay put, mother was off in the blink of an eye to get a cotton swab, a Band-Aid, and some Dettol disinfectant. Zoom. She returned within moments, carrying these. Mother tended to my bite. The first bee bite in my life.

However, even after mother had finished with me, I realized that my bite still hurt stubbornly hard, and I could think of little else except the throbbing pain for the duration of the day.

And I learned only one other thing: getting kissed by an angry bee at the age of three, which I now was, was baaaaad! "Baaaa!" This is what every little person customarily says when circumstances disrupt one's life. Little people cry. Little folks always have to make sure that everybody within a mile radius of them know about their discomfort. That way they figure to get more sympathy from mom and dad. Little folks are pretty clever, huh?

But, I was a man and I did not cry from a bee sting that day. And nowadays, I can't see myself getting anything more than a bit peeved should a bumblebee ever decide to kiss me again. I know that I've little to worry about. I don't know of too many a bee—or anything else except the odd mosquito—that might want to try its luck with me before I resign it to the netherworld. I guess that I am just not as attractive as I used to beeeee!

FOR ALL OF MY LIFE I've been explorative by nature. At the age of three, I managed to raise the eyebrows of one flustered young mother. Her little girl, a lass with curly brown hair, and she about the same age and size as myself, had stood in the center of an aisle in a Vancouver department store. I recall the store and the incident well enough, I just don't remember the name of the store, nor its location within the city.

Anyhow, on this day long past, the child had strayed a mite too far from the protective side of her mommy. So, naturally, I had to do what any gentleman who suffers from a total lack of common sense and etiquette could only have done. I did the unthinkable. The unforgettable. And to the little girl's mom, my act was unforgivable. I breached the unspoken law of decency.

Very casually, as though I were practiced in so doing, I went up to the tot and lifted the decorative hem of her dress to have a good look at whatever I'd find beneath her attire. And, as I peered upward, I obtained a mighty fine look at her panties. Please do not ask me if I remember what color her undershorts were, though. Like the color of her dress—I just don't remember.

I have another, better excuse for my forgetfulness as well. In the case of her lingerie, it was fairly dark beneath the flap of the dress then. This, I feel, should do for an excuse. And I have to admit it—during my quick examination then I couldn't see anything which struck me as being particularly interesting. Nothing of monumental noteworthiness or historic value, certainly.

My curiosity having been appeased then, I ducked out from beneath the tot's dress; it was a mighty good thing that I had not tarried in my inspection. Yes, for my sake. And for the sake of the tot's mother, who, very likely, nearly suffered a heart attack.

I was still standing beside the little girl, wondering if she wanted to be my friend and play with me. But her mother, who was not far off, responded with the stern tone of urgency in her voice. "Katie! Come here now!" And on hearing her mother's command, the little girl ambled off. Her mother, if she was the girl's mother as she seemed, made no attempt to conceal her considerable displeasure as she stood there in the aisle, utterly aghast.

Sorry about that, mom. Please accept my sincere apology. And accept my very late excuse: remember that I was only three years old at the time of my indiscretion. In fact, as you will no doubt be happy to know, I had to endure a great deal of ribbing from my own mother in the years following this incident. My mother, you see, had witnessed it all from afar.

A child's interest is prone to wander. Back at the store, I soon found something to distract my attention. Someone had dropped a green pen on the floor of the establishment. I picked it up without a second thought and pocketed it, much to the amusement of mother and father, who half-playfully admonished me in turn, I having been told that I would find myself promptly marched off to jail if I was, in carrying out such an act, ever caught by the store's detectives.

I reasoned at the time that whatever small items I found on the floors of stores had been accidently dropped by unlucky customers, and that these items belonged to the stores no more than a lost coin, which I sometimes discovered, did. Hence, a lost pen or a coin were always fair game for me. My behavior was in no way remarkable. All children pick small items up, off the floors of stores and other public places, and carry such things away.

What else did I do when I was three? Well, let's see. Once, when I was almost four, I got caught at a downtown Vancouver bank. No. No. No. I know what your overall impression of me must be by now, but peppy-please with peppermint on it—do not consider me as having been an aspiring career criminal who'd started this young. The pop bottles and bubble gum that I stole later in life do not mean that I am a lifelong thief, either. And I was never in the same league as Al Capone in his prime.

Besides, I would never have considered using the only means at my disposal with which to make a threat—the squirt gun, to hold up a bank. I am, er-uh, was much too professional to be caught using such a useless piece of weaponry. What I really mean is that I got sort of entangled. You know. Those revolving doors of see-through glass that don't seem to offer any means of exit once ingress has been gained. They just go round and round and well, you get the picture. And I went round and round and, you get the picture.

Compounding my frustration at the time, I could see mother standing ten feet beyond the door, outside, on the sidewalk, as clearly as she could see me, and of course, she wondering what the hold up was. Today, I wonder who the genius was who invented the revolving door. Please remember to remind me to let the air out of that troublemaker's car's tires.

I still feel this way because, at the time of the action I was getting pretty dizzy and winded as I fought for my freedom in the clutch of this particular revolving door. More dizzy and more winded I became with each rotation as I'd spin around for a minute that would seem eternity to me. In fact, I was being spun around by the door's acquired momentum and will. Spun around in a hopeless circle inside of this awful passage, while I did my very best to cry out one word: "Mommy!"

My plight was an amusing spectacle for all the bank's clientele who happened to witness the free show. Mother was the most amused.

And after mommy had dragged me clear of the infernal device she exclaimed merrily, "So you like to play with that door, do you?" Laughing, mother bent over and drew me close to her. Mother patted me on the head to soothe my shattered nerves. I was still very frightened by my momentary separation from her and she knew it.

As I recovered from my ordeal, mother took me by the hand, and we walked to Woodward's, where she bought for me a small bag of potato chips. The chips had been slightly overdone along the edges, a feature I found interesting. And I thought, because the chips were wrinkled so badly, that they looked exactly like the wrinkled face of an old man who sat across the aisle from us, after mother and me had boarded the city bus to go home. I did not know that my potato chips were called wrinkle chips.

Mother and I were seated near to opposite the driver, on the long bench at the front of the bus. The old man faced us from across the aisle, his steady gaze lifeless, he seemingly oblivious of our existence. As I stared vacantly at the old man, I bit into the blackened portion of one chip. I kind of lost my appetite then. It would take me several years to regain my appetite for potato chips.

I still remember the old man like it was but yesterday that I saw him. I remember the hunched back and crooked nose. And of course the look of hopelessness in his sunken eyes.

Back in yesterday, I could *see* even then that his eyes were eyes that had nearly lived their life. His mouth was shut tight; I could not see whether he was missing any teeth, but I guessed that at his age he probably was.

An old man on a city bus. A man with a wooden cane. And a black raincoat to shield him from the elements. Where he was going, I didn't know then. Yet the old man might just as well have been on a journey into *The Twilight Zone.*

With the tip of the cane in his left hand resting on the floor of the bus, the old man turned halfway about on the bench and pulled a cord beneath the window at his back, signaling a stop. He rose slowly and approached the front exit.

It was eerie watching him. He stood at the front of the bus, framed in the gray light of the day, his bent back toward us. It was a cold, miserable, rainy day so typical of Vancouver. For all that the old man seemed to care, he might just as well have been standing at the edge of a wormhole leading to another universe. Into another place. Into another time. And into another life.

Perhaps into infinity. With no memories to remember. With no memories that could make him smile. And no memories to flog him. Time itself seemed to freeze about him. He had that unusual quality. A quality that even one so young as myself then, could not miss. And I was not given to missing anything that aroused my interest.

I could clearly see that whatever the old man had been in his youth was of no concern to him: the old man was on a journey. A journey into the unknown. I now know what I was too young to know then. The old man was on a journey of apathy, which so many people fall victim to at the end of life. Like every old man, he was a traveler. Traveling alone to where he knew not. In enough time, all of us complete this journey. But what, if anything, might lie beyond I cannot say. I am not entirely sure of everything. Only a total fool ever is.

I doubt that, had he been so inclined to do, the old man could have told me anything of value then, that I do not know today: in parting, he did not turn about to tell me anything then. He did not have to. The diary of his life and the hardships he had faced along the way were written into the weathered crevices of his face. The old man's worn face, the look of tired despair in his eyes, were a mirror of his inner self. I understand this now.

I would have no wish to divulge to you the details of another man's life even could I do so with no mistake, which I cannot. And what secrets he held within him will remain forever unknown for another reason as well. You see, those secrets no longer exist because he certainly no longer exists.

The door of the bus swung wide open. "Sunaprava!", a newspaper vendor, another old man, shouted from a downtown street corner. The old man with the cane got off of the bus. The darkening light of dusk closed about him, and I never saw him again.

AS MOTHER AND I WALKED HOME from the bus stop, a question continued to nag at my mind. The old man on the bus had made me think. I felt quite uneasy. And as soon as we arrived back home, I asked mother about the nature of my interest. What, I wanted to know, do old people do when they become really old.

I had presented my question to mother in a jumble of Finnish words that you would understand only if you speak the language yourself. "What on Earth do you mean, Roy?" So replied my all-knowing mother.

"What happens to them mother?" I persisted, curious to know the answer. My mother looked at me with an expression on her face that I had never seen before. She looked grave.

And mother's answer, when it came, struck me with almost the force that a bolt of lightning would have. "They die," mother said. "We all die someday, Roy." I had heard of people who had died in accidents. I knew, also, that these people had vanished into thin air, never to return.

I began to cry. I was worried about mother. And me. I knew that I simply could not live without the love of the one person in the entire world who really cared about me. And mother could do nothing to stop the torrent of tears that were now running down my face. A cascade of tears that picked up speed and ran like an untamed river, the droplets of saltwater hitting the rug on the parquet floor of our living room. This was the very first time in my life that I could see the far future clearly, yes, and on this day I saw the river of eternal despair.

Heartbroken, I rushed away to my room and hid beneath my bed. There, I cried for a long, long, time.

As I grew a little older, I listened to Marilyn Monroe on radio as she sang about the same river. This river from which no one can ever come back.

CHAPTER TEN

ANOTHER DAY in the life of a little boy. "I have—nothing—to say!" Exactly why I said it, I do not recall. It is as much a mystery to me now as it must be to you, since, undoubtedly, you will recall that which I told you at the outset of this book, that mother called me Happy. And I guess that except for the rare occasion, I was just that—happy.

As I say, I recall the fact that I had nothing to say, nothing to say on this particular bright summer morning. I recall it as though it were only yesterday. Was I sad then? Perhaps. Perhaps on this day I was.

I was four years old now, as I sat idly on the front porch of our house on Lanark Street. A seventeen-year-old chap, whose first name was Denny, delivered *The Vancouver Sun* to our door in the evenings, every day of the week except on Sundays. Yet a half block away, I could see Denny taking a stroll on the sidewalk this early morning, on his way to somewhere.

I knew Denny to be a cheerful kid who I'd hardly ever had any dialogue with. I also knew that mother liked Denny and sometimes chatted briefly with him. "Hello Roy. How are you today?" the smiling lad queried myself as soon as he came within earshot. From mother, Denny knew enough about me to call me by my first name.

But about Denny's question. At first, it seemed to fall upon deaf ears. But I was not deaf. I had heard Denny's question well enough. Yet, only after what must have seemed like eternity to the waiting lad, did I choose to respond.

With both of my elbows resting on my lap, and the palm of each hand firmly supporting the underside of my chin, I replied in a fashion befitting an old man. A very wise old man. A sage of countless years in experience. A man who had seen the peaks and valleys of his life go by, like the advancing and retreating glaciers of an untold number of ice ages gone by. With my gaze now riveted on our porch, without the slightest interest to acknowledge Denny's existence on my face, I said what I said before that I had said on that long gone day, "I have—nothing—to say!"

I wonder what Denny thought on hearing such seemingly profound words from the mouth of a little boy. A little boy who looked to be lost deep in thought. The words must have sounded strange to the youth. Words that supplied the aura of a young mind already resigned to whatever the future held in store, and these were words that had been spoken with all the assurance of a true prophet.

Words spoken, as though I had been rendering a binding statement on the future of the human race. Words that might have seemed to the listening lad, to speak of vast knowledge of all events in the faraway future. The distant future, and the distant past.

Mere words. But words that had been uttered with lazy indifference as though the entire world lay at my feet, and I had only the task of judging the trials, failures, and triumphs of humanity. I might just as well have been sitting on a silver cloud on this day, immersed in meditation. Certainly, my spoken words will have made no sense to Denny, and to anyone who might have chanced to hear them while hiding in the camouflage of our neighbors' hedge.

Or—to Denny, and to others like Denny, these words from an innocent little boy might, just as likely, have come from the morally advanced inhabitants of a parallel universe, who had tried, and failed miserably, to warn mankind of some impending disaster. I don't know what

I meant on this day in the past. Maybe, like an old man, I was a trifle despondent for some reason. (Perhaps it be that all little boys are really very old men in disguise.) Or I was just pooped. I know that I will never remember now. It is far too late. I feel the crushing weight of the doors of time as they steal their way in on my memory of this long gone day—and close.

As for those of my memories which remain stubbornly intact, I shall need to think hard and fast, and try to beat these doors before my memory is wiped away by the encroaching ravages of feeble old age.

Time is like that. Time always produces change as it moves forward. Sometimes for the better. Sometimes for the worse. And by the time that I turned five years of age, my disposition, usually obedient, had slowly undergone a mild but noticeable transformation. My personality had developed a stubborn streak. A streak of defiance.

Now, whenever I felt that I had been needlessly chastised I made no secret of it, by mouthing my protest aloud. In Finnish, mother would ask me whether I still objected to do this or that, after mother had issued an order. Then I'd respond. *Hantiin (hun-teen)* is the Finnish word that I reserved for use on occasions when I wished to convey my deep dissatisfaction. Hantiin, which has but one meaning, means to resist. At the old age of five I felt old enough to use that word to convey my staunch resistance to mother's demands. The unyielding demands of a physically superior power.

Oh, mother may have given me the odd tap on my behind, now and then. Yet if she did, these would have been more like playful love taps.

But that mother beguiled me on one occasion, this I remember. Positively. You see, my dear mother could act. And the unrecognizable, furry entity that she became was frightening enough then. I know that I did sweat with fear when mommy, with her head and shoulders completely hidden beneath a black bear skin throw, pursued me throughout our house until I ran to safety beneath my bed.

I am truly glad that my legs and feet had responded to the surge of adrenaline I'd felt back then, this having allowed me quick flight. And back then, it mattered not to me that a good long section of mommy's pants' legs had showed from under the bear skin. I was fooled. Completely. Call me stupid. STOOOO-PED. Boy, did that mysterious bundle of black fur e'er scare the crap out of me! Credit mother. The fearsome boogyman could have done no better.

Years later, mother recounted that I had appeared, at the time, to object for the mere joy of it. For the joy of resistance. I would vociferously object then, mother recalled, even on those occasions when I was not certain what it was that I was objecting to. "Hantiiiin!" To any bystander, the bear rug ruse that mother deployed this once would have been hilarious to watch. Some costumes can be so doggone frightful.

BIRDS LOVE TO LAY EGGS. Before I was five and, naturally, well-informed about life's many mysteries, just as well as any grown-up, I'd wondered why birds went through the trouble of laying eggs at all. And I still wondered about it. I knew that, had I been born as a bird, I would not have wished to sit on my butt for hours on end, keeping some white, or brown, or turquoise colored, rock warm. What a useless activity this was. I can think of lots of things that I would rather have done, and sat on, had I been a bird, I thought. For instance, I could have spent most of my time sitting atop the soft cushions of a nice, comfy sofa or armchair.

About eggs. The only eggs that I really liked were the chocolate variety. The kind that the Easter bunny would always bring when he made a delivery to our household. Turquoise eggs, the eatable non-rock kind, were a nice touch too. My only complaint was that once inside of my mouth, they tasted almost exactly the same as the eatable pink or yellow colored eggs. There was no real variety in flavor for my sensitive, unboring, young taste buds. Oh well.

But what a busy fellow the Easter bunny must be, I thought. I assumed that just like Santa Claus who I knew had many elves, the Easter bunny had little workers of his own. Workers that were always passionate about their work. Workers who never complained. That never ate. And never slept. Workers that never get tired of laying eggs, both eatable and not, or never get tired of pilfering them from somewhere, I figured.

Where, exactly, the Easter bunny obtained his eggs from was not my concern. How he got them was none of my business, either. I had a lot of time to think about the Easter bunny and Santa Claus. I had all day. And um. I slept during the night. Night, which is a delightful time when no one can be expected to be thinking about them, I thought.

I knew that I always got awfully tired thinking about the Easter bunny, who had nothing better to do really, than any dumb bird did. And—*if* the birds actually layed all of their eggs, which they probably did rather than resort to theft, then the birds did all the work. The Easter bunny, like Santa, just walked amongst his "flock," congratulating them all the while on their productivity, as his workers toiled on. Being birds—they had bird brains. As such, they can never be expected to be overly smart, I thought. Enough about them and the Easter bunny.

CHAPTER ELEVEN

A CHANGE WAS IN THE WIND. Our house had been up for sale for some time. My parents had decided that a new home was desirable over an older dwelling. So it was that the day came when our house on Lanark Street was sold, and our life at 6152 Lanark merged with the past to become but a memory.

We moved south, over the Knight Street Bridge to the township of Richmond.

I noticed a pleasant difference between our new home and our old one. As soon as the first heavy rainstorm hit. The roof of our new home did not leak; our old abode had under driving rain so common to Vancouver and its environs.

Our new home sat on a mud lot as flat as the Saskatchewan prairie. At 620 Kalamalka Crescent.

Called the "Elm" by the development corporation that had sold the house to my parents, this house of ours, situated amidst an entire community of new homes, was a big change for all of us.

Our house was two floors high. The color of the exterior was predominantly gray; mostly siding, some brick of a color I wouldn't recall later, had been used.

Looking back in time, I am of the opinion that the primary color of the exterior lent a conservative, even drab, atmosphere to the home.

Back then: I checked out the inside of our new dig. There were, I discovered quickly, many closets for me to hide in on those days when I was sure to misbehave and would have to scurry to a safe place to park my scared butt.

Along the first floor of our home was an unfinished area that would become, for the purpose of myself and my siblings, our vacuous playground. We would soon be using this empty space to engage ourselves in matches of ping-pong and, to throw darts into what else—but a dart board, of course.

Father lost little time in building a sauna, right next to a spacious laundry room that abutted on the carport. The second floor of our dwelling boasted a large living room-dining area. Like each of we children had had at Lanark, we kids each had our own bedroom.

It rains less in Richmond than it does in Vancouver. This is due to the influence of the north shore mountains across Burrard Inlet, a narrow expanse of ocean that penetrates east fifteen miles from the open water of the Strait of Georgia. Mountains always attract rain clouds. That is why the north shore receives the most precipitation annually, and the heaviest rains in the area.

Being further from these heights, Richmond is often spared a good soak that Vancouver is not. Still, even though nature favors Richmond with less rain, the sky here is often burdened with somber, gray rain clouds. Mostly gray house. Too often gray sky. Even a child will instinctively recognize too much of one color. I did.

For me, life in this otherwise utopian, ultramodern community would have been without problems—except for school. Grade one was knockin' on my door, and I was not eager to begin the most important learning experience of my life.

Yet before I was drafted into the first grade, our family headed out on a late summer vacation. Into the wild interior of British Columbia. By car of course. Not by pack mule. The Cariboo gold rush days were long over. Just like the men who went there in search of the prized yellow metal. Went to where a lucky few did manage to stumble upon gold, and thus, financial security and bliss. And from where others, enormously enduring of spirit, trekked further north to the Yukon to begin a gold rush that was destined to make colorful history. But we did not journey north in search of gold. Only fun.

WE CAMPED AT PAVILION LAKE, near the tiny village of Pavilion, which is north of Lillooet, for three nights. Then we headed deeper into the interior, with father driving us up the Cariboo Highway, all the way to the small community of Quesnel.

It was cold and drizzly in Quesnel. So, we did not linger there for long before father turned our recently acquired red-and-white Dodge station wagon around, and drove us back south the way that we had come. Drove us to Lac La Hache, where we spent the night. From here, father drove our party to Cache Creek, and from there, on to Kamloops. Then, on Highway 5, father headed north again. We stopped at a dot on the map, a dot called Little Fort.

And from what I'd seen Little Fort wasn't any more than that. In America, a dot and name on a U.S.-made map usually means, at the very least, a good-size town or village with real, live people. In Canada, especially in the far north, it can mean little more than the sight of a long-since abandoned mine, slowly fallen into decay, with a ghost town having sprung up around it.

Anyhow, we'd be staying for two nights in Little Fort now, camping in a rocky pasture, on a slight slope littered with the white skulls of long-dead cattle beside our makeshift campsite. I noted the small creek below our site, and thick woods on either side of us.

Father, who was concerned about bears, especially grizzly bears, had made sure that we had come prepared. Well. Sort of. Father had brought his starter's pistol. And if that did not provide us with a false sense of security, then perhaps the thin, quarter-inch-thick wall of our homemade plywood camper, painted ferocious baby-blue on the exterior, did. This camper, our home away from home, was mounted on the roof of our station wagon by rack and rope. Here, in our supposedly secure hotel, we slept peacefully but uncomfortably for two chilly nights.

The days had been somewhat warmer though. And during this time me and Helen imagined that we rode horses. By the creek, we each found the straightest stick that we could, one proportionate to Helen's height and the other to mine. Then we tucked the rough shafts of these betwixt our legs as we frolicked about the pasture. Lacking sleeping bags, the five of us slept on inflated vinyl mattresses, with a couple of wool blankets each, these to help keep us from freezing to death. And we each had a pillow, to rest one's head on.

At the end of our brief, six-day adventure, we all felt ready to go home. The nights were too cold here. And—there were too many hungry mosquitoes. We left for home.

BUT ONCE WE WERE ALL SAFELY BACK HOME I had to face reality. The next day, in the afternoon to be specific, I accompanied mother on a half-mile walk to the one place in my world that I had really begun to dread, now that my family's camping trip was over. School. To be precise, Samuel Brighouse Elementary School. A modern building in 1964, my former jailhouse still stands today. At least the structure had been aptly named. Brighouse.

Once mother and I'd arrived and stepped in through the jailhouse door, I was introduced to my first-grade teacher. Mrs. Mulder. A tall woman, she was then. And thin.

I must say that if there was anything about this woman that impressed me straight off the bat—it was her height. First impressions are often right, because from this point onward I would find nothing else to admire about my teacher. Our meeting over with now, mother and me walked home.

That evening, the sight of mother packing my lunch pail with peanut butter and jam sandwiches on *the* eve before I was to be conscripted did not make me happy. And if there was any question about it in my mind then, I knew for a certainty that my years of freedom were about to end, when I stood with my lunch bucket in hand, on the sidewalk beside Helen, a block from our house, early the next morning.

Yes, I knew exactly what the big yellow bus, moving at a moderate clip toward me, meant: long years of forced obedience and silent suffering.

I was still sleepy from the uncivilized hour at which I had been awakened by mommy. Parallel to the sidewalk and the school bus, two long lines of children stood waiting to board. Just now I was in for a rude surprise. A girl of my age stood at the head of the other line. Right beside me, she did. The door of the bus was already open, and several children had boarded the vehicle. Despite my silent misgiving about going to school, I was about to myself. But. "Ladies first." the mature, sandpaper-rough voice of the school bus driver barked at me.

I bristled. So rude, I thought. Still, I'd back down and let the young lady at my side in first; although, not before I'd protest. "Let's take turns," I said, defiantly looking up at the chubby, middle-aged fellow who drove the bus. I, as if to stare him down to my level of height with my pirate's evil eye, the right eye; my left orb was closed.

The driver had shut his yap. And with no further interruption to plague my first day of school, I stepped onto the bus with Helen close behind. I found a seat near the front and *I* sat down. But. Soon I discovered that the racket, which the older children on the bus made, disturbed me. Even though Helen sat in the seat right behind me, I felt quite bewildered and afraid. I wanted to go back home to mommy. And play with my toys. I did not want to go to school.

Yet, I knew that it was too late to jump out of the half-open window next to me. My school was but a short drive from home. The bus had arrived at its destination. Yes, it was too late to make a mad dash for my freedom now. Even had I, I would not have known how to get back home.

The bus driver put his foot on the brake as he eased the leviathan to a stop in the schoolyard. I did not like this at all. I thought again about slipping away. Maybe I did know how to get home. I knew if I walked along the nearby railway tracks, these would, eventually, lead me home. I knew home for me was a long ways away. And just as I was internally debating this issue, whether I should flee or not, Helen seized hold of my coat sleeve and bade me to follow her into my new school. I should have jumped out of the open bus window, I thought.

There were lots of little kids, just like me, inside the building. As there had been on the school bus, there was lots of noise here, and like me, some of the little kids appeared startled and confused. Every little body clung beside a mom. None of the children who were about my age looked bored.

Mother had given Helen a note. A note that told my sister which room to take me to. Being the old kid that sis was, seasoned in finding her way in the big world of school, Helen didn't have any trouble in finding the right room for me, either. Groan. I would have welcomed a delay, no matter how fleeting. Any delay, just to postpone the beginning of my jail sentence. Helen's good sense of direction was just one more nail in my coffin.

Well, sis and me had arrived. Helen left me in my teacher's care and vanished from sight into the corridor, to see herself to her own classroom. Wherever on Earth that was.

Chapter Twelve

I JUDGE that Mrs. Mulder was thirtysomething years old at the time of my inauguration into the first year of school.

Mrs. Mulder bade me to sit at a desk in the second row nearest the door. Through the entrance, children were walking in from the hall, a guiding mother at the side of each kid. By now, my brain was starting to acclimatize to the situation at hand. I now surveyed the humdrum scene about me with strong disinterest, mingled with anxiety. I peered unhappily about me.

Scarcely a minute into my new surroundings, if you had asked me as to what single word would have defined my feelings about this place I would, without any doubt, have said—yuck! This—to me, looked like a very boring environment. For an unboring kid like me then, it did. And, if you had reminded me that I would spend the next twelve long years, except for summer holidays and other holidays, in such a place as this, I would, positively, have thrown-up out of sheer spite. If I had been sitting in some nice lady's warm and comfortable lap, you can imagine the terrible mess I would have made.

But there was no warm, comfy lap here. Only a hard wooden chair to sit in, a chair hard enough to petrify anyone's butt and make it sore by the end of the school day—and an equally hard wooden desktop, to place my hands on.

I construed that the empty, dark-green metal cubical beneath the top was meant to hold something important.

Perhaps bubble gum, I thought. Just then my train of thought was interrupted by my teacher's voice. Mrs. Mulder was announcing, in quick succession, each of my classmates' names. Because Mrs. Mulder had begun with the row of desks next to the door, it was no more than a matter of seconds before I heard my own name announced. Having just had my name read out loud in a public place made me nervous, and I looked about to see whether anyone else, besides my teacher, was paying attention to me. No one was. Whew!

From this point onward, in terms of events which I know for a fact that you will not find (snicker) interesting, my life in the classroom went steadily downhill. The boredom was already beginning to kill me. There were no toys for me to play with here. There was no television to watch cartoons on. And, having given up my much-worn rubber pacifier not even one short year since, my lower teeth were already gnawing at my upper lip in bored frustration. There was nothing here to keep my mind awake.

There was only an authoritarian figure who I was beginning to think of as being a kind of jail-lord. My teacher gave me and everyone else a yellow lead pencil which had to be sharpened. Walking to the pencil sharpener stuck to a wall, beside the door, Mrs. Mulder proceeded to give us a demonstration. Then, one by one each boy and girl in my class had to get up from his or her seat as Mrs. Mulder called out each child's first name. Get up and walk to the pencil sharpener. And crank the handle while pushing the pencil into a hole. Boy, this teacher sure seems an unwilling hostess, I thought. Uh-huh. What must she be thinking, requiring us to sharpen our own pencils?

As I wondered that, I wondered if there were any termites inside of the hole. How else could a pencil sharpener be expected to work? And if there were termites inside the hole—they sure worked fast. Incredibly fast. My pencil had come out plenty sharp. I returned to my desk and sat down in my chair.

I faced another problem now. What to do with a sharp pencil? I was not a bad boy, so I did not think, even momentarily, about jabbing the little girl who sat in front of me in the butt, with the finely sharpened tip. No. All that I wished to do, was to go home to mommy and play with my two miniature plastic tigers, and set of cowboy and Indian action figures. Enjoy a *donut* while watching cartoons on TV. *And* have a daytime nap. Yawn.

I looked about. Each boy and girl had finished sharpening a pencil, and each sat snugly in a chair. Mrs. Mulder, who had been sitting at her desk at the front of the class, probably daydreaming, now rose from her seat and demanded our attention. Taking a big stick in her hand, Mrs. Mulder turned about and pointed her stick at a row of strange-looking black characters printed on a long ribbon of white paper above the green, boring chalkboard. Mrs. Mulder was speaking.

My teacher claimed that the weird-looking things were a must for us to learn to use so that we could read books. Who would want to read books, anyway? Mrs. Mulder called the weird-looking things, letters. And the entire collection of letters—the alphabet. Strange name too. My teacher was continuing to jabber about this alphabet thing.

According to Mrs. Mulder, some letters were more important than other letters. These special letters, as many as the fingers on my hand, were called vowels. A, E, I, O, U. All five of them. My teacher had stopped explaining. Mrs. Mulder was giving us orders again. She wanted every boy and girl to draw the five letters, as best we could, on a sheet of lined paper. Which our teacher gave each of us next.

Every kid drew the five letters in miniature on his or her sheet of paper. Even me. Then Mrs. Mulder changed the subject.

My teacher was talking about an unknown called numbers. Mrs. Mulder drew the number 1 on the chalkboard. She said that this simple, unimpressive-looking line was the first real number in the world of numbers. From what my teacher said, I understood that there was only one number, which was not really a number at all, before the number 1. Then, so that we pupils could get a good look at this fake number, Mrs. Mulder drew an Easter egg on the chalkboard. This figure, my teacher explained, is called zero.

Now, I know that we are all well acquainted with the alphabet and numbers. We all know how to read, spell, and count. And therefore, my dear readers, I shall not bore you needlessly with the details of my first days, weeks, and months in school where I was supposed to be acquiring a solid foundation in these fundamental skills.

Though, I will say again, that school sure was an unexciting way to spend my day, perched stiffly, as I hate to remember, with my ass on that none-too-comfortable wood seat of my chair, staring at a green chalkboard, and listening to Mrs. Mulder's chatter. Enough about boring matters.

When my first full day of purgatory was at last finished, I returned home the old-fashioned way. I walked. Along the railway tracks. But come the next day, I would take the big yellow coach home. And on every school day thereafter, I would face the same routine. Five agonizing days every week. Helen's school day was not yet over. Helen would arrive home later on the coach.

I WISH TO REVEAL to you good folks, out there elsewhere on Earth, the particulars regarding the only classroom catastrophe of my first grade. I shall not keep you waiting and guessing as to the topic. I now refer to the event as my loose-poop-in-the-pants episode.

It happened thus. A slow learner, I was not doing well in language and numerical studies at school. In part, the problem of my poor performance in the classroom stemmed, I believe, from the glaring fact that Mrs. Mulder simply was not cut out to be a teacher of very young pupils. She did not seem to understand the needs of children my age. Or could it be that she did not care about us kids? Whichever, she may also have had the tendency to assume without proof.

You see, one morning as I sat at my desk I was heavily burdened and in dire need of a toilet for a poop. And so, during class (I would not have been sitting at my desk otherwise) I raised my hand and requested permission from Mrs. Mulder, that I be allowed to go to the boys' lavatory.

Since I was a trusting kid, I considered the necessity of obtaining my teacher's permission but a formality when one had a pressing matter to attend to. It was quite a shock when Mrs. M refused my request.

Perhaps my teacher believed that I wished to gain leave from class for a no-good purpose (hooky). If so, it was not a valid excuse for her refusal. Reason: in this situation or in any that bears a possible serious consequence to someone else, to merely assume in the absence of any proof is indicative of faulty reasoning; without proof the conclusion formed cannot be relied on and if it is—that may lead to an act of injustice. In other words, when one is in doubt about another person, one must give that individual the benefit of a doubt.

Whatever the impetus for my teacher's decision was, it is sufficient to say that I was more than a bit dismayed by Mrs. M's refusal then—the strong, unrelieved silent pressure inside, mounting swiftly, was becoming unmanageable.

I was trying, desperately, to fight the urge to crap in my underpants. I was trying to hold the chocolate back, sitting stock-still and squeezing my buttocks together like a vise, in the futile hope that I could prevent a spill. I was giving it my all. The best effort that I could muster.

However, it was not a wee, insignificant poop that fought to poke its ugly brown head into my clean underwear. It was a monstrous poop fighting savagely for its freedom. Fighting against me, just as hard as I fought against it. Needless to say, with this action going on in me, I was not doing any learning. I twisted back and forth in my seat, hoping that I could make it to the morning recess period. I continued to fight, tooth and nail, against my attacker. But I never made it.

Chocolate sausage slid into my underpants. And at this awkward instant then, which you might consider to have been the instant of my surrender even though I do not, I likely could not have told you whether my name was Roy. It is equally doubtful, at this moment in the past, that I could have concentrated long enough to tell you whether I was a boy. And, I certainly could not have told you, had you been there to ask me, that I was Roy, the er-um-boy.

Recess time came. But it did not matter much now. I waited impatiently until everyone else, including Mrs. Mulder, had left the classroom. Then I rose from my seat and slipped quickly into the boys' washroom.

I was glad that it was near. I slipped my trousers down and surveyed the scene in my underwear. What I saw was a disaster. My white brief was stained clear through, with a thick layer of rich brown paste on the inside.

In hindsight, I should have had the sense to discard my underwear. I should have. Yet I was only six years old then, and I had never faced such a situation. Even though it challenged me to do so, there was nothing else which I saw that I could do on this miserable day except pull my light-gray slacks, which bore on the exterior as well as the interior—between my two back pockets—this same dark-brown discoloration—an ugly stain that spoke volumes to anyone who was interested, back onto me—along with my soiled underwear which was even worse off.

Now as I returned to my classroom early, in the hope that no curious spectator would be about to notice my rear predicament, I knew that there was nothing else for me to do except attempt to be as inconspicuous as I possibly could. I mean, for the r-e-s-t of the school day.

I sat down at my desk. I sat down endeavoring to cover as much of my seat with my posterior as I could.

But even with the scrupulous care I took to minimize my disaster ghastly fumes rose into the air about me. The putrid odor lingered in my nostrils, reminding me that I was different now.

If I would have had any doubt as to whether anyone else had become aware that something in my immediate vicinity was terribly awry with the air quality—that forlorn hope would have been coldly destroyed when the brown-haired, doe-eyed little girl, who had heretofore sat in silent misery in front of me, suddenly turned around in her seat and popped the ultimate question. "Do you smell something?" the lass asked me innocently enough.

"No," I said, trying to be as calmly reassuring to her as I could manage.

The little girl shook her head in obvious confusion. Then she said, "I smell something terrible".

I made it through the lunch hour, the same way that I had made it through the morning recess, by being as inconspicuous as possible. I stayed glued to my seat in the classroom. No use risking detection by venturing to the lavatory to hide, I figured.

The remainder of my school day seemed to crawl by at a snail's pace. Then at last—school ended for the day.

The bus pushed its way down the road while I sat on the door side, in the front seat. I had chosen this spot for its strategic location. It was as close to the exit as I could hope. And I hoped to be off that bus and home to a warm, cleansing bath as soon as I could. But Father Fate, ever watchful, must have said—not so hastily, little bud! Absolutely, for, every time that the bus came to a sudden stop, I would lurch forward a bit in my seat. And I have no doubt that each time the bus hit a bump in the road, the solidifying paste stubbornly clinging to my rear end—assumed a new shape.

At last, the bus rolled into my neighborhood and turned onto Kalamalka Crescent. This was my stop. I rose slowly, rather than quickly from my seat, like an old man who has witnessed and experienced many things. I stepped off the school bus.

My face was downcast as I trudged toward home like a beaten puppy. Mother saw me coming while I was still a block away. And she told me later that she knew, instantly, something had gone wrong in my day. At the moment that she opened our basement door to welcome me home after a long day of learning, she guessed the reason for my despair. The liberated, pungent stench of poop wafted past mother's keen nose, into our house.

"Oh!" mother said, holding her nose in disgust with her left hand while she turned me about with her right. "Uh-huh," she said. I stepped into our house and mother closed the front door. Then mommy turned to face me again.

"Okay Roy—off with the pants!" I took my soiled slacks off. And my discolored underpants.

Mother spoke not a word as she washed me from head to toe in the bathtub. Finished! "Now." she said. "What happened?" I told mother about Mrs. Mulder's refusal to permit me to go to the washroom when I had badly needed to. And when I was finished explaining, mother did not scold me. She knew that it was not my fault. Just like I did.

I was physically ill the next day and had to stay home from school. But the following morning mother gave me a short penned note to take to my teacher. The message was quite terse. It explained the reason for my absence from class. The note also stated this: "The next time that Roy asks to go to the washroom—let him go!!!!"

I handed Mrs. Mulder the note as I stepped into her classroom. Whereupon my teacher read the note and asked me whether I wished to go to the washroom. I did not smile when I said: "No."

With a teacher like Mrs. Mulder, who could be difficult for any kid and adult to understand, it is a wonder that I learned a thing at all in class. And what small, isolated fragments of knowledge I did manage to pick up were usually unrelated to the three Rs—reading, 'riting, and 'rithmetic, which were so very hard for me to understand. And—if these basics in education were not difficult enough for myself—there was more.

The long music hour. Tell me about it, you say? Okay. I shall. Between my daydreaming about home and toys, I actually learned a few odd lines of lyrics. In one melody these lyrics describe a small rooster who is a child's play companion; in another, they describe a snowman who magically comes to life and, in so doing, acquires the ability to walk and run. And to speak and smile just like Frosty, the ever jovial snowman. Frosty, who unfroze and evaporated away. Then sprang into being again on another cold and snowy winter's day.

Now. Please consider the "cock-of". Though I was much confused as to what a cock-of was, I later guessed that I was singing about a clock, and that my garbled rendition of the lyrics probably had not impressed my teacher.

At home, I would sing "Secret Agent Man," who I mumbled about as, "elva man". Why?

Well, supposedly, as much as Raimo had said that he could make out from the sound track of "Secret Agent Man," one line of this very famous song, sung by Johnny Rivers, says that he is "One helluva man". Sure-sure. There are no such words in the lyrics of this song.

Albeit, inasmuch as the words are slurred in the driving rhythm of the music itself, for me, "elva man" will do the trick, so long as one's voice doesn't squeak too badly—and one's ear for music is in key.

Even though I was failing my first grade in school, my life was not entirely dismal every day. There were happy occasions at home. In particular, Christmas of 1964 in our spacious modern home was very rewarding for me. Not amongst other toys that I cannot dredge from my subconscious to conscious mind, I received a road-racing set with two miniature, electrically powered Ferrari cars, one red, and the other, white, which sped at high velocity along a wonderful grooved track built of numerous sections that snapped together in a jiffy, creating an oval circuit, or, if one desired, the more sporty number eight with almost equal ease.

Both patterns incorporated a white guardrail, but only the figure eight had an overpass built into the plan. The cars were guided by the usual handheld controls, and could be speeded up or slowed down as two competitors squared off against one another. When assembled, the layout fit into a space just four feet long.

CHAPTER THIRTEEN

To where he must ride is from whence he came
On the wind brews the tale of a gun with no name:

"Fast Gun of Silver—Money Can't Buy"
HIS JUSTICE spins from a groove of steel
One fast gun a man's fate shall deal
His swift hand will bow to no law
Except the one which he makes in the flash of his draw

The word of this man travels on by his deeds
The soul of his gun measures the life he leads
His deck ace of trust no money can buy
He'll soldier on to the day he dies
                                    —the author

TO ANY MACHO MAN, TERRITORY IS IMPORTANT. To me, it is not. That is, excluding the comforting worn familiarity of my fairly private berth, it is not. Not any more. I outgrew territorial disputes eons ago. I am anything but macho now. While it is true that I usually find myself attired in dark-blue or black denim, and likewise true that I always wear a black military belt about my waist, still, I am certainly not the Lone Ranger type by any stretch of anyone's imagination who might believe that he or she knows something of me.

For instance, am I resilient like the Lone Ranger? Well—maybe. Silent? Only when I am in deep sleep. And I never snore. Resourceful? Who cares? And just because I wear a military band about my middle, does not necessarily mean that I harbor a flagrant suicidal desire to be recruited into the ranks of the army of any nation on this small world of ours. I am a pacifist. Not a warmonger.

With those thoughts on my mind, it is difficult to explain my behavior. Not at the precise moment that the clock ticking on our living room wall told me that I had just turned six years of age. That was a couple of months ago. And, I didn't know then that forty years later I would finish penning an often-crusty autobiography of my early exploits in life—called *Timewalker Forever*. This book. Your book. All I did know then, was that every man worth his salt—must protect what is his own. His territory.

My territory included amongst other things an empty corrugated refrigerator carton that sat in our carport. Back in 1964, which was the present then, I was the John Wayne type: rough and ready. That I was when a pretty, little, brown-haired lass by the name of Karen, who was from our neighbors' house, came on over from her side to my side, and, asked me if she and her few friends could play with me. In MY territory.

I have to give credit to five-year-old Karen. Her then sparkling brown eyes and little-girl femininity would nearly persuade me to shelve, for the next hour or two, my sole ownership to the empty fridge-box when she asked me so wistfully, "Wanna bite?" As Karen asked me this, she thrust the orange frozen confection on a stick, that she had been sucking on, practically into my mouth. Fortunate it was that my mouth was closed.

Bribery might well work wonders on me now. But back in my early manhood I was, in my view at least if no one else's, the hygienic type. Hygienic with regard to what went into my so-o-o-o-o clean mouth. Karen's well-meaning offer appalled me.

And, should you refuse to believe that I was a clean-mouthed kid because of my unfortunate incident with poop in Mrs. Mulder's classroom, you may still redeem yourself in my eyes if you agree, even against your will, to believe that I was indeed a R-E-E-L man. I am not jabbering about fishing, either.

As obviously eager as sweet, innocent, little Karen was to have me for a friend then, I nonetheless rebuffed her. I regret it now. But I did. I wasn't the least bit interested in Karen's treat. Especially after where it had been. I was, however, quite impressed by Karen's apparent generosity of spirit. And her sincerity. If I ever get married, I would marry someone with Karen's personality.

Yet, as you all know, this time of which I speak was not the present, and the hair at the nape of my clean-shaven neck would surely have risen, had there been any hair there. My valid concern about hygiene aside momentarily then, I was not about to be bribed into relinquishing my claim to my box by a mere sugary snack. Even temporarily. I was not to be duped. I knew what any amount of time spent inside my box was worth.

I asserted my right of ownership. "This is MY territory," I said to Karen.

Whereon the little lass objected in instant indignation. "This is not your territory!"

Karen had spoken with absolute defiance in her tone.

"It IS SO MY territory!" I vehemently insisted.

But my emphasis of this point did nothing to convince Karen. "Humph! No, it's not!" said she. And Karen walked away, taking her friends with her.

Territory. Many books have been written about who owns what. As for myself today, I have all the territory I need. I have memories. The hidden little boy inside me wishes to tell you more about his past. I am Timewalker. Got brain—travel I must. The mission continues.

I hope that you do not judge me too harshly. It was never my intention to look for trouble by telling trespassers that they were infringing on my territory. Karen was a nice little kid. Not so the dirty imp on the opposite side of our lawn.

I had good cause to wish to be rid of him. I found this mischievous small guy taking a long, satisfying piss—in mother's rose patch. That, in broad daylight, in full view of passersby on our street. So, I did the responsible thing and promptly apprehended him. You can imagine the scene. I was one six-year-old boy—quite determined to perform a citizen's arrest of a three-year-old. I deemed my intended course of action fair, inasmuch as I had caught the peewee red-handed.

As the tyke casually zipped up his fly, I asked him what his name was. "That's me," the smart aleck rascal replied. I saw that not only had the kid committed an unpardonable sin in having discharged his pee on mother's roses, but that he was being evasive with me.

I was about to lay hold of his shoulder and give the brat a thorough shaking. I was surely about to. Had I been a betting sort of gentleman, I would not have given pee-pants any more of a chance to escape a good shake, than I would have given myself a chance of jumping on a trampoline— and landing on the moon.

But mother bruin was near and watching. Glowering at me she was, from an open window on the upper floor of the said anonymous rascal's house. "Don't you dare touch him!" she screamed at me, such ferocity in her voice that it made me quake in my undershorts and nearly caused me to wet them. "Let him go! Jamie come home!" mother bruin told me and her kid. I was outgunned and I knew it. So! Even though I regarded myself as the sheriff of my mother's rose patch, sworn to uphold the law, I had no choice but to let this Jamie feller go.

With often this kind of luck, rotten luck, no wonder that I'd never make it to become a real sheriff. And no paladin. I guess that I was just never meant to sport a tin badge of justice, and ride a white horse. Oh, what dangers could be found in my environment then were cause enough to have had the strong, unyielding arm of the law about. About the law. Forget about it. Okay? This damned law thing is too damaging for my pride to stomach. Right now.

Snicker.

I heard that!

A few months later, mother and I witnessed Jamie's mom going tooth and nail at the neighbor lady—whose name, incidentally, was Jeannie—who lived across the street from us. It was quite a fight with Jamie's mom tearing at Jeannie's long, raven hair. Though, with myself being a pacifist these days, you will never get me to admit that their brief match was at all interesting for me to watch then. Women! Born to scrap like women they are. Anything goes, it seems.

I, of course, fight like a man. Whenever I am in doubt about victory I can always be counted on to walk away, and thereby, spare myself possible humiliation. Knew that you did. You can always depend on me. That too. I prefer to save my hide. My hair t-o-o.

And just so that you need not ask. Back then, I was strongly rooting for the underdog, Jeannie, who was, mother said, a true lady. My mother was always right.

DOES THE NAME Scott X mean anything to you? To me, it R-E-A-L-L-Y did once, but for the X—which is a mere symbol of anonymity for his last name that shall remain ungiven.

Scott was supposed to have been my friend. However, during the short time that I'd played games with him this kid had turned out to be anything except that. With friends like Scott had been, who would have wanted enemies? Not me.

Here's the story—you be the judge: Being six years old then, Scott was my age. And, he was as pugnacious as a six-year-old kid can be. Scott had not only a problem getting along with myself, Scott had an enormous problem getting along with the entire world. Or, at least the world immediately about him.

I admit that my introduction to Scott had been my fault. My fault alone. But, let us be realistic in laying blame. How, on Earth, could I have known just what I was in for on the unhappy day that I'd knocked on Mr. X's front door, requesting permission to play with his son?

As viewed from the street, the X household lay a ways to the right of Karen's place and ours. To be purposely vague on the basis of legal prudence, the X house was a healthy pack rat's jaunt to our right. The elder X, I thought, was a gruff sort of human being. I was later surprised to learn that he was a teacher because he was as unpolished as a slab of granite newly cut. A dark-haired bear of a man with a huge pillow for a tummy. He towered over me. In fact, looking at him, I was half-scared shitless.

Anyhow, the fact that I had asked for instant company was not lost upon Mr. X. Indeed no, he knew a golden opportunity when he spotted one. My fault. Totally. At least, that is how I felt the very next day after school was out, when mother was conscripted as a baby-sitter. She would watch over Scott while the kid played with me. Played with my toy tow-truck and miniature set of cowboys and Indians.

Unfortunately, Scott was pure trouble from the outset of our brief association. He was as aggressive in personality and action as a shrew. Scott's favorite line, which he repeated often, probably for dramatic effect, was: "Evlyboty say I'm meeeen and nasteeee—but—I'm only nasteeee!" If Scott was intending to instill laughter within our house, I did not see anything to laugh about, at the time.

We argued about everything. Like who should get which toys to play with. A trivial matter, sure. The problem was that Scott liked my favorite toys as much as I did. This naturally created friction between us. Okay, so I had invited him to come on over. Yes, I officially admit that I had called on Mr. X, in a buoyant spirit of a child's inexperience and innocence, asking him to dump the brat somewhere in the vicinity of our home. Yet this, in itself, was no reason for mother and I to be saddled with the kid indefinitely.

Not this kid. Was Father Fate watching? I figure so. And I think that Fate, looking on as an amused spectator then, understood my fast-growing exasperation with Scott. Fate, who can be indescribably cruel, can also be quite the opposite, sometimes. And I guess that it was Fate—who wisely decided that Scott would have to go. Fate. And me. And Scott's own vanity.

My difficulties with Scott came to a timely end. Permit me to assert that I am a refined gentleman at the best of times. And no gentleman at all when I am mercilessly pestered beyond the threshold of my considerable patience. And besides: Scott had asked for it.

As suited his mean temperament, Scott had wanted to play war games, using rocks. But what Scott had been too vain to consider was the possibility that I was a better marksman than he. More than Fate, it was this which had proved to be his undoing. And my liberation, as well as my mother's, from the well of virtual hell.

It happened thus. Scott and I were hunkered in parallel ditches, close to home, with a mound of earth and rocks between us. Scott started it. And I would end it. He picked up a plum-size stone from the ground, and squatting, threw it over the mound. In having done so, Scott had made only one mistake. A tactical blunder that I would never have been guilty of making. Scott hadn't looked over from his trench to pinpoint my exact location immediately before he'd launched his missile. I guess that Scott, being Scott, figured to show me his future military potential. A crack arm in an elite commando unit, dispatching grenades at the enemy? Maybe. He missed my unprotected head, but narrowly. Had Scott been engaged in a real war, his oversight might well have meant the sudden termination of a promising career in the military.

Squatting in my trench, from beside me I picked up a rock of the same size and weight as the stone that had sped harmlessly through space, so close to my head. But unlike Scott, I did not fail to look over the mound the moment before I launched my stone. And—unlike Scott—I did not miss.

The stone caught Scott on the right side of his bean. I knew, instantly, that I had scored a hit. Not just because a split second before that I'd seen the projectile land, but because Scott promptly let out a wail that shook the whole neighborhood.

Fortunately, it was late afternoon on this particular weekday and our neighbors were already long wide awake. Scott leaped out of his trench and began to run toward the X home. Wailing he—all the while. As sorry a sight as Scott was, and as loud as his wailing was, I was not grief-stricken for Scott. I was panic-stricken for myself. Poop-a-gooooook! What do I do now? This question I nervously asked myself.

It was, I knew, essential that I find suitable refuge. It would not be long before the elder X showed up, pounding his fist on our front door. And my sweet mother, a bleeding heart when it came to a crying little boy, even a hopelessly mean one like Scott, would be horrified beyond words when Scott's dad told her of my deed. Scott would see to that. If anyone would ever try to drain an ounce of sympathy from a bleeding heart—it was Scott.

The reality that I had acted in self-defense, I knew, meant nothing to Scott. In his brain, his own violent act would be shunted aside. I knew this, for, I had come to know Scott well in the short time that I had been involved with the X household. I knew that Scott would portray me as the aggressor.

And knowing what Scott planned to do, I was equally determined that he fail in this regard, just as he had failed to strike my bean with his rock. I did the only thing that I could think of doing at the time, guaranteed to buy myself time, while I hoped like hell that the initial shock of what I had done to Scott would wear off a little on Mr. X and, my dear mother. If THEY could not find me.

I hid behind a twenty-foot-high cone of fresh earth, a long stone-throw behind our house. I should, I thought, have been wise enough to carry a pair of earplugs on me at all times. Earplugs can come in mighty handy in all kinds of emergencies. With both of my ears plugged, I would certainly have possessed a valid excuse, to not answer mother's siren call. "Roy!!!! Come out from wherever you are," her stern voice demanded. Earplugs. Every small mischievous boy should have his own pair.

As I prepared to face the music, I thought what a pity it was that Santa had never brought me earplugs for Christmas. For an emergency like this when I needed them the most, earplugs must be considered indispensible. And had I been wearing earplugs, I would not have heard myself being forced to apologize to Scott and his dad on our front step; yet, neither would I have had the pleasure of hearing Scott's father extract an apology from between Scott's clenched teeth.

The X duo left, and I'd have nothing more to do with them. Believe me, mother and I would always be glad for that.

And then, again the power that was had decided on a family move. And that power, as always, was father. Father, who persuaded mother. During our time at Lanark Street, and in Richmond, I know that father had been in the employ of a company called Auto Marine Electric, situated in Vancouver. That was before. This was now.

CHAPTER FOURTEEN

YOU MAY WONDER WHAT REASON had been good enough for us to have abandoned our dream house. All that I know is, difficulties had arisen between my parents and the land development corporation that had sold the Elm to them. So it had come to pass, that in early spring of 1965, father had locked the doors of the house that had been our home for the past ten months then, and we'd departed immediately for Campbell River, to the island which Captain George Vancouver visited in 1778, along with James Cook.

Captain George, and other early European explorers like his English compatriot James, should have stayed home, I think. They should have, because it was the white man who had brought an unseen hitchhiker in the form of smallpox, which had decimated the native population scattered along the long isle. But, enough about the sad history of Vancouver Island.

After the ferry trip from the mainland, a trip on which I'd not become seasick at all, we stayed for a short month at an unknown motel in Campbell River. From the motel we then moved to a second-floor apartment in town. And from what I can recall about the location of the apartment building, I know that it was situated near my new school. I do not remember the name of the street on which our residence stood.

My school was Helen's school too. Cedar Elementary. The school had been built fronting Cedar Street, an average street in an average neighborhood. From our apartment we would soon relocate to the oceanfront. It was yet during our stay in the apartment that the following would transpire, which has caused me in these later times—to conclude that Helen should have tried out for a part on *E.R.*

Helen would have been well suited for the job. One doesn't need a whole lot of brain matter to play doctor. And if one has little or no brain matter, one can always play the part of the comatose patient near death's door. The latter is what my sister chose to do. The only problem was that on this day Helen would carry her portrayal of the dying (or dead) patient, too far. And truth be told, I'd fall for her act. No wonder, then, that Helen would come to refer to me as, well, you don't really want to know.

Stretched out motionless on our living room couch was Helen. I, at first, believed that my sister was pretending. Still, Helen did not budge a single millimeter when I lifted the edge of her T-shirt and tickled her tummy with a feather, which, had fallen out of my Indian chief ceremonial headdress, a novelty of unauthentic manufacture that I had received as a gift on my sixth birthday, back in Richmond.

Seeing that this method of torture, which I thought extremely difficult for anyone subjected to it when awake to have to bear, had done nothing to get my sister off the couch, I decided to try another avenue of sparkling promise. I turned about, and, standing beside the sofa with my rear end pointed toward my sister, farted as though I were positioned with my butt stuck right in Helen's face.

Much to my dismay this tangency failed as well. So I opted to try a more conventional, sane, and less insulting approach to the problem. I screamed in each of my sister's ears, in turn. And I noted that this sound each time, quite unpleasant I thought, did not produce any result.

Next, I tugged hard on Helen's ears, hoping that the pain would elicit a response from Helen. But, this course of action did not arouse the patient, either.

Now I was really confounded. I tried other methods of forcible arousal, not all of which I can recall, but none worked to waken the patient. If my sister is truly in deep slumber, I reasoned, surely she would have woken by now. By this time, I was commencing to become very worried. I thought that maybe Helen had died. The thought shook me, and becoming suddenly frantic with concern, I was about to run and tell mother that something awful had befallen Helen.

I would soon have to give Helen her due. Her sense of timing had been well thought-out. Yes, because it was just then that Helen stirred, yawning, as though wakening from a deep slumber. And it was then, that I realized I'd been duped.

Helen looked at me with a mischievous grin on her face. "You're mean," I said. "I thought that you were a goner. But you were just acting all along." This said, in the next second I was off to the kitchen to tell mother all about Helen's liking for the extreme scare.

That memory brought me back into the present. I got up from my place on my favorite rock behind Lavers. The sky was still overcast and a light rain had begun to fall. There was little wind in the air. I looked out to sea—secure in the knowledge that I knew who I was. Then I turned my steps toward home, I having had my time to think.

ANOTHER DAY IN CAMPBELL RIVER. Another day in the life of a small boy. I still knew for sure who I was. But I was changing. I was ever-so-slowly becoming wiser about the sometimes mysterious ways of society. Sometimes, I was beginning to learn, one does not ask questions of people. Yet, I was still inquisitive about any matter that even slightly was taboo.

Some folks who believe that they know me well, might be inclined to tell you that my natural inquisitiveness has always been my one major drawback. These people, and there are not many who have known me since I was a kid, believe what they choose to believe. Not that it matters overly much to me, what they believe. What do they know? Are not *all* boys, especially little boys, naturally inquisitive? Some more so than others?

Well anyhow, if you do choose to believe that I was more inquisitive than all of my peers at the age of seven—so be it. But before you judge me in absentia, know this about me: As a child I was for the most part an introvert, and I still am.

Meeting people and learning to trust them have always been problems for me. That's because there are so many crooks and other undesirables amidst the decent citizens of society; the bad folks I don't care to meet.

As a kid, Helen was an extrovert, and still is. In Campbell River, Helen had a bosom buddy by the first name of Sandra. A chubby, light-haired, and freckled twelve-year-old girl Sandra was. Now, I do not recall her last name, and my sister would never tell me for fear that I will print it here and, so cause embarrassment to her longtime friend. Anyhow, I must get on with my account of events.

Adolescent girls often do silly things that adolescent boys never do. Like boys of this age, girls of this age chat, but unlike boys, they giggle while they chat. And they make funny faces while they giggle. See. Now you know what I mean. Plus, girls can act quite unpredictably in the company of boys. Girls may do this—if there are a minimum of two girls.

And you all, my loyal readers, know that I was at the time I speak of, just a kid barely out of my diapers. Right? Just a kid because I still had some of my baby teeth, you know. Forsooth, Helen and Sandra knew that I was just a kid, too. In my presence, they always seemed so smug together that I am sure that is what they must have thought about me.

So, it was quite unexpected and unsettling for Helen, who was always concerned about her self-image and the impression of our family in the eyes of her friends, when I broached what I assumed an innocent question. Questions must always be given the benefit of a doubt and be considered innocent when they come flying with reckless determination from the mouth of a little boy.

In truth, I was just a wet-behind-the-ears youngster, who but a couple of years before had still been sucking on a much-worn rubber pacifier. Remember? I did that too. Even at five years of age. At that ripe age, I was practically an old man. I'll tell you more, right after I am finished with my sister's friend Sandra.

While it is true that I was often timid around adults and most everyone of my age, for some inexplicable reason I never took it into my head to be shy around Sandra. Or Mary. Oops. I know that you fine folks do not know it yet because I have not yet introduced Mary to you, but it does seem like I am beginning to trip over my words here. And, lest you all should think me dishonest, I shall wait until the next page or so, or perhaps much later, to impart my news and, thereby give everyone the chance to mentally crucify my worthless butt. You all need have no fear. Your chance to do so is coming. But about Sandra.

How can I describe this? Or them? Sandra had these two very conspicuous and, in my estimation then, totally useless identical masses which grew, as far as I could tell, from straight out of her chest. And whatever these things were, they were fairly large, round in shape, and, they just hung there in front of her. As if, it appeared as I gazed in open wonder at them then, each one of these curious balls, which is how I thought of them, had a mind of its own to allow it to work with the other, so that both could simultaneously take off in flight.

I say that because I can recall thinking that the very air which surrounded them, also seemed to support them.

Even the tireless force of gravity (I would later discover that Isaac Newton had discovered gravity long ago—of course, gravity is what had caused Newton's apple to fall from its tree limb to the earth) did not appear to have an effect on these mysterious-looking orbs then.

To me, this was something that just called out on its own for an explanation.

Whatever they were, I knew that mother had these same things. Things that she always liked to conceal beneath mounds of clothing. Helen had these spooky-looking things too. These things on Helen were nowhere near as big as these same things were on Sandra, though. If all women and big girls have such stupid-looking attachments—and those that I'd seen do, I reasoned, then these things must surely possess a purpose of some kind. Whatever that purpose was I knew not. I only knew what I saw. Whatever these things were, they looked alien on the people on which they clung.

And they looked to be equally at odds with the environment around them. In my whole life, I had never seen anything quite so grotesque. Also. Please remember that I had already lived for a very long time.

At last, I could no longer bear the suspense of the question really gnawing at me. What on planet Earth were they? I pushed the question out from within me: "What are those bumps?" I blurted to Sandra, while I pointed at her chest with my finger. Helen flinched instantly, looking at her friend. Then my sister looked at me, and her tormented face shook me.

I was not completely stupid. A strange mixture of anger, pity, and amusement lay on Helen's countenance. But now, I wasn't looking at Helen any more. I was looking at Sandra.

Sandra's broad moon-like face was turning very red. Very, very, very red. More red with each passing second. Her face now looked like a monstrously overgrown beet. It was that red.

I was already beginning to wonder if Sandra had suddenly become ill. She looked ill. The silence was deafening. We were out-of-doors, but I would have sworn that you could have heard a pin drop, even with all of the considerable noise that cars driving by on the street made. We were many seconds into the aftermath of my question and Sandra's face still looked quite red.

And—like it was about to explode. I shuddered, wondering whether it was possible for a girl's head to explode. I was debating that intangible within myself even as I began to sense that Sandra was not ill. No, but that she was speechlessly suffering in the throes of embarrassment. If this were so, and it now appeared to be, I yet could not understand why. I had only asked a simple question of her. What unspeakable harm could there possibly be in asking a question?

I had, after all, been encouraged by mother and father to always ask questions whenever I was uncertain about something. I had never been told that there was a definite limit to what I could ask. I had never been made to understand that there were questions in life I could not ask of other people. At school, even my teacher Mrs. Case, encouraged me and my classmates to always ask questions when in doubt. I had, to my knowledge, committed no crime. I might well have visited other places of thought except for a sudden burst of laughter that instantly brought me back to the immediate reality.

It was my sister. Helen had a laugh which sounded like a nervous hyena with a rusty coat-hanger stuck in its throat.

By this time the complexion of Sandra's face had returned to its usual pale self. Both girls giggled uncontrollably, looking at one another and, completely ignoring me. Curiosity gnawed at me. But I kept my mouth shut.

Sandra never did tell me what those two plump bumps on her chest were. Yet, it didn't really matter. Later in life I found out all about bumps. Why girls and women have them. And why boys and men don't.

I would never want to have bumps anywhere on me, I thought. Never, because all of the boys at school would make fun of me. I was very glad that I was not a girl.

At the time, I did not have a clear conception of how babies were created. I knew only what I said before that mother had told me. I had come from inside of her. I had wondered about this matter a lot, and I still wondered how that was possible. I thought that I didn't even look anything like mother.

But one thing I knew for sure. Ever since the age of three, and this was almost as far back in time as I could recollect, I had instinctively maintained that I had burst into this world, complete with a short wooden stool, light-green of color, to sit on. In fact, I should have remembered to tell you of this when I told you of my family's trip to Finland. I should have remembered, but I did not. So I shall briefly touch upon this now.

I HAD ARGUED LONG IN DEFENSE of my stool theory with my Aunt Kepa in Finland. My aunt, you see, had assured me in no uncertain manner that I was minus the stool when I'd entered reality. And Aunt Kepa had been as adamant in her opinion as I was in mine. But I had known that I was right, of course. I had known that my aunt was wrong. Yes, I was mighty sure about what I knew. Yes I was. I knew that I had been born into life, fully equipped with a wood stool, nicely painted at that, to sit on while I, bladeless, whittled away much time in thought.

I had, I figured, nearly succeeded in convincing my by then subdued and silent aunt that I would never have come into the world unprepared. I would never have come without a stool to sit on. I had reasoned my stool shebang out, all by myself. As my thoughts returned momentarily to the present, I began to wonder what had happened to my light-green stool. Things always disappeared in this life and I never found them again.

But, unlike the mystery of what fate had befallen my beloved stool, I did know where my pacifier was. It was at the North Pole with Santa.

Father had kept buying me pacifiers ever since I was a baby, thereby extending my infancy psychologically. I guess that I had looked irresistibly cute with one stuck in my mouth. This, in part, was the reasoning for the deluge of pacifiers I had gone through.

I am sure of it now, because I was never prone to be a loudmouth. I was never so noisy, that either of my parents would have been tempted to shove the adult equivalent of a toilet plunger over my yap. No; the cute-kid argument is, I believe, a formidable reason; I was, in fact, encouraged by father to indulge myself—sucking on a pacifier then, gave me an aura of angelic innocence.

Sucking on a pacifier was, as well, something that I had become used to. Sucking on one gave me not only something to do, it provided me with a sense of security important to my emotional well-being.

I admit that at the old age of five, my habit, which I now see as having been an emotional addiction, had, at odd times, led me to seek refuge beneath my bed when visitors had unexpectedly showed up. At this age I was old enough to know what strangers, and family friends alike, would have thought had they seen me blissfully engaged in my pursuit.

And under my bed then, hidden from the curious eyes of onlookers who might have questioned my manhood out loud, or to put it another way—shielded from the instant embarrassment that their finding and subsequent elation would have brought me, I sucked on my pacifier whenever I felt the need.

Because I had very sharp, young teeth, the poor thing that I held prisoner in my mouth was pretty badly chewed up, with a large piece missing from the tip. And it smelled quite unheavenly.

When at last the time came that mother demanded I give my pacifier up, it was as hard a day for me as parting with a dear, old friend would've been. But please do not feel too sorry for me, I had known many a good time with my pacifier.

Tearful, I carefully wrapped my lifelong companion within a Kleenex, and with a heavy heart full of the most wretched dread of being forced to face the uncertainty of life's many twists without my friend, I pressed my pacifier into mother's hand. The Finnish word for a pacifier is *tutti (toot-tee)*. Tutti, I used to self-describe as a "kilo"(kee-lo). "Here is my kilo," I said to mother, sobbing. Then, I promptly went to my bed and hid myself beneath it.

Beneath my bed, where no one could see my misery, I sought solace in isolation. You good folks know that I would never have given my kilo up willingly. Right? Well, I guess that I shouldn't say never. Anyhow, mother knew exactly how my brain worked. Her trump card, in having convinced me to bravely take the inevitable plunge toward manhood, couldn't have been contested. Mother, dear mother, had used blackmail. A weapon of persuasion as old as the human race itself. Blackmail, which is in my humble opinion more likely to be practiced by a woman than a man.

For, the time of this emotional upheaval of mine had not been dictated by chance. It had been, you see, late afternoon of Christmas Eve, of the year 1963. And Santa, mother had said, would never make an entrance if I did not first hand my most-prized possession over to her. And, as I have already explained to you, I had complied in full with mother's demand.

Now, if you are at all curious as to what happened to my pacifier—this is what mother told me. Mother let me know that she would give my *former* friend to Santa, for safekeeping. Talk about me having been gullible.

I guess that gullible was a good word to describe me by, back then. I knew that Santa Claus was a nice guy, who could, generally, be relied on to bring some kind of neat new toy with him. I figured that his elves were probably watching myself with great interest that very moment. What moment? Who cares? Hidden in the kitchen cupboard, peering at me from a cabinet door slightly ajar. Or from beneath the chesterfield in the living room. Or—from behind the TV set. Or from wherever. I knew it when I was being watched.

I felt a fuzzy sensation. I was full of nervous excitement. I knew all of Santa's principal elves by their first names too. There was: Lolly, Linky, Winky, Twinky, Blinky, and Stinky.

All six were, of course, of the very highest integrity. They never stole anything. And, I was sure that Santa would have told anyone who asked, that they never complained. They were Santa's trusted helpers.

And even now, I am almost convinced that on the instant I'd relinquished my kilo, all six had run back to the North Pole in a flash to inform Santa that I had indeed been an especially good boy, and done exactly as my mother had told me.

What I knew then, was that Santa's elves would inform Santa of the fact that I had forfeited my kilo to my mother, unprotestingly.

I knew that Santa knew that the act of my having done so broke my heart. Yet I knew that Santa sometimes thought just like a businessman. I knew that it was on Santa's order that mother had asked for my kilo. Santa, I knew, could be quite uncompromising sometimes. And, he had an incredible knack of always getting me to do, unprotesting, the very things that mother and father had wished me to do.

Looking back at that time now, I must say that there must have been great communication and comraderie between the trio. I never doubted, even for a moment, that Santa Claus existed back then. No, even though I had observed that father was always absent when Santa showed up. And that, when Santa saw fit to leave, father would soon appear from the bedroom, stretching his arms wide and yawning, and telling everyone what a wonderful sleep he had just had.

That father never looked *fresh* from a good sleep then, mother said years later, was a thought which never crossed my mind.

I still wonder why I never noticed it. Had I, my suspicion *might* well have been aroused. And yet, who knows whether I would have correctly interpreted that and other signs. As a child, I was always so trusting of family. Small wonder, that I got duped so many times.

But even dummies learn eventually. Every dummy must. Even me. I say this, because I did not find out that there is no real Santa Claus, who lives along with his pack of elves and small herd of flying reindeer at the North Pole, until the age of ten. I had realized that I'd been—as some folks say—had, when I'd finally noticed father's black leather boots were exactly like St. Nick's. For me, it had been a breakthrough long in coming.

With my kind of deductive brainpower, it is a good thing that I never applied to study at Harvard. Nor ever tried to land a job at Mission Control. Landing folks on the moon, in one piece, is a bit out of my league.

CHAPTER FIFTEEN

I ADMIT THAT I DO NOT FIT the stereotype of a James Bond kind of guy. All of the other kids at school—all the other guys, that is—carried a lunch bucket with Sean Connery's image plastered on the front. Whose image did I have stuck to my dull lunch pail? Take a guess. Superman? No. Batman? No. Spiderman? No. No. No. Snow White and the Seven Dwarves? Well—no. As usual with everything, my lunch bucket was a notch above that. What could a well-disposed kid like me then, expect? I know that I told you that I had been forced by necessity to wear sneakers as cardinal as a pretty girl's lips. And that is after a girl touches up her lips with rouge, in preparation for her first date. My lunch bucket featured Lassie.

I guess the wholesome collie was a very good role model that I should have tried to emulate. In mother's eyes. Maybe that is why she had picked this bucket for me. Picked it off the shelf in the store. Whatever store it was does not matter, but the bucket had come to be in my possession before I'd started the first grade of school, back in Richmond.

"Would you like this one, sweetie?" mother had said. I mean, how could I possibly have said no, when my two ears had heard the persuasive tone in her voice which had clearly told me that Lassie the dog was mother's favorite from amongst the various characters planted on both sides of every lunch bucket. All women possess such a saintly, subtle touch when it comes to persuading a helpless child. No, I am afraid that I had definitely not been properly equipped by my mother for a sometime career as the illustrious James Bond.

In regard to James, I used to wonder what the pair of Easter eggs and the lucky seven stood for. Please forgive me. Remember, I have never been all that lucky. And actually, as concerns the two zeroes, I still don't know for sure. Maybe the zeroes represent what is left of a man's face after James does what is natural for any cool dude, and reduces it to fine dust with a single well-aimed bullet. Booty-loo-tooty-too. All really cool guys always use after-shave fragrance too. They use it to spice themselves up for the ladies once the heart-pumping action is over. I figure that James did then, and still does, even though Sean Connery left the portrayal of his famous movie character to his successors long since.

As a boy I knew that James Bond got to sport a nice suit as well, no doubt tailored to his exact specifications. Back from the dry cleaner, just in time for more action. And smelling as pure as a daisy on a fresh day of May.

There were never any unsightly holes eaten into this fine attire of his by a voracious slug, either. I'm not talking about ammunition here. I am talking about hungry mollusks that had not eaten for a month.

Danger, I knew, was integral to James. And, as I think of Connery's occupation now, he, like every actor who has played the invincible secret agent, really had the very best job that any man could have: as James, he got to experience all the hair-raising excitement that only James could actually crave, but unlike James—with none of the risk, as lead actor—a fat contract with Hollywood, and a beautiful blonde, brunette, or redhead lady in his (as Bond) ever-capable arms.

I figure that given Connery's character's luck with women, J.B. probably had reinforced steel springs for arms. Uh-huh, bionic attachments hidden deep in his flesh. It is too bad that there was never a movie about James that would prove my suspicion. In this movie, every doll within a fifty mile radius of James would have been requested to jump into his extended arms from a second-floor balcony to poolside, where James would have stood, ready and waiting, on the tile walk one floor below. All that James would have had to do, is to have caught each babe in turn, before any of these poor girls, who would've been too many for our hero who wouldn't have bothered to count them all, would have fallen one after another into the swimming pool and gotten all wet.

I don't know whether James would prefer his many girlfriends dry. I suppose he would. That's because it would be much easier for him to hold onto them.

With all of the variety in ladies that James Bond could pick from in the movies, I very much doubt that he ever had a chance to suffer boredom. Besides his coterie of lady friends, James had use of such a sleek sports car. If my memory does not fail me, his car was outfitted with a high-velocity ejection seat, just in case he needed to hastily dump an unwelcome guest.

And his car came complete with such fine skunk spray. James used this to repel all of the meanest crooks with. What? You say that you never saw this movie? Shame on you. Yep—James had it all. He had all of the best bosom babes and high-tech gadgets that any man would want to play with—in addition to his personal style of attending to business. Ah, that never-failing charisma of his, which so many men would kill for to have. Indeed, James could kiss a woman at the same time that he was comforting her with one hand and, shooting her would-be assailant in the heart, with a ready revolver gripped in the other. Talk about him having had his hands full during filming. No, they don't make gents like they once did. Except in the movies where James Bond lives on. He, always quite ready to, sort of, kick the bucket on some other day.

As a kid I wondered whether James ever used mouthwash to prevent his breath from stinking. I wondered, too, about what brand he might use. Every man as cool and effective in bed as James was—had to have an equally effective program of oral hygiene. I now doubt that any of his many dates were obsessed with such minor details, though.

As for me, I never used mouthwash. And my breath never stunk because I brushed my teeth twice daily. Come to think of it, I never saw James brush his teeth. Maybe James wore dentures that he cleaned like mother did hers when she removed her dentures from her mouth. Before mother went to bed, she always scrubbed her dentures plenty clean, and left them to sit in a cup on her night table—until the next morning when she would place them back into her mouth for the day. I guess that mother's dentures did not fit her mouth properly and caused her a bit of pain.

I return to the cool topic of J.B. I am just guessing of course, when I say the following. But I now believe that James did not comb his fine head of thick dark hair with a greasy kitchen fork, like I do mine every morning when I get up from a good night's snooze. Just foolin'. You hope. And about James' hair. His hair always looked so well kept and shiny, so shiny that I am now almost sure that Sean Connery wore a toupee. A man just doesn't get all that experience in negotiating persistent peril without losing a few follicles of hair, now and then.

Back to style. Yes, I admire James for his style. Especially the Bond of my boyhood, who made almost everything that he did, look so carelessly easy.

To begin with, there was that smooth, sinewy walk; catlike. And even though I tried stubbornly hard, I never could copy it well enough to impress any girls with.

Too, Mr. Bond probably never got his clothes soiled without getting them back, clean and ironed, the very same day. And we never saw him fighting off mosquitoes at the beach while getting a suntan lying next to some bronzed goddess.

We positively never saw a tiger shark tear his swim shorts off for a snack. That would indeed have been the ultimate in humiliation for James, who, I'm sure, never belonged to a nudist cult. No, James Bond led a perfect, charmed life.

On screen, he had an image to uphold. He was James Bond, two eggs plus number seven. One of a kind.

Me, well, I could always redouble my efforts to become James Bond once I grow bigger, I thought then. But as the youngster I still was, I couldn't quite figure out how to manufacture that casual manner of his in not just his walk, but his talk.

Speech, which always slid from between his teeth with all of the refined elegance of the schooled elite operative he really was. How he managed this feat while inhaling the poisonous vapor of a Cuban cigar was beyond my grasp.

I noted, also, he always spoke his last name first, which was unusual. Yet more than that, somehow, it seemed to me that he was trying to impress whoever he happened to be speaking to, with an air of importance. His last name— was more than a mere name. In the movies, the renowned name Bond stood unabashedly for quality amongst both his superiors in the secret service as amongst his clique of contacts who knew his reputation. James Bond was the Rolls Royce trademark of this man.

LIKE THE NAME AND MARK of another man. The classic, enduring mark of—one Zorro. Zorro, the wiliest of foxes. Another legendary boyhood favorite of mine, Zorro was a man forever shrouded in the magnificence of mystery. Like James Bond, a character of his creator's imagination, Zorro still *is* a name we all know and trust. To myself as a boy, a character of make-believe he was, and to many folks then, he was nothing more. But not in Hollywood. There, Zorro was the swashbuckling hero of the silver screen, whose courage, wit, and superb swordplay—knew no equal.

Zorro had a habit of leaving his mark whenever he could, and the zigzag became his signature trademark. A scrawl and nothing else by which anyone could identify its author with. Always drawn with the razor-sharp tip of his épée, into a door.

In his expert swordsman's hands, his fine weapon drained the lifeblood of many a foe. Yes, as a master swordsman (and tactician) Zorro was incomparable. That he was deadly good at his chosen craft was without question—the épée had to have been born into his skilled hand, and being unrivaled in its excellence for speed and accuracy, only his lightning-quick hand could maneuver such a weapon with the revered finesse that made Zorro who he was.

With their swords' tips, his antagonists never could quite taste the mortal red blood that coursed in his veins and powered his noble heart. It was as though the black cape on his back protected him from all manner of harm, front and rear.

And Zorro, he always smiled from behind the dark exterior of his mask. Even when he was fighting single-handedly for his life in a pitched battle against seemingly insurmountable odds, he did. The black mask of el Zorro. The avenging blade of señor Zorro. And his clothes—were like the mask and cape he wore. From the black gentleman's hat to the black riding boots, everything was—solid black. Had it not been for the areas of his face unconcealed by his mask, and the smile of his impeccably white teeth, teeth which positively gleamed in the moonlight—mocking his enemies, Zorro would have been invisible in the cloak of night.

Guy Williams, alias Zorro, a man who performed the best impersonation of a character of fiction (1957-'59) from amongst those who played the part of the masked crusader since the creation of the first Zorro movie in 1920, probably spent no less than a good half-hour brushing his teeth every day in preparation for his role on the set of the Walt Disney TV series.

Like Robin Hood, Zorro took from the rich and gave to the masses of the poor. Often endangering his own life for a good cause—Zorro always thought of others. He was the ultimate champion of the downtrodden, the innocent, and the weak of his society. Zorro had the rare purity of the clearest diamond in his heart, as befits the heart of a true warrior. This, was the heart of a man who knew no fear of death. Oh, he cheated death often enough to know death well, and always, he laughed in its venerable face.

Yes, the mark of Zorro was the mark of excellence in character. And like our friend James in the world of all things Bond—when Zorro turned on that effervescent smile and natural charm of his—you knew then that he had no equal. Nor ever could he. Zorro, whose title and real name on the screen was Don Diego de la Vega, was the son of a wealthy gent, Don Alejandro, in the aristocracy of Los Angeles under Spanish martial rule in the year 1820. As Don Diego, his casual manner and seeming incompetence in swordplay never failed to disarm the suspicions of his powerful adversaries. In order to protect his secret identity he portrayed himself as a bungling idiot, a joker to all appearances. We all know that this was the public persona of the man. To myself, and likely to any other child who had ever watched a Zorro movie—either at home on television like I had because no one took me to the cinema—or on the big screen itself, the sudden and remarkable transformation of Don Diego into Zorro, when complete, was as striking as the difference between night and day.

And so, as Zorro has always been well-known as the champion of the poor, it is not at all strange that, for his many enemies, no possible comparison was made between the wealthy, privileged, flamboyant playboy, and—the purposeful and deadly sword arm' of Zorro. Stupid fools that they were, they could never place the two men together. Suspicion did fall on Diego's broad shoulders but, his enemies could never substantiate the notion that he was Zorro. They could never prove who it was that Don Diego became when he donned his black attire and rode out into the countryside upon his midnight steed, as the majesty of twilight enveloped the land and blended into night.

And when the blackness of night, in turn, gave way to the purple of dawn and the early morning sunlight descended from the heights into the valley far below, the only proof of what action had taken place during the sleeping hours lay on the ground, when the Spanish military forces counted the unlucky in their midst. And the single letter Z, which they so feared, would always be scrawled nearby.

And what was there for them to fear but a single brave man, pitted of his choosing and indomitable will, against a fortress of well-armed soldiers. A man to whom personal wealth and a privileged position in life meant nothing, as these were far outweighed by his concern for the very poor amongst the peasant population.

Nothing about Zorro has changed since I was a boy. I know now, just as I knew it then, that Zorro will forever remain impervious to death on the screen. In Hollywood, more than that most renowned warrior of all time—the mighty Achilles, given to us from the fertile imagination of the Greek writer Homer, near to three thousand years ago in eternal time.

And offscreen, the answer to the question of whether Zorro could ever die in the heat of battle shall always be unclear to me. Perhaps death will finally muster the courage to take our hero away from us. Whatever happens, I know that Zorro's reputation of unrivaled swordsmanship will certainly stand the test of time, untarnished with age, as will his bravery and rapier cunning.

To me, it is every aspect of the character which has the power to cut through all dimensions of thought—in a single, potent thrust. A thrust aimed dead center. A thrust aimed at the heart. Indubitably, the equality that Zorro fought so hard to gain for his people will, as I say, ensure that an icon of his stature will live on in the medium of film. Vanquished never. Triumphant ever. As any true hero should be.

Perhaps, like my other boyhood hero, Tarzan, who drank from the fountain of youth as a young man and who for this reason could never die of old age, Zorro had found that same, special fountain, wherever it may lie on Earth. The fountain of immortality. Yes, perhaps.

Looking back at 1965, I now know that I would not have made it as Zorro, in real life. Nor James Bond. At three feet in stature then, I figure that I didn't look much like either of them. Especially James. And besides that, I didn't own a fencing sword like Zorro's épée, nor, in comparing myself to James, did I own a Remington revolver or whatever make of pistol it was that James was fond of using to deadly effect. In that regard, the firearm James used, maybe I am confusing James with TV's *Remington Steele* series from years past. However, I do know that Remington was only a few short years out of his diapers when James was out doing the wild thing.

Like Zorro, Mr. James Bond never stepped into trouble without stepping out of it. To the very best of my knowledge, neither of these guys ever suffered the misfortune to step into cow dung. And me, though I always used to step into trouble feet-first and get mired in it, I didn't even once step into cow manure in Campbell River. There just weren't any cows on the loose about town. Otherwise—I probably would have. But I shall tell you what it was that I did step into. Or maybe I should say—what stepped into me.

I HAD SET OFF for school one day, alone. Helen had already left for school, on this morning a few minutes earlier than she usually did on each weekday morning. Usually, we walked to school together. Helen was in grade seven now, and I, being only in grade two, would most always tag along beside her like a pet puppy.

But, on this day as I'd set off for school alone I had overlooked a little something of importance. The hair atop my head was well groomed. My shirt collar was clean, and my pants had seen a hot iron. Even my shoelaces were in order. Tied the way I had learned to tie them.

I'd said good-bye to mother and father for the day, and I'd managed to slip out of our shop without their noticing what was wrong about me. As I say, I had no knowledge of the one tiny detail that had somehow fallen between the cracks and eluded discovery. How it had, I don't know. As I walked to school, a wide ribbon of white, three feet long, trailed from the lip of my trousers to the ground.

Now, I think of myself as being a nice guy. Yes—these days. With that in mind, I shall refrain from blaming the manufacturer of Royale for having made a product so strong, so incredibly resilient (they still make the stuff this strong and tough), that it had actually withstood the tension of having been dragged along on the ground behind me for a mile—almost to school then. A stream of white originally, now somewhat discolored in spots by having been unstylishly towed in my wake. Drawn along to a center of higher learning. A center of academic potential. An esteemed place where authority reigns.

A center where small mischievous faces would surely have looked down upon me in pity, and where an unstoppable torrent of laughter would just as surely have ensued, falling upon me from many a merry young throat. A torrent of laughter that would have instantly rendered me a marked man for the rest of my life.

Doubtless, I would have been better off dead. Quite so, because I know that I would have been reviled to the end of my time. To my very last breath. And, after I'd have departed from earth, my reputation, never perfect, would have been turned into that of a total misfit in the eyes of society. My doom would have been sealed for the rest of eternity.

I could go on with my description of the bleak future with my name in perpetual purgatory, just for the sake of showing you how I would have viewed my demise. But it was not to be, after all. Fate, ever watchful, was kind on this day. Perhaps it took pity on the little boy with the red running shoes.

Only this I know. A dog barked behind me then, causing me to check my rear for possible attack from that direction. And you know, I have almost liked that particular dog ever since. Even though I have no fondness for four-footed creatures in general.

As my attention shifted from the low, green picket fence that the dog sat behind I happened to glance downward. It was then, that I noticed what so many others amongst the schoolchildren would never reap the joy of noticing. My name is Roy. And in keeping with such a first name, everything that I do, must be done with style. Everything must be done ROYALLY.

I have been called "Royalite" by certain of my foes while in primary school.

And my friends have badgered me jokingly in high school. "Roy, my boy!", my peers have quipped. And yes, of course I am Roy. In all honesty, I could not have been else. Must I say it, so that all can mock me? Must I spell out exactly what it was that had accompanied me so faithfully then, like the tail I had not on my entry into this world? This thing that had accompanied me to the brink of disaster? To the brink of my ultimate humiliation at the hands of my peers in the second grade? Only one block from school—when time and space—and a dog barking in its yard in the early morn—intervened to save me. That. And probability. This was my ultimate saviour. It could easily have been for me a worst-case scenario born into reality. Yet it would never come to be.

As I lifted the tail of toilet paper, still clinging with that famous Royale resilience, out of my undershorts, I looked about me to see if anyone, anybody at all, might have seen. Though, I guessed that no one who really mattered, had.

No one in my class at school knew of this. Only I knew. And I thought that I would never tell anyone about this incident. But I have. And now, as my mind drifts toward peaceful sleep I know that time and space will be mine to relive and roam again on another day, on another day in memory of the past.

My adventures continue.

THERE WERE MANY IDOLS IN MY LIFE who I tried to emulate. Think both superheroes blessed with exceptional physical means and ordinary men with exceptional bravery and skill. Strengths, which ensured their survival in seemingly impossible situations that would easily have defeated the average human.

As I learned to read better each day, I would temporarily assume the identities of those of my heroes that could be found inside of comic books at the Beehive. And it was because of my interest in these comic books that my reading skills improved measurably, without my fine head of hair being further tugged on by my brother, for cause of failure.

Like every red-blooded boy who has ever imagined himself as a hero, I would imagine myself grown to manhood, dreamily captivated by my high-flung fantasies as I raced time as Superman—in a desperate bid to save Earth from evils such as Lex Luthor, or failing that, swinging half-naked through the African brush on a leafy, green vine, while blurting out ooo-ooo-ooo-ooo-ooo. Just to let my ape friends know that I—Tarzan—ruler of the vine—was in the vicinity, and (beating chest) I was not one to be trifled with. Yum-yum banana.

Could it be that this is one of my dreams even now? To suck on a ripe yellow banana while beating my bare chest with a fist and to holler ooo-ooo-ooo-ooo-ooo? I hope not—if I have descended to the social level of an ape, I certainly don't have much of a future in the job market!

Whatever. Whatever. Whatever. I shall let my brother take the blame. You see, it was his cunning mind that had contrived a scheme to let him enjoy the benefit of indulging his own interest in comics at a bargain rate, while facilitating my struggle to improve my reading ability.

As it was, I would always go the Beehive, where the establishment had a fine rack of comics at the back. Out of habit, I would then buy a comic with my hard-earned money. In turn, Raimo would partially reimburse me for the cost of my expenditure.

Yes, Raimo figured that I would learn vital language skills, while he always got to enjoy the best comics, delivered to him by yours truly, at a reduced cost to his wallet. What a shrewd fellow brother Raimo could be!

In regard to his having kindled an interest for the printed word in my mind then, or rather, the story behind each word, I must say that Raimo's plan worked. Had it not, you would not be reading this book now. We have all heard the adage: you can lead a horse to water, but you can't make it drink. Even though the strict hair-pulling measure (a better way of describing that is to use the word, Draconian) had appeared to have the desired effect in helping me toward literacy in the English language then, my brother must have felt that, by him making reading enjoyable for me, I would master this necessary skill much more quickly. Very clever indeed.

Which reminds me. Any man, well-read or not, needs a stool. So! Lo and behold! I impart to you a little something about an old wooden stool of father's making. It had an oval top which was just large enough to sit on, and it had the usual four legs that any self-respectin' stool must in order to be self-respectin'. Father had painted the stool, light-green, after he'd cut a round hole through the center of the top, making it easy to carry. Remember? Yes, it was the same stool whose origin my Aunt Kepa and I had disagreed over. And yes, I had found my stool, which, as you recall, I had been unable to locate earlier. Whew! I say it *again* I do! Every man must have his own stool to sit on! Indeed he must! Pirate's honor!!!

The hole was the width of a Canadian or U.S. quarter. This was a significant detail I made use of.

Whenever I caught someone roosting on the stool, I would approach silently from behind the unsuspecting party (the victim was usually my brother or sister) and poke my pinkie up through the hole into someone's rump. Quite often, a family conversation was interrupted in this way by a startled exclamation of surprise.

Hunters know that wise ducks and geese soon get wise to decoys. They get wise to being shot at, too. After a while, no one but me in our family desired to sit atop the stool. Which, sort of left it all to me. What a welcome coincidence! But I was not to enjoy any long-term squatter's rights. And it was always my brother or sister who would return to exact vengeance for those ill deeds of other days—and spoil my fun.

Chapter Sixteen

I DID PROMISE TO TELL YOU about um, well um—someone by the name of Mary, didn't I? I know that I did. So I guess that I had better get this very private matter finally over with.

Mary was a waitress in her early twenties who worked at the Beehive, alongside mother. Mary was about five feet and ten inches tall. Slim she was, with straight dark-brown hair that barely touched her shoulders. She wore spectacles all of the time while she attended to the clientele. Come to think of it, I never knew Mary to not wear her glasses.

Mary was kind of quiet and shy around strangers. But she had a nice personality. At the Beehive, Mary was mother's best friend. Mary had a little boy about my age, and maybe it was for this reason that she'd taken an instant liking to me.

Yet, I didn't know that Mary thought I was cute until mother persuaded me to go and sit on Mary's lap. Of course I, already a full-grown man then, was quite happy to have the opportunity to do just that. And so, with Mary (who was—thankfully—willing to accommodate me) atop a bar stool, we posed for a photo-op, I nestled securely in the grip of warm comfort.

At the time I must have thought that a fellow could get used to lounging in the lap of a pretty, young lady, because after I had spent such a wonderful time in Mary's comforting lap, I considered Mary, who was more than three times my age and married, my girlfriend.

And, although I sat in her lap but that once, I don't mean that I pictured Mary as just a girl who happened to be my friend. No. I thought of Mary in the same way that Popeye, the sailing dude, took Olive Oyl to be his sweetheart.

I think Mary knew that I had a young man's crush on her. Shortly after our family left Campbell River for California, mother penned a letter to Mary, from San Diego, telling her about the details of our trip to the Southland. Mommy had urged me to drop a few lines of print to Mary too. Unfortunately, I cannot recollect what of substance I wrote to Mary. I do know that my message was only a sentence or two long, though.

Mary never wrote back to us. And I still half-wonder whether an equal amount of spinach to that which Popeye ate would build huge muscles for me if I ate it. After all, spinach put PEP into Popeye's muscles—which gave him a chance to hang onto Olive Oyl.

Nah. All that spinach (yuck) sounds a snig too corny for me to really try to eat. I never was cut out to be a sailorman, anyway. The last is how I feel this instant.

But back in yesterday, I could well act the part of a ruffian, fresh from the briny. With a black patch that mother had cut out from an old pair of jeans, over one eye, I remember swaggering down main street in mock drunkenness one day, singing Tappu's adopted song, singing in Finnish the old sea dog's tune I told you about many bananas ago.

People took notice of me, even though they couldn't understand what it was that I was singing about. The truth is, insofar as my singing this song went, I had never been allowed to taste whiskey or any spirits in my life. And neither of my parents drank. Still, those realities did not stop me from singing about the joys of alcohol.

Ah, what dreams a youngster like me could have with a bottle of whiskey to soothe the palate. Oh yes, the joys of this drink I had never tasted in my life were very real to me then.

Without the eye-patch, when I sang the described piece in Finnish and in that tongue I always did, but rarely, and in tune to a good ear for melodies, people smiled even though, as I say, they had no idea of the meaning of the lyrics. I, as well, sang another song. But when I sang the words to that song in English, the looks on people's faces changed abruptly from astonishment to outright horror. Every adult shuddered in my presence. As for the subject, I'll give you this. In Richmond, I had picked up the riveting vocabulary from a western movie by the name of *The Hanging Tree*.

Yes, I was quite a character as a kid. No surfboard have I to ride a high wave! Big, furry thing am I, it's the cave I crave!!! Well—almost. I've never had a yen for claustrophobic life in any cave, and I guess that I can't boast of my having ever straddled a surfboard with which to mount a tall wave, either. As for excessive body hair. Get lost. I never was cut out for life as a sasquatch. Tarzan yes. No sasquatch, no. Life as a sasquatch would have meant forever eating unpleasant things like worms, cockroaches, and tree roots. Certainly, not foods that I ever had a taste for.

MIND YOU, I DID have a taste for French fries eons ago, and I still have some of these every day. I must thank the French for their excellent recipe. Burp.

Mother quite often made my fries. At the Beehive. And the fries mother made were always superbly prepared.

One morning, I walked into the Beehive with twenty-five cents tucked safely in my shirt pocket. This was the cost for a whole plateful of my favorite food. Mother had slipped me the quarter on this morning, before she had left for work on the day shift. I guess that mother liked the feeling of seeing me happy, gorging on a full dish of glorious golden fries topped with oodles of spicy tomato ketchup. If you are about to ask me—you need not. I tell you in no uncertain terms that mother's French fries were my thirty minutes in heaven. And when I was finished, my tummy always thanked mother in spades.

It seemed to me that I could never quite eat my fill of French fries. I felt that the whole world did not grow enough potatoes to have sated me when the spuds had swum in a hot, bubbling vat of lard oil, been rescued and left untouched for a while to drain the excess oil away. Now I know why Napoleon was chubby. Indeed, if I had been he, I wouldn't have bothered going to war and a stinging defeat at Waterloo. I would have just stayed at home in the lap of luxury, comfort, and of course—safety. Tinkered in peace with my toys. Dined on French fries, and strawberry-jam-filled donuts. Incidentally, I cannot imagine a distinguished gentleman like Napoleon Bonaparte ever having been forced to peel spuds. And they didn't have electrically-driven potato peelers back in his time.

As chance had it, this morning, back at the Beehive, would've been uneventful. Except for a pair of fellow diners. One man and one woman. Each about thirty years old.

As I was seated at a table, patiently waiting for mother to bring me a plate of fries, I noticed the level gaze of the couple, on me. In no way did either of them look like anything hostile. They just sat there, at their table like I did at mine, waiting for their orders to arrive. They didn't say anything to one another. But I noticed that both seemed rather fascinated by me. I wondered if I had a booger hanging from my nose. I must have a booger, I thought.

A napkin dispenser stood at the center of every table in the Beehive. I reached for a napkin to wipe my snout with. I wiped my nose with the paper napkin and glanced at it, before stuffing the napkin into my shirt pocket. Nope. There was no dried snot on the napkin. Now. What could it be, I thought, that had attracted the couple's undivided attention toward me? Maybe my shoelaces were untied. I looked down, checking my red running shoes. But no. My shoelaces were tied.

Now I was really confounded. Why, on Earth, were these people staring at me? I have, in all of my life, never liked to be stared at by anyone. The couple's undivided attention toward me was making me nervous. Very, very, nervous.

To me, a concentrated look—a stare—usually means one of three things. Sometimes, it can be a kind of unspoken challenge. At other times, it might be an attempt to penetrate my thoughts by way of facial expression, so that the starer can form an opinion of myself, or my intent. Like in a game of poker, which I have never played. Believe me, I don't appreciate either of these.

The third possibility (on occasion), is that I have somehow acquired a not-so-secret admirer. And here, I shall state for the record, I have never catered to secret admirers in my life. And I solemnly vow never to do so. Unless, of course, my secret admirer happens to be a very pretty girl without a menacing-looking boyfriend. Even minus the ugly boyfriend, a very pretty girl's longing look, when it is cast in my specific direction, will cause me to become a little nervous.

But. No very pretty girl need be concerned for my welfare. Believe me, it's nothing serious. I just undergo total internal incineration. Emotionally, that is. Yet, she need remember only this. Despite my outward appearance which may suggest the contrary, my meltdown is internal. Not external. What? You just don't believe me? Okay-okay. How about this? When it comes to the matter of love, I am an emotional basket case—and—this tends to show. *Er-wait a sec! Not show.* I will make an exception for any very pretty girl and instantly abandon my rule of never catering to any secret admirer in my life (copyright, circa 1965). *Not instantly!* What man would not? Any very pretty girl, will INSTANTLY be welcomed into the fold of my adoring fan club. *What club?* Total membership at this time? Zero. But hey, please do not feel sorry for me. You know, it will only take one very special girl to make my club complete. I gotta go now. I have to get back to the past before my time-travel machine breaks down from a leak of hydraulic fluid within the circumflex drivel-drive, and I begin to mutter unmentionables.

Zoom. There. I'm sitting in a chair back at the Beehive now, and I am starting to become quite flustered by all the unwarranted attention I appear a victim of.

You know, it just occurred to me that I have never picked at the inside of my nose with a loose finger, as an adult. When I was seven years old I didn't, either. Leastwise, not in public.

But I really did think now, in my padded chair back at the Beehive, that some serious nose-picking would have done me a heap of good. At least I would have been accomplishing something constructive, rather than having Mr. and Mrs. YOUR-BUSINESS-IS-MY-BUSINESS continue their silent, creepy, methodical, roast-me-slowly brand of torture.

Roast me yes, I was beginning to feel like I was a condemned goose, and the oven was set on bake. Beads of perspiration began to stream down in tiny rivulets beneath my long-sleeved red-and-white, flannel checkerboard shirt.

I decided to try fastening my eyes on the glass ketchup bottle already in place on the tabletop. I'd never known that Heinz ketchup was made in a place called Ontario. Wherever that was, I couldn't recall having ever heard of such a place. No matter. I wouldn't have been sure that I could even have told you what my shoe size was right then. If someone had bothered to ask. I was just as preoccupied in my thoughts now as I'd been on that one day in Mrs. Mulder's class in Richmond—that terrible day.

I looked up from the ketchup bottle to see whether I was still under surveillance. I was. The snoopy pair still sat at their table, waiting, it seemed to me, like vultures waiting for me to drop. Neither of them, man nor woman, had relaxed a single facial muscle.

I knew that I had to do something. I looked quickly to the rear—to see whether mommy would come soon and save me from my predicament. But mother was still cooking the fries. She had apparently noticed nothing. I could positively bear the suspense no longer.

Then it happened. Abruptly, instinctively, my hands were yanked upward as if they were drawn by some mysterious, invisible force—to cover my eyes, while a blush settled over my face, admitting my cowardliness of spirit for all the world to see.

In hindsight, I guess that I sort of did what ostriches in Africa do when a hungry lion is about to pounce upon and devour them. Silly birds that they are, they bury their heads in the desert sand, thinking that, by so doing, they will escape certain destruction. Ostriches are not too bright. In no way am I implying that I am as stupid as an ostrich.

It turned out that mother, her work complete, had found the time to be a quiet spectator, after all. She came forward with a plateful of French fries well-done, and smiled at the man and woman. They nodded at mother and smiled back. I didn't see it, though. My eyes were still covered in the shame of my shyness. Of course, mother told me about it later. But how did I feel at the time? Well, I was just a little homebody in a very big restaurant and—I was glad that mommy had saved me. I was especially glad for the fries. As always, though I would have much preferred to eat them in solitude, with no probing eyes to watch me.

Chapter Seventeen

HAVING JUST FINISHED READING ALL OF THAT, you will know that I meant a very great deal of joy to my mother when I was a kid. I loved mother dearly, as any child will a good mother. And mother loved me right back, with all the tenderness that only a good mother could bestow on a child.

Case by example. I remember my first pair of real jeans, which mother had bought. Navy-blue, with the logo "Mommy's Sweetheart" stitched in cursive letters, with red string, on the seat. This was when I was three years old. Then four years later, I no longer had those pants. I don't know what had happened to them. I guess that I'd eventually outgrown them. But you know, as much as I loved and respected mother then, I would not have wished to go to school with my ass jammed into those pants.

Nowadays, I think I couldn't have slid my rump into them at the old age of seven, anyway. No, not even if my naked rear end had been greased with petroleum jelly. I had gained so much in size then. I was still a scrawny kid. Yet I was getting bigger with each passing day.

And, as I grew in stature, my confidence grew with me. But growing up can be an agonizingly slow process. There were so many variables in life. So many uncertainties, that I could not even count them all. I was just a small boy, stuck in a cosmic sea of destiny. A sea of matter and energy, shaped by time and chance.

I thought of myself as being transparent. Never would I have considered myself deceitful. But that thought never struck me.

Our bottle-snatching operations from Safeway, which Helen and I seldom visited now, I had, as you know, previously carried out with my sister on a grand scale. Just to ensure my survival I had. In my mind, I was still a good kid.

Even if you do not agree with me on this point, I contend that I was just a small rock in a big universe with lots of rocks. Some rocks were sharp, very jagged affairs. Others were smooth. Like the rocks that lay on the seabed; these rocks were hidden from my sight, beneath the surface of my friend, the ocean.

As you know, my fascination with rocks, early in life, was exemplified by that communist-looking rock I had discovered on the beach. The rock that looked so much like father's head. I don't remember what happened to this particular rock. Maybe I threw it back into the ocean. Back to where its real home was.

SOME ROCKS, I KNEW, WERE MORE IMPORTANT than other rocks. I knew this because I had heard about rocks that grown-ups liked to collect. These were called diamonds. And rubies. And sapphires. And emeralds.

Diamonds were held in the highest esteem by all big people. I wondered why. I much preferred the mysterious, inviting green of the emerald. As a kid, deep-green was my favorite color. Now—it's black. Black, to me, is the most magnificent of all colors. Actually, black is not even a color in scientific terms. What black is—is the absence of color. I am sure that you already knew this.

No matter, to me, black is very much a living color. There is, at least to my artist's eyes, kind of a dark and rare beauty to black. Kind of an eternal sadness seems to reside where black is.

Black is almost like the night sky with the stars to illuminate the great expanse of the universe. Infinitely mysterious. Infinitely romantic. I can sit for hours, steadfastly gazing upward at this cosmic marvel. The universe seems to tell me everything I really need to know. Things about myself. Things that happened long before I came squealing into being as a newborn babe. Things about the future.

Black, the dark, melancholic spirit of the cosmic domain, lives within me now. Dark, yes. But I shall have you know that I am no Darth Vader, the one who was overcome by the force of darkness lurking in himself as it does in most of humankind, I bent upon the destruction of moral order in *this* or any galaxy. Nor can I say that I am a knight, shining of armor, in the opposite cause. Good and evil. Most of us know them.

Also, what I can tell you about myself is that money means virtually nothing to me at this point in time. As you're aware, I cannot say that it never has. The reason for the first is simple. As I have come to the present day, time and the experiences of life have taken their toll, jaded the depths of my inner being. *Déjà vu*: not all of my memories in life are happy ones. And though time itself has worked to soften the vividness of my recollections measurably, dulling both bad and good memories, the many rivers of pain still run deep through my heart, embedded in the very fiber of my existence. In my physical mind. I am emotionally-oriented; this is in stark contrast to those amongst humanity who are possessed by the all-consuming desire for reams of wealth, those motivated by greed and obsessed by money.

Yes—money, that old evil of our society. While I recognize money to be a means toward an end, I am as I say, infected by no lust for vast riches today. As I've shown, not so did I think about money in my early boyhood. This is a sad fact I have already well established in this book. But even as a kid of seven years in age, while I liked the dream of great wealth, riches which I hoped to eventually realize by my plan of becoming a professional diamond-seeker once the small matter of my growing up was over with, I was nonetheless more intrigued by the brilliant flash of color that cut precious stones display when a light is shone on them. And with light, one may see how unadorned dainty little fingers will attract a doting mother's attention.

I had my own little ring in this time of long ago. Indeed I did. It was a dandy ring too, and mother had bought it. A ring with a shiny golden band, and a polished glass stone—the color of an emerald—set squarely in the center of the ring.

As I remember, I was quite proud of my ring, even though I knew that the emerald was only a fake, and even though I knew that the gold band was, at best, just gold-plated. Yes, my ring made me feel so very special. Like I was one of a kind.

By their very masculine nature, most young boys of my time spent as a kid believed that effeminate appendages (like my ring) were meant only for mollycoddles to wear. Real men, they believed, did not wear such things. A beautiful ring like mine, these boys believed, was not just not manly: in their narrow view my ring would have been considered, on sight, as the indelible mark of a sissy.

Which is exactly why I never wore my ring to school. My being forced, by necessity, to wear red running shoes then was bad enough. I try to not mention here, anything of my Lassie lunch bucket. Oops! Well, I look on the bright side. At least I didn't have to wear my lunch pail on my feet.

But I always wore my special ring at home. And out of sight of my old classmates, I can SAFELY say I never felt that my ring somehow detracted from who I was. Honestly.

CHAPTER EIGHTEEN

'SIDES the always present gulls, only a few crows, ravens, starlings, and robins did I usually see about the waterfront. I never chanced to spot an eagle, falcon, or osprey. Yet, I am no bird-lover. I never wasted any of my time searching the air currents above the rooftops for their presence.

As for the other birds I have made mention of here, I would often witness them picking at scraps of food in the open trash bins that sat in the alleys behind the few commercial enterprises which sold food.

Food is sure to lure a hungry animal, be it a bird, bear, cougar, coyote, or, in my neighborhood then, a stray dog. A strange thought just struck me. You know, I don't believe there is a Fido in the whole world that would have felt maternal had it been forced to share a cot with my sister's cat. As we all know, cats and dogs don't mix. People who fight like cats and dogs don't mix, either. Except to bean each other. I was always able to defend myself against people of my size, provided that I faced no more than one antagonist. But I knew instinctively that I was no match for a trio of dogs that nagged at my heels as I now regularly traversed alone the mile from school to home.

Because Helen got out of class later than I, about one hour later, there was no point in me sticking around our school to wait for her, not when I could go home earlier than my sister. And my return home on each school day afternoon would have been without incident, had it not been for these three dogs that had banded together.

I'd encounter these canine misfits, who were all entirely lacking in manners, at the top of the short, steep hill that gave me access to main street below, across which stood our shop. Father always came to get me from across the brisk run of vehicle traffic, to ensure that I made it home without getting run over by a car; the heavier than usual midafternoon flow was always dangerous.

Now, I will be the first to admit from amongst me, myself, and I, that I do not know much about the many different breeds of dogs inhabiting our society. However, one of these three dogs had looked to be a Great Dane. During medieval times in Europe, this breed of dog was used to attack bears that had been blindfolded and chained to poles. Needless to say, these unfortunate bears were almost helpless to defend themselves, and each bear ended up being literally torn apart by several Great Danes unleashed upon a single bear at once. The cruel acts were a kind of sport for royalty and the well-heeled to watch.

If you know something of dogs, and I am reasonably sure that you know more than I do of the strains of dogs in existence, you will know that Great Danes are huge dogs. But despite his awesome size, for— this dog stood taller with all four of his feet planted solidly on the ground than I did standing on my two then, he was no mean beast. He did try taking a nip at me sometimes. He just wasn't too serious about it. He was, for the most part, a territorial creature that should have been kept behind a high fence in his owner's yard. Not running loose on the street.

The Dane's associates, two poodles, were despite their much smaller size more ferocious in nature. All three of this gang would wait for me, without fail, on the afternoon of each school day. The poodles, which were both ivory in color, would come at me from the rear and try to tear at the flesh of my legs. Cowards that these were, they didn't try to attack me from the front. I supposed that the pair wished to see what either of my legs would taste like. And, inasmuch as meeting the approval of their refined palates was not foremost on my agenda of ambitions in life—I quite naturally resisted their eager, dogged efforts to make a meal of my means of transport.

My synopsis of this matter is as follows: Whenever the trio of dogs would accost me on their dead end street then, I'd holler and try to evade them. This only made the poodles so much more inclined to make my life as miserable as they could. Of course, these two were nothing but small dogs full of animosity toward me. They were much smaller than I was. Much, much smaller. They were only poodles, even though they were full-grown poodles. Being only seven years old then, I wasn't big myself. Still, I was a whole lot bigger than they were. I often lunged as though I would hit the poodles with my lunch bucket, which I always kept handy, between their sharp teeth and myself.

Dogs, both good and bad, do not live long like we humans do when we live without illness and accident to a ripe old age, and I am sure that these two tormentors of mine left the earth ages since; although, during the time that my family and I lived seaside in Campbell River, this pair of rat canines would make my heart beat almost twice as fast on every school day afternoon when I'd encounter them. Rerun programming, just like on TV. Yep, rain or shine—all three dogs would be out there on the street—waiting for me to attempt a safe passage home. That the threesome were (obviously) incredibly dedicated to their shared cause of harassing me, is the only respectful observation I can make about this collection of canine miscreants.

I RETURN to the previously mentioned topic of marbles. Beyond the parochial sphere of chewing gum, marbles is an interesting word with a couple of applications.

For instance, one might mention were one so disposed to do, that anyone who has lost his marbles, has lost his sanity. Done! I lost mine, eons ago. Exactly why I am pluggin' away at this unfinished book now it is—to inform all who are willing to read it—about my many misadventures during boyhood.

Seriously now, marbles, the kind that boys play with, come in but one shape and two sizes. Naturally, in order for marbles to roll smoothly on a dirt, cement, or an asphalt surface, marbles have to be spherical. And marbles must have weight. To possess that smooth roll on uneven surfaces, marbles need to be made of solid construction. This is why marbles are made of glass, which lends weight.

If the game of marbles has a drawback, it is that marbles is strictly a boys' game. Or, at least it was when I was a kid. Anyhow, I am sure that you would not find many girls who play the game today.

So far as games go, marbles is one of the most simple games that I have ever played. Though it is a game that requires a fair degree of skill, it's v-e-r-y simple. All one has to do, is hit as many of one's opponent's marbles with as few of one's own as possible.

In the beginning of the game, the players, of which there are but two, square off against each other with each side's line of marbles parallel to the other's, separated by a distance of no more than a couple feet. Each player might have a half-dozen marbles in his arsenal. And each player shoots to hit the marble directly opposing one of his own. The competing players take turns, regardless of whether a competitor hits or misses his opponent's marble.

But, just how easy is it to speed a marble on its way? Easy. One simply bends down into a squat, or, one may kneel with one knee, or both, touching the ground. Then, one places a marble between the first finger and the thumbnail of his shooting hand. One then "kicks" the marble into transit using his thumb. But before he shoots, he must make sure to accurately aim his bullet toward a strike. Like in bowling.

Sad though it be for the loser of a match to have to contemplate, in this game a straight eye and steady hand usually prevail over dumb luck. Customarily, each side gets to pocket every marble on which he has scored a hit, and of course, he does not forfeit the marble used to make a hit. The player who wins more of his opponent's marbles than he loses of his own, wins the match. Oh yes, he gets something else too. By tradition, he is entitled to bragging rights. Inasmuch as this is sure to enhance his reputation as a formidable player amongst his fellows of the same age, this may be the most important gain to a youngster.

Since I usually won more than I lost, I felt a little sorry for my opponents most of the time. Still, I guess someone had to lose. So someone else could win. That's capitalism. Maybe that's why bankers like it so much.

Banks like to collect your money. I used to like looking at postage stamps. I knew that like old coins and unlike marbles, old stamps could be worth a lot. It's what my siblings had told me.

As a bonus, I found perusing stamps not only enjoyable as I scrutinized the features of every one of my stamps with a novice's eager interest, but a hobby that gave me something to do on those Saturdays and Sundays when I was forced to stay indoors by inclement weather. A cold, overcast day, with rain pouring down in sheets. This was always a nice time to stay indoors.

During these gray times out of the elements the three of us siblings would occasionally exchange philatelic specimens to pass the time. Trading stamps was a good way of ensuring that we all had a wide assortment of specimens in our individual collections. None of us knew the true value of the old stamps we bartered between us, and had we known the value of every stamp we swapped, such knowledge might have detracted considerably from our pleasure in trading them.

To some people, bartering is an art. To we three, trading stamps was just fun. I no longer retain my stamp collection in this day and age. For whatever reason, and I'll not guess, I have lost my once avid interest in collecting stamps.

CHAPTER NINETEEN

WE KIDS DID NOT GET MUCH IN THE WAY OF PRESENTS from our parents during our stay in Campbell River. Not even on a birthday. Cash was much too tight. For my parents, putting food on the kitchen table was the priority. Thus, in spite of my memorable experiences in the place, life in Campbell River was less than idyllic for me then. And with economic hardship being a reality of life then for our family, our time in this town would come to an abrupt end. Father had decided to pull up his stakes and immigrate south to the land of a sunny clime, and, he hoped, prosperity.

The picked location was San Diego, California. In comparison to cold, rainy, and dreary Campbell River, father figured then, as many a resident of a northern land would have been likely to do, southern California meant paradise itself. Eventually, uncertainty over the raging Vietnam War, begun years before our arrival in the United States, would force us back to Canada. Or would it? There were other reasons.

With our expected move to California almost in sight then, Helen became concerned for the welfare of her two pet turtles. Turtles? What turtles? You all must say. Remember, I told everyone earlier that my sister kept a lonely pair of hard-shelled, little, green Martians inside of a bowl.

Aside from the turtles whose fates *were* uncertain, Helen would've had Tiger the cat to worry about, but Helen planned to give her cherished cat to Sandra. Unhappily for sis, Tiger would later meet his fate beneath the wheel of a truck in the brisk traffic flow on our street. Helen, of course, did not know of her cat's pending tragic end at the time, and believing her cat's future safe—my sister had only her duo of turtles to look out for.

Reluctant, Helen was to abandon her pets, though she knew that she had to leave them behind. Father had decreed that it be so. U.S. immigration policy, father had told Helen, did not permit the transport of animals from another land across U.S. borders.

Apart from the U.S. Immigration and Naturalization Service, (what its policy on domestic animals was at the time I don't know) Helen's turtles were on another list. The same list my sister's cat was on. My list of dislikes in life. After all, these were two ugly-faced turtles that swam around in the stagnant water of a round, clear plastic dish, which stunk of turtle manure.

Unlike her cat, I had some sympathy for Helen's turtles; these stinky little guys lived a hard life, sequestered from the rest of the world behind a four-inch-high wall, encompassing a space no more than one foot across. A space no larger than the width of your dinner plate.

It is my wish to make a long account regarding the fate of Helen's two little buddies real short. Here be the upshot of what happened to them.

Helen spoke with father. Father then made a decision to accommodate sis's wish that her turtles be set free in a wilderness lake. So our family took a leisurely drive in our faded army-green Volkswagen van. Father had traded our Dodge station wagon for the much-weathered van a while back. Since father had no preference as to where Helen should release her turtles, father drove we five, plus Helen's turtles, around for a spell. Until we came to an unknown lake not far from town. A mountain lake with fir and spruce forest bordering its quiet stillness.

And here it was that Helen released her two friends. Were her turtles happy to be free at last? I don't know. But I suppose that lives of cramped captivity had been no lives at all, even for turtles—slow-of-feet—and probably slow-of-minds too. Yet—who really knows how a turtle thinks? Except another turtle. If Helen's turtles thought of their newfound freedom at all then—perhaps they were both overjoyed.

The gloomy side of the picture is that domesticated turtles do not possess keen survival instincts. For sure, their senses, long since all but atrophied by the security of a controlled indoor environment, are not as keenly attuned to their surroundings as the senses of their untamed cousins who have spent a lifetime in the wild, who can feel peril closing in on them and escape into the safety of deep water, or into their shells where the danger cannot pursue. I strongly suspect that these little bosom buddies of Helen's perished from starvation, cold, or predators within a matter of days following their liberation into the wild.

When we returned home, all of us immediately set to packing our personal belongings in preparation for the long journey southward by car. It was October 31, 1965. And because it was Halloween, me and Helen decided to make the most of it; our last days in Campbell River might as well be *filling*. So that evening, with a starry sky above our heads, we two kids went trick-or-treating.

Me and sis would end up going to a couple hundred households.

I WAS DRESSED AS A PIRATE and Helen was garbed as a gypsy. My having no real pirate's mask to cover my face with then, posed no problem. I wore a black tuque on my crown; indeed, the night air was cold enough for this. Mother had previously used her sharp sewing scissors to cut an oval black eye-patch out of an old pair of jeans; this patch I mentioned and not long since, I had wisely kept for future use. To each end of the patch, mother had fastened a large rubber band, and tied these together at the back. Wearing both the tuque and the eye-patch with the stretch band about my head—I was instantly transformed into a bloodthirsty buccaneer.

As I think of how I looked, even Robert Louis Stevenson's fictional character, the one-legged Long John Silver, would likely have nodded in approval had he been plucked from his everlasting home in the classic novel *Treasure Island*, and then been brought before me as I was. The old pirate king has acquired quite a notorious reputation since the publication of Stevenson's epic tale in 1883. Yet, somehow I know that he would not have been at all ruthless, for which he was so feared by many of his kind, toward a pint-size ragamuffin like me then.

Had I known of Long John Silver on Halloween night of 1965—and I swear that I did not, and had I been endowed with the powers of a warlock—which I have never claimed that I possess, I am sure that Long John would have fallen out of his book feet-first. And into a time warp leading him to the thirty-first day of the tenth month of the most recently mentioned year here, to present himself before me then, safe and sober, for the sole purpose of providing me with his seasoned pirate's opinion as to what, er, trivial improvements, if any, he might have wished to make on my overall appearance—to allow me to better portray the role of the vicious scoundrel I so desired to be.

And, had I known of Silver on Halloween of 1965, I am sure I would have declared to you, with no uncertainty in my voice, that the only recognizable difference between us was that Long John had just one good leg—and I had two.

Men of war must always look stern. My black eye-patch was an indispensible fixture for a youngster who mightily wished to look not just merely stern, but fantastically fearsome of face. True pirates always have to display an ugly face in order that the ordinary folks who they threaten and intend to rob, take them seriously—because not being taken seriously is no fun for any pirate. Especially for an upstart pirate it's not.

Before Helen and me had left on our outing, mother had applied some red lipstick to my cheeks, in a manner that mimicked the blood of battle. As we walked to our first house, and on to others in quick succession, an exaggerated savagery shone from my painted face and one good eye. With my makeup and amusing make-believe, seemingly perpetual, scowl, plus my diminutive size for a pirate, I resembled the caricature of ferocity.

However, had you seen into my mind at the time, this unflattering appraisal of myself, by myself now, would have gravely upset me then. Had I known of it—it would have. I fancied my representation of a pirate to resemble ferocity itself.

Safely hidden behind my grim mask, or so I believed, I flung myself with pounding fist into door after door. Ah, I could only marvel at the sweetness of the hearts that gave so considerately to poor folk such as we. The cistern of generosity flowed as unsullied as angels' breath from these kind souls. Fabulously so; the amount and variety of candy we children had collected gave me no reason to doubt the profitability of my venture and Helen's. Our shopping bags were bulging with goodies when I turned toward my sister.

I was getting pretty tired by now; I decided to let Helen in on this fact. "My feet hurt," I said. "Can we go home now?"

I wasn't looking for sympathy from Helen. When it came to me, Helen, I knew, was not the sympathetic sort. And as usual, sympathy I sure wasn't about to get. "You're such a little baby," came the stern response. "We'll go to one more house." So we trudged toward one last door.

I did not have to knock. This door had a doorbell. Helen pressed the doorbell. Helen was tall; fittingly then, it was always Helen who pressed doorbells. She usually had to. Most doorbells, and certainly every door-knocker, lay beyond my short reach.

WE HAD NOT WAITED LONG behind this door when a man answered. A middle-aged, heavyset man with a receding hairline. A fat man whose equally robust wife stood in their kitchen, twenty paces behind his right shoulder with her back turned toward me, setting dinner plates on their table.

Like I said, I was drained from all the walking I had done. In fact, it was about eight o'clock in the evening. I knew that my bedtime hour would soon be due. Fatigue weighed heavily on me and it must have influenced my mind. This excuse, I hope, will explain to you my subsequent action. In truth, I can give you no other explanation for my behavior.

I looked at the man in the doorway. I looked at his potbelly. I smelled the unmistakable odor of well-done steak that wafted to my nostrils from the kitchen. The warmth of the home's interior was not lost upon me, either. These things do not at all explain what I was about to say to this man. "All your dollars or your wife I'll take!" I blurted out.

Standing beside sis, I could almost feel Helen shrink by a good foot and a half; I wasn't looking at Helen. I was looking at the man. And looking at him I tried to smile sincerely. Like my hero Zorro would have done when he was about to rob somebody.

Right now, I was hoping that by charming the fat man with my tired but still razor-sharp wit I could induce him to hand me a spare chocolate bar or two. It did not occur to me that he might actually take me at my word. Or pretend to.

"Young fellow," said the man—not smiling at all, "let me get this straight now. You want—to steal—my wife?" His even voice seemed to blare through the few feet of distance between us like the foghorn of a ship. I mentally pinched myself. The man had obviously misunderstood. I didn't actually care to own his wife, I just wanted the man's candy.

I thought of explaining this to him. Yet as I looked up into his poker face, I noted for the very first time that he was a very large man looking down on a very little boy, and, I was beginning to think that maybe, just maybe, I had bitten off much more than I could chew.

But you know, I had already learned one thing in life long before this. This was that, when one has made a real big mistake—one should never admit it. Yes never, because if one does admit it—one will look like a complete idiot.

Certainly, I was *not* about to let this man make me look like an idiot. *Nor* could I let him see me back down from my position.

I am, you know, quite confident you will agree with me now, when I say that I used to be a cocky, stubborn runt. I stared the fat man in the eyes with determination worthy of only a desperate rogue. At the time I was quite sure that I looked quite menacing to his towering figure so far above me. And, I was sure that I did appear thus to him because my blood was pirate blood. Plus, with the nice paint job that mother had performed on my face, and the black patch that she had outfitted me with, I knew that I was, indeed, a very frightful sight.

I had been born to sail the seven seas, plundering at will like so many others of my kind before me. (Did I say something like that before? Oh well. I guess that I felt the need to reassure myself in my own mind then. You know. Bolster my ever-so-slowly flagging courage. No snickering please.) I *knew* that Helen was right beside me, ready to help out in case her little brother got himself into big trouble. Right? With my sister as backup, what had I to fear?

"All your dollars or your wife I'll take!" I demanded a second time. And this time, I'd slightly emphasized the word *wife*. I wanted the dolt to get the idea that I meant business. My habitual shyness around adults looked as though it had deserted me. Was I getting peeved? Well. Heck—yes. It was this man's inert response to my nonnegotiable demand that really stuck in my craw.

I was feeling hot under my shirt collar because I was not being accorded the respect that I felt I was entitled to as a trick-or-treater. Who did the fellow think that he was? Trick-or-treaters do not grow on trees. Nor do we t.o.ts grow on vines, either, I thought.

Yes, I officially admit it. I was riled, and rightfully so. And had it not been for this anger, I would probably have let my shyness show, and been squirming quite miserably in front of the man by now. Or been running toward home

167

like I had fire ants inside my pants. Just so that I could get out of his sight.

Had I been Batman, I could have spread my wings into the night sky to avert an uncomfortable situation. Batman, as you must guess by this time, used to be another hero of mine. But Batman was not foremost in my mind the next instant.

I was now wondering if the man had wax stuck inside his ears. I say this because the man just stood there, barely within the vestibule of his home, looking down at me with his mouth agape, dreadfully so, yes he was. In fact, I could clearly see his pink tongue resting on the floor of his yap. At a complete loss for words, he did appear to me. And the strange expression on his face made me doubt that the man had wax plugging his ears.

I thought about my own ears. Mother always cleaned the inside of my ears with a cotton-tipped toothpick. If the man did have wax in his ears, I figured, then he would not have heard me. The man would not have heard a single word of what I had said to him. But from his earlier reply to my greeting, I knew that the man could not possibly have wax in his ears. The man's silence, I reasoned, must therefore be due to another cause. Possibly shock.

I was not concerned about the man. Too much. Of mystery to myself was the now burning question of how I could be so daft to have threatened to run off with the man's wife in the first place. Tiredness was no excuse. For Pete's sake, I didn't own a bicycle. Nor, for that matter, did I own even a tricycle. And quite frankly, packing an unwilling hostage who likely weighed a couple hundred pounds at least, four times my weight, onto the back seat of a bicycle built for two—would have taken some doing.

Add to this the glaring fact that I did not yet even know how to ride a bicycle and you will instantly see just how empty, and ridiculous, my infantile threat to steal this man's wife really was. Of course I knew this truth well enough. But hey, don't you all ever underestimate my willingness to challenge the seemingly impossible, because I am a very stubborn fellow. Exceedingly stubborn. As stubborn as a screeching doornail—as my saying goes.

Still, in considering the situation that was, the man's wife was the size of a full-grown female gorilla. So you might well ask what I could have done, had I attempted to move her by whatever mechanical means—had she strenuously objected to being kidnapped? What little could I have done then? Other than reprimand her, and advise her of worse things yet to come. Or stomp on her big feet with all the might of my running shoes?

I admit it. Those speculative thoughts of mine now are utterly ludicrous. And thoughts are all that they are.

The man had recovered his composure; though, I believed, and it was awfully hard for me to be absolutely sure about this because the bright light that flowed into my face from the interior of the home was playing tricks on my one weary good eye, that the man had aged somewhat in the brief span of time elapsed since me and Helen had showed up on his doorstep. It looked to me that he had aged at least ten years in a span of seconds. I wondered if this had anything to do with what I had said to him.

More than before, his potbelly seemed to sag closer to the floor. And his receding hairline, an unlikely feature to flatter him at the best of times, looked like it had lost a few more follicles of hair. I thought of looking at the floor to see if there were any orphaned strands of hair lying about, but I immediately thought better of my first impulse, canceling it. What other very interesting thoughts might have happened in my mind next, I and you will never know.

Never, because just then the spell that bound the three of us broke as the man reached down and put his left arm inside a bowl which sat on a small table beside the open door. "Here you go, my young friend," he said smiling, as he tossed a lemon lollipop into my candy bag. And then another into Helen's. "But please," said the man—pausing to look me square in the eye, "don't take my wife. She's all I've got."

Friend? Had I heard the words right? I had not known that the man is my friend, I thought. It is mighty strange how a body can pick up friends just like that, I thought also. And—I had not even tried to be friendly. Boy! I mused. If I started treating everyone that I would ever meet during the course of my life—in a friendly manner—maybe I could suck them all into giving me something worth having.

I felt sorry for the man with the kind heart. I felt so sorry for him that I decided to let him know what I thought, just so that he would not have to worry about me showing up on some other day to lay claim to his wife. "Don't worry." I said to the man as Helen and me were leaving. "I won't steal your wife. She's too heavy for me to carry." We thanked the man, and me and sis trudged toward home happy, each of us having amassed a full bag of candy.

I decided right then that if I ever should actually get it into my mind to steal another man's wife—I would focus— on someone slim. By so doing I might be able to avoid getting a flat tire, if, of course, I ever should acquire enough money to afford a bicycle, I thought.

AS OF THIS MOMENT I am half convinced that both me and my harebrained accounts will never make it anywhere. Certainly not into the vacuous confine of the prestigious, hallowed hall of literary fame in Canada. This place is strictly for suckholes who cater to the unspoken rule of the ancient art of writing: a certain praiseworthy style exhibiting a rigid, bland conformity to the norm must be inherent in all such work in order that it receive the King's stamp of approval.

B-O-R-I-N-G.

All such work, you see, needs to be liberally sprinkled throughout its length with an ambiguous array of words that sound imposing in a doctoral manner. My style of writing, employing the clear language of the layman, is just not boring enough by way of its being confusing enough. My work is just too easy to understand. Too basic to even cut through the shallow, retarding layer of surface frost on a mentally-frozen head. Too exciting.

No, my work is just not boring enough for me to *really* hope to join such an elite club. I am never dull. I am just not a boring-enough fellow. What a shame. But—about this club. It be only the dullest *and* dumbest dimwits in this strange land of Canada that gain admittance, you say that I say? Dumbest, you say? It can't be! Else I would be in the club.

Today, I passionately believe that no man should ever embark on the highly dangerous undertaking of attempting to steal a woman who he does not know, from beneath the very nose of her husband. Unless, he is willing to clean the crevices between her teeth with a toothpick every day. And twice on Sundays. No reason given. None asked?

Needless to say, my Halloween was a roaring success. Halloween was a success for Helen too, until the next morning when I sold our catch for fifty cents to an occasional customer at our shop, a man who father had nicknamed, "Danny Boy". Father had named him thus on account of the man's high-spirited rendition of this classic Irish melody.

While I flatly admit that I am guilty of having sold my sister's portion of our take, and I never did share the proceeds of the sale with Helen, I entirely reject the crude notion that likely exists in your mind—I am nothing more than a common brigand. In other words, I am just another ordinary thief, slick of tongue. Banish the likely thought because—this—I feel—is outrageous. In no uncertain way, I shall have you know that I am not ordinary at just about everything. I still have pride, you know.

In late evening of the day that followed Halloween and this of course was the first day of November, father addressed a long-standing problem of mine. The problem was a wobbly tooth.

Having converted nearly all of their currency into American greenbacks in preparation for our immigration south, my parents were short of Canadian dollars. And besides that, seeing a dentist in town at this hour and late stage in time, on the eve before our exodus, was out of question.

I knew that father intended to pull my tooth out. But I didn't fully comprehend what father was up to as he told me to open my mouth wide. He then proceeded to tie some twine securely about the base of the tooth, lapping it several times. Father next led me to the washroom. Here he tied the other end of the string to the doorknob.

Telling me to say "Cheez"—father suddenly slammed the door shut. My tooth came flying out of my mouth. I shrieked in mingled pain and shocked disbelief. I stormed out of the washroom and immediately took refuge beneath my bed, my trust in father shattered by his clever, but traitorous, act.

I knew that I was safe beneath my bed. Once here, the tears began to flow from my eyes. And you know, with this barbaric demonstration of his unrefined and sometimes openly cruel nature, from this point in time onward, I never truly trusted father again.

THE NEXT MORNING BEGAN AT FIVE-THIRTY. Father had already loaded our possessions into the Volkswagen. The interior of our van, from the floor to the ceiling, was mostly taken up by neatly placed rows of corrugated boxes crammed full. In addition to the boxes of various sizes inside of the van, there was a two-foot-high load of spring mattresses strapped by thick rope to the roof rack.

From the appearance of our van, we would be traveling like gypsies. As light as we could. And as compact as we could. All that we owned father had squeezed to fit inside of that van, save for the stacked mattresses on the roof. As with any long move by sensible people, some items which had not made it into or onto our van had been discarded, including my seashells. Sacrificed, the unnecessary had been, as we all knew that we would not be coming back to Campbell River ever again.

Neither will we ever return to Canada, we thought at the time. Why would we want to return? Return to a country which did not even seem to know its own identity. This was a time when the symbolic yoke of the once mighty British Empire had just been cast aside with a new national flag—the red of the maple leaf, on a white background that I have (ever since the new flag made its debut) thought of as representing snow.

The van was ready and waiting. Father was inside of it and waiting for the rest of us. The rest of us jumped inside. And the five of us, without any of us bothering to take one last look at the gray brick building that we had all known as home for the past seven months, hit the road on the long journey to California.

CHAPTER TWENTY

THERE WAS BARELY ENOUGH ROOM inside the crowded van for my companions, except father, to sit. I had to lie down on some pillows, in a small space near the ceiling, a space not taken up by encroaching boxes. This was just behind the front bench, where mother sat nearest the passenger-side door.

To my rear, the back seat was buried beneath a mound of boxes. Four people, my parents and siblings, took up the front seat in a tight fit. Crowded together like a company of sardines inside a fish tin. I lay stretched out on my stomach, like an eel; in hindsight, that may have been for the better.

Besides my parents' wish to conserve space in the van, I had been allocated my lofty perch, where I had a bird's-eye view of the road and roadside ahead, for a reason other than sightseeing. Everyone, not just mother and father, knew that whenever I sat in the seat of a moving vehicle I would become lightheaded and I'd begin to vomit. And it wasn't just the motion of the vehicle that was the cause, it was in good measure due to the poisoning influence of the gasoline fumes, that drifted from I know not where on our van, which would assail my nostrils.

Since the motor of our vehicle was situated at its rear, I have often wondered how it was possible, with the wind working against us as our van had moved forward at fifty miles per hour, for the odor of gas to have persisted in the van while every window was shut tight, thus, one will think, this having eliminated the possibility of an external source for the bothersome fumes then.

We drove south along the Island Highway to Nanaimo. Here, father pulled the van up before the ferry dock. There was a slight problem now. It was a problem that I was already well aware of. Remember, I told you that my parents had already converted most of their Canadian currency into U.S. greenbacks. Well, our troop needed to get on a ferry bound for Horseshoe Bay on the mainland. And father—had to pay the toll so that we could board the boat. But, father was about ten dollars short of the required amount. Fortunately for our party, my M.J.B. piggy bank was not.

So, the coins that I had managed to obtain, often by less than virtuous means, came in real handy to save the day for us. (Father later repaid me the amount that he'd borrowed.) I did not complain in the least. No. I was mighty proud that my coins were of assistance for the greater good of my family. We boarded the ferry with father driving the van into the ship's parkade.

Our crossing to the mainland was uneventful. This was good, because I remember with relish, the great-tasting slice of blueberry pie that I'd purchased in the ship's cafeteria. A slice of pie which I would manage to not throw up because I wasn't seasick. On a smooth journey through flawlessly calm waves, no true sailorman ever gets seasick. Did I ever tell you that I was not a real sailorman?

Having arrived in Horseshoe Bay after a pleasant two-hour voyage, we disembarked to shore. From here it was but an hour's drive to the Canadian border. All of us were interestedly looking at the sights beside the road. And talking.

Father, who much preferred the feel of the open road to the congestion of the border traffic, shared my sentiment. Continual stops and starts. What a total waste of time.

Stops and starts would have ordinarily made me queasy: I was not thinking that I might vomit right now; had I been thinking that I would vomit, and had I vomited, the vomit would have dropped on dear mother's head. I wasn't carsick. Mother's Gravol pill in my butt was doing its work.

I recollect that we stayed the night in an old motel that had gray siding, a motel on the Canadian side of the International Peace Arch.

Next morning, bright and early: The traffic ahead had ever so slowly thinned as our van edged forward, past the Canadian border post to U.S. Immigration. Here, a man sporting a blue uniform, greeted us. Father had rolled his window down. Father handed the man some papers. I thought that the man looked important standing there on the road in his uniform and policeman's hat on a sunny morning. The man would not have looked so important had it been instead a miserable rainy day with him standing there on the road with a soaked, dripping hat on his head. Before I grow up, I will have to find myself an important-looking uniform too, I thought.

The man had finished his examination of father's papers. That was fast. The important-looking man looked at the load of mattresses on our van's roof. He peered within the van. Addressing father with several questions, the man then requested father and mother to accompany him inside a building at the roadside. But first, the man motioned father to park the van to the rear of the building. During father's and mother's absence we three kids chatted, and yawned while we chatted. A considerable while later, father and mother emerged from the building, father holding documentation in hand.

Thus it was that with the sun's fresh celestial glow looking down upon us, as if to assure us that all bode well for us on our trip southward, we now resumed our journey.

Although my memory of events this far back in time is vague with respect to a few specific locations we visited then, I do remember the interesting features of our passage through the American landscape with fair accuracy. With the border behind us I recall, in a series of snapshots of time still intact in my memory, that we stopped at a roadside diner in northern Washington State in the late afternoon.

And I recall the fact that except for father, who chewed on a burger, the rest of us each had a large plateful of delicious, golden fries. And, while our parents drank coffee, we kiddies each savored our own bottle of soda pop. Orange Crush for Helen and me. Coke for Raimo.

A few miles further down Interstate 5, father rented a large motel suite for the night. Our life at the back of father's shop in Campbell River had been without luxury. Here in the motel I had the opportunity to watch television for the first time in months. *Flipper*. More than a bit on the boring side for me, though. Not at all in the same league as being entertained by the highly amusing antics of Jack Tripper.

It is too bad that *Three's Company* wasn't around in 1965. If this show had been around then, I would have learned from Tripper's masterly example all about the do's and don'ts in life when one is looking for a girlfriend. But I'll not complain too much. I look on the bright side. Watching a show as dull as *Flipper* certainly helped put me to sleep once again, and at the time the show had been free entertainment. So, what the heck?

The morning thereafter I had quite an appetite. That did not go unnoticed by mother, who had made toast for me and everyone else except father. Father had mother make him a sweet-pickle sandwich. Which he, being father, gulped down with coffee—of course. I didn't complain. I would not have willingly traded toast with strawberry jam slathered on it—for any sandwich. Num-num. Having eaten, we all piled into the Volkswagen and took up the long drive to the south.

The VW blew on by the hills and flatland of Washington and Oregon. Effortlessly, it seemed to me, whilst another Gravol saw to no bothersome ejection from within my belly, nothing to result in a sudden nasty, slimy spill. Our day was uneventful until we reached the small township of Roseburg, Oregon just after dusk. If we had not paid much attention to the deepening shadows earlier, we couldn't now. It was plenty dark now. I was about to learn a lesson this evening. Reliability, I would learn, is often not considered adequately in life when an old or old-looking mechanical device is called on to perform to someone's too-hopeful expectation.

Maybe we'd all learn a lesson. Excluding father, that is, who was mechanically-minded and experienced in the ways of man's mechanical pony. A worn pony this was, yes. But father understood everything about motors. He had to because he fixed motors in his occupation every day.

I did not yet understand the difference between gasoline-powered motors and the electric engines that father tended to in his work. To me, motors were motors. All motors are doubtless the same, I thought. To myself now, it's kind of funny how an experienced hand like father, to whom all motors were first nature, had doubtless seen what could happen next, long before it would happen. And, in spite of his intuition to warn him, father had chosen to gamble.

As our van limped into the lights of Roseburg, it was pretty clear to us that something was terribly askew with it. From the back of the van a thick cloud of gray smoke spewed in our wake, and a medley of low noise emanated. As we listened to the ominous sound we knew that our metal carriage was quickly falling apart. Then, as the van stumbled slowly onward, Raimo hopped out of the vehicle and helped the ailing bucket of bolts ascend a low hill by pushing hard against the dashboard while the front passenger door lay wide open. Luckily, with Raimo's muscle power we reached the crest of the hill. At the top of which the inevitable finally caught up with us. And it was here that the inevitable broke our pony's back. The van's motor blew out. With a dead engine, we rolled down the other side of the rise and came to a halt.

The lump in our throats was heavy as we each felt the uncertainty of the immediate future. But it was not to be all bad news for us. There is usually a silver lining to every smoking, gray cloud in life. Thanks in part to gravity, the momentum of the van coming down this strip of highway had carried us into the yard of the very first gas station hereabouts, and—thanks to the fact that none of our transport's four wheels had fallen off. We were now in Roseburg proper. The date was November 4, 1965.

FATHER GOT OUT OF THE DRIVER'S SEAT and stepped out of the van. The rest of us followed his example, evacuating the silent vehicle like we were all rats fleeing in desperation from a sinking ship. Father walked around to the rear of the van and opened the engine cover to have a look at what he already knew that he would find. He bent over and quickly examined the dead engine with a flashlight. Father straightened himself. Then father dug his hands inside his pants' front pockets. I followed father's example.

Father was the leader of our party. Standing straight with his hands sunk deep into his pants' pockets was what father always did whenever his nuts-and-bolts mind was lost in concentration. Being a lady, mother was wearing a dress, and mother had had no pockets cut into her dress to put her hands into. I was not paying attention to what my siblings were doing with their hands, though I knew that pockets are always handy when a body has them.

Speaking in a low tone to us all, father took his hands out of his pockets and clinched the butt of a cigarette, pulling the cigarette from his shirt's front pocket. Father dug his lighter out and lit his cigarette. Then father stuck the tobacco stick between his teeth and inhaled the poisonous cloud that rose from it into his lungs. I could not emulate father's bad example. I had no chocolate cigarettes to pretend with. So, each of my hands stayed in its pocket.

The loss of the engine that drove the VW van slowed down our journey toward the south by a bit, and we all sat in a Roseburg motel during this time while the heart of father's van was replaced. Once this was done, the Volkswagen was ready to roll again. Ready to roll down the highways of America, the land of promise, to a new home. And roll we did.

We crossed the border from Oregon territory into the State of California. Our van's new engine purred like a well-fed cat. Content to be of service and operating well. A good four hundred miles later, along Interstate 101, as we came to the Golden Gate Bridge in San Francisco we sighted a most unusual fellow. A heavily bearded old man with a lion's mane of silver hair. Standing alone at the roadside, at the entrance to the bridge. Standing in his sandals, white dress slacks, and white long-sleeved shirt. Holding a homemade sign, roughly hand-painted. A sign with an unusual message. And about that sign of his with the unusual message.

His sign read precisely this:

> "THIS IS GOD'S COUNTRY.
> PLEASE DON'T DRIVE
> THROUGH IT LIKE HELL."

And you know, that old man had already struck fame somewhere along the line of time then. I know for sure that he had. I know this because I later spotted his mirror image on a postcard at a convenience store we had stopped at because the business had a gas bar out front and, inside the store, mother knew that they would carry cool treats in their freezer. Anyhow, that's California for you. A place where you might occasionally catch a glimpse of (did I not tell you?) a (but you know it, anyway) movie star. And see all kinds of other stars. Even if some of them do appear homemade.

Five-hundred-or-so miles further down the road we met the most picturesque community that I would ever see in California. Santa Barbara. A beautiful place which, in my opinion, has the finest sand beach in the Golden State. Plus, all of the very prettiest "skirts" on this side of the Continental Divide.

I knew, then, that I had to act like I wasn't noticing the girls. I had to act cool. Yes, I was noticing them, even as

I was fooling everybody in our clan into believing that I was not.

Were my traveling companions to know the truth of my discovery, I mused, I'll never find another quiet moment to myself for the balance of our trip. Helen, always a pest, will surely see to that, even if no one else pokes fun at me for possessing a romantic desire at my young age.

In Santa Barbara, we would stay at a pleasant, older motel, near the beach, one week, enjoying the sunshine and the sight of huge palm trees as any tourist would. Just a stone's throw from the sand beach. Unfortunately, it was early November and the ocean water was very cool. Even for northerners like us. Brrrrrr! Cold! We left Santa Barbara with reluctance; we had to resume our journey. Our next rest would be at our new home in the city of San Diego.

Ah, what a paradise I'd just lost, I thought then; I mention that now even though the seawater in Santa Barbara was far too chilly, at this time in mid fall then, for any one of those pretty girls, that I'd seen walking as tourists about town, to have been dipping her skin into the waves. Nor had I spotted anyone wrapped in a bikini, lying on the golden sand beach.

It was in midafternoon when Interstate 101 led us into the sprawling metropolis of Los Angeles. As I beheld America's second-largest city, I could not help but feel awestruck by the spider's web of freeways that ran out from central L.A. in every direction, like the limbs of a tree. Impressive. But we did not drop anchor here for a moment. And once Tinseltown was behind us, even father, usually reserved, seemed more than a bit relieved. Next stop: San Diego.

Begun in 1769 when the first Spanish mission was built on the site, San Diego is a city with a strong Spanish history. Even today the early Spanish influence can be readily seen: many of the street signs display Spanish names. With the early Spanish activity having been so recognizable a force in settling the area, one might think that the early French explorers had no interest in it. I think this. Yet I cannot explain the name of the street to which father drove us, the street on which our next residence was to be then. La Salle Street. Named after a Frenchman. Possibly the early French voyager, René Robert Cavalier, Sieur de La Salle.

CHAPTER TWENTY-ONE

IT WAS ABOUT FOUR O'CLOCK IN THE AFTERNOON when we cruised into San Diego, and at last arrived at our new home on La Salle Street.

From the exterior our residence looked just like any other place. Our quarters were in a small, ground-level apartment complex, with a well manicured green lawn out by the "side" entrance where our front door was. The caretaker and owner, a Japanese lady in her very late forties, by the first name of Masuko, was hosing down the cement drive out front with a garden hose.

Masuko greeted us warmly, and immediately led our travel-weary party to our suite. Masuko unlocked the front door and commenced to give us a tour of the premises, whilst she explained in passable English, laden with a strong Japanese accent, that she and her husband lived in the suite behind us. Once we'd entered the interior of the apartment I could see that, unlike our former spartan quarters in Campbell River, there was plenty of space inside this abode. It was a three-bedroom unit, modern and clean.

Masuko was married to a Japanese-American serviceman who was usually absent from home; involved he was in the Vietnam War campaign. I have no idea what Masuko and her husband (he I later met along with their twentysomething-year-old daughter who lived elsewhere) thought about this war. And I certainly don't remember the man's first name, or the first name of their daughter any more than I can recall what their family name was.

About the Vietnam War. I, of course, had no idea how prominently this war would contribute to my parents' decision to later return to Canada, then. As a man now, I think back on the Vietnam conflict.

As I see it this day, the Vietnam War was just another war for America to fight. Another war, another opportunity for good men to die. I say this solemnly as I remember newscasts of this troubled time in U.S. history when so many American soldiers came back to their native soil in sealed bodybags. It was a time when growing numbers of conscripts were taken into the U.S. military machine—to help wage a war that most of them did not believe in.

A time when so many others amongst the peace movement spreading throughout America, left the country for the security of Canada, and were labeled as draft dodgers by the U.S. Government. Fortunately, U.S. politicians were not hard of sight and hearing. Witnessing the growing protests in the nation's streets, a rising sea of voices clamoring for peace, the U.S. Government would, as we all now know, eventually give in to hardening public opinion against this war. A war that every sensible American had been against from the very beginning.

But not until 1973 did the war which should never have involved the United States of America, finally end. I have no desire to bore America with a recap of its bloody history.

In mid autumn of 1965, the gravity of the Vietnam War concerned me not. Being just a kid then, there was no reason that a faraway war in a foreign land, should have. My immediate concern was my education.

For, again I had a new school to adjust to. And the name Barnard still lives in my memory as the name of my school. A continuation of second grade. My teacher was Mrs. Posterick. Her first name? I don't recall. Not that it much matters.

At the time, Mrs. Posterick was past thirty years in age. About thirty-five, I will guess. She was tall and slim with bushy, raven hair cut fairly short. Of course, when a fellow is seven years old and short in comparison, every grown-up looks huge. (Just like the Empire State Building in the Big Apple.) Even so, Mrs. Posterick was extra tall for a lady. And she'd seemed to like me from our first meeting.

Shortly thereafter, as Mrs. Posterick worked with me to improve my poor math and unimpressive word skills, she bonded steadfast to me. I knew not why. Of all the students enrolled in her class, my teacher probably liked me the most.

I say this with affection for Mrs. Posterick. In her presence I felt warm inside. And totally at ease. I knew that Mrs. Posterick adored me as a mother will her own child. I knew this because I was one of the very few children who Mrs. Posterick would always pick from out of the many pupils in her class—who she'd take to her lap. In Mrs. Posterick's class I quickly became what is customarily described as a teacher's pet.

Odd enough though it was for myself at first, here in Mrs. Posterick's class none of the other kids, boy or girl, made fun of me on the basis of my special, almost exclusive, seat. No one did, because every child in her room, liked Mrs. Posterick. Apart from my teacher's affection for children there was another reason, I believe now, as to why no kid *ever* poked fun at me for my preferential standing in class. This. It was only grade two then and every child had worries. For every child, there was so much to learn. And so quickly.

But you know, to me, Mrs. Posterick could never be just a mere teacher who treated her students with ultimate kindness. To me, my teacher made the hours that I spent in class on each school day, worthwhile. I felt then, that if I should ever need a true friend at school, a comforting shoulder to cry on, Mrs. Posterick could be counted on to be such a friend.

My mentor's inner warmth was directly reflected in the atmosphere of cooperation between herself and her students. Unlike the rigid mood of Mrs. Mulder's class in Richmond—back in frozen Canada, here the mood was so passive. So warm. And I flowered.

In Mrs. Posterick's class my spirit had at last emerged from its ice age. For my parents, this was the break that they had awaited. Yes, here—my spirit—was now free. Free at last. And everyone around me saw the change. In hindsight, my awakening was not surprising, as the spirit of my teacher had begun to rub off on me. Mrs. Posterick, you see, had touched my heart with her own.

BACK AT HOME IN OUR APARTMENT on La Salle Street we Kellosalmis had already well acclimatized to our new dig. We were quite comfortably settled in now. Then—the invaders came. I am not referring to the extraterrestrials who always landed in our living room via a popular TV series of the time. Those aliens never looked like they were from another world, anyway. Another world? Aliens!!! These most always seem to possess such a sinister agenda, don't they? C'mon. Sure they do. An evil seen lurking in the preamble to each episode of *The Invaders*, where we witnessed the lone occupant of a solitary car, caught out on a remote country road in the dead of night. Shielding his eyes from the glare of an alien saucer about to land on Earth. No. The invaders I speak of hadn't arrived in our home via a spaceship. These invaders were small. I awoke early one Saturday morning, before anyone else had stirred from bed, to witness a column of these audacious intruders marching into our private space—pouring in through the crack of sunlight that showed from beneath our kitchen door. These invaders were not just small, they were tiny.

I still entertained the thought of getting myself a biscuit or two for breakfast. I soon banished the idea from mind, since I noticed immediately as I opened one door of the kitchen cupboard, that the marching troop had beat a direct path to the paper sack of white granulated sugar on the bottom shelf. I picked the bag up and examined it.

The sack had not been opened by mother or anyone else. The lip of the bag was completely glued shut. Yet, somehow the sugar sack had suffered a miniscule slit at the bottom of the bag. This was all that a legion of black ants would have needed, but some of the crystals of sugar had spilled from the bag onto the lower shelf itself. And now, two-hundred-or-so black ants were busy licking up every granule of sugar that they could squeeze into their greedy little bellies.

Some of the intruders had already taken, as is the survival-dictated custom amongst ants, to carrying off as many specks of sustenance as they could manage. After satisfying its own hunger for sweets, each member from this colony of ants would, as I watched in interest mingled with horror, crawl back down the edge of the kitchen vanity and onto the floor. Each ant with a pack of sugar on its back, each ant bound for the door exit, all while other eager participants from their colony rushed in from outdoors to join the free-for-all.

I didn't know who it was that had invited these little burglars into our home. Some fool had to have leaked the word out. Like hung a sign on the exterior of our kitchen door, that had persuaded the foreign legion to move in.

A welcoming sign saying:

ALL YOU CAN EAT.
ALL YOU CAN CARRY.
NO CASH. NO CREDIT. NO PROBLEM.
BRING APPETITE.

I was sure that their queen would be delighted with her subordinates' find when they would arrive back at headquarters to provide her with a briefing of every detail of their mission, and their exceptional good fortune in particular; so brazen were these ants, they have made me wonder since then as to whether they had all been trained by the recruiters of the vaunted spy-thriller TV series of the time, *Mission Impossible*.

Certainly, these ants had to have believed from the outset that an impossible mission their early morning jaunt would not be. And please, do not tell me that an ant's I.Q. is commensurate with the weight of its brain, because I don't, and won't, believe you. I tell you—these little guys have the inside track on humanity. Like me specifically, ants have a one-track mind. Note that you will never convince me that ants are stupid on the basis that they have a little less free space in their beans with which to daydream than I do. Yes, ants are actually pretty smart.

They are—because ants regularly conduct reconnaissance missions to pinpoint the whereabouts of food. And like bees in search of honey, ants will find and devour your sweets. A small spill and the slightest air space beneath your door is all that it takes. You need not hang out your INTRUDER WELCOME sign. No. Ants are smart. Very smart.

Ants be salty food. Did you know that to any bear it is a well-known fact that devouring ants by the drove will make for thirst? I have never eaten ants myself and I never plan to, but I learned this about ants by reading Ernest Seton's *The Biography of a Grizzly*. A handy book it was.

I received this sad book, detailing the hard life of one orphaned grizzly bear cub, for my eleventh birthday in Portland, Oregon. Our move north to Portland would come much later in time.

For now, I was just a seven-year-old kid who fancied himself, believe it or not, as a big-game hunter. On an African safari I was. And all of this heart-gripping action was packed into the safe confines of our apartment on La Salle Street.

Being then, as I have always been throughout my life, infected with that active imagination I mentioned before, on this day I saw myself to be in pursuit of an enemy—on a highly dangerous expedition from which I knew not whether I would return alive. And, being the ultimate hunter—in search of the ultimate quarry, the wily, miniscule black ant—which is so small that it was difficult for me to spot from standing up, meant that I had to crawl along the hardwood floor of our apartment. Armed only with a loose elastic band and a twelve-inch-long school ruler of wood, the first—stretched out when firing, over little more than half the length of the latter.

As I say, ants are not dumb. These ants had spread out. And they liked to travel along our floor, next to the baseboards; they did this, I believe, because they soon learned that it was not quite as easy for me to zap them there, as it was when they ventured out into the middle of the floor space in each room. However, as you might expect, the evasive efforts of the enemy then, would prove futile. I was a determined hunter on the prowl. And I stalked and met the tiny black critters face-to-face.

I found the enemy in great numbers beneath our new Scandinavian sofa in the living room. So I slaughtered the intruders to the last ant. Even at the demarcation line—the baseboards, where the hostile forces tried to sneak through my territory undetected, my deadly rubber band found their worthless, sleek black butts, and stung them.

I met the enemy in every room. I found them in the bathroom, at the base of the toilet. I discovered them in the dark closets, trying to scurry for cover beneath miscellaneous items when the beam of instant day from my flashlight lit up their tiny, startled faces. And of course, I met them at their entry point beneath our kitchen door. Thus the battle waged on, and a legion of black ants, one ant at a time, reluctantly gave their immortal souls to their common deity in ant heaven.

It was almost dinnertime for me when the last black ant drew his last breath. Strewn about on the floor were bodies and bodies. I had slain a good two hundred and thirty-six soldiers of the ant army on this day. All KIA they were—I had taken no prisoners. And although there were no hostiles lurking about that I could see, a few dozen of the enemy had either deserted their common cause or become lost during the searing action, and were now classified by me as MIA.

I had respect for the bulk of the enemy, though. Just like General Custer did for his at the Little Big Horn in 1876.

Oh, if he got scalped, that respect will not have lasted long, I thought.

Unlike them ants, my star was definitely arising in the world. Having successfully crushed the enemy offensive with the efficiency of a hungry anteater, it was natural for me to feel this way.

In fact, the worst part of my whole Saturday was when mother announced that I needed to clean the floor of all the corpses littering it. After that, I knew that mother wanted me to take a bath. Mommy always scrubbed me real good with soap behind my ears. Like some wise folks say: a mother's work is never over.

This had been a long day for me. Yet, it was just another day in the life of a small boy. What had been the most dangerous part of my successful mission? Answer: I had accidently bumped my head on the underside of our sofa. Wood frames, you know, are not healthy for helmetless heads.

CHAPTER TWENTY-TWO

IT WAS AROUND THIS TIME that my parents made the acquaintance of a young family in San Diego, who became fast friends of ours. This couple, whose surname was Lampinen, were recent immigrants from Finland. Jukka Lampinen, was a likable fellow who was employed as a photocopier technician. His charming wife, Annelli, worked as a hairdresser. And the pair had an infant daughter by the name of Heini.

This easygoing couple, and little Heini, would visit us occasionally, just as we'd visit them in their apartment, here in town. The Lampinens would later add a son, Petri, to their family. And, like many folks with one young child and another yet to come, they'd already purchased a nice house. Besides the Lampinen family, during the three short years that my family and I would spend in San Diego, my parents would have little association with other folks, excepting people in the workplace environment. The end. Yawn.

I remember that I was supposed to build Heini a sturdy wood stool once. Now, you really should not laugh at me when I tell you this, and I must try to not dwell on this matter long to avoid needless embarrassment to myself in the often critical eyes of the public. I have to be fair to myself, you know. My project did get off the ground. Those seven derisive words seem, equally, apologetically lame to me—my creation went further than that. But Heini's stool was never fit for anyone, even a baby, to actually sit on. To anybody terribly poor in vision it might have looked okay in a darkened room, but I believe that my piece of carefully constructed handiwork would likely have collapsed under the weight of a full carton of Kleenex tissue. I never was much of a carpenter. Then, and now.

However, let us look on the bright side of this complicated matter. My stool project convinced me that I was not made of the right stuff to become a carpenter. Ever. And I am sure that you would not want me to be the guy who you hire to build your dream house. You really should know this too. Beside' buggering up my stool project, I had managed to score a direct hit with a hammer, on the thumb of my left hand—when I had attempted to strike an unhelpful finishing nail of hard steel with the full force of my right. Oh well. That's life. Ouch!

Under Mrs. Posterick's caring guidance, my studies in school were proceeding smoothly. And in the evenings after every school day, my sister drilled me in arithmetic at home. You know, when a body is indoors a lot during a severe Canadian winter it's an indication that it feels the biting cold of this season. However, here in southern California there were no real seasons.

True, it was cooler during the autumnal equinox. And while the ground lay barren of snow, the school Christmas break came and went. There had been no drastic change from fall to winter, a rapid change that often occurs even in southern Canada.

Although, these days with global warming influencing the weather on our planet, the seasonal changes in the north are more gradual, with the result that an average winter in Canada is not as severe as it was twenty or more years ago. You know that.

And San Diego was dry. Really dry. Here in San Diego, a city with the Mexican border as a southern boundary to future growth, rarely did it rain, even in winter. And when it did rain in winter, it rained in buckets. On one occasion it rained so hard that the storm drains at curbside on every street in our area became clogged with rainwater, forcing mother to accompany me on my morning walk to school.

Across a waterlogged intersection, a swift-flowing torrent of angry water, she carried me in her arms to the other side of the street, and to safety.

Yes wet—and in particular cold from a wet sky, were rare occurrences here. And as 1965 advanced into the spring of 1966, the quickly warming rays of the southern sun had defrosted the last vestige of weather-related northern cold from within me.

The monotony of the weather, a seemingly never-ending cascade of sunny days without a single miserly drop of rain, did not bother us at first. No, because everyone in the family, with the exception of father who deplored any setting which reminded him of luxury, was much happier here in decent, modern lodging than we had been while living in the back of our gray brick workshop in Campbell River.

Back to my education now. I was nearing the end of grade two at Barnard School. I had under Mrs. Posterick's guidance, coupled with my parents' desire to see me succeed as was evidenced by Helen's tutoring which I could not have done without, mastered the spelling of most simple English words. Basic math, too, was becoming much easier for me to understand.

One day in late June, Mrs. Posterick announced that she would hold a spelling bee. This contest, she told us students, would determine which children would need to devote some of their leisure time, during summer vacation, to upgrade their spelling skills. Because this would be a contest, and because my teacher believed in rewarding competence gained through study, Mrs. Posterick explained to we pupils in her class that she would award a prize to each of the two best spellers.

My teacher stood at the front of her class, in the center of the classroom. Mrs. Posterick asked every student to stand. Next, my teacher split the class in half. Every child whose desk lay on her right side, moved toward the center of the classroom and formed one line. And every kid whose desk lay to my teacher's left, formed another line which faced the right.

The contest began. Each contestant stood and listened carefully as Mrs. Posterick read aloud her chosen words. None of we pupils fidgeted. Every child knew that Mrs. Posterick was a friend, first. And a teacher, second. No one amongst us students appeared at all uncomfortable. Even the poorest spellers in Mrs. Posterick's class had little to fear.

But any word that is spelled incorrectly by a contestant during a spelling bee, generally spells instant elimination from the ranks of those still left standing. It was not long before the length of the two opposing lines began to shorten, and, as the contest advanced and child after child went down to defeat at his desk, I was beginning to feel the heat of the tourney. Though, outwardly I was quite calm.

Knowing that it would take but one word to spell my defeat, I tried to concentrate solely on each word that Mrs. Posterick requested I spell. And when, at last, the once long ribbon of children on either side of the classroom wound down to just one left standing on either side—all the children in the room, seated or standing, listened with keen ears, waiting for their teacher to continue with the contest.

THE TWO WHO STILL STOOD faced each other from across time and space. These kids, one little girl and one little boy, stood, it seemed to me back then, like opposing gunfighters straight from out of the historic wild west.

Was this, as it appeared to me at the time, to be a battle of wits to the very end? Which of these instant rivals would crumble to ignominious defeat? And who would stand? My classmates were, as always, exceptionally well-behaved. There was no rooting for either contestant. This in no way surprised me, since Mrs. Posterick had a calming effect on young ones. In any contest between the sexes, boys can usually be expected to applaud their own kind. And girls usually can be expected to do the same for their kind. Not in Mrs. Posterick's classroom. Here, there was only intense interest showing on every little face.

Then—there was Susan. It was Susan who faced me now. Susan, I knew to be an intelligent, quiet, shy girl. Susan was also the prettiest girl in Mrs. Posterick's class. Easily. Indeed, with her long, straight, dark-brown hair to grace her face, Susan—was a perfect meld of raw physical beauty and brain.

At the moment, Susan was avoiding my eyes. Probably, I figured then, for the same reason that I was trying to not look directly into hers. Not because we be gentlefolks, but because we each felt that we needed to do so in order to think.

And as Susan and I stood there at the front of the class facing each other, I knew that Susan knew that we were two equals of mind and spirit. Locked together for a brief eternity in time. Two equals locked in one unpredictable showdown.

Mrs. Posterick looked at Susan. Then at me. My teacher and friend smiled. Was it that the bell would eventually ring, signaling the start of the lunch hour? Or was it that Mrs. Posterick simply felt that the contest had to end? Was it that she knew what the outcome would likely be were she to allow the match to continue? And if it was the last of these possibilities which was reality, was my teacher afraid for me? Or for Susan? Whatever the case was, I knew that Mrs. Posterick was wise in the ways of the world. She was wise beyond her years. Wisdom and kindness. These often go hand in hand.

Mrs. Posterick had made a decision. A draw would immediately be held. A lottery governed by chance. Mrs. Posterick held a numbered card facedown in her hand. I don't remember which hand. I do remember that Susan and I were told to pick a number between one and ten. The number closest to the number printed on the reverse side of the card in my teacher's hand then, would win. Meaning that either Susan or myself would be entitled to select first from one of two prizes, those which Mrs. Posterick now displayed before her class.

I saw that both of these prizes were well-illustrated, fact-filled children's books. One was a slender book on dinosaurs. The other was a larger and thicker book, detailing every well-known species of animal, from A to Z, on our world. And here this particular account will end. I do not remember which number Susan chose. Nor do I remember which number I picked. But ladies never come second, some folks say. Leaving Master Fate to end the play. It was a gamble. And Susan won—fair and square.

Susan chose the book on the long-extinct dino's. Had I gotten to pick first, I would have made the same choice that she did—dinosaurs are a subject more likely to intrigue a child's mind than any other. Yet, I can't say that I was too displeased with the outcome of my first spelling bee, because I was left to enjoy, *The World of Animals*. A great book for an inquisitive youngster like me then.

Chapter Twenty-three

WRITING, reading, and arithmetic again. Well, actually, just writing. I've conveniently chucked aside the other two essentials in life to reveal my penchant for writing. My promising, early writing career which never came to fruition once I had graduated from high school, began in the comfort of home, long ago.

I tried writing short stories, purely fiction of course, since I had no experience of the world such as journalists possess, 'specially those of them who cover international events of significance. Yeah, I tried to write stories, all right. Tried, and did. Really short stories. Like this one about my sister's schoolgirl heroine, X, who, though undeniably a character of fiction, was very popular amongst a loyal readership of teenage girls. See whether you can guess X's true identity.

My story, minus the then existing epilogue, essentially went thus: "X was in trouble. The house was haunted. The other girl was lost. But then X saw a big boat come down the sea. To X it came. X was saved. But the other girl was still lost." As for the name quiz. You didn't get it, did you? Oh well.

I don't remember how the rest of my tale turned out. Please excuse me for my lapse in memory: I printed the funny words in pencil—one-half of a lifetime ago. Writing was my favorite pastime now. That would soon change. For a while.

On La Salle Street, I had a good buddy by the first name of Manuel. His last name? It was half of a lifetime ago. I have never been much good at recalling last names. How many times have I demonstrated thus in this book of recollection? Anyhow, my friend Manuel was like myself then, seven years of age.

Like me, he attended Barnard Elementary School. Manuel was in my class, the class of Mrs. Posterick.

Manuel was a kid of Spanish heritage and he was from Puerto Rico. And after I showed Manuel some of my stories, he got himself all fired up and began writing as a hobby too. (Unlike myself, my friend Manuel chose to not write fiction.) And 'sides writing, Manuel liked dinosaurs a whole lot. So, naturally he chose to write of them.

Never should we underestimate the intelligence of a seven-year-old. Manuel knew everything that most kids of his age then would not have known about the giant reptiles that once roamed Earth. I didn't know much about dinosaurs initially, but I learned a fair bit about them, from what Manuel wrote of them. I learned how all of the really vicious meat-eating dinosaurs, such as T. Rex, feasted on benign giants like the much larger Brontosaurus who had gone about minding their own business, living their entire lives hiding in and around the deep water of swamps. And every Brontosaurus existing then had tried hard to not fart too loud so that T. Rex would not hear him or her. Before Manuel taught me about them, I had only known about the dinosaurs that I saw daily on *The Flintstones*.

Obviously, writing stories was fun for me at my age. That said, I had no overwhelming aspiration to eventually become a writer. As a matter of fact, if you'd asked me what I'd want to be, I would have told you that I really don't know. I don't know what career path Manuel chose to follow. Besides writing stuff then, Manuel and I played together as kids do. And being boys, we played war games.

Because we lacked the body armor that the splendidly clad knights of medieval times had the good fortune to own, we made do with what we had, and fought in our shirt-sleeves. Each of us had a shield, cut out from a large corrugated box, to which we had affixed a handle of thick rope. And with wood-bladed swords, on the side lawn at La Salle where mother was less likely to keep a watchful eye on our pursuits, Manuel and me, battled back and forth.

Sometimes, we would play out our duels in Manuel's folks' yard, which was only a block away. And it was a fair fight every time that we battled: Manuel was a match in height, weight, and strength, to myself. But my desire to win exceeded my friend's, and Manuel eventually lost interest in swordplay because I'd usually ended up gaining the upper hand in these mock battles.

This is understandable for another reason also: the tips of our swords were hard and sharp enough to hurt some when they were thrust into the thin fabric of a shirt-sleeve, or into a pants' leg. Or when these weapons of play were jabbed into the belly or groin, where a sharp tip really hurt. Foolish we both were, and fortunate it was that neither of us boys lost an eye.

LIKE I SAID, MANUEL LIVED on La Salle Street. Just that short city block from where I did. Distinctly etched in my memory is the time that Manuel and I were playing with my small dart-pistol, on the sidewalk. Halfway between his folks' place and mine.

Now, we all know that accidents do happen in life. And we know that the results are not pretty to look at. Anyhow, it so happened on this warm, bright afternoon in late spring of 1966, that I, who had the dart gun in hand, sprung a rubber dart from the tightly coiled spring in my toy's barrel and that dart flew over a five-foot chainlink fence, and landed some thirty feet beyond it in an enclosed dirt lot. Manuel grinned. I didn't.

"I'll get it," said Manuel without hesitancy.

Seeing that the top of the fence had been cut, leaving a ragged, knife-sharp row of wire, and knowing Manuel's usual carefree way well, I feared for my friend's safety. So I volunteered to climb over the fence and retrieve the dart.

After all, it was my dart and my responsibility to secure it. But Manuel was Manuel. He had already said that he would be the one to return the dart. Like myself, Manuel was a proud kid.

To any red-blooded boy, being a boy automatically means that when peril is present, one must conduct oneself as a warrior would. At the young age of seven, that is how every boy would like the world to see him as, a warrior. Plainly, Manuel feared that I would see him as less of a man than I was, if he allowed me to go fetch the dart. And in spite of Manuel's objection, that I was still ready to do. No question about it. Unfortunately, Manuel would have none of my offer.

My friend's decision was a classic mistake. Yet it was a mistake that any man could have made. I knew that at the time, and I was an experienced climber. I knew that Manuel was not. I knew well the inherent danger in climbing over this fence and I knew enough that I would have been very cautious in Manuel's stead. Manuel, I knew, was almost never cautious. Yet, Manuel had made up his mind.

Up Manuel went, over the fence to get this dart back. And then, what I feared would happen, happened. Just as Manuel was negotiating his way back over the fence, the tip of his right running shoe slipped in a space between the chain links. Instantly Manuel's body plunged downward, dragging the underside of the upper part of his right arm straight into line with the sharp column of wire—which impaled his arm. Manuel screamed in pain, his left shoe torn free of the fence as he shot toward the ground. He landed on his back with a sickening thud.

And there, on the other side of the fence, Manuel lay bleeding from a gaping wound to his right arm. A crimson flow stained a dry patch of weeds beside him. My friend was now helpless, trapped behind five feet of wire. I knew, instantly, that I alone could not help him much. Without Manuel being able to assist me, I could not drag the writhing dead weight of his body over the fence. Further, I could not help my friend by remaining where I was, either. The only reasonable thing to do, was for me to get Manuel's mom.

I ran one quick half-block to Manuel's folks' ground-level apartment and pounded loudly on the front door. I was relieved beyond words when Manuel's mother answered my pounding. Manuel's mother was a slim, black-haired lady, in her late thirties or early forties. Briefly I explained to her what had happened to her son. Whereon the good lady immediately got on the phone and called for an ambulance.

Manuel's mom and I then hurried up the block to where Manuel lay stranded and bleeding in the weed lot beyond the fence. Manuel's mother scaled the fence to attend to her son. Having alerted her, I could do nothing more than watch.

Within a few minutes an ambulance arrived on the scene with two men. One of the paramedics climbed over the wall of wire, his emergency medical kit in hand. He tightly bandaged the deeply torn flesh on Manuel's right arm with layer after layer of gauze. Then he gingerly hoisted Manuel over the fence to the other man. Manuel was rushed to hospital.

All is well that ends quite well. Manuel had made an excellent recovery. And we two adventurous boys were soon back at play. I shall never forget Manuel as a spirited boy. A true soldier with a heart of silver.

ANOTHER DAY. My parents had been looking for a house, to lay our family's name to. And once they discovered a house that suited their taste and budget, my association with Manuel ended. Small items such as kitchen cutlery and dinnerware were packed into boxes, just as these had been before our move south from Campbell River. Large items like our Scandinavian couch, coffee table, bedroom dressers, and dining room unit, were carried out of our front door and loaded into our van. We kids already knew what our next home looked like from the outside. And from the inside, because we had viewed the premises earlier.

The house that would be our home stood at 3850 Demus Street. And it was more toward the east side of town than in the center of it. This was a new home for us, even though it was an older house. All of it had been built on one convenient level. Not like our former home back in Richmond, where I'd always had to run all the way upstairs to hide inside my favorite closet whenever my fearsome brother had been about, seeking to dole out a licking to me.

I'd almost gotten even with Raimo once. That had been one time at the Elm, sure. The glorious time that I saw him lose his balance and nearly fall over backwards as he slipped in the hallway on our thin runner, beneath which I had purposely let loose a dozen of my best marbles to float atop a slick, freshly waxed hardwood floor. For the creative effort I had managed to snare for myself a severe licking. That was then.

Now, we in the tribe of five unpacked our small belongings. It was not long before we were settled into our residence.

Our house on Demus Street was perched on flat earth. Our front yard, with a large rock garden of roughly cut red and gray gravel, sloped slightly downward from our house to meet the street. Our backyard had a fairly narrow section of unkempt grass, long of stalk, which was nothing more than a strip of hay. And in appearance the long-neglected lawn, about three feet high, did look quite dead. Our backyard did not end there. Beyond a chainlink fence the level yard fell away into a steep, dry canyon of desert weed, of which our property encompassed a settler's share. Below this miniature wasteland was the bottom of the canyon, which was populated by houses.

Standing in our front yard, I saw that the lot on which our house stood lay halfway down a long, steep hill that ended in a quiet cul-de-sac. The homes on both sides of our street had been built thirty or forty years before our arrival. All these homes, like ours, were one-story affairs, coated in stucco.

I could go on to describe the layout of our new home then, but I am almost certain that you all would fall into a deep slumber from instant boredom. Maybe even into a coma. I don't want that and neither do any of you. So, I shall keep my narrative on what was our house, very short.

I am a, er, wannabe-cool guy, and the only cool thing about this residence was that our front yard had a real banana tree. To any northerner, a banana tree is exotic. Exotic, even though our tree would never sprout a single banana for us. And like the color of the plantains that I'd never see this tree grow as its leafy maze looked down upon our kitchen table then, the exterior of our house was light-yellow. A faded yellow, which mother would later see fit to change to coral.

CHAPTER TWENTY-FOUR

IF YOU'RE STILL WITH ME, I shall elaborate a bit more on the weather in sunny San Diego. And there you have it. In one word, almost always hopelessly SUNNY. In the summer. And almost as hot as the inside of an operating oil furnace. Gone nova? Well, not quite so uncomfortable as that. Like I said before, only in the winter months did we ever witness any significant precipitation. On these unexpected occasions when it did rain—it rained like a monsoon.

I recall my trying to walk up the near side of our rain-swollen street, on my way to school one morning, with high gum-boots on, stumbling about for balance, and nearly losing my footing. Caught I was in a furious flow of water that spilled down from the top of our hill. Caught in a deluge of rainwater freed from the sky, after its evaporation from the Pacific Ocean. Drawn downward by gravity, the escaping force ran as one ribbon down the sharp decline of Demus Street, causing the storm drains at streetside to become swamped, which, in turn, caused the excess water to run amok and rise above the six-inch-high concrete curbs. To my eyes then, as I recall the experience, this raging brook looked to have the vitality of spirit, the ambition, that it might have wished to be something more. Perhaps the steady onslaught of water aspired to become a river. I still don't know. Back then, I did not stop to ask it what it may have wished to be.

I made it to school. The rainstorm passed. The flow of water stopped. And never again, during the time that my family and I lived on Demus Street, did I see the sky open dangerously wide with grief and the water rise enough to threaten the homes on our street. Though, I wondered about the homeowner at the bottom of the cul-de-sac on our street then. With the possible exception of that homeowner, so far as I knew, people on our street had suffered no water damage to their homes.

Indeed, here in drought-ridden southern California folks seldom complained of flooding; they generally regarded a sudden freak rainstorm as a generous gift from nature. An opportunity for nature to replenish the tortured spirit of a landscape usually bankrupt of cooling moisture from the heavens. So—here rain was good.

And in summer, a rare wet day offered a much welcome respite from the searing heat.

Too much sun is no good. No, for the land, nor is it good for the people who must exist on the land. Positively, and without the fresh water of the Colorado River having been diverted from its pristine mountain source many miles to the northeast in order to quench the thirst of nearly all who call southern California their home, and to replenish the farm soil with precious moisture by means of irrigation, besides keeping the many parks and golf courses looking green, San Diego and most of southern California would surely have resembled a parched wasteland. In the absence of water from the Colorado to furnish liquid sustenance for life, the scene here in the low-lying areas would have been a cactus-strewn desert of sun-scorched earth where only rattlesnakes, and the kinds of creatures that they eat, would have thrived. Make sense?

Without an adequate supply of fresh water, humans certainly could not have lived here in large numbers. In cities. In tall buildings of concrete, steel, and darkly tinted glass. San Diego's Balboa Park—home of the world's largest zoo, nearby elsewhere in S.D.—the Sea World aquarium, and to the north in L.A.—the city of smog, perhaps even Sunset Strip, the well-traveled thoroughfare between Crescent Heights and Beverly Hills, would never have existed.

Beside' the booming agricultural sector and tourist industry predominant in the southern half of the State of California, the sunny clime that has long fueled these mainstays of the region's economy provided for mother a relief from osteoarthritis. Noticeable too, was the fact that when they were strung out on a line in our backyard, just six miles inland, away from the moisture-laden breath of the placid, cooling Pacific Ocean, wet clothes, fresh out of mother's old-style ringer washing machine, dried in the hot, windless desert air of summer in a matter of several minutes, faster than wet clothes dry here in the north in the average electric clothes-dryer.

No surprise this was to us, as during summer the sun beat down upon humankind and their pets mercilessly, day after burning day. Whether scalp hair grows faster in a hot climate than in a cool one—I don't pretend to know. Mother believed that it does. She now routinely cut we menfolks' hair each weekend. Even during the winter months. But she was less eager with her electric hair-clipper when it came to her own hair. And Helen's long locks.

Even I, an immature kid, perfectly understood the reason for the seeming oversight. No woman or girl will look feminine sporting a navy crew-cut on both sides of her head, above the ears. Women and girls are not at all like us men, who were left with almost as little fur at the back of our heads, as the meager amount left surrounding our ears after mother was finished snipping.

We in the family all had a lighter tone of hair now. The powerful southern sun had bleached our hair and given each of us a light-brown tan. The penetrating California sun gave us lots of vitamin D, too. Straight from the sky. Straight from the sun's magical rays. Straight from the yellow giant who gave it away for free. Straight from the sun, who, like a rock, never asked questions. Straight from the sun, who hung steady in the azure subtropic sky from early morning to late evening, then dropped below the horizon and left us with night.

With no air conditioning system in our home, the sweltering days of summer gave each of us quite a number of discomforting muggy nights, lying on our sheets in bed, each beside an open window equipped with netting to keep the creepy crawlers of the night, who were all lurking in the darkness outside, from violating the sanctity of our home.

Late evening was a time when the crickets on our backyard lawn began to chirp in chorus, and miniature monsters like the praying mantis would roam about seeking their food. I call this ugly creature a monster because this term best describes the appearance, mannerisms, and temperament of this insect which thrives in tropical and subtropical regions of Earth, though it is also found in areas that have a moderate climate.

I believe you'll agree with me that the mantis is a monster in light of the fact that a female mantis, depending on the species and there are in excess of a couple thousand, will—as does the female black widow spider, sometimes feast on its smaller mate during or after the ritual of intercourse. I don't know whether this beastly urge arises solely from hunger, and I'll not speculate further other than to offer you this. If not, I think that the gruesome act of decapitating the male during or after sex is about as kinky a finale as anyone can imagine. Don't laugh. After all, I am talking about genocide here.

In the looks department: I cannot say that I find the species attractive in the least. For those of you who may be unacquainted with this insect, I extend the invitation that you view it on the Internet. Even a text covering the broad world of insect species, at your local library, should contain an introductory photo of the mantis.

I virtually guarantee that when you take just one look at the praying mantis—you will agree with me that this insect has never bothered to head down to the nearest beauty parlor. Please bear in mind, in no way am I insinuating that a beauty salon would do the mantis any good. In fact, female or male, it is doubtful that any one special treatment, such as a complete manicure, for instance, would do the creature any great favor in terms of its appearance. The praying mantis needs no manicure. What it needs, is a whole new body. It is, by far, the ugliest insect I have ever set my eyes on, with manners (or rather a lack of them)— and a vile temper to match its looks.

The praying mantis, female and male, also has formidable size for a lowly insect, and though some mantises reach a length of about half a foot in equatorial regions that experience a true tropical climate, the species I'm familiar with from San Diego is not to be compared to the bird-eating spider of the Amazon rain forest. The mantis here is not built to anywhere near such a colossal scale.

But the mantis here is very large for an insect. It is about the same length as an adult grasshopper, and has an elongated neck, like a stork. Much taller than a grasshopper as it stands on its hind legs, it, no doubt, uses its advantage in height to locate its quarry, and kill it. Light-green of skin like a grasshopper, with a narrow jaw anchoring a demon-like face—and possessed of that personality to match, this is one creature that not many folks would care to keep as a house pet.

Perching on a tree limb in the protective shadow of leaves, away from that furnace-like heat of the southern sun, I suppose that the praying mantis prefers to avoid direct sunlight. What it does on rainy days, I have no idea. And camouflaged perfectly by its body color while it lies in wait within the dense foliage of any deciduous tree of the southern latitudes, the praying mantis may escape the notice of a casual observer. Like the aphid, one type of insect amongst its smaller prey in a varied menu, the mantis' color allows it to blend into a backdrop of leaves, making it hard to spot.

I am glad that the largest mantises prefer a tropical clime. And, I am especially glad that I am far too large to be on their common list of appetizers. I conclude my account of the praying mantis by saying that every specimen of this insect that I ever ran into as a kid—I felt obligated to remove from this world.

CHAPTER TWENTY-FIVE

IN THIS WINDLESS LAND, a Sahara so close to the cool breeze flowing off the mighty Pacific Ocean, I spent much of my time in the lazy days of a southern summer doing exactly what I, in 1966, might have been expected to do. Whenever I had nothing else to do and I was left in peace to think, I would eventually try to find some activity which would provide me with something tangible to do.

One thing naturally led to another. I enjoyed a good fart. Hence, my brother's not-so-creative nickname for me: "Little Fart."

Named thus, I did not bristle in indignation. No. I understood humor, and I simply returned the sarcasm by labeling Raimo as a "Medium-size Fart". And father, being the kingpin of our family, I discreetly referred to as, "Big Fart". Believe me, I know what you are thinking. This. Oh, what a farty threesome us guys were.

Besides the activity of farting, I would daydream. For me, when conducted in moderation, daydreaming always was a worthwhile pursuit. In life, daydreaming was my favorite activity now. Yet, too much of this alone, done at one time was no good. Hence, my other need then—to be constructive. Thus we obtain the fart, much maligned by the crème of society though it was, and is.

My blissful preoccupations then, did not escape Raimo's notice. How could these have? For me, farting and daydreaming went together, a fact about myself that Raimo well knew. He knew from those times that he'd been around me, around to catch me deeply engrossed in a state of silent thoughtfulness.

And silent I was. Except for those of my always smelly gas leaks which were quite audible to the human ear. Unlike my rear end, my mind, of course, made no noise, but I reassure you that my mind was full of thought, incredibly so. It always was.

In comparison to myself then, the silent but smelly thinker, most folks would probably tell you that they prefer to make use of their hands, rather than sit like a bump on a log and dream, and fart away most of their day. If their preference be that, as a kid I would surely have felt sorry for these poor folks, who I would have considered to be missing out on the best combination of things in life then. But, don't get me wrong. When I was a boy, I did use my hands too.

However, whether my summertime activities then, bordered on my being constructive, or just plain destructive, I care not to ponder any more. Let's just assume the worst, that the line of demarcation between bad and good had, over the course of my earlier years, become a little blurred in my mind as has my vision now. And since I believe that I am a man of, well, childlike forthrightness, I would like to take this opportunity to confess to you that I had nothing but boredom to plague me on one Sunday evening in the summer of '66 as I lazed about our backyard, with seemingly nothing better to do.

In our backyard grew two sizable trees. One was a peach tree which supplied us with excellent fruit. Now, because my lack of expertise in the field of botany leaves much to be desired, I shall ask for your forgiveness, as I am driven by necessity to label the other tree as nothing more complicated than your average, er-um, berry tree. What are you laughing at? A berry tree is a tree. And this tree, a deciduous tree, bore a large crop of small, orange berries, equivalent in size to your average-size wild Juneberry, a blueberry. A berry tree. What's wrong with that?

Beside' the berries that grew amidst the thick verdure, a platoon of garden snails liked to call this tree their home, as it afforded them plenty of sustenance while they quietly went about their business nibbling tunnels through the leafy maze. I have to hand these snails their due credit. They'd picked a damned good tree in which to proliferate their slimy kind, safely hidden from potential predators in the privacy of green—with so much to eat. Except for me, no one in our family ever bothered them.

I hardly ever did, either. Naturally, I had a perfectly sound rationale which will instantly explain my ostensible act of kindness toward these snails. Most boys of my age then, like to climb trees just for the fun of it. But snail tracks are sticky. Climbing a tree with this kind of gunk on it, was not worth the effort of scrubbing my hands afterwards with soap and water. So for the most part I let the snails be.

I was eight years old now, tall enough that I could, with extended arms, reach the lowest branches of the berry tree, to pick the berries. I was old enough, wise enough, to know that these berries could be toxic, and therefore, I did not try to eat them. No. I had another purpose in mind for these berries.

An act of malfeasance. Yes, an act of pure evil, to which I would occasionally stoop on those days when boredom weighed more heavily on my adventurous mind than it did on the average day in my life during summer. To alleviate this mental discomfort during the long hours of summer when thoughts of school were far removed from my mind, I had earlier devised an audacious plan. A very bold plan that I put into action on this day.

From our berry tree, I proceeded to pull down a good many berries, let's say between fifty to one hundred of the very plumpest specimens. I trust that you all will concur with me. The precise number of berries that I usually picked whenever I engaged in the following activity makes little difference. I usually gathered my take of the ample supply of berries into an empty receptacle, such as a discarded margarine dish. Then, after I had amassed a sufficient quantity of berries for the less-than-angelic purpose I intended to use these berries for, I would run inside our house and find my wood slingshot from beneath my bed.

This homemade slingshot, devastatingly functional when firmly gripped in my left hand, had come from father's creativity. Fashioned from three-quarter-inch-thick fir plywood to lend it strength, father had smoothed the rough edges of his saw's cuts with a sharp knife, and fitted his creation with a sling of red rubber. Less than handsome the toy was, and the sling required considerable effort for any boy of my age to draw, which meant that the slingshot did sometimes tend to move about ever so slightly as I flexed my arm and drew a bead on a target. No matter.

IN NO UNCERTAIN TERMS, I would like you to know that I had never aspired to be *Dennis the Menace.* That smug kid from the comic strip by this name was everything that I, as an eight-year-old boy, felt I was not. And I still think that I was, basically, a good boy then. A good Roy. A good Roy, though sometimes, a very bored Roy-the-boy.

Every very bored boy craves action. I was certainly no exception to this rule which governs boys' behavior. To alleviate my bored suffering I needed action—the grist of life—to survive. I needed it in the same way that a thirsty man, stranded in the sand of a desert, beneath the heat of an equatorial sun, seeks water and shade to cool himself with. And back then, whenever action did not present itself to me, I felt in such case, that action had to be sought out in life by me. Action, for the sole sake of my amusement, had to be made by me.

Each house on Demus Street is perched on a slope; every house is perched on its own terrace. I say *is,* because this street still exists today just as it did when I was a boy. And the last word that I heard not too long ago is that our former home still stands, but since I'm not sure whether this is true *now,* elsewhere in this book I've used the word *stood* to denote past tense.

Onward. While the front of each house faces the street as is customary amongst houses, one side wall of every home on our former street looks down on the one below it. On recall, there is about three feet of height differential between each lot. Three feet between each step in the long chain of houses on Demus Street.

Back in the past, I had no sure idea where the neighbors above us were at during the early evening hours when the heat of the summer sun was at its peak. Wherever they were, I could see that they were not in their yard on this Sunday evening. If they were present inside their home, and I assumed they were, they were keeping to themselves. Nowhere near a window, and watching, could they be, I thought.

I know that my observation then, must have been correct, since I am sure that I would have been instantly apprehended had my activity ever been observed by these neighbors. Indeed, their two side windows, windows that faced our backyard, were always vacant of the scrutiny of penetrating eyes then. A fortysomething-year-old man. And his wife. Plus, their adult daughter. The threesome must live a life of almost perpetual slumber within their home, I thought then, because I rarely see any of the three. And I never speak with them.

In fact, given their silent refusal to acknowledge my existence, I felt that I pretty much could, as always, do as I wished. So, in broad daylight, I stood in full view of the line of sight from their side windows. I then proceeded to pepper the entire side wall of their nicely painted light-blue house, with my berries. No kidding. I plastered this one wall with so much goo that, after my unsolicited artwork was completed I was half horror-struck with the severity of the outcome. And while the other half of me, the evil half, naturally admired my handiwork, that wall, I swear, could have used a new stucco job. At the very least—some serious cleaning with soap and water.

In truth, I had seen the Great Wall of China looking in better health on postcards than our neighbors' wall did now. If that fact strikes you as insignificant, please realize that the Great Wall has seen its share of serious insults too.

Since its glorious arrival as a man-made barrier in the third century B.C., much of this time spent under siege by generations of intruders, that now ancient wall has absorbed a gamut of bloody inhumane treatment.

I suspect that each of the Wall's defenders had had a field day as he'd peed down on the heads of the attacking forces. Doubtless, engrossed in the blood and sweat of mortal combat as the centuries had flowed by into obscurity and were lost forever, I wager that the hordes of unnamed assaulting armies had seen no sense of humor in the free shower of urine that must have been disposed upon each army from above.

Having worn no shower caps then, and with their hairdos having been all messed up as a result, the morale of the enemy forces, in all cases, in every attack, must have struck rock bottom. Fighting stubbornly and stupidly to the death over the questionable value of a stone wall, is one thing. Being humiliated in the process *is* quite another.

Yes, plain boredom can make a good boy, like I was, do many undesirable things in life. Things that any well-behaved boy would otherwise not do. Yet, I am not being completely honest here. There was another very good reason as to why I did what I did to our neighbors' wall. Because. Because is an excellent reason, you know.

I assure you, you need not scratch your head in worry over our old neighbors. Being just as sane as the rest of us, they probably did the sensible thing—painted that wall of theirs a sensible color. A suitable color to hide the berry stains. Perhaps orange.

Fret not. By this date in time, the whole exterior of their home has likely been repainted five or six times. Even if their house has acquired a new owner, which I know not, it probably has. As I said, I never once spoke with any of the trio, but I believe that our former neighbors had the sense to do the right thing.

Fuch. This was the surname of our other neighbor. He was a stout, old fellow of German descent, who lived, then, peacefully with his wife on the property below us, and who never gave us any trouble. Not that our other neighbors ever did, either. Rats. I truly hope that you shall immediately realize the subtle drift of my last statement and extend to me your heartfelt sympathy, while I am still trying devilishly hard to justify to my every reader, by means of the slightest excuse at my disposal, my berry bombardment of our other neighbors' wall. Well anyway, back to Fuch.

Mr. Fuch gave us a greeting card at Yuletide each year. In my book, this thoughtful recurring action automatically qualified him and his wife as swell people. Partially, it was this act of repeated kindness that kept me from peppering the near wall of the Fuchs' house with berries. That, and their tall, thick hedge which stood in my line of fire.

In addition to that, the Fuchs' house of yesterday sat, as we know, on the next lower step in the long terrace of lots on Demus Street. And since the difference between each terrace was three feet, this means that the Fuchs' residence sat three feet beneath ground level, as viewed from our side of their hedge.

With the hedge and the difficult topography in mind, I dare say that even if Lucifer himself were to seize my soul for a moment, I could only pepper the very top of the wall of the Fuchs' one-floor home with berries. That's how I thought then. Oh well.

I never spoke with Mrs. Fuch. Only Mr. Fuch. Nevertheless, somehow I know that the pair were such nice people. Somehow.

I have no idea what the neighbors above us, nor the Fuch couple below us, did for a living. And if I ever knew that, I have forgotten long since. Oh. Another thing. One bright Saturday morning with not a single cloud in sight, Raimo had shot the Fuchs' gray tabby in its behind from our open living room window, with his air pistol, when he'd caught the strayed house-cat stalking a small bird perched in a low tree at the side of our house then. A sadistic act? You bet.

215

Interestingly, even though Raimo was a sadist then, he was, one might argue to his benefit, a selective sadist. He chose all his targets with utmost care. Defenseless targets, me included.

And I swear that just as soon as the tiny pellet had bit into its butt, the Fuchs' cat had jumped so high that its flight had almost carried it over its owners' hedge, into their yard.

But we need not be too worried about the feline. After all, cats have many lives. Just like me. You may rest assured that the Fuchs' cat survived the incident in fine style. I believe that the tabby learned something too, as it never showed itself in our yard again. This is a fact, which, I am sure, made every local bird happy then.

MY FIRST SUMMER BREAK IN SAN DIEGO was at an end now. Moved by rare emotion, father had purchased a green plastic pup tent for me. He'd erected the tent on our back lawn a few months back.

Here, inside of my comfortable wilderness retreat I'd lain flat on my belly most every Saturday morning when the sun shone warmly. Early mornings during early summer had been pleasant. However, by the time that the clock had struck nine, the temperature had risen enough to be uncomfortable. Uncomfortable, even though my tent was entirely open at each end. Uncomfortable, even though I wore only a T-shirt and swim shorts.

And in late summer, although I could have spent the early morning hours, when the air was cool, napping in my tent, I did not. I did not because I wasn't given the chance to completely degenerate of mind and body with idle complacency, and thus become a true couch-potato. Saturday mornings meant homework, after school had begun. My arithmetic skills, never impressive, were still being honed by Helen. On father's orders.

If I have any complaint to make of Helen's tutoring then, which I do, it is that one lousy squeal from her always-willing-mouth and father would have made my rear end into chop suey. I used to feel that my survival during the school year, from one day to the next, hung on nothing more than my ability to learn, a fact I deeply resented.

My new school, Darnell Elementary, was a leisurely fifteen-minute walk from home. A half-mile away. In grade three I, Roy-the-boy, was now. My teacher was an elderly lady by the name of Mrs. Bell. And Mrs. Bell, I shall have you all know, could have passed for a near double of my former teacher Mrs. Case, from Campbell River.

And though these elderly, gray-haired women looked much alike, this was not the only similarity they shared. Like Mrs. Case, Mrs. Bell was kind. This quality in her made me take an instant liking to my new teacher. By my reckoning now, Mrs. Bell, like Mrs. Case, must have been born very close to the turn of the century. It saddens me greatly that the last century is dead now, and I would be pleasantly surprised were Mrs. Bell still alive.

Mrs. Bell, and I never came to know her first name, was blessed with an artistic flair. Out of view in my bedroom closet, there still rests two two-tone paper silhouettes of me. Cutouts, with identical poses, facing one another, once handily fitted into a thin black wood frame and sprayed in each corner of the square frame with silver paint. Mother it was who had cut the frame and done the assembly and paintwork. But Mrs. Bell had done the portrait.

My teacher had asked every child in her class to pose solo for her, as she had worked in quick succession with each of we pupils. I'd gotten my chance to remain stock-still then. And, while I'd sat motionless in a chair, a short distance in front of my teacher who had also been seated, a white beam of bright light from a projector had shone the outline of my head and upper body onto a film screen. In wonder, I'd almost felt the sharp tip of the pencil that had etched the smooth contours of my face onto light-blue art paper. And felt I had, the mind that had driven the pencil. Today, I still marvel at the quality of the finished product.

In my mind I can still relive the past. I can still see Mrs. Bell penciling, one at a time, the features of the many children in her class. A considerable undertaking. And, my teacher had done this for every year of her career, I know not how long.

Her artistic ability aside, Mrs. Bell, like Mrs. Case and Mrs. Posterick, knew what children were all about. She understood me and every child. I shall always remember with fondness, both her and the closing remarks that she had penned on the fourth and final report card of my third grade: "Roy is a good student and a fine boy. I am pleased to have had the chance to work with him during the school year." Flattering.

Try as I am, I don't remember that anyone else in my early years of school—other than Mrs. Posterick in my second grade, ever praised anything about me. Myself, I did not think then, and I still do not think so, that there was much in me to praise.

CHAPTER TWENTY-SIX

LET'S MOVE ON. But wait. Back up a belch. A big one. I'm not done with grade three yet. So: It is a cryin' shame that not everybody in my school thought as kindly of me as did Mrs. Bell. Case by example. Darnell was a single-level structure and it was a small school. Of the two grade three classes being taught at Darnell—the other—had a bully. I'd come to know him, one year later, as Marty, when I'd be placed into the same classroom as he. From the time of our first meeting in grade three, Marty, I'd already quickly discovered, could be quite an irascible fellow.

Picture it now: One noon hour, on the dust field behind my school, I was playing dodge ball with the other boys in my class. Marty and his pals were playing nearby. And on this day trouble threatened to erupt in my face when a volleyball, struck by one of Marty's classmates, ventured off course and, strayed far into occupied territory.

The misbehaving ball fell out of the clear blue sky and landed smack in the center of our field of operation. As lousy luck glowered upon me (as usual) on this day in time, the delinquent orb, naturally, had chosen to strike the earth directly in front of me. Without a second thought I reacted instinctively and used the tip of my running shoe to send the alien object streaking back to its point of origin.

Shucks. I didn't know it at the time, but this act, as innocent as it seemed to me, was, according to the school rules, a no-no. Volleyballs were not to be kicked. Just ask Marty. But I didn't. I didn't need to. And I didn't need to because I could clearly see Marty's displeasure written on his freckled countenance.

Marty's face was twisted into a menacing scowl. This, while the tousled black mop of hair growing out of his head angrily shook with the pounding of his feet as he ran toward me, the volleyball clutched tightly to his side, beneath his right armpit.

In the next few seconds I found that Marty obviously did not hold myself in high regard, because he felt quite free to exert what he believed was his authority, loud on me. Marty knew—that I had transgressed the school rule. In his brain, Marty figured that *he* was right; though, at the time of this encounter, remember that I did not yet know his name. No matter. I could see that the boy was looking for trouble. And nothing but trouble.

Marty spoke: "Hey you idiot! Whudge you kick the ball for? You're not supposed to kick a volleyball you moron!"

I shot back: "It was on our side. Its your friend's fault!" My indignation was showing as I looked at Marty. I have no exact idea what might have happened next.

Marty, I should mention, had the build of a natural athlete. And, though he was no taller than me, I knew from his physical appearance that Marty would be a really tough customer for me to take on, in the event of a fight. A fight that now appeared imminent. But. Standing at my side, I had a robust friend in one Robert Lee. Sensing the threat to myself from Marty, Robert stepped in between me and the other boy, challenging him. Marty's left cheek twitched, uncertainty showing plain on his countenance. Robert could see that Marty wished to pulverize me, just as well as I could. Unfortunately for Marty's wish—it was about to go the way of the dodo. You all remember the dodo, don't you? Surely we have all heard of the dodo: The dodo: an extinct, flightless bird that vanished from our world in the late 1600s. Robert, Marty saw, was a hefty kid. A big kid, who was more than a match for Marty.

I do not feel the least bit sorry for Marty today. But it must have been terribly hard on Marty's self-esteem then, to see himself being forced to back down from a fight. Hard for Marty to shelve his pugnacious spirit and have to walk away from it all with an uneasy truce. Marty grimaced at me as he left. Yet back down Marty did. Thanks to my friend Robert.

I later visited Robert at his folks' place. This lay in the same direction as Demus Street, from our school. Like our school, Robert's home lay on Hughes Street, the artery for vehicle traffic in our neighborhood. Robert's place was twice as far from school as our house on Demus Street was. In Robert's backyard, overlooking his home, my friend had built for himself a private retreat. A fortress made of old, weathered gray boards, that fit securely within the sprawling embrace of mighty branches, twenty feet above the ground. A tree house. As in the case of any tree house constructed with convenience having been foremost in the builder's mind, access to Robert's fort was by way of ladder. Not rope. Robert may have been too heavy for that.

I only visited Robert once at his home. And he never did return the favor by dropping by to see me at Demus Street. Although, on this day that I'd paid Robert a visit, we had spent a couple of hours in his lofty shack, talking away.

I'd learned that Robert's wish was to join the U.S. Army when he got out of school. Now, this I thought somewhat unusual because I knew that most young boys of the time were not keen on joining the military, especially when their country was already engaged in a war against a formidable power. But Robert was a Cub Scout. He was a kid who always wore his dark-blue scout uniform and its appurtenances when he came to school. These Robert took very seriously.

Don't get me wrong. I understand Robert's wish to serve his country. I just hope that Robert never suffered misfortune on account of his wish.

As you know, I have never liked the thought of war. My picture of war is that of people dying here, just as there, people dying everywhere. Many are innocent enough. Some are not. But somber thoughts of war and death were not on my mind on February 14 of 1967 when St. Valentine's Day arrived. Being eight years old and being a boy, I was like every other red-blooded boy. I liked pretty girls. A lot. I liked nice girls who were not pretty for their softness too. Ideally, a truly attractive girl with a kind heart—blended with just the right amount of gentle, seductive femininity, would have impressed me.

Yet, in the real world of my third year of elementary school, my dream of finding a really pretty girl, who, to boot, owned a nice, loving disposition, was much easier for me to continue to idly dream about than it was to witness my dream become reality. On this day of the heart, so long ago, I had yet to learn from experience that dreaming about the perfect girl is one thing—but finding her first, is quite another.

On this day of the heart, I had, as well, yet to learn from experience that, when it comes to girls who are physically very attractive, opening a heartfelt dialogue is often not as easy as it should be. In fact, when a love-struck boy makes his amorous thoughts known to the wrong girl, it can be a monstrous mistake. A mistake that he should never forget.

And there was one girl in Mrs. Bell's class at school whose face and slender graceful figure had captured my heart. In respect of this girl's appearance, my heart had fallen head over heels in love with her when I'd first set my eyes on her. And in having let my heart do so, I'd made a classic error. This girl had a face that was not just pretty. She had a face that was very beautiful. Very beautiful to behold. But ice-cold toward me. But—so beautiful.

I had a young man's crush on the dark-brown-haired, long-haired and long-legged, blue-eyed girl who sat next to me. I had a crush on a girl who I shall only refer to as, school Helen. I call her this because I no longer remember her last name, only her first.

School Helen knew that I had a crush on her. In fact, once Helen had realized that I had feelings for her, she'd begun to detest me. The situation was made even worse when I left Helen an anonymous greeting card on St. Valentine's Day.

Because I had left my card anonymous, I assumed that I was safe from detection.

I assumed that also, because Mrs. Bell had decreed St. Valentine's Day in her classroom the day of the compulsory card-swap between the boys and girls. With Valentine cards flying thick and furious, I asked myself—how was Helen to know which card, directed to her desktop from amongst all her gentlemanly admirers in class, was from me? In reasoning so, I made a huge mistake. How so?

Because first, each boy in class had written his name on the card that he sent to each girl in the classroom. Each boy had done this. But me. Helen might have forgiven myself for this omission. She truly might have. Except for one teeny-weeny message I'd written on the card I'd left for her. That message rankled Helen.

I was quite jealous of her friendship with another boy in Mrs. Bell's class. I may be mistaken, though I chance to recall the name Michael—this could have been the boy's name. Michael (I think this was the kid's name) was a small boy then, shorter than myself. And Michael was quite a lot shorter than Helen. As I look back on the time now, I believe that Helen could not possibly have been in love with a runt like Michael was. However, I know that Michael loved Helen. Just like every boy in class loved Helen.

At the time I feared the worst. Suspicious I was that Helen was more than amused by the attention Michael showered on her. Could it be that Helen had feelings for Michael? That question annoyed myself as much as Michael did.

TODAY, you would be hard pressed to find anyone who would describe me as the jealous type. Today, I am anything but that. Anything nice, that is. But on St. Valentine's Day of 1967 I had done what schoolboy jealousy had prompted me to do. I cannot remember exactly what words I'd written on the inside flap of my card to Helen, words for her to read and wonder over as to the identity of their author, across from the factory-printed message on the card's right inner face. I recall only that the tone of my one-line message was mockingly critical of Helen's and Michael's relationship. All be acceptable in love and battle. Right?

Alas for me then. Helen was not only a very beautiful girl, she was very smart. And given the circumstances I have described for your wise analysis, I doubt there is any question in your mind too, that I was guilty of a serious blunder in thinking. An unforgivable blunder in thinking that, by my having left Helen the only unsigned card in class, the only anonymous card she had received from among her fraternity of worshippers in class—with every other card accounted for with a signed name, Helen would not put one and one together, and quickly figure out exactly who it was who had left her a nameless Valentine greeting.

Regardless of these established facts, Helen's girl intuition alone would have been sufficient to inform her, with pinpoint accuracy, as to who it was that had given her this card to read.

I found out that Helen knew about my Valentine's Day message to her, the usual way that I find things out. The hard way. Uh-huh, because Helen soon ratted on me, telling Mrs. Bell that I had not bothered to read a particular story while a small group of we kids were gathered in a circle about our teacher during story session. What can I say? I was guilty of the heinous crime of not having read one story? Psssst! Actually, I used to do this with stories all the time. But officially you don't know it. Right?

In conclusion, this is what I learned from my less-than-idyllic, one-sided premarital relationship with a girl who was so beautiful on the exterior. Yet so frigid toward me, on the interior. I learned that I should never again venture to tell such a girl my true feelings. Not to her face. Nor indirectly through written communication.

And, if I were ever to play the part of an honest fool with my feelings again, I learned from this one encounter that I should expect to run the risk of making my predicament doubly worse.

And I learned that if a girl is ice-cold toward me—it means that she has no interest in me. For sure it does. School Helen was an iceberg. And guess what? Girl icebergs don't ever melt. Truly, they never do. One-sided puppy love can be so sad. Believe me, there exists nothing remotely like a girl's scorn. It is a comment which, quite naturally, invites this intriguing question. Would I ever again be foolish enough to dispatch a card of love to another beautiful girl? Well. Maybe. Or—yes. I would be dumb enough to try to win a girl's love. But the next time that I *try* such an adventure, I shall remember to wear a coat of heavy-gauge armor. Just so that my feelings don't get trampled on again.

In fact, I would definitely advise any upstart Romeo in pursuit of a pretty girl, to wear not only an armored suit of the sturdiest workmanship—he should remember to take an Aspirin in the unfortunate event that he encounter an iceberg. Remember the *Titanic*. Unsinkable, some folks had said that it was.

And, 'sides the armored suit and the Aspirin, Romeo should remember to call his doctor A.S.A.P.

Notwithstanding the excellent advice of mine to Romeo, if Romeo's love-fogged mind still doggedly persists in its destructive desire, I would refer him not to some time-walking extraterrestrial psychiatrist freak with a Ph.D. in alien bullshit—advanced bullshit, a weirdo who, whilst suffering from an overly aggressive other-world ego, could never recognize the dissimilarity betwixt the hole in his or her own rigid, reeking rump and the result of a meteor strike in the turf! No. In this darkest-possible scenario, were it to come true, I would send Romeo to his local denturist, instead. The denturist, a true earthbound professional, would be pleased to provide Romeo with a new set of fake teeth, once Romeo's love interest has finished pounding all his originals out of his aching mouth. For a grand "wee fee" a cosmetic smile *really* can be recaptured.

CHAPTER TWENTY-SEVEN

ANY MAJOR CITY HAS ITS SHARE OF EVENTS INVOLVING FIRE. Fire that nature causes. And fire that's man-made. Or, was in my case, boy-made. Tinder-dry at most any time during the year, San Diego is. Here, a fire, if it is allowed to become a runaway blaze in this large of an urban center, will cause a lot of destruction. For boys of my age once, fire, and too much time on one's mischievous hands, can lead to disaster. Even so, being for myself a time of precious freedom then, summer vacation was prone to draw forth the experimenter in me, just as it will with almost any boy. Even the ones who get lots of lickings. Like I always did.

For me, continual boredom was no life at all. And with this belief firmly entrenched in my mind, it was on one summer morning in early July, after mother and father had disappeared to their workplace environments, that I decided to conduct an experiment, which at the time, appealed to my scientific curiosity. As a preamble to the following account, you all must understand that I have long aspired to use the word *scientific*, and the word *curiosity*, in combination. In relation to myself, of course. Psssst! I am not conceited. Okay-okay. Maybe I am. But just a bit. Satisfied?

Anyhow, this test would be groundbreaking for me. Nothing as earthshaking as Albert Einstein's *General Theory of Relativity*. Nonetheless, close to it, I hoped.

Unsuspecting of what it would eventually be used for, on an earlier day mother had given me an empty, cylindrical,

226

cardboard carton of Quaker Oats. She had trusted it to me so that I could play with it. Had mother not done this, she surely would have discarded the container into the trash can. I know that today, in these environmentally sensitive times, a lot of people, myself included, recycle such refuse. But back in the 1960s recycling was not a buzzword or tradition.

I took the carton out to our patio, at the rear of our house, and set it on the cement floor. Father, as was his wont, kept his long-handled magnifying glass on the coffee table in our living room. Except for himself and mother, who rarely used it, no one in our clan found any real use for the optical piece. We kids didn't because we all had good eyesight then.

I knew that only Helen was home. Raimo had already left for his summer job at Krasne's, on his scooter. Krasne's was a downtown sporting goods store, and Raimo sold firearms there. Being careful to not arouse Helen's suspicion, I reentered the house. For my experiment, I expropriated father's magnifying glass from where it lay beside a candy dish, on the coffee table. Helen was nowhere in sight. But I could hear her chattering playfully to her two pet budgies, which she had acquired shortly after our relocation to San Diego. Helen was safely out of my way—on her side of a wooden partition in our shared room.

I returned to our patio. As patios usually do, our patio had a roof. This roof was made of fiber glass, to allow some light to enter, while the cover blocked those of the sun's rays that are harmful to exposed skin.

At the edge of the patio, the sun's strong light shone from a cloudless sky to the cement below. And so, with the magnifying glass in hand, I bent over Mr. Quaker, and focused the sun's incoming rays into the smallest dot I could create on the level top surface of my carton.

I did not wait long. In fact, I was amazed by the speed of the reaction. The carton burst into flame. Although I had anticipated combustion as being highly probable, the miniature inferno that had resulted scared the dickens out of me, and jolted myself into action. I scampered for our garden hose and put the blaze out.

I admit that I never felt the urge to try this experiment again. Once was enough. Now, if I had been foolish enough to have told my brother about my once-upon-a-time pet blaze in our patio, I would have received a licking, for sure. As a reward for my honesty. But there was no sense in my taking an extra drubbing, I'd thought. Though it be true that I had taken the precautions of having set my test on solid concrete and nowhere near anything combustible like our house, these measures would have done nothing to discourage my brother from doling out a licking to me. Neither would the ready water hose I'd had. Thus, it is only now that I mention this incident.

IN AUGUST OF 1967 our family embarked on what would be a seven-day vacation in the Sierra Nevada Mountains. I was finding hot the long drive north as was everyone else. Too, practically moaning under the heat of the sun and weight of five people was our Volkswagen van. Father and Raimo were taking turns at the helm, driving.

First, father drove us into the desert. Mojave Desert, that is. A place even more torrid than our home in San Diego. Here, somewhere along Highway 395 in the Mojave, father stopped the van. We all got out of the van. And I went for a leak in a shallow gully because I had to. Returning to the van parked nearby, I found everyone else withering in the desert heat while each surveyed the tableau of heavily needled spires of saguaro cactus, some, thirty feet high, that rose into the baking air on either side of the highway.

Because of the oppressive heat we did not tarry here. Indeed, the desert air was cooking-hot from the sun's radiation. Every window on our van, every window which could be opened, was open to full.

What other roads we took to get where we were going then I can't be sure, but by four o'clock in the afternoon we had reached the end of the flat desert land. Then, as cactus grew sparse, we climbed over the low foothills and into the purple mountains. Our climb was not only steep, but slow. Volkswagen vans are not famous for their horsepower—and thus—speed. Our Volkswagen van of the late 1950s was not suited to climbing steep hills. It was not adept at handling a heavy load with any more spirit than the average pack mule. That is my opinion.

Midway to the higher altitudes we stopped at a small unfrequented lake in the shadow of the Sierra Nevada, hoping to bathe the streaks of sweat off our bodies. It was here on the sand beach that an awful sight met our eyes. Lying on the sand, punctuated with large droppings of cow manure, were thousands of dead fish. About six inches in length, on average.

What type of fish these were I had no idea then, nor do I now. Though both the dead, rotting fish, and cow crap were revolting, the awful sight did not deter me, as it did not Helen and mother, from plunging feet-first into the water, regardless of the sanitation hazard the carcasses of the decaying fish and the cow manure on the shore then, and likely in the water also, posed to us.

We found the temperature of the stagnant lake water to be warm. So warm, we knew that the legions of expired fish cluttering the beach must have all died of exposure to heat. And since the time of their deaths, the level of water in the lake had, through evaporation, exposed the corpses. This result, we knew, was possible if the flow of water from the nearby mountain peaks that had fed the lake, had dried up. Being late August in east central California, the temperature of the water in the lake had just been too-hot-to-handle for these fish, which had found no place to swim to in their futile efforts to escape the rising water temperature. So far as anyone in our party could deduce, there was no other likely explanation for this phenomenon.

I will guess that the temperature of the lake water lay beyond eighty degrees Fahrenheit. Not enough to fry a fish. Still, warm enough to kill it. And warm though the water here was then, it nonetheless invigorated us who took the foul bath (father and Raimo hadn't); as well, we had rid ourselves of body sweat. Our brief dip done, we clambered back inside the van, and our party hit the road again.

As we drove onward and upward, stately pine and fir trees now appeared in the changed landscape all about us. We continued on the drive until, in the early evening, we at last came upon what would be the first campsite of our trip. The Kern River tumbled forward in a short falls before us, whilst behind our site stood the picturesque backdrop of a mountain, that looked, I thought, much like Mt. Rushmore in South Dakota. It did indeed, though this mountain, whatever its name, had not the visage of honest Abe, or the visages of his three friends on that distant rock, George, Thomas, and Theodore, to adorn it.

After our journey through the desert country the mountain-bred water of the river was delightfully cool. Pure, mountain kind of cool. We three kids went for a swim, as did mother. Father, who as you know didn't believe in bathing himself more than once a week, again declined the opportunity to get wet and refresh himself. But us four intrepid souls who'd taken the plunge, now had to be careful as we swam about in the river. Careful, since the swift-flowing water of the Kern can easily sweep a careless swimmer over the falls, and to serious injury below it. Or to oblivion.

We slept in our van at the Kern site for just one warm night. And in the morning, as the newborn sun ascended from the surrounding mountains and the other campers, as had we before breakfast, stirred to greet the day, we broke ties, and father drove us deeper into the wilderness. He drove and drove and hours flew by.

Our van now climbed and climbed. Finally, our long ascent over with, we came to a bridge. A terrifying framework of rickety, weatherworn gray timbers this was, clinging, I observed, by iron spikes that had been struck into the rough mountainside. Given the appearance of advanced age in the timbers beneath our van's tires, I figured that these spikes must have been driven into the cliff face a good fifty-or-so years before our arrival here.

With father piloting, our van inched slowly, very slowly, on its way across the mountaintop bridge. I looked out of the window beside me as a timber beneath one of our vehicle's tires creaked. We were high in altitude. Maybe a mile high. It was an awful long way down to the bottom of the gorge that yawned below us. I was scared for my life—just as everyone else was for his or hers.

Each of us waited—as though each butt rested on needles—as father moved our mortal souls forward, the first foot. Then, the next. And so on. Still nothing happened. Needless to say, it was only when we reached the end of the bridge, and our van rolled back onto terra firma, that we all breathed a heavy sigh of relief.

I have never liked extreme heights. Having successfully crossed the harrowing bridge then, there now stood before us a small plywood cabin. A ranger lookout. Boarded up were the windows, and long deserted it looked like. Smokey, the big brown bear, smiled at us from the door. But we had no reason to linger here. No. Father turned us about and we retraced our path along the bridge.

Then we descended, dropping slowly in altitude as father negotiated our winding passage down from the high Sierra. Fifteen minutes later, we reached the bottom of the gorge. Here, there were no other visitors. Only the stillness of the wilderness.

Since it was late in the day with night soon to move in, we decided to make camp here, beside a small river. It might even have been the Kern, shrunken by proximity to its source. Mother had sandwiches on hand. And we roasted wieners over an open fire. We talked late into the evening as we each listened, between conversation, with hound's ears to the sounds of the forest in the night.

Close by in the wilderness, the yelp of a coyote caught my ear; the quieter music of the forest was drowned out by the waterway. Unlike our first campsite along the Kern, the night air was cold here. As we all were bushed, we finally retreated to our mattresses and wool blankets in the van, as the orange glow faded from the dying embers of our campfire.

In the fresh innocence of early dawn we awakened from sleep to near shivers, and exiting the van, had a breakfast of sandwiches, each of us ready to resume our adventure. And as the chipmunks rushed about our picnic table in search of discarded scraps of food, we humans departed, leaving our small, furry friends with a few slices of white bread to nibble on. Into the rain forest, father drove. Or, as much of a rain forest as one can find hereabouts. It was barely early afternoon when we came to another campground.

As we were moving on we saw that this place was often crowded with people at points of interest. And every campsite in front of us looked taken. Not quite. We found the best site of all.

Our campsite lay across a paved road, opposite a small dammed up stream, which I dubbed, "Poo-poo Dam". I called it that because somebody, or his dog, had carelessly discarded the finest brown sausage into the shallow water near the bank. Using a long tree branch, I prodded the piece of floating shit to shore. I then used a strip of tree bark to chuck the memento into the woods. That done, the small pond of this waterway was now clean enough for a dip.

Our party stayed at this campsite in Sequoia Nat'l Park for four nights. Then we all got up from our lawn chairs, and father drove us to what would be our final overnighter in the California wilderness. Coffee Camp, the popular site was called.

The air here was hot. Hotter than it had been at our first site along the Kern. In fact, the heat was so stifling here, that in late evening even father decided to join everyone else in a deep pool along a small waterway, name unknown.

The next day we journeyed back to our original campsite beside the Kern River. I climbed a pine tree to collect a souvenir of our trip, a giant-size cone that measured no less than eight inches in length. The huge cone was nearly as wide too. We all posed for a final snap of the camera's shutter. (We did? No, mother had to take the shot.) Me, in my patched and badly faded blue jeans, with a straw hat atop my head—just like the headwear that father and Raimo wore. And to better beat the savage heat, besides the shade afforded us by our covered crowns, we men each wore a white T-shirt. Mother and Helen were wearing hats as well. Who wouldn't have? Yes, the sun had become so burning that even Helen, the ultimate rebel, had had to swallow her pride for once and don a hat.

Following the photo shoot, we stepped into our van and father dug up the dust along the gravel road as we headed for home. Father took the short route to Bakersfield, thereby avoiding the incinerating heat we'd encountered earlier in the Mojave Desert. Our camping trip was over. Soon—the summer would be too.

CHAPTER TWENTY-EIGHT

SCHOOL WAS KNOCKIN' ON MY DOOR, AGAIN. That time of year I most dreaded was here. And when the new school year began, I heaved a huge sigh of relief. The last couple of weeks before the start of school were always a time of tension for me.

Of course, I had a new homeroom and a new teacher. Forget the homeroom. It's not worth me telling you about it. But my teacher, in year four of my education, is worth having myself tell you about her. So, here goes. My new instructor was a personable lady who went by the somewhat rhythmic-sounding name of Mildred J. Miller. Mrs., that is.

Mildred, who I would never fail to speak to respectfully as Mrs. Miller for the course of nine and one half months that I would sit at my desk in her classroom then, was a teacher who had that great American propensity to support the striving underdog in the pack. That great American personality. A magnanimous personality. Large in spirit like an eagle soaring above the clouds. A very special, endearing quality this is that Lady Mildred shared with my two earlier American teachers, Mrs. Posterick and Mrs. Bell. And like Mrs. Posterick and Mrs. Bell, who were both first-rate teachers, Mrs. Miller was large in kindness.

I recall the day that I took part in the second spelling bee of my life. Throughout my elementary school years I both hated and liked spelling bees a lot. Half of me would hate them because the intense competition strained my nerves—while my other half welcomed the chance to kick ass.

As is usual when a spelling bee is held, Mrs. Miller had divided her class of students into two opposing factions of equal size. We pupils all stood. And, as had been the case in Mrs. Posterick's classroom two years earlier, I saw the weakest spellers go down to defeat and humiliation first.

Midway through the day's competition, my best and only good friend, Wayne Hare, stumbled on his given word and was instantly eliminated from the contest and forced to return to his seat. More about Wayne, very shortly. Anyhow, as one line of verbal combatants engaged and re-engaged the other—one by one my remaining comrades were retired to sit at their desks, in disgrace.

With the opposing line having been stronger than my side, it was then that I found myself in an awkward situation, facing three of the finest spellers in my class. Alone. The word echoed in my mind. Even though I knew that I was only a participant in a game, faced with this trio from the opposing side I could not help but feel tense. A frozen gaseous mass, as hard as the Abominable Snowman's fart, had welled up in my belly—gripping it like a giant clam.

Besides that, shades of various defiant characters of heroic fame, all from the realm of make-believe, were beginning to happen in my mind now. This was the kind of unspoken defiance that the badly repressed fictional gent Walter Mitty would imagine each time his overbearing wife proceeded to nag him.

And it was with the same cool poise that Walter had faced his end, that I stood before my nemesis of three, as the slim, blue barrel of my six-gun lay quietly ready in its holster at my right side. One against three. L-o-n-g odds, no question. I knew what it meant. I would lose—eventually. But I would go down fighting, even as the storm of bullets that I expected, pierced my flesh and vanquished my mortal body. But not my spirit: this—the other side could never defeat. Not ever.

Even as these morbid thoughts played out in my imagination, I considered sending a telepathic communique to my opponents, as would have Mr. Spock in my stead, the Vulcan half-breed with the pointed ears on the original cast of *Star Trek.*

Doggone! I now believe that my message, dispatched in groovy, true psychedelic language then, would have convinced my classmates to lay down their arms and retreat peacefully. That would've left me with the spoil of the contest!

My not-so-subtle broadcast would have implied something such as this: drop dead. Stay dead. Sort of.

The hour ended. So did the school day. I was glad for the reprieve from the pending execution. Or was I? A delay is always delightful for a condemned man to have to bear. Especially an unexpected delay.

THE NEXT DAY, approximately 10:30 in the morning— P.S.T., I had already prepared myself for my date with Fate. What day of the week was this? A school day. Specifics don't matter when a body is about to be taken out of commission for good. Neither does the month. (I suspect that the general frame in time was early 1968. Perhaps February.)

Now, I faced my three classmates again. Oh, didn't I introduce my opponents to you? No? Shame on my soul. Let me try to recollect this as best I can. I recall that Cory Bradley was one of the three. Cory, I knew as a quiet, thoughtful, highly likable fellow who wore spectacles and had a high I.Q. And despite his being smart, he was no bookworm given to spending his free time at home as a couch potato. And like the rest of the kids in Mrs. Miller's class of 1967 to 1968, Cory was not fat.

Of my other two opponents: One was a chap named Mark—this was the boy's first name. Like Cory, Mark wasn't stupid. Nor, for the record, was my third foe—a girl whose name and face I cannot recall.

Not one of these kids was what I would call a mean kid. In fact, all three were quite the opposite. Not that it much matters now whether they were mean or not. I suppose that even Mrs. Miller's spelling contest doesn't matter much now. But back in 1968—it sure did to me.

Unfortunately for myself then, the odds on this day would be stacked too heavily against me. In that, I believe I have a legitimate complaint now. You see, for every three words that I'd be required to pronounce and then spell correctly in order to stave off my elimination then, each of my opponents would have only one word to contend with. Yet, I dared hope that they would not finish me off too easily so that I would be able to avoid, at least partially, the embarrassment of having lost along with my team.

The contest began once more. And about halfway through the hour that Mrs. Miller had reserved for the s.b.—I faltered (the word—strangely enough—I am unable to recollect). However, my teacher was a generous lady. And, instead of resigning me to my desk and a brutal defeat that would resound in my mind for the next couple of years to come, Lady Mildred did an extraordinary thing. Even though I had failed miserably, she bade me to remain standing.

I suppose that Lady Mildred, like myself who did at better times, must have believed in the dauntless spirit shown by the fictional medieval Saxon knight, Ivanhoe. And the only notable problems with my teacher's highly supportive action of me then, were that first, I was of course not the revered warrior of book and film (never been), and second, I was as badly outgunned as Noah's ark would have been stacked up against some full-scale, haughty warship with an intimidating name like—*Destroyer Of The Seas*.

Lady Mildred's boon was but a respite. A temporary stay of execution that could not last. Three against one. Notwithstanding the unusual grace my teacher had shown me, the odds against me were still of issue and the result predictable. I faltered a second time.

On just an ordinary seven-letter word. An easy word it should have been for me to spell. And for a long while after Lady Mildred's contest it would be a word that would make me ashamed of myself whenever I'd hear it spoken. The word was, soldier. I spelled it minus the i.

Defeat to me has always been almost as bad as dying. I took a silver bullet to the center of my heart on this day in 1968, a day now lost forever. A bullet—sort of. A bullet that I'd seen coming—and had known that I could not dodge.

ENOUGH ABOUT SPELLING. I can recall another interesting happening from our time in San Diego.

My buddy Wayne Hare and I were astride our bicycles in our schoolyard—when we were rudely accosted by interlopers. It had happened that the two of us had been riding our wheels about the field at Darnell on a Saturday near noon when a pair of young teenage boys, who were each much bigger than Wayne or myself, had approached us.

One should never make the mistake of underrating dark evil. And these delinquents had presented themselves as just that. Two immature thugs waiting to grow up. Being what they were, they'd not greeted Wayne and I with niceness.

"Why did you do it?" one of these meanies had just asked us in a flippant tone.

"Do what?" said Wayne now, looking apprehensive.

"Do what?" sarcastically replied the meanie who had spoken. Then, with equal venom in his voice, he continued. "Do what?" the same meanie stated again. As he looked at Wayne, my friend appeared to shrink before his malevolent gaze. "Why did you break the school windows you . . . ?" he demanded of Wayne.

Grrrr, I didn't like these two buggers any more than Wayne, who was taking direct heat, did. My buddy and me would confer about this incident on another day, and we'd guessed that these guys had broken a dozen of our school's windows, an act of vandalism that we had discovered earlier on the day of our encounter.

The foremost punk's accusation seemed to stun Wayne. Not myself. I perked up. "We didn't break any windows. And we don't know what you're talking about." Like I said,

Wayne and I had seen our school's busted windows. Most of these were on the other side of the school. Of course, I knew that our accusers were thinking what the guilty always think. Guilty minds always dread the worst possibility. And in so doing, the guilty sometimes hang themselves.

I also knew that Wayne and I had to be smart. By playing stupid. Indeed, inviting suicide was not my intention. I knew as well that in this situation I had to be as tough as I could appear. By looking tough and ready I hoped to avoid an ugly brawl that I knew me and my friend would lose. Our accusers were just too big for me and Wayne to take on in a fistfight. If it came to that. Given the two meanies' superior size and strength, I had a sane man's desire to avoid a physical altercation with but the said conceivable result.

My train of thought was interrupted when the second boy of the meanie pair spoke. "You brats did it. Tell us you did it and we'll let both of you go." I didn't like it. The second meanie's accusation, direct as it was, smacked of a boast. Sure, I knew that our accusers had us. And they knew that we knew it.

Wayne was beginning to cry now. He must be thinking that he will never see his parents again, I figured.

Me? I was not going to cry. At least, not on account of the two disreputable meatheads.

Had I known of him then, I would sure have wished that I was, well, this: *The Last Electric Knight.* Unfortunately, I had never seen that movie; that movie's diminutive martial art champion would not be born onto the TV screen for nigh onto twenty years. And not having seen the movie, I didn't know the first thing about kung fu.

In fact, lacking deadly hands and feet, I was, instead, starting to think that perhaps Wayne and I should do the sensible thing: make a mad dash for freedom atop our bikes. After all, our detainers had no wheels. They had only feet and long legs.

Right then, the boy who had first talked had a sudden, unexpected change of heart. This surprised me. Up until this moment, I had been darned sure that he and his associate in crime possessed no heart. But this he said: "Okay. Both of you can go. Just don't you tell anybody about us." Almost amusing. The boy's statement implied to me that he and his pea-brained partner were just as guilty of having broken our school's windows, as your average jailbird attired in an orange-and-white striped suit is of having broken the law.

What Wayne thought at the time was the same thing that I did. But like myself, Wayne was not up to making a fuss with our captors about who broke what. Not when our liberation was at stake. "We won't," said Wayne. And without bothering to see whether I was coming along, my friend began pedaling his bike toward home.

I caught up with Wayne, on my bike. But Wayne was in no mood to talk about the incident. I guessed that he was still pretty badly shaken by the experience. Me? I wasn't shaken by anything. At least, not by those two clowns in our schoolyard, posing as self-styled magistrates. And fooling no one. Except maybe themselves.

Humans are wily. These two bastards had sought to lay our suspicions to rest by blaming their ill deed on Wayne and I. Just in case we had thought of squealing about them to the school authority. Which was unlikely. For Pete's sake, we didn't even know their names. But they must have figured that the police would be able to track them down— which explains why the two attempted subterfuge.

ONCE I WAS SAFELY AT HOME I shed my persona of manliness on the instant that I walked in through our front door. I knew how to act when I was under duress. And I knew how to act when I was not under serious duress. Like this: "I'm telling mommy about you." I would always threaten Helen in this way whenever Helen saw fit to undertake some ill deed that impacted on myself. But, on one occasion at Demus Street there was no need for me to utter from my lips so much as a single, tortured word.

Here be the details of my electrifying experience with my sister's teenage self-centeredness and indifference toward me, two dangerous realities with which she chose to wreak on my fine head of hair an indignity, and a near tragedy. My account now.

Helen, who was fourteen years old at the time, attended a junior high school by the name of Horace Mann. And inasmuch as necessity would be the mother of invention in regard to the act of evil experimentation I describe in the text that follows, please be forewarned that my sister had to appear in a school play. Sis needed a guinea pig. And there were no volunteers handy—anywhere within Helen's range of vision.

Believe it: I be no fool in most any matter which involves wheeling and dealing. But—I used to have a really powerful hankering for a good match of the popular word game, Scrabble.

Being a contest that requires a knowledge of words, Scrabble, as a cerebral game, has always intrigued me. Whenever I played against sis in this game I would look forward to boasting of a win to Wayne. If I won. Helen knew of my weakness for this game very well. And sis, always an unsavory character whenever she needed something of value to herself then, had decided on this day to make full use of my fondness for the board game.

Being then, as I had been trained to be, always trusting of my older siblings, I failed to *see* into Helen's mind in time, and so did not realize her hidden motive of wishing to avoid any risk to herself, when she struck me with a carefully crafted proposition. A chiseled proposition designed to overcome any objection that I would, sis knew, almost certainly voice otherwise. A proposition which, Helen calculated in her shrewd mind, would almost instantly wear away my expected objection to her proposal. Praise sis. Helen had calculated correctly. Without much thought, I quickly accepted Helen's offering.

And thus—was I crucified. Easily. Helen's portrayal of her character, in this school act, would require that short, thin strips of gold foil be affixed to her hair, with transparent tape. And sis wished to discover, comfortably in advance, what the probable appearance of her head would be like when her hair underwent the explained procedure.

Because Helen had no one else of questionable intelligence about her, Helen had done what I might have expected her to do under the pressing circumstances, had I been older and wiser. As part of our deal, Helen's harebrained experiment demanded that I surrender my hairy head to her seriously twisted judgement, and less than deft skill of hand. To my sister who had never believed in sacrificing herself in the pursuit of knowledge if a willing conscript, brainwashed of all reason beforehand if necessary, could be enticed by a game of Scrabble to volunteer in her stead was to be found, her perfect plan must have indeed seemed without fault.

Surely, Helen had figured that there was no sense in jeopardizing her fine head of hair and cozy composure if her experiment somehow began to go wrong. Not if my younger brother, who is a dolt, can be bribed and duped into saving my fine follicles of hair, blonde hair at that, from suffering possible distress, she'd cleverly thought. So, as my part of Helen's bargain then, much more so Helen's than mine, I sat atop a bar stool while Helen taped her add-ons to my hairy crown, using the tape. And being a total idiot on this day, I never bothered to protest, until I saw for myself the result of my sister's doing in the reflection of our bathroom mirror.

It was at this time that mother and father, who had been away on a local shopping trip, chose to return home. And once mother and father discovered the new look of my head, their initial astonishment quickly turned into displeasure with Helen's handiwork.

For, my head now resembled that of a golden chicken with a menacing case of hypothermia—who, for the past ten years or so, had lain in stasis within a freezing vat of liquid nitrogen. A chicken who had experienced the bone-numbing cold of a temperature equivalent to that of outer space. Bereft of brains, a white chicken whose golden scalp feathers stood in the air like a headdress of an Indian chief of the Great Plains.

I shall end this account by saying that Helen ended up being amply scolded, and then ordered to remove the tape from my light-brown locks without resorting to the use of scissors. Happily for me, the removal did not prove impossible. Although, the task of extracting the tape from my hair had taken Helen a couple of hours to complete. And do you all know what bothers me the most? This. For all of the pain that I'd had to endure as Helen had ever-so-slowly removed the pieces of tape from my hair—I got only one measly Scrabble game out of our deal. Whoever says that modeling work isn't hectic, has got to be kidding. That Helen!!!

Today, after all these years, rightfully I should still be waiting for a full apology from Helen. I should. And not just for this reprehensible act, but for all of the other imaginative tortures that she had seen fit to devise for my poor damned soul in this life.

In regard to the apology that I should be awaiting: Either verbal or written would do. But it would need to be sincere. No condescending get-well card would be accepted by me. Neither would a drop-dead message.

Yet, knowing my sister, I harbor no fool's expectation that my wish will ever be realized. Ever, because the reality is that neither Helen, nor Raimo, nor my father, ever did apologize for any ill deed they'd done me. And believe me, I have never had the slightest doubt that *self-humiliation* was never a phrase in the vocabulary of these three, but this, in itself, should not have stopped any of them. Yes, it is just that none of this trio were ever sorry about anything.

Chapter Twenty-nine

A LOT OF FOLKS nowadays are obsessed with their teeth. These are not yellowed teeth like so many carnivorous and herbivorous animals of the wild have inside of their mouths, but teeth which must be the pearliest white that teeth can, for a stiff gut-wrenching price, be transformed into.

All that it takes is a thorough bleaching with a concentrated solution of hydrogen peroxide, done by a dentist, and presto—the coffee stains instantly disappear for about six months. After this time it is, for these fortunate people who have lots of surplus cash on hand or a great dental insurance plan on which hefty annual premiums must be paid by either themselves or their employer if they have one, time to schedule another appointment with the tooth doctor.

I am barely smart enough to know that a license as a dental surgeon means big bucks for any dentist. Regardless, I have never had any interest to go to tooth school so that I can try the trade myself and probably get dragged over red-hot coals in a malpractice suit for my incompetence on the job site. Plus, who amongst me, myself, and I, would want the glorified, unwholesome job of being an oral janitor? Certainly not me, myself, and I. How unfortunate. Indeed, the cleaning *and* removal, repair, *and* replacement of teeth mean no beggar's gruel for that personable, enterprising dentist who is, I am sure, always quite happy to take his or her payment: be it from a dental plan or from a thick wallet.

For me, my teeth have always been a struggle. Literally. And a nuisance. In fact, I swear by my molars—if I would not absolutely require teeth to protect myself against the occasional nasty city bus driver—I would have had all my teeth pulled right out of my mouth, eons ago. Just kidding about some of that stuff.

Unlike me, aggressive animals like wild lions need fabulous teeth. With teeth, they can make impressive sounds that scare away most of the other animals that live on the African savanna. Wild elephants have a different mindset. They do not need to have great teeth, with which to make lots of noise, because they are big. Being big, elephants are not afraid of the other denizens of the plain and jungle.

But I really do not feel that I would ever like to be an elephant. And no lion. Yet, if I had been born as one or the other—I could have skipped school and homework. I would not have had to put up with fussy teachers who were all driven by the parochial thought of wishing to teach me a bunch of things of debatable value. Who cares about dumb things like letters and numbers? Who cares how many times any one teacher might fart in one whole day, or in one whole year, when he or she bends over now and then to add the odd paper airplane found lying on the tile floor, to the wastepaper basket? I don't.

And I do not care to keep track of time. I do not care to keep track of every second, minute, hour, and day in my life. Nor the accumulated number of years that these units of time combine to create, just so I can impart to you a statement unveiling exactly how much time, if my example as a patient is to be considered the norm, any one dentist will spend with clientele in the course of a hopelessly monotonous career.

And, I speculate when I say this next. I really feel that dentists, as a group, don't much like me because I very seldom visit a dental clinic.

When I was a kid, my parents did not like to give the dental profession money on my behalf. You know that, but it might be a good clue to help explain why I had to quietly endure the insufferable so many times. For instance, I could badly have used partial braces when I was nine years old. My teeth were crooked enough to warrant braces. But even partial braces cost a lot of hard-earned cash, back in 1967. And even in America, supposedly the land of prosperity, for my parents, the money to fix my mouth by their acquiring partial braces for me to straighten my teeth, did not exist. And yet, something needed to be done about these teeth.

It is true that all the teeth in the front upper half and front lower half of my mouth could have used an alignment job. So true, because the inside of my mouth looked as though someone had tried to ram too many teeth into too small a space. Some teeth stood forth like the gray pillars of rock at Stonehenge. Resolute. Defiant. Overlapping other teeth they were. And some of the lesser were laid back noticeably at a sharp angle.

In the top row of teeth, in the direct center at the front of my mouth, were my two incisors. There was nothing wrong about the incisor on my left side, but the chomper on my right was laid back severely. So severely that I often bit my tongue with the tooth while masticating on a hardy meal.

This errant tooth was bent inward as though it possessed a mind and will of its own, as though it actually intended to spike my tongue out of sheer spite. And so, faced with that problem, what could I do? As mentioned, partial braces were a luxury that I had to do without; there was no hope of such kind. For my parents, money was just too tight. A tooth implant? Same thing; too, this method of tooth repair did not exist in the 1960s.

But? My mother had it in her to be a great sales lady. And, great English language skills are not a prerequisite when a mother knows how to communicate her wish to her child in Finnish. At first, mother tried the soft approach as befits a sales lady. That didn't work. Gentle persuasion seldom, if ever, works in the face of physical discomfort. And a sweet pep-talk does not work, at all, for straightening a crooked tooth by hand. At least for me, the pep-chat did not, and could not, work as a lever of motivation, because there is no inspiration in manually attempting to align a tooth by one's dogged will, using just a couple primeval tools. End result—no result.

About the tools. These consisted of a wood clothespin and a silver spoon. I had received my instructions again. Instructions that I applied in measure to the task before me.

The clothespin I kept set dead center over my two upper front teeth so that the make-do clamp covered one-half of each tooth, plus the sliver of a gap between them. A proper alignment was necessary, crude though this technique in home dentistry was. And though it hurt some, I had no choice. I did not use the spoon.

Unfortunately, the clothespin did not produce the anticipated result. That sure surprised me some, because the clothespin mother had given me had a vice grip much like a steel trap for animals. That was my opinion. But, the bottom line here is that the clothespin, by itself, did not work.

It was then that mother re-reminded me to make use of the spoon. She instructed me once again. I would have to use the spoon to push against my crooked tooth. I'd have to push outward from the inside of my mouth with the curved face of the spoon, or the handle, after which I'd again apply the clothespin.

And push I did. I pushed and pushed and pushed. I pushed day after day. Still—the recalcitrant tooth had not budged much. To my parents, my depth of will was now in question. It didn't occur to mother, or to father, that perhaps the task they had laid before me was near to Herculean in nature. I was very much aware that the desired results were not being seen. I did not need to be reminded of this every day. And every sensible excuse I thought of, was of no avail to me. Every excuse fell upon deaf ears.

With the failure on mother's part and mine, my parents conferred with one another, and they decided that it was now time for the artillery to be brought in. Heavy artillery.

Once again, they sought out the services of my older brother.

Enter Raimo. I was given what my brother described as a choice. Some choice! In multicolor, Raimo proceeded to paint for me a perfect picture of what punitive action would soon befall me, were I to continue to fail to produce a satisfactory result. A matching pair of teeth, properly aligned, were needed inside my mouth. Soon. Very soon.

Where punishment was concerned Raimo need not have elaborated. I was already quite familiar with reality. If I did not work magic and straighten my crooked tooth within one short week—I would be handed the usual reward for failure to comply with my elders' deepest wishes. I would be handed a thorough thrashing with Raimo's favorite tool of persuasion—the thin, black, leather belt.

I knew that Raimo was only heeding the will of our parents. In his own way. His own sadistic way. I knew enough about Raimo's affinity for doling out a licking to myself, at the slightest excuse and whenever he could, to know that his iron directive was, as always, a nonnegotiable ultimatum, not to be ignored. Or else. I got the message, alright. There was no need for Raimo to repeat it. No need for him to spell it all out in a threatening letter. The spoken words were sufficient for me, when the message came from my brother. A very big brother.

And so, wishing to live as much as I did, I pushed against my crooked, troublemaking tooth as only a wise man will do. Day after day, after school, after homework, I pushed against my crooked tooth with all of my will. I pushed with every exhausted ounce of my will—feeding the strength in my young arms with the desperation of a man about to be lynched and—hoping like mad to stave my execution off for one more day of precious life.

Despite my facial tan, beneath it I had the ashen look of a man about to be strung from a lonely treetop, a man soon to be left to dry in the desert. A dead man for the wind to cuss. A dead man for the hot desert sun to bake. A dead man for the buzzards to peck at. And I, I decided, was not that man.

I increased my efforts to put straight the crooked tooth in my mouth as I broke the threshold of my will (or so I thought), time and again.

My increased efforts were not in vain. Grudgingly, almost imperceptibly, the leaning tooth responded. Slowly it did. But surely it did. Slowly but surely, the wicked lean became less and less. And one day not far removed, yet more than a scant week later—with no dire punishment received, the once crooked tooth was gone. Gone, like the desert wind of my overextended imagination.

MOTHER WAS WORKING STEADY, as a maid, at a place called the Hitching Post Motel. For reasons that I shall not disclose here, one day she would quit her job. Much later, mother would move on to a Travelodge Motel and continue in the same line of employment.

Mother would have preferred to stay home and tend to domestic chores, but she was forced to work because father had quit his job at the California Electric Works facility. Father had gone into business for himself by reestablishing AC/DC Electric. Since a reliable cash flow was needed, and since father's enterprise wasn't bringing a heck of a lot of cash home, mother found it necessary to provide an adequate cash flow by working outside home.

For a while, and I don't know exactly when, mother worked solely at the food bar of the Newberry's department store in the College Grove Shopping Center, too.

As I look back in time I believe that, for my dad then, his business venture in San Diego was more like a drawn out holiday. San Diego was more of a tourist mecca than an industrial city. With little heavy industry in town, father's prospective clientele base was severely limited. Sound familiar? Remember Princeton? Naturally, this reality meant that father's motor-repair business was doomed to fail from the day that he'd opened his shop door to legions of nonexisting customers, regardless of the fact that father was no longer in his prime—so far as patience went.

During our summer break from school, me and Helen would sometimes walk to Newberry's just to see mother at work. I also remember that Newberry's was once the site of a most humiliating experience for myself. It was an experience that saw me pitted against a machine. It was an experience that I still regret. For me then, not being more like my hero Superman, proved very costly to my self-esteem.

On this day, stubborn young fool that I was—I chose to challenge, of all loony-toony things conceivable, the escalator at Newberry's. (As you all know in having read this book thus far, I have had my share of problems in life. Not the least embarrassing of these was that nasty revolving door that had blocked my exit to freedom from that Vancouver bank I spoke of earlier.) Yet, not until this point in time had I encountered such a stubborn opponent as an escalator.

While I was supposed to be tagging along behind mother and sis then, I had unintentionally lagged too far behind, and found myself at the base of the store's escalator. This, while my shopping companions had already ascended to the second floor of the building via the escalator.

Now, from where I stood on the wrong side at the bottom of the two oppositely headed chains, I did not do what any sensible kid would have done: proceeded to look over a couple feet to the other side, then taken the upward-moving steel stairs to the top.

But, as you know by now—I am Roy. And quite a boy. Anyone can do things the easy way. Even a regular fool usually can. But I am Roy-the-boy. I repeat. I am Roy-the-boy. But you already knew that—because I have told you that before. Being Roy, I am no regular fool. I will never do things the easy way—whenever I can do things the hard way.

And, on this day which was no exception in my life, I swear that I tried devilishly hard to do just that. I never glanced at the easy passage so near at hand. No. Instead, I jumped on the empty section of chain taking people to the ground floor. A foregone conclusion to your perfect logic no doubt, the outcome of my action was less clear to me. Did I ever in this book hint at my being wise? If so—I herewith surrender my pride and proclaim my gullibility for believing that I could outdo a machine. I can't.

Yes, what I did on this day was certainly not the wise thing to do. It was even less wise for me then to remain where I was and continue to fight the downward momentum of the fast-moving chain in a bid to stubbornly claw my way to the top of the chain and the floor above, step-by-step. Yes yes, the hard way. I know now that it is not always the best way. Not too bright—you say?

Unknown to myself at the time, a large crowd of curious onlookers had gathered at the foot of the escalator now below me, while mother and Helen watched from the floor above in astonished disbelief, mingled, I am sure, with a good dose of pity for me. *Why-oh-why does he always insist on doing things the hardest way, and thereby needlessly subject himself to certain ridicule?* —they must have both thought that. And, how stupidly stubborn can a person be? I know that thought surely crossed their minds also. I know that now.

But even as mother and sis watched in shocked silence the amazing spectacle taking place below them then, along with the growing gathering of folks below me, by this time I had succeeded in beating an arduous path to the midpoint of the downflowing chain—as I strove in accelerated drive to reach the second floor.

The only problem was that I, being Roy, had, of course, from the outset of my unfortunate misadventure drastically underestimated the speed of the downflow. And yes, there was another problem. As much as it hurts me to admit this, it seems that I had substantially overestimated my capability to overcome an obstacle. Despite my best effort to make further headway, I now found myself running furiously on the spot, unable to gain another inch of progress towards the top floor, and insofar as the interested spectators below were concerned, who knew my way not, I must have appeared to them quite determined to wear a path through the steel chain with my running shoes!

And let me assure you all that my legs were swiftly becoming numb from fatigue. In a few more seconds the up-and-down pumping action of my lower limbs had slowed markedly from their previous feverish velocity. The inevitable reigned supreme on this day: the quick flow of the escalator soon dragged me back to the bottom floor, to face defeat and public humiliation.

I was exceedingly frustrated. Frustrated I was that I'd been beaten by a mere machine. So frustrated, that tears welled up from my eyes while I bit my lower lip. No! Wait a sec. I bit my lower lip? No I didn't! As the curious crowd looked on, I cried standing.

Mother came down the escalator (the proper side of it—the proper way) to fetch my pathetic soul. She was quite amused, I am sure. What I knew that sis was thinking did not count. No comments from the goober gallery, either. Being a man whose pride has absorbed innumerable beatings during the course of my life, you should not find it at all surprising that I have never told anyone that I was once bested by an escalator in a department store. Never farted a word about it! Until now.

THE COLLEGE GROVE SHOPPING CENTER was the site of another notable encounter. As this meeting did not involve me and machines, nothing as riveting as the account I just finished telling you took place.

It involved Helen, who told me of it. And, the awestruck young lad who had asked Leonard Nimoy of *Star Trek* fame this question. "Mister, where is your starship now?"

Leanard had replied cheerfully: "It is in orbit around the sun." Comfortable, the actor had looked in the weak December sun while garbed in a light sweater and slacks—and minus the sharply pointed Vulcan ears that had propelled him to international stardom as the characteristically stoic, always pragmatic Mr. Spock, amongst his many loyal TV fans. Fans! Ah! The everlasting fame of a screen star!

That Christmas, the Christmas of 1967, I received amongst many other gifts a model kit of the original starship *Enterprise*. And after I had spent all of Christmas Day trying to assemble the miniature replica myself, and without much success, Raimo, who I suspect had had a hand in buying me the kit, noticed my sorry predicament—and decided to intervene.

By this time, I am sure Raimo had realized that I wasn't too handy with my hands. An instruction sheet to assist assembly had been included with the kit, but this information had proven of little use to me. Yes because—there was the significant problem of properly connecting the electrical wiring from double batteries placed end-to-end where the matter-antimatter reactor and high-performance engine that drove the vessel through space at phenomenal speeds were supposed to be located in the TV version of the *Enterprise*, to the saucer housing the command deck above, which would be highlighted by a powerful glow coming from the bridge. Well, to make a very long story very short, my brother lent me a helping hand. Or, make that two hands. Two hands, plus experience which he had gained in those nearly ten years that separate we two in age.

It was good that Raimo interfered in the assembly—by the time that he'd seen fit to do so, I'd been hopelessly confused and frustrated. Frustrated too I'd been with the hookup of the twin pods, though this had been because the model glue wouldn't dry fast enough for my liking.

Raimo had wound up finishing the piece. That suited me just fine then, thank-you. In the end now, the *U.S.S. Enterprise* looked nothing short of magnificent in a darkened room. I was sure that her master, Captain James T. Kirk, would have thanked Raimo for his perseverance in having completed the task of constructing *his* prized possession. Oh, I know. Kirk didn't really own the *Enterprise*, he just traveled *The Galaxy* in it. Lounging in his comfortable swivel chair on the bridge of his great starship thirty-seven years ago as he prepared to leave Earth orbit, I could almost see him smile, this as he ordered the helm of the *Enterprise* turned toward another sizzling galactic adventure. For myself, *Star Trek* has always represented the ultimate voyage in imaginative sci-fi.

Chapter Thirty

MUSIC HAS ALWAYS INSPIRED ME, providing a lift to my psyche in the same way that it does for everyone else. With the exception of jazz, which I cannot stand to listen to, I will quietly listen to any song that packs a decent melody. In my boyhood I liked most of the songs that my brother did. And Raimo liked many of the songs that father did. And, although Helen is older than myself by a fair stretch in years, back in the latter half of the 1960s anyone who might have happened to know nothing of our difference in age, would have thought myself the older sibling of we two. Sight unseen.

Anyone would have thought so because, based upon Helen's choice of tunes, which she would frequently listen to in her spare time, my sister was definitely of a younger generation, a younger mindset than I.

In regard to her choice of music, I don't know whether I would have gone so far as to label Helen a rebel, like father had. I do know that Helen had most always been found in her half of our shared room, listening to the sometime music of the hard-rock generation. Helen's preferred brand of music ran completely counter to the classical tunes of the 1950s, and most of the contemporary songs of the early sixties. Being soft-rock, Helen's music did not go so far as to rave against the establishment in the bold, noisy way that heavy-hitting hard-rock did. But in the way father saw Helen, a proclamation that read LIBERATE ME might just as well have been tattooed on my sister's forehead.

255

I shall not take a side in that dispute now. I will say that I didn't think much of sis's favorite song by far. This was a song with one line of lyrics that made my whole body shudder every time that my ears were forced to hear it. Never mind the lyrics. I am tryin' very hard to forget 'em—'cause in my mind I still shudder uncontrollably, as though my brain were stricken by ague, whenever I happen to recall but the song's title. Which is, "Look at Me".

Truly, I heard this single song played by Helen on her record player so often on each day then, summer and winter, spring and fall, with no change foreseeable in my sister's menu of music, that I had begun to think I was in serious danger of going bananas. After school, during the weekend, in the summer all day, it made no difference to sis how many times my tortured soul had to listen to the bland rhythm of her pet tune. I figure that a good pair of earplugs would have done wonders for me.

Now, I didn't know it at the time, but Helen had a huge crush on a blond boy at her school. Had I known about him then, I would undoubtedly have thought this: who would want to be forced to look at sis? Yuk! I would have thought this also: that poor guy.

Let us for a while forget everything that involves Helen. The memory of it all makes my mind groan. Instead, let me brief you good readers on my musical career that never blossomed to bear fruit.

My career that never came to be, began innocently enough. In fact, it began from father's interest in classical and contemporary music. Making music came easily to father, for, he possessed a good ear for such. On weekends, father would strum his mandolin whenever the mood seized him. Not often. Just sometimes. Yet, what father really liked to do was to smoke a cigarette while he'd listen to the classical music hour on radio. Father reveled in this.

And while he sat in his easy chair, listening to songs in his-and-mother's bedroom, father used his background in electricity to help him build a tape recorder, modeled after another that Raimo had received as a gift on Christmas when we were in Richmond. Once father had built his own recorder, he set about using his new machine as a draft net, raking in classical and contemporary songs playing on radio.

After he had taped a song, father would sit in his chair and play it over and over. Some years later father would tape a popular tune called "Love is Blue." He'd already taped melodies such as "Sunrise Sunset," "From Russia with Love," "Waves of the Danube" and, the unforgettable, unrivaled love song of the time—"Treasure of Your Love".

"Treasure of Your Love" was sung on record by Eileen Rodgers in 1958. And I've not heard this very beautiful love song in years, but trust me—this song is raw emotion at its very best. In accord with the superb voice of Rodgers, who'd belted this song out of her lungs, in my estimation, "Treasure of Your Love" is one of the greatest love songs I have ever heard sung on this planet. Probably largely unheard now because it is, likely, seldom played on radio, this song is a true classic of almost mythical proportions. As a song, it is complete in every respect that one could want. It lacks absolutely nothing. "Treasure of Your Love" is endowed with a driving energy much like Celine Dion's vocal perfection in the theme song of the widely acclaimed motion picture—*Titanic*. You'll recall: "My Heart Will Go On".

Anyone who has heard these songs will appreciate their beauty as musical masterpieces. It doesn't take much of a musical ear. Mother was not at all as musically gifted as father was, and mother had just a few tunes she liked to hear playing from a music box. Brenda Lee's "All Alone Am I" was her favorite song. And Wayne Newton was mother's favorite male vocalist. If I know women, and I do, Wayne's fine looks surely had something to do with that. And I am sure that mother felt drawn toward that silky-smooth voice of his, because any good-looking man with a good voice—singing emotionally-charged love songs that pack a decent melody—and delivering the lyrics with sincerity—will always make a big splash with any woman.

Like I said though, my father, unlike my mother, did possess a good ear for tunes. And after he learned from me that I had been selected to sing in my school's choir, he put to me a proposal. In hindsight, I figure that I should have considered father's offer much more seriously in the beginning. I really should have. Father's offer had been conditional.

Pop's offer had gone like this. Father would rent a violin for me so that I would have the opportunity to partake of music lessons under the tutorship of my school's music instructor. An older gentleman this was, whose name, incidentally, has long been absent from my mind. Without much thought, I had accepted father's proposal.

Unknown to Roy on that day, I'd made a terrible mistake. A mistake that would cost me dearly for years to come. And my mistake it surely had been—I'd misunderstood the way of my father. I'd not realized the serious repercussion that my decision to take up the task of learning to play the violin would have on my life—I wouldn't realize the truth until six full months had passed by. And by that time it was far too late for me to back out of father's deal.

As an adult, I have always felt that I should not, as a nine-year-old boy then, have been held accountable by father for the choice that I'd made on the day of his offer. I strongly feel this way because, in my mind now, it stands to reason that any kid, when offered an opportunity to try something new in his, or her, young life, something which looks like fun, will be sure to make the same mistake I'd made.

Further, a kid will feel compelled to accept such an offer as this when it comes from a parent simply because he or she knows that when an offer is put forth by a parent, the offer is not to be rejected. Any child is certain to feel this way.

Why else would a parent make such an offer to begin with? The child shall reason thus.

But to father then, the fact that I was only a nine-year-old boy made no difference at all. Father held me fully responsible for my earlier decision. And after one year of drawing my bow across my instrument's quartet of steel strings, when I at last realized with certainty that I did not have it in me to ever become a great violinist, I was quickly reminded by father that I had willingly entered with him into an agreement. I had told father that I wished to quit playing the violin.

And, to complicate the matter of my wish to retire from the laborious task of being forced to play this instrument for an hour each day then, my parents, on father's lead, had gone forth just before the arrival of Christmas of 1967, and purchased for me a used violin. And unlike my shiny rented instrument had been, my new quite-old violin was a full-size replica of the famous Stradivarius violins.

But as I say, my wish to retire from the chore of being forced to play every day was met by resistance from father. Stern resistance. Father was as rigid as a mountainside of rock in the face of my wish to quit my instrument. In fact, once father had heard my protest, he enlisted Helen to make sure, when no one else was at home, that I did not renege on our verbal agreement by failing to carry out my daily practice on the strings. Yes, a grueling full hour every day. No excuses accepted.

Now, as every reader shall find out this instant and later, this narrative of my childhood essentially ends when my family and I reenter Canada in late summer of 1970. And here I shall momentarily break from the time line covered in the main frame of this book to tell you this. I finally was able to maneuver an end to my compulsory music practice. Even so, at this later time in the last days of this year, 1970, in Murrayville B.C., Canada—I paid a heavy price for my precious freedom.

I found freedom thus. On each weekday after school was over, and on the weekend when I was forced to practice also, I tried drawing my bow across the strings of my violin in such a rough manner that the screeching racket I made would have awakened even *Frankenstein's monster* lying in deep slumber in his graveyard coffin. Be aware that I was not so naive that I would have thought I was fooling anyone with the noise I generated, and I did not have to wait long for father's reaction. Oh, father did not react at once.

Father waited. Then, on a weekend afternoon he bade me to watch a symphony orchestra playing on TV. And I, finding the dull hour-long program exceedingly difficult for me to have to patiently bear, voiced my opinion to Raimo.

I said no more to my brother than two words: "You're lucky." I said that just as Raimo was leaving the combined kitchen and living room area of our travel trailer for his back room to study his medical books.

Father, who was sitting atop a stool near myself who was likewise seated, rose. He shut the TV off. Father undid the thin, black leather belt he wore about his waist. To my horror, he then laid hold of me, pushing myself toward the floor. Father strapped me with all of his adult might across my back—he thrashed me soundly.

And on this day my father won the battle. However, I certainly won the war—father would never attempt to force me to play the violin again.

Being the sort of man he was, father would try to gain his revenge against me though. Yeah, one week after father had whipped me with his belt, he asked me to step outside from our trailer. And then, while he looked at myself with a baleful gaze in his eyes, father told me to go and walk the road. And out of his life forever.

The road that father wanted me, a boy of twelve, to walk, was the ice-cold and windswept Fraser Highway. In very early January of 1971.

The winter of 1970-'71 was tough, temperatures outdoors often having hovered scarcely above zero degrees Fahrenheit for days on end. A real Canadian winter this was, with nearly two feet of snow still on the ground, and a chill wind almost always at one's back. Or in one's half-frozen face.

At the time that father told me to walk, mother was inside the trailer and knew nothing about what was transpiring.

Mother did not know until I told her, a little later. I knew that mother likely believed me, but out of her fear of father then, I figured, mother would not, to my knowledge, raise the incident as an issue with father. How was I to know for sure, what mother thought at the time? I didn't. Perhaps, then, mother had not taken me seriously. Or, she having known father longer than I, maybe mother had guessed what I now am sure of.

When this incident is judged strictly at face value, I know but this. I know that what father had asked me to do on that one day in January of 1971 would have spelled tragedy for me. It would have, had I not refused to obey father's direct order to leave home and begin the grim walk to my death. And died I would have along the icy highway, if I would not have been picked up by a police patrol, or a good Samaritan somewhere along the length of the Fraser. In the minus temperatures that existed then, and with nothing to eat—nothing to warm the inside of my body, within days, one week at the very most, I would have lapsed into unconsciousness and frozen to death, even though I was covered from head to toe in heavy winter gear.

In this later time, I have oft traveled the gloomy road of what once was. Many times, yes. And I have this to remark. My father, as you can appreciate from my unflattering description of him in this book, was no saint. Yes, unquestionably he wasn't. He *was*, as I've depicted, a difficult and sometimes cruel man, always calculating, who was not, as I happen to recall other incidents (unvisited here) of similar nature that occurred over the years since that mentioned here, above staging an extreme bluff (holy blipperzit bleeperpoop!!!!) for maximal effect, regardless of the detrimental psychological impact of his action on an impressionable youngster. His own son.

Where does all this lead us? Here. Had I been intimidated enough by father to have heeded his command, would he have stopped me before I would have trod too far along the shoulder of the cold, uninviting road? I am sure that he would have. For other than the reason I've expressed here

I believe this, and for good cause. Like strong, unbendable iron bars. Yep. Father's penchant for boogyman theatrics aside, I believe this because the fallout of father's action—had he further pushed me to walk—could have temporarily landed him in the slammer (besides reaping for him the condemnation of the rest of our gang), just ask any police officer who might have retrieved me alive from the roadside, and who might have then heard my explanation for having been there.

Father was not stupid, but a man stubbornly set in his petty, domineering way.

I have since disposed of the violin that had come to cause me so much emotional torment; I sold the instrument to an elderly couple over three years ago. And, even today, each time that I see a violin anywhere—be it on display in a storefront, on TV, or captured as an image in the newspaper—I see the beauty that lies in the intricate woodwork of the instrument. But I see also into the distant past, for, I am always reminded of the jail that I, a nine-year-old boy then, walked into on a day long ago. Unsuspecting of the harm that in time would befall me.

Chapter Thirty-one

I HAVE NEVER BEEN FAVORABLY IMPRESSED by people who have wanted to force their will down my gullet because of my smaller size. At one time, people like my father, brother, and sister. Being younger, smaller, and physically weaker as I still then was, I always had to endure a lot of my being pushed around. Especially by my siblings. Unlike father and Raimo, who only a foolish child would have stood up to because of their size, Helen was not yet an adult. Thus Helen I felt safe enough to contest whenever the situation demanded that I retaliate to her teenage pushy nature.

Whenever I was left with no choice, I did not hesitate to take my sister on in a physical fight now. Helen, being nearly five and a half years older than I, was still capable, though barely, of getting the better of me. Because I was younger, smaller, and less powerful, I was always the underdog. But I was a young boy with strong pride. In my mind, I preferred to think that I was underrated. In a serious fight my temper always boiled beyond my skinny frame. I suppose it was because I felt that I held my own against sis very well which led me to consider myself as her equal. Forsooth, powered I was by a spirit which had in it the savagery of a boy who believed that he always fought for a just cause.

I'd hardly ever initiate a fight with Helen. As bystanders viewing events so many years later—every reader of this book shall know that I speak the truth. The proof is in the pudding. At my size and age then, who, in his right mind, would have begun a fight against a larger, stronger opponent? Not me, certainly. Except, as I say, I would on the very rare occasion then. Again, this was whenever I felt that I had no option. But, regardless of which one of us kids would pick a quarrel with the other, I concur with what you should suspect—once begun, in a fight I'd always fight like my life depended on a successful defense. Unfortunately, Helen must have believed in exactly the same thing. She must have. Helen usually fought like a tiger.

And the things that we two kids, as adversaries, would fight about then were mostly pretty stupid things. Things that seem silly to me now. Things like—well—this. Helen had this, to me, terribly annoying habit of letting her pet budgies loose from their shared cage. This window of freedom was, sis said then, the only freedom that her small avian friends knew in their entire boring days. And so, once every day this pair of winged bombers would fly freely. Throughout our house. The problem being that practically each time they did, the pair would let loose a couple of sickening droplets of white goo from their tiny rear ends.

The single positive aspect I found to the budgies' exercise period was the fact that parakeets cannot speak as can larger parrots. Had they been able to, I am sure that Helen's two feathered friends would have yelled out, "Bombs dig ya boy!" Yes, loud and clear as each bird flew over my fine head of hair then.

Whenever these guided bombs happened to come too close to finding their mark, a fighting match between myself and Helen would erupt within the blink of an eye. I would scream at my sister. And Helen would scream her undying hatred at me. The very next thing we knew was that we then found ourselves engaged in seemingly mortal combat with one another.

On these occasions when I and Helen tangled over her birds, I sometimes struck my sister first. Or sis struck me first. Whatever. I learned that girls can fight very dirty, because Helen, I know, tried to utilize every method of grappling with a foe. She used every method known to her. She used every trick in the book, so to speak. Like trying her damnedest to yank out each sturdy follicle of brown hair, attached by a healthy root to the top of my head. And once I learned that no holds, no matter how reprehensible they were to my ethics in combat, were barred in my sister's rule book, I, for my part, naturally adopted that prudent strategy and applied Helen's own technique against her with such devastating efficiency that Helen found me, in nearly no time at all, an unpalatable adversary.

Unpalatable, metaphorically speaking. Getting eaten is what usually happens to smaller, weaker creatures in the wild; and metaphorically speaking, I did not wish to lose badly to sis then and wind up being the eaten one.

One of the things about me which always drove Helen raving nuts was whenever I acted like a baby. And I, being the last of mother's children, was indeed superbaby then. Mother still liked to dote on me. I didn't know whether Helen was just jealous. I knew only what I observed and heard.

I knew that Helen hated my less-than-manly persona with blistering vehemence, because she complained about my act so often to mother and myself. And not surprisingly, with Helen's intolerance of my budding thespianism to spur her on then, the two of us nearly managed to become embroiled in a physical altercation about this trivial matter too. On the one hand there was I, who obstinately claimed that I had every right to act like a baby if I so wished. Opposing me was sis who boisterously, adamantly, insisted that I, by carrying on like a much younger child, and I, being not really a baby at all, was doing nothing less criminal than what her outrage led me to believe was, in sis's mind, its equivalent: breaking a Federal statute. Helen's laughable condemnation of myself in this regard was approached just as seriously in her muddled mind as upholding the Fifth Amendment of the United States would have been by any legal beagle representing a client in criminal court.

The result was: I would wisely try my best to persevere and ignore my sister's sporadic periods of infantile rage. For me, this proved easier thought than done. Yet, at least I tried.

And what was my reason for behaving in a docile way before mother, as befits a superbaby? This. Being sensitive beyond belief as I am, I sensed mother's need to receive love. As well, I sensed her need to give love to her children. I, being one of her precious children, mattered to her. Prolonging my earlier innocence in life seemed to make mother happy.

Father Time is slipping by me again. In reverse. Sorry— nevertheless, I really do need to backtrack a bit here. Back to the summer of 1966. About Raimo and work now. Oh, I didn't have to worry about the latter then, only the first. I was too young to worry about a job. So was Helen. But like mother and father, my brother was employed. I gathered that Raimo found his summer job at Krasne's much like Lavers had been for him, back in Campbell River. *That's it?*

N-o-o. Raimo, I figured, must have felt rotten to have had to leave all the pretty girls in his grade twelve class behind when he'd graduated as an honor student from San D.'s Point Loma High School. I took one swift look at his face each morning and I always thought that he looked more stern now. I knew that in the coming fall Raimo would attend his first year of premedical studies at San Diego State University. He would then be quite absorbed in his studies.

I was thankful that my brother had to WORK in the summer to pay for his tuition at school in the fall. I was very glad, actually; with him being absent from home during much of the day, left him with less leisure time in which to pull my hair. In these days of yore, being then an habitual sadist like father, Raimo was always too eager, as if anyone should even be eager to mete out nastiness to another, to dispense me a good yank. Or worse. For myself, an always existing threat the former especially still was. And when he pulled my hair, given the considerable advantage afforded him by his size and age in comparison to mine then, for Raimo to do thus is simply wrong of him, I felt. During these painful sessions my head would oscillate, yes, from side to side just like a yo-yo, at what felt like faster-than-light speed.

And at other times, for the slightest of reasons conceivable, Raimo would threaten to use the thin black leather belt he wore about his man's waist to strap my backside; carrying out the threat my brother was always ready to do.

Other than the understanding that my designation of Raimo as a sadist then can provide you, I can but speculate as to a likely-contributing cause of Raimo's wish to see me suffer then. I believe that Raimo's desire to vent his inner tension, always discernible outwardly, arose from the pressure of him rising to meet the significant challenge then ahead of him, fueled by not only Raimo's own wish to succeed in life, but the knowledge that our parents wished him to graduate to a degree in medicine. Like father and Helen, but more like father, whose consideration toward myself had evaporated once he'd seen me slowly shed the appearance of an adorable younger child, all too often Raimo showed not the kindness that comes from deeper caring, toward me. Far from it, throughout my childhood years Raimo was, much too often, that abusive enforcer.

Parcel to this candid critique, whilst it be true that Raimo is my biological brother, he is a brother who has been, frankly, somewhat condescending of my intelligence in my adult years, though just once has he actually called me stupid, and my build felt his criticism—but that was long ago. And yet, it should be no surprise that an older sibling who once continually subordinated a much younger and smaller family member in the guise of discipline, has not, by force or threats then, and by the odd vocal barb in later years, endeared himself to me.

I don't believe that I really need to tell you all, all of the immediately following. Most of you who read this book already know that the physical abuse of any given child, early in life, will still impact on that individual when he or

267

she becomes an adult. Physical abuse, particularly constant physical abuse, always leaves unseen scars that linger in mind for years after the fact. Invisible though these scars be, they usually last for a lifetime. Certainly, by its very destructive nature, physical abuse of children cannot assist their emotional stability later in life. Gosh no, the more sensitive a child is, the worse will be the emotional damage resulting from such abuse. I know, because my heart is marked for life by these invisible scars. To me, these wounds are tentacled reminders of that other time.

Whether it is called heavy-handed discipline, or physical and emotional abuse—which is what I speak of really is, makes no difference to me any more. It doesn't: the bleak reminder of my past has made my memory of these events numb in my mind for a very long time. The horror is gone. But the sadness still remains.

I remember my boyhood fairly well. Of San Diego and summertime, I remember when my brother would don his dark sunglasses in the face of yet another stifling-hot, sunny day. On his way to work, in our driveway I remember him stepping onto his motor scooter on each weekday morning. He would step on the gas pedal and crank the small engine into ignition, and as blue smoke would curl upward from his bike's tailpipe, Raimo would wave good-bye to mother and me as we'd look on from behind the large window of my parents' bedroom.

When the early morning sun was not too hot for him, Raimo would wear his thin, medium-blue Windbreaker. Always a short-sleeved white dress shirt, a long tie, and black dress slacks. Atop his motor machine he never wore a helmet.

Raimo had purchased the scooter used, for seventy-five dollars. And he had spray painted most of the old, white metal body of his bike so that it presented a two-tone format. Blue-green and white. I thought this combination of colors a rather strange mix. But an old can of blue-green paint was the only color of paint that Raimo had found in our house, which was, in hindsight, suitable for a motorbike.

One of the few other cans of paint that we had then was coral, which had been left over from mother's paint job of our home, and mother's house paint was not suited for metal surfaces. Aside from that, as a color, coral ain't suited for use on a motorbike driven by a man. Pink never was a man's color and never will be.

About the same time that Raimo had bought his bike, father, who was wise in the ways of old used cars and their tendency to break down on occasion, had acquired a second vehicle which mother sometimes drove, as she had obtained her driver's license. Though seldom did she drive it. This car was an aging Hillman sedan. Quite tiny the Hillman was for a car. The light-green paint on this Hillman had faded through the many years that the car had spent outdoors, likely beneath the southern sun.

Father's Volkswagen van received a new look too. Father had painted it baby-blue. The whole exterior of his van. And because father had used a brush to apply the paint, instead of a spray gun, father's handiwork was noticeably uneven. The result was no surprise to mother, who knew how to paint properly. When it came to artistry and color, father, who always wore one of his drab gray work shirts and pants to match even at home, never was Michelangelo.

Chapter Thirty-two

THE ALLURE OF SOUTHERN CALIFORNIA as a semitropical paradise is soon lost upon many a snowbird who call the arid region a year-round home, as the novelty of seeing palm trees and sunshine every day dims with time. Aye, this feeling comes quickly. Or slowly. But, eventually the tall palms and the radiant yellow ball in the sky shed their attraction for so many as the years wear by in the senseless heat. At least, these did for everyone in our gang except mother, she—who always liked the sunshine and heat.

Throw out the mountaintops and in southern California there is almost never any real snow. In fact, the only location in the southern part of the State at which *I* ever did see snow was a small stretch of forest known as Torrey Pines. Torrey Pines has slight elevation, rising just enough above the rest of the city of San Diego that the area can capture snow. Very, very, seldom, though at the top it can. Or, it could, before global warming.

When our bunch had visited Torrey Pines on a weekend, I remember that I'd felt strange, seeing, for the first time since our arrival in San Diego, isolated patches of fresh white snow from the night before, on the ground. Not hail. Genuine snow. It was early morning when we'd visited, and on that day we three kids had had ourselves the only snowball fight that we ever had the joy of participating in, in the State of California.

For most of we North Americans, really hot summers are bearable only in the comfort of indoor air conditioning.

But you know that our clan never owned an air conditioner. No. Not unless we all stifle a chuckle and resort to calling a portable fan an air conditioner. Or a wide-open window an A.C. In my view, the many fine vistas of southern California do not atone for the almost constant sunshine. Not if there is too much of the latter. Not if both the days and nights are too hot. But who am I to complain? As a kid, I got to see some pretty nice sights. I mean, apart from the darling girls in swimsuits. Other than the girls, er—women I mean, so many of whom always look adorable in bikini-wear, there are many beautiful sights worth seeing within the urban sprawl of San Diego itself.

Foremost, there is the beach at La Jolla, where a cool, refreshing ocean breeze will entice the summer swimmer or surfboard enthusiast into glistening waters of cobalt-blue. Here, a wide variety of marine life inhabit the nearshore.

It was here on the rock beach that my findings in the sand so pleased me that I'd soon begin another seashell collection then, identifying every unbroken specimen of shell I'd come across.

You'll recall that my shells from Campbell River hadn't made the move south.

There were a number of shells I had never seen the likes of in the northern waters of Canada. There were: smallish moon shells; I found worm shells, even a sand dollar. In all, from La Jolla, I collected two shoe boxes filled with seashells.

I took my bounty home and placed my catch into our bathroom sink. I turned the hot water tap on, and let the water run for a bit until it was plenty hot. Then I donned latex gloves and inserted the rubber plug into the bottom of the sink, letting the sink fill up completely. To this, I then added a full cup of Comet disinfectant powder, and I stirred the cleanser in well with the water. I let my shells sit in the sink for a half-hour.

In addition to cleaning my shells, I wanted to make damn sure that no sea slugs which might have hitchhiked into our home, inside of the shells, could possibly have been left alive and breathin'. I have never been fond of slugs. Not land, or sea, slugs.

When I finally drained the sink and flushed each shell individually with cold water I *was* damn sure that no alien life was left alive, hiding aboard my shells, and ready to sneak out in the dead of night to attack me or my family.

Another beautiful spot that father took us to is called Shelter Island. This is not an island. It's a bay, on the shore of which I discovered another type of seashell. Though these shells are no more than a half-inch long, they possess the glossiest exterior and the best colors I'd run across. These shells have a pleasing mellow turquoise body—smoothly tapered at either end, with an orange-brown turret. The contrasting colors impart a rare charm sure to make any necklace made from the shells stand out. For one's special lady, of course.

The marina here at Shelter Island provided a berth to not only single-hulled sloops, but to three-pod trimaran as well. Father rented a trimaran on a weekend afternoon, and we five slowly navigated the calm water of the bay. I could easily have dozed off in the sailboat.

Not so at San Diego Zoo. I became very tired in the legs and feet just by walking leisurely around that huge place. Some people like zoos. I don't. San Diego Zoo is the world's largest zoo.

And even with all of that space for *people* to stroll about in, I know that I would never want to be a monkey, for instance, destined to live my entire life out behind an inescapable fortress of iron bars. Or, was that unshatterable glass, or unbreakable plastic? I would not wish to be forced to waste my life as a captive polar bear, either, sunk into the bowel of a deep, refrigerated pit. I feel that way in regard to every animal in every zoo on this planet.

Nor, as the principle of confining a wild species to a limited space is the same, would I wish to be an orca at Sea World, which you'd figured. An orca whose assigned purpose is to provide pleasure for the millions of human beings who come to watch marine animals in their artificial habitat. A prison.

In my mind I have always championed the right of every wild species of animal, as species of sentient creatures, to live in the freedom of the wild. The wild—from birth to death, the native habitat of all these animals. An environment that imprisoned wild species do not share.

It was, in part, because I did not have to stare at jailed animals that I thoroughly enjoyed one trip which our tribe took on another weekend. This was an overnight excursion to L.A.

We were in Los Angeles on Boxing Day of 1967. Having arrived in town in the care of father and his spartan VW van, we, as tourists, did what tourists always do. We shopped the numerous downtown shops, parked ourselves in a hotel overlooking the core of downtown L.A., and we visited the forecourt at the Chinese theater to view the imprints of the stars' at 6925 Hollywood Boulevard. Hands and shoes, some nose impressions and what not. Quite a few of Hollywood's biggest stars had left their marks here in fresh cement. On the sidewalk. Bob Hope, John Wayne, Judy Garland, Elizabeth Taylor, Frank Sinatra, Marilyn Monroe are those whose imprints I can either remember or, er, achoo, predict to be here. There were so many others whose castings I saw but I don't recollect their names. And the impressions the celebrities had left in the concrete will probably last for another fifty years, at least. Unless of course, California is split into two by a major earthquake. Fate forbid.

And speaking of stars: We traveled by what we thought may have been Lucille Ball's home, a modest home in Beverly Hills. We had to. We were Californians. But like I said, we were also tourists. The curiosity bug had bitten each of us. It was left to our real bug—the VW van, and father, to take us all back home to Demus Street.

NOW, ABOUT MY GOOD BUDDY, WAYNE, and his parents. I often visited Wayne, whose folks' house was about a mile from ours, and in the direction of the College

Grove Shopping Center. Wayne's mom was a teacher, who taught at Jack & Jill Elementary School. She was a fine lady, like you'd expect most any teacher of young ones to be. Wayne's mother was not like that woman of an undying disturbing memory in my life—Mrs. Mulder. Wayne's pop was a computer programmer, who sometimes fell asleep while he watched football on the boob tube. Like his dad, Wayne liked football. The Green Bay Packers were one of Wayne's favorite football teams.

Um, I shall get down to business now and change the topic of activity from football—to swimming. We had one of those small, circular, galvanized steel swimming pools with a plastic liner on the interior, in our backyard. In his folks' backyard Wayne had one of these popular kiddie pools too. Swimming pools, I found, are complicated: swimming pools can be a source of trouble for youngsters like me and Wayne then. And trouble between my mother and Wayne's mother, and thus friction betwixt myself and Wayne, threatened to materialize when my mother insisted that Wayne would have to take a shower in our bathroom before he could clamber into our pool.

I reckon that Wayne's mom kind of took offense to this formality. Kind of, because the next time that I showed up for a dip in Wayne's swim can, I was asked by Wayne, likely on his mother's prodding, whether I had bothered to take a shower. I hadn't, actually. Yep, I told Wayne that I had.

Despite our disagreement in regard to swimming pool hygiene, Wayne Hare was a good friend. Later on, as a token of our friendship just before our family left San Diego, I gave Wayne all of my old comic books. A whole two-inch-high stack of 'em. My finest Superman, Tarzan, and Batman editions these were.

Given the age of these comics today, should they have survived the decades intact, they will have significant value. They would be worth even more had I not repeatedly scribbled this—"Helen is a bum." with a light shade of pencil, in randomly selected areas over many of the pages. Erasable—yes, albeit not without telltale imprints being left behind on the pages where I had always pressed my reliably dull pencil into them—hard, and not without a loss of color in the illustrations on those pages.

Of course, we all know why I'd marked the pages? Yes? Yes, I'd done it to vent my frustration with sis whenever me and Helen had butted heads in just another sibling power struggle.

I am sure that Wayne, as he stopped to read my scrawled messages then, chuckled at least once or twice in boyish amusement when he saw the same message of my dissatisfaction with my sister leap at his eyes from so many a marked page. POSITIVELY. I entertain no doubt in my mind that Wayne, who was a good student, ever had any difficulty in deciphering my messy pencilmanship. What a numbskull I am!

WHAT CAN I REMEMBER of our family's time spent in San Diego in addition to what I have already told you folks about our experiences there? I shall strive to remember forever, the following: A young dark-haired American girl of Mexican heritage, whose name I know not any more—swinging valiantly, while blindfolded, at a pin yata strung from a basketball hoop behind my school Darnell. And unlike her name long forgotten, I vaguely remember the pin yata shattering beneath the force of the baseball bat in her hands. And candy falling out everywhere as my eager classmates and I rush in for a treat under the watchful eyes of Mrs. Miller.

And, I shall try to remember forever the one gingerbread cookie that each of we pupils received on another day at school. Along with the tall, cool cup of sparkling red punch that accompanied it. Both the cookie and the punch had been supplied through the courtesy of a classmate's mother who knew how to bake. Divinely.

And I shall remember forever another venerable slugger, my own mother, striking a softball, with concentrated desire, on a lazy Sunday afternoon in my schoolyard. She—sending the ball high into the air where it loved to be—

before it had to obey the force of gravity and fall back to earth. Just short of the faraway fence marking the boundary between the school field and the desert canyon beneath it. My mom. Given a decent pitch, she sure could whack that ball true. As good as any major league slugger I'd ever heard of. Except for "Babe" Ruth of course, who would have sent that ball rocketing over the fence into the canyon itself.

CHAPTER THIRTY-THREE

BY THE END OF 1967, father had begun to talk of leaving San Diego for a destination to the north. Where, exactly, he intended to take the rest of us, father wasn't sure. In our family it was no secret that he had grown tired of the long, hot summers. And as always, whenever father was involved, there was change for the mere sake of change itself to be had now. In other ways. Father could smell the future.

Mother would have preferred to remain in San Diego, as it was the south. As I have stated, in the subtropical climate she never experienced osteoarthritis as she had back in Canada, and thus, she never complained of suffering from it here. But mother agreed to abide by father's wish for two reasons. First, mother was not an argumentative lady. Second, she agreed too because of her concern for Raimo. Raimo, who despite his high scholastic standing in his premedical studies at school was, mother believed, left open to the possibility of being conscripted into the raging Vietnam conflict. Someday. Perhaps someday, mother thought.

Mother need not have worried about anyone in the family. Only U.S. citizens were being drafted into the grim, deadly arena of that awful war then. And in order to be drafted, by law an immigrant had to voluntarily apply for U.S. citizenship. Point made.

The preparations for the move, now. The following summer, in August of 1968, a plan was devised. Doubly weary of heat by this time, father wished to travel as far north as he could while remaining in Uncle Sam's territory. Yet, father wished to drop our anchor far enough to the south to be free of that persistent Canadian-like winter of snow and ice. Or so he wished.

Oregon appealed to father because, in addition to a change in climate, Oregon provided an outlet to satisfy his craving for other forms of change, and father was looking for a job in heavy industry. For this purpose, father sought a large urban center. And the only such center in the entire State of Oregon, was then in 1968, and still is, Portland. Nestled in the Multnomah County, with picturesque Mt. Hood fifty miles east, the Portland of this earlier time was home to some 370,000 people.

The statistic of population was lost on me. I only knew that two months later the packing commenced. Father did not ask me whether I wished to leave. And in fact, I would gladly have stayed behind for one reason which was very important to me. This reason was that mother would be left behind in San Diego, to oversee the sale of our house through a real estate agent. I was not opposed to the move itself. I was opposed to leaving mother. The sad reality was that most everything father planned, and did, showed not the least bit of concern for my feelings, and for those of others' in our family.

I knew that Helen was not keen to leave San Diego, either. This was because of mother, yes. I knew, also, that my sister had taken a real shine to a handsome lad at her school, a boy she now called David. Remember? I alluded briefly to his existence earlier. Like Raimo, that dude would go on to university and become a medical doctor. I knew that Helen liked David a lot. I'd known that on the day that she had brought home her class photo from school. I'd known instantly, because Helen's face had developed an unmistakable rosy tinge when mother had asked her who the good-looking boy in the class photo was.

Anyhow, I did not wish to go north. I did not wish to make the trek to a far-off place unless mother came too. I was mother's son. Period. And when the morning to depart came in late October, I felt as though my heart was literally being wrenched from my chest, and—I was in a never-ending free fall over the darkness of the ocean.

Devastated almost beyond description I was. I felt as though I were plunging to my death. I cried, and I would have run away had I possessed the individuality in character to think of it. Looking back now, I figure that I should have hid myself on the dark hillside behind our house, and lain on the ground to avoid detection. Then let father's van leave for the north, carrying only father and Helen. Not Raimo, though. He was already attending university in Portland then, my brother having begun his third year, his final year, of premed back in September, his first in the City of Roses.

Father was *oblivious* to the emotional upheaval he had created for me. I was being forced to abandon mother for I knew not how long a time. That, in black and white, was the way I saw the situation then, and that is how I still see it.

I know that you all shall remember with some humor what I declared at the beginning of this book, my statement that at six years of age in life I had already felt myself to be a man. I said that even though I know that at ten years of age I was still very much a child trying to cope with circumstances beyond my control. I knew that I had to leave mother by order. And when the front passenger door of father's van slammed shut by his hand—I was not on earth any more.

Mother came and stood beside the open window where I sat in teary-eyed despair. Mother knew what I was going through. She always knew. And knowing just how miserable I felt, she comforted me. Mother kissed my forehead as she had done ever since I was a baby in diapers. Reluctantly, she bade me good-bye. I was sure that mother's gentle soul nearly broke in her as she watched the van back out of our driveway onto Demus Street. And as the wheels gripped the surface of the road in forward motion, I felt the sorrow in her heart through her moist eyes when she waved a final good-bye to us. I learned then, that a child's misery is only equaled by a mother's misery for her child.

In the darkness of early morning, chugging under a heavy load, our van moved up to the top of our street; a small, demasted plywood-hull sailboat of my brother's creation was strung, bottom up as dictates logic and wise custom when transporting an untrailered boat by motor vehicle, to the roof of the van, whilst the inside of the van was packed with boxes full of goods.

From here father drove us through dimly lit streets onto the freeway. Well, not quite. Father had taken the wrong exit and we'd strayed onto a new freeway still under construction. So, father backed up the van, and he drove us around until he located the right road. We resumed our journey toward the north.

Father drove as fast as his van would allow. An hour and a half later we hit L.A. Except for a pit stop to take on fuel, we did not linger here but continued our steady advance northward. It was midafternoon when we came upon San Fran. under gray sky and drizzle. Here, father stopped the van at a restaurant that appeared a popular truck stop, to buy for Helen and me each a small tray of fries. For himself, some coffee and a burger. Having finished our repast, we were soon on the beaten path toward the north again.

We found lodging in a motel near Redding, California that evening. Here, we three further "rested" our butts, which had grown stiff and sore from inactivity during the day. My ass was really sore, and I was sure that Helen's rump was too.

And sleep would not come easily. I was thinking of mother who was now alone, back at our house on Demus Street. I knew that mother would be thinking of us. And about me. During the long night my every thought was burdened by the sadness of my having had to leave home. But just before sunrise I must have dozed off a bit. Away from my emotional misery.

An hour after sunrise, Father Time saw us when we drove past the snow-laden peak of Mt. Shasta in the distance, resplendent in the new day's glory as the sun shone on its unspoiled majesty. Not too long after that we crossed the California-Oregon border. Later, it was in the full light of midmorning that I caught sight of a small black bear, likely a yearling, as it ran up a forested incline to the left of the highway. To the right of our passage was the serenity of a mountain lake.

By early afternoon our van had made it into Eugene, where we stopped to take on fuel. Helen, who was under physical stress, had now begun to complain, and without bothering to poll me for my opinion, Helen insisted that from hereon we periodically exchange the position of our feet (in my view then, so that her tender tootsies would not petrify into stone during the remainder of our trip—the trip had already been, I observed, an extended period of inactivity).

I didn't much like Helen's simple solution which made for a crisscross. And the most awkward X this was, because my lower legs and feet now took up the space where Helen's should have been, while Helen's comparatively long stilts ran along the floor of the van diagonally, and into the corner where mine had a right to be. Helen's screwball idea, now meant that my feet ran beneath my sister's lower-body bulk. Given the oddity of what had been sis's demand, which I would afterwards always consider to have been ridiculous, I thought that, rather than her legs and feet, perhaps it is Helen's brain which has been gripped in the throes of a severe circulatory malfunction. Yes, not her legs and feet.

Yet, I had done as Helen had told me to do, I knowing full well that if I had refused a direct order from my older sibling, I would have been subject to either a stiff reprimand or punishment from the executive ruler. Meaning dad of course. I knew that Helen, being a girl and therefore father's favorite child, would always prevail over me in the war of public opinion. Helen had done so on several occasions in the past. Yes, no matter how unfair I judged my sister's directive to have been, I knew then, that I was doing myself a big favor by complying with sis's wish.

WE ARRIVED AT THE CITY OF PORTLAND in late afternoon of the day which followed our departure from San Diego. A twelve-hundred-plus mile drive for father. The sky was overcast and it was raining as father eased the van into the parking stall beneath our next home, and that was on Thirtieth Place. Raimo came downstairs to open the door of Apartment Five to us.

Raimo looked happy to see us. And after we all made small talk, I sized our pad up. Fairly new it was. And it was a two-level townhouse.

Well, it was not long before we newcomers were settled in. But I could not help it. I was thinking of mother again. I wondered how long I would have to wait to see her.

When morning arrived with the glow of the sun, father drove me and Helen to school, and enrolled me straight into grade five. Yes. Yet another school in another city. Kern Elementary School. Only a half-mile it stood from where we would live, as far as I knew, indefinitely. Helen's high school was called Adams. It lay in the opposite direction from our dwelling than my school. My homeroom teacher at Kern was an affable lady called Mrs. Hale. I shall give you my complete impression of her later.

Silence, some folks say, is priceless. On every weekday after school me and my siblings had to keep as quiet as we could in the late afternoon and evening hours when father was still asleep. And with the exception of my hour of violin practice each day, which father made sure that I did, we kids kept noise to an absolute minimum. Not only because father commanded that it be so, but because father worked the graveyard shift at Crown Zellerbach's pulp and paper mill in Portland.

Father didn't care to be on the graveyard shift and he made no secret of this fact. In fact, father hated the night shift so much, that he would quit his job at C.Z. after just three months and go to work for a small firm called Machinery Sales, located on the outskirts of town.

Prior to our move north, Raimo and father had made a preparatory trip to Portland together, and father had phoned us back in San Diego to apprise mother, Helen, and I, of the fact that they had reserved a roomy townhouse. Having left Raimo to look after the rental pad in town while he attended Portland State University, father had returned to San Diego shortly. But not before he'd found work as a maintenance electrician at C.Z.

THEN WORD CAME by phone one evening. Mother had sold our house in San Diego. Mother had spoken briefly with father, first. After this, in compliance with father's order, all of us kids lined up in the kitchen where our phone was. I was first in line, and father told me to make my conversation short. I took his meaning literally. I greeted mother with a standard welcome. "Hi," I said. And I didn't say much more than that. I had not forgotten mother. Not at all. It was just that I did not wish to run afoul of father's iron rule: obey at any cost. Or else. This was the rule.

I bade mother good-bye, and reluctantly handed the phone over to Helen, who seized the extra time given her by my very brief exchange with mother, and sis had a nice long chat at my expense. Raimo spoke after that, and took his sweet time. Being twenty, and big in body, he didn't have to worry about getting a licking from father for dillydallying. Then father spoke again. Because he was father, he always got the last word.

A month later, mother joined us in Portland. I was physically ill, and mother said that she would have me healed and up in no time. In bed, with a sore stomach I was. But, from the instant that I was reunited with mother, my ailment, whatever its cause, quickly disappeared. It is a wonder what the simple pleasure of a boy being able to see his mother, after a long absence, can do for him.

And boy-oh-boy was I ever glad to see mother, who was equally glad to see me. Everyone in our family was together again, and the Christmas of 1968 was the happiest I can remember.

CHAPTER THIRTY-FOUR

THE WINTER OF 1968-'69 WOULD BE COLD AND HARD. Portland had already received a foot of snow. Christmas was past now. It was now the beginning of 1969. And our Christmas tree, like any cut Christmas tree, had outlived its usefulness. Like Christmas now past, our tree was now a ghost. Stripped of its former glory, mother had resigned it to the carport beneath our building. A truck would take it away, come garbage day.

Removing the knitted pair of slippers that mother had made for me, I put on my navy-blue bomber jacket. This was a jacket that mother had purchased back in San Diego, she having known that the climate of the Pacific Northwest would demand such outerwear be worn. As for the foot-deep snow, it was the first significant snowfall I had seen in years. For the snow, I put on my tan steerhide construction boots. Whenever outdoors I wore these always. Even to school.

Leaving our apartment, I bent my steps toward the underground carport. Here, relegated to one corner of the parking area, lay our Christmas tree, along with a few others just like it. All shorn of their pride and clinically dead.

I examined our tree closely. As I looked at the brown bark and dark-green needles curiosity struck me, and I began to consider the type of tree it was. I didn't know much about trees. Just enough I did know about them to know that our Xmas tree belonged to a genus of trees called the evergreens. Supposedly, this name had once come from the observation that this kind of tree is always green, in winter, in summer, and in the seasons in between, I thought. What I did not know is that an evergreen is also called a conifer. And if someone had asked me then, when unseen side by side, I could not have told the asker the differences between a spruce and Douglas fir.

Some folks like to keep a stately pine tree in their home at Christmastime just for the extra sweet fragrance this tree exudes, especially when fresh cut. We never had one, though.

For anyone with a sensitivity to tree sap, the type of tree that one comes into bodily contact with—be it coniferous or deciduous—will mean the difference between no aftereffect, and a severe skin reaction known as eczema.

I had a project in mind. For this I donned a thick pair of black knitted gloves, albeit loosely woven these were. I knew that I had suffered from eczema at the age of three. I remembered well the painful water-filled blisters that had broken open on my hands. Still, with my gloves on I thought that my hands would be protected well enough to permit me to handle the task at hand. Alas, I was terribly wrong.

Our tree on this past Yule was a spruce tree. And spruce trees contain the most-acidic sap of conifers. In conifers, the sap beneath the bark is the substance which is, for any susceptible person who suffers from eczema, the agent that will cause an eruption in one's skin, on any part of the body which happens to come into contact with the tree sap.

Without further consideration to my safety, just as soon as I had located my toy saw with a real steel blade, a tool which I had been given for Christmas at the age of five, I set to my labor. I proceeded to lop a good three feet off the crown of our Christmas tree, cutting our tree in half. Next, I sliced through the tree again, cutting a specimen of the ring structure, about one inch long, off the bottom of the top half of our tree. As I'd done so, the sap had oozed out from under the cut friction-heated bark and now, as I viewed the small specimen in my gloved hands, the sap clinging to the piece somehow penetrated through or between the fabric of my gloves, onto my bare hands beneath. At the time I was too preoccupied with the thought of creating a collection of specimens, from native trees that grow in northwest Oregon, to pay much notice to my mishap.

But it was not long before I felt a reaction. I had believed that I'd satisfactorily attended to my hands with bar soap and warm water beneath the bathroom faucet after my little saw-job was finished. I don't know to this day whether I actually had performed the mundane task adequately. It is possible that I had failed to entirely remove a smidgen or two of sticky spruce sap from my skin.

What would happen in the next day then would catch me off-guard. My hands began to blister, with scores of tiny pimples filled with water. About the water inside the pimples: I had found this out when I'd poked a sewing needle into a few of 'em. Before I drained the pimple infestation that had overrun my hands, on mother's advice I sterilized the tip of the needle with a lit match.

Mother was concerned. And we both knew what the cause of my allergic outbreak was. Yet, neither mother, who could clearly remember my earlier instance of eczema from when I was three, nor I, could appreciate the tenacity of the burgeoning army of pimples I would soon face this time around.

In fact, I quickly discovered that my ultrasensitive skin proceeded to erupt with new pimples more quickly than I could dispatch of them with my sewing needle. The skin on my hands itched horribly. I clawed at the grip side of my fingers and the palm of each hand, in turn, with my free hand, my short fingernails scratching in vain at the broken and bleeding surface of these. Because of the incessant itch I rubbed my fingers and palms into any sharp surface, a failing attempt to appease the itch. And continually, I ran to the bathroom to let cold water from the tap wash over the flaming discomfort my hands were in.

The worst was yet to come. From my hands my ailment had now leapt to the soles of my feet, feet that were alive with growing colonies of blisters. As with my hands, I now scratched at my feet. Even my personal appendage, the mark of any boy and man, itched from the unrestricted spread of the pimple army. Risking infection, I savagely scraped at the intruders. My deliverance into hell went on for a couple of days. To mother, my plight and growing desperation were obvious.

And mother had decided that my case now required a professional's medical intervention. Mother made an appointment for me and I accompanied her to a local doctor's office. That dude had a familiar last name. Hale. The same name as my teacher, Mrs. Hale. I was slightly curious about his surname in regard to whether he was any relation to Mrs. Hale. I wanted to ask him if he was, but as Dr. Hale was a gruff-looking old man I kept silent.

The doctor examined my hands and feet. Except for my socks which I'd had to remove, I was glad that the doctor had not asked me to remove my apparel.

DR. HALE had completed his examination of me. Because my hands were red raw, mother rose from her seat, she intending to make life for my hands a bit easier by tying the rough laces of my construction boots. But Dr. Hale would have none of that. He told mother to let me tie my own boots. I always did when my hands were in better health. Another coarse old man like my father, I thought. However, neither mother nor I said anything to the geezer. And I still doubt, as I did in my mind then, that the doctor was any relation to my teacher. Mrs. Hale was so different.

Anyhow, the titled old man prescribed a familiar drug, cortisone, to deal with my skin allergy. Oh, 'sides this medication, I'd have to soak my hands and feet in a solution of potassium permanganate and water, daily, which would leave a durable purple stain on these members. Wear gloves in the classroom at school. Stay away from both chocolate and cheese for a while. And, not so much as brush my hands against the skin of an unpeeled orange because I am quite allergic to such.

Life, I could see, had suddenly gotten complicated for me. Especially so, as I'd still have to play my violin during band practice at school. And then I'd have to play this instrument at home. With my gloves pulled on tight over my hands.

And, my-oh-my, what gloves these gloves that mother soon had me wear, were; these gloves of mine would have attracted attention most anywhere, not just in Mrs. Hale's classroom. They surely would have, because my gloves were white, ladies' dress gloves, bleached white, and small in size to accommodate my underage hands. Attached to the backside of these, between my knuckles and each wrist, mother had sewn the large figure of a black horsehead. Just to make my gloves more masculine.

Your question now. In spite of mother's good intention as demonstrated by her installation of the pair of dark horsehead, why did mother have me don ladies' gloves, she having known well in advance that I might face a measure of ridicule from my classmates, especially at the ready hands of my male peers? Simple. Comfortable, breathable, gender-neutral, cotton, garden gloves would have been too loose about my slender fingers. Much too bulky these would have been for me to use when I played the violin. What's more, with the pimple infestation well underway then, mother feared that the supersensitivity of my hands' ravaged skin might be further aggravated by long, sweaty contact with any material that had been manufactured using a dyed fabric. Hence, in mother's view, black gloves to cover my hands with posed too much of a risk to my hands' health.

Unfortunately, with the exception of the few friends that I had yet to make amongst the kids in the schoolroom, my classmates had begun to think that I was afflicted by a disease which might be highly contagious. Even deadly.

Deadly? A deadly kid? Me? That thought damn near made me laugh but particularly the boys thought so. For sure, my malady of the skin, along with my unusual gloves, were freaking out many of the fellows in Mrs. Hale's classroom. In psychedelic colors, baby. The result was that even the meanest bullies amongst the boys in the classroom now feared for their own safety as though I were afflicted by nothing less than the bubonic plague, and, so would give myself a wide berth during the time that I'd wear my fancy gloves.

Yet, as I say, the downside to my situation was equally obvious by the fear and unpopularity that now surrounded me in the classroom. Oh well, I guess that some souls, like me, are destined to live out a lonely life—if this is the case, then so be it, I thought.

The year 1969 is long gone. But when it was not, I waited patiently. And when, at last, the day did arrive that I took my distinctive, never-to-be-forgotten-gloves off of my hands "forever," I knew on this momentous day that I had stepped back within the fold of the human race.

FOR OUR FAMILY, life at Apartment Five was nothing to complain of. Life for me at Kern School was now about the same. Since starting school at Kern I had gotten to know my teacher very well, and I would always remember her as a truly nice lady of character. Besides her being possessed of a caring disposition, a teacher who'd always support her students, the one thing which was obvious about Mrs. Hale on the instant that anyone first met her was that she was tall. Even from a distance as she sat behind her desk at the back of her classroom, it is the first thing one noticed about her. Tall she was for a lady. Tall, in spite of the fact that when a kid is only ten years old and short in stature, every teacher looks tall. (Hmm. Too much talk about tall people too often.)

I wish for you to understand that I have never run across a midget-size teacher in my life. And if you can follow my boy's thinking back in the late 1960s, I figured that all full-time teachers made a good living by teaching. Which full-time teachers did even then. A good living from a decent paycheck, which of course, allowed him or her plenty to eat. And thus, by this reasoning one might expect any teacher blessed with many paid hours of classroom time—to grow tall. Not short.

Because she was the caring person that I knew her as, Mrs. Hale had been quite concerned about me. At first she'd been, because I hadn't any friends amongst the other children in her classroom then. I didn't make friends easily. And I didn't find relationships easily because I was, and as you know still am at heart, something of an introvert.

In fact, the closest thing to a friend that I had back then was the basketball court. Here it was that I played in self-imposed isolation, away from my classmates. Thus I would always spend the morning recess and noon hour. Playing by myself with a basketball, while the other children took turns kicking a bigger, bouncy, red rubber ball over the baseball diamond. Of their use of the diamond, the listless spirit of Babe Ruth, if he was looking on at the time, surely couldn't have much liked what he saw. But sometimes, if he did happen to be near then, old Babe's ghost must have been pleased. And this was when the other children played the game that the diamond was intended for.

My loneliness must have been pretty apparent to the watchful eyes of Mrs. Hale then. Indeed, she expressed her concern on my report card. I guess that my solitary existence had not gone over too well with her. In time a skinny, straw-haired lad by the label of Jerry Bursack changed the course of the matter.

Jerry played in the school band. He blew air. Into a trumpet, that is. This was Mr. Buzzell's band, where I always squeaked the strings of my violin even though I tried my best not to. My overt incompetence on the strings was probably much to my music teacher's dismay. So I figure that Mr. Buzzell's heart must have been very large—because he gave me an "A" on my report card.

Swell. I of course did not deserve an A. But Jerry did. Unlike myself, Jerry was a born instrument musician. I shall always remember the evening that my friend blew hard on his trumpet before a packed auditorium, in a solo presentation.

Solo, save for the accompaniment of Mr. Buzzell's expert fingers on a grand piano. On that evening in mid-June of 1969 Jerry did what I could never have done. He stood bravely, square in his shoes, and played his youthful heart out. And the adult audience of mothers and fathers loved his marvelous performance right down to the last note he blew on his instrument. And him. I know because I was in the auditorium.

Earlier in the evening I had taken part in a presentation along with Jerry and the other student musicians in Mr. Buzzell's ensemble. When our group had finished its work, Jerry had taken the stage by himself. Trying desperately to remember, I nonetheless am unable to recall the name of Jerry's musical piece, though I do recall the fact that just as Jerry finished his one song, the auditorium burst into applause. Judging by the wild clapping of hands, everyone in the chamber then, knew that Jerry Bursack had become the instant celebrity of our school. And by his talented performance Jerry had earned every bit of that recognition.

A celebrity though he was, I knew Jerry Bursack very well as a person too. Jerry lived just one street behind our street. Jerry lived in a large old white house on Thirtieth Avenue. Jerry delivered newspapers. Jerry had a friend by the first name of Matt, and a girlfriend called Linda. Linda played a violin beside myself in the school band.

I remember the time during spring break when we three boys walked on over to Laurelhurst Park, which was about a half-mile from home. All of us were, one can say, a tad bored. So Matt, who was always a creative fellow, proceeded to lessen our boredom by resetting the controls guiding the path of spray on several of the park's sprinklers. His mischief done, now, instead of discharging water in a semicircle, each sprinkler sprayed water in a full circle. All over the sidewalk during the park's public hours!

The park caretaker soon discovered us, as we'd taken to running just ahead of a rotating sprinkler (in order to see which one of us boys could be the most daring, and escape getting wet). Well anyhow, after we were discovered, we got off the park grounds real fast.

I thought that my two friends were real cool. Especially Jerry. I figured that Jerry was extra cool because he had a girlfriend. Any fellow as cool as Jerry was, had to have a girlfriend. Jerry was a handsome boy and his blonde girlfriend Linda was a real looker. To this day I owe Linda a debt of gratitude, a debt that, naturally, I forgot to tell you about. I'm talkin' three months before Matt's sprinkler job would take place, on one afternoon in mid-January of 1969, with school barely finished for the day, I found myself besieged by my classmates. Excluding Jerry, Linda, and Matt. Under heavy bombardment I was in a snowball fight. I now call this friendly assault, pack mentality.

Like I said, Jerry was taking no part in the free-for-all then. Nor was Matt. But Linda. What did she do now? This. Linda rallied instantly to my defense. She probably knew, because she was well-liked—and a girl, that she was practically immune to assault by the surrounding gents as well as the ladyfolk of our class, who were all feverishly busy it seemed, trying to bury me beneath a landslide of snowballs. And even though it was I who was getting buried by the snowballs then, not Linda, I must give Jerry's girlfriend her long-due credit here. Must, because Linda had come to my aid and had stood her ground beside me. And even though this snowball fight had been all play, I respect the gesture. By deflecting some attention toward herself, Linda must have known that I would get an easier go of it.

I will never forget any of my three friends. As for the lopsided snowball fight itself on that January day—I was stung by more of my adversaries' projectiles than I care to remember.

I guess that stubborn resistance is the American way. Even in the face of overwhelming numbers. But I—and Linda too, are in no way different in this respect—that of stubborn defiance—from most people. When under assault, a body tends to fight with everything at its disposal. Just ask Bob A.

Bob was one of the biggest boys in Mrs. Hale's classroom. He was taller than myself by a good six inches. Bob was not fat. And he had a much sturdier physique than I. Not surprisingly, Bob was strong. Plenty strong.

Long after the winter's snows had melted, Bob sought to take his jealous frustration about his seeming lack of popularity in the classroom out on me. Bob had a well-planned strategy to his thinking. Bob had picked me because he viewed me as the weakest link in the threesome of Jerry, Matt, and myself. But in having picked me, big Bob had already made a big mistake.

Bob came at me in the hallway, one afternoon, after the final bell at school had rung. It was time for we kids to go home. The corridor that I took to exit the building was crowded with children. The attack was entirely unexpected. And cowardly.

Bob caught me from behind. I remember, somewhere in the upper back I felt the sudden impact. It was either a fist or an open hand, driven with powerful intent, that jarred me. As I turned around to confront my attacker, he pinned me against a wall, then—he began flailing away at me—with both fists. Now, I was pretty shocked by Bob's surprise attack. I knew that I had done nothing to Bob. And I never would have guessed earlier that he was near to losing his marbles.

Knowing me as well as you do by now, you will know that I have never liked people who have wished to use my body as a human punching-bag. And because of the righteous rage I felt, I didn't stand there in Bob's face, with my back against the hard wall for more than a second. My blood verily—nearly—boiled. I retaliated immediately, hitting Bob in return. Blow after blow with my fists.

In quick succession, as hard as I could deliver the blows, I hit Bob in the head and stomach even as Bob struck at me. Hit back in desperation Bob did. Yet, by the end of just one minute of ferocious seesaw fighting I had, much to Bob's dismay I'm sure, successfully repelled his attack and driven

Bob against a wall, himself. The stern voice of authority snapped me to my senses.

It was Mrs. Hale, who, being ever vigilant, had heard the bedlam from the hall. It was she who broke up our fight.

I am sure that Bob had learned a hard lesson: never again should he initiate a fight. And I surely hope that Bob's lesson will stay with him for the rest of his life. I know that I'd learned my lesson: know who your friends are—but paramount to that—know who your enemy is.

From time to time I still think of Jerry, Matt, and Linda. And when I walk alone off of the beaten path I sometimes tend to dwell on the question of whether Jerry eventually tied the knot with Linda. And if so, did they realize connubial bliss? Or did Linda marry someone else? Jerry and Linda. From the way this ten-year-old boy and girl got along then, I think that these two were custom-made for each other.

CHAPTER THIRTY-FIVE

WHEN THE MOVE FROM APARTMENT FIVE CAME, I was not surprised, simply because maintaining our family's existence within an urban townhouse had been putting too much stress on father, who had been looking for cheaper lodging to park us all in. No change here. Another move was all just a part of father's long-established pattern.

My parents had coughed up a mere two thousand dollars in cash. The former owners had moved out. Then we in the company of Kellosalmi settled ourselves into cramped quarters in a much-weathered narrow home on wheels.

No, not into a rail diesel car had we shoved our way into. No. This time our home was a trailer on a rented pad in the Portland Mobile Home and Trailer Court. I shall briefly describe the layout of our then-new environs before I commence to dwell upon the trailer itself.

The Court lay on a large flat field below a major thoroughfare called Union Avenue. A three-building department superstore called G.I. Joe's stood on the other side of the highway from the trailer park. I still recall the address of the park: 9000 northeast Union Avenue.

An artery of clear water, large enough to be noted as a stream, ran near the east end of the park. A busy manufacturing firm called Boden Brothers sat on a sizable section of industrial land; that was next to a low rise—on the opposite side of which was a ravine and the waterway. Looking down from a highway overpass in the year 1969 when I was there, both the waterway to the right of the overpass arch, and the trailer park to the left, were easily visible.

I haven't been back to visit my old haunts since I and my family moved back to Canada in August of 1970, and I have little idea what the area I speak of here has seen in the way of change. I know only one building still remains to house G.I. Joe's now.

As for the trailer: as you must have guessed from the price it sold for, it was an old trailer. Eight feet wide and thirty-eight feet long. This trailer had been built in Illinois, back in the thirties or forties; while still in the factory, it had been dubbed the St. Croix. That handle is what the nameplate at the bow, read.

In the summer of 1969 I wasn't too interested in the nameplate. The only thing I had to be interested in was the bleak fact that this timeworn relic would be our home for the indefinite future.

No sooner had the sale been consummated that father had begun work, making structural alterations. Within. But first without. Father first reshaped the bow, which had had an overhang built into it above the kitchen window that sat smack in the center of that wall. The helm of the kitchen had suddenly become from the sloped roof onward a vertical drop to floor level. To accommodate this change, in lieu of the original aluminum sheeting on the exterior, father had used a galvanized sheet to transform the hull. Throughout our trailer's length a faded coat of flaking white paint covering the aluminum shell was removed and replaced with a new coat of white, thanks to mother and her ready scraper, sandpaper, and roller.

It's father's turn again. Father had moved his attention and tools inside the premises. The kitchen sink had remained in its place during father's transformation of the helm. So had the narrow propane stove and the refrigerator. The kitchen cabinets father had had to modify and reposition, so that the single row of cabinets, which ran the width of the kitchen, now hung three feet above the sink.

Father had started his alterations at the bow, but now he moved backward. Using light of weight mahogany paneling, which was cheap and thus affordable in the 1960s, father then built a thin wall sectioning off the kitchen and living room area as one unit; to accomplish this father had had to tear down a preexisting wall, though. If there was a dining room to be found in the cramped kitchen, I didn't notice it. In fact, owing to the lack of free space in our home, father mounted his Admiral TV, which offered imagery in black-and-white as so many TVs built in the early '60s did, a couple feet above the kitchen counter.

This large portable TV father hung from the ceiling in such a way that it could be swung from side to side for better viewing because it was mounted from above to a swivel base. The TV had nothing but air between it and the counter. Four feet from the counter, father built for himself and mother a common bed. Not only would my parents sleep here, they could watch TV straight from bed. But let me be clear: both of them could not do both of those things at the same time. As a matter of fact, I have never heard of any couple that can.

My parents' tiny bedroom was so small that father's hand-built double bed had no more than a foot of leeway on mother's side of their bed. And on father's side there was but the side wall. Just two mahogany panels, each, one-quarter of an inch thick and separated by an air space of one inch, lay between the backs of my parents' pillows and my resting place in the next room, midway—toward the rear of our home.

As you might expect, my bedroom was not much of a room. It was more like a standard-size house closet. Father had made it so because space in our new home was at a premium. I have no special reason to complain now, because Helen's room, which was next to mine, was not one inch larger. And Helen was still bigger than I was.

Another flimsy wall of father's making divided our quarters. Just so that Helen and me would not get overly testy with one another in the small confines of our home and start tangling with each other's hair. In width, our rooms measured exactly five feet. In length, our rooms were five feet and six inches long. Sis, who was five-foot-six and still is, had zero inches to spare between her big, nasty-smelling toes and the side wall. Although I was shorter, my room was plenty cramped for me, even though the distance between my clean, nice-smelling feet and the side wall was a good foot. My observation: *The Road Warrior* would not have liked this setup.

With so little space for us to maneuver in, our storage compartments had to be built with efficiency in mind. That is precisely what father did. Beneath my bed and that of Helen's, father constructed two drawers from the same mahogany paneling that formed the partition between my room and my sister's room, paneling identical to that which he'd used on the wall dividing my space from that of his and mom's. Father had managed to tuck a drawer in his and mom's wood bedframe too—a fully walled frame he'd created that had a solid plywood platform to rest on, before he'd tackled the other rooms.

From birch-veneered plywood three-quarter-inch-thick, father constructed a door for every room in our trailer. These doors naturally provided access to the hallway beyond. Guess what? I soon realized that ingress to my room could be prevented while I was inside of it. All that I would have to do would be to pull out my bed's drawers halfway, to back my door. Since these drawers are attached to the frame of my bed, I thought, they'll combine to effectively block all unwelcome intruders from disturbing me; this will be convenient whenever my sister or brother will feel the compulsion to pick on someone smaller and still weaker than either of them. Whenever I'm threatened I can quickly pull my drawers out, and so prevent the undesirable party from entering my room. In an emergency with no option left to me, Helen, I can take on. (Not willingly of course, though I could.) But a physical fight with Raimo is out of question, I figured. So yes, my bed's drawers will come in mighty handy. Unfortunately, Raimo will get back to me, I thought.

There was one small window in my room. Another in Helen's. Each of these windows were identical, measuring about twenty inches in height and about two feet across. These windows allowed a modicum of light to enter our rooms. Both utilized a screw thread with a rotating lever that opened and closed them.

A small varnished birch desk with one drawer, a piece of furniture that father had modified from a cabinet, was mounted atop the wheel housing. The desk—and the housing that supported it which enabled the top of the desk to rise to a height roughly in line with the bottom of the window—were identical in my room and Helen's.

In these rooms, commencing from three feet above the bed and rising to the height of the original varnished birch panel ceiling, father constructed a vanity from a light tone of mahogany paneling. It was the same paneling that father had used to separate his and mother's quarters from my room. Intended for clothes, the vanity ran wall to wall for the full length of my bed. The doors of this cabinet would slide open in wooden grooves that father, the ultimate handyman, had cut with a self-made table saw.

Father had the ability to build a lot of interesting and useful things from scratch. Near the ceiling, above my desk, and Helen's on the opposite side of our wall—a wall which kept me from going insane—which I surely would have done had I been forced to bear my sister's company within the same room, father built two rows of shelves for books and other collectibles. One thing that father did not touch was the floor, which was dark-green tile and much worn. The other thing that father left alone was the birch ceiling, which was beautiful.

The hallway that led past my room and Helen's began in the comparatively expansive kitchen area and shot, as straight as a birdshit will drop under the influence of horizontal gravity, to the door of my brother's secluded residence, which, unlike the two other rooms, met the long, narrow hallway head on. Oh, I almost forgot. On the way to Raimo's place the hallway did streak past a tiny bathroom. More on that place in seconds.

Raimo's room was spacious in comparison to any other in our home. My brother actually possessed sufficient space beside his bed to enable him to stretch himself out on the floor, on his stomach, and do push-ups. Not that I can recall him ever doing any.

Added to privacy and space then, Raimo had for his private enjoyment three windows, one on each side of his room, excepting the wall of his room that abutted the bathroom. And not just three windows to surround him from which he could always part mother's homemade curtains to sneak a peek at the world outside. The world beyond his cozy room. No, brother Raimo actually had in his room enough space to store his few suits and dress slacks, etc., in a decent-size closet.

Yes, wonder of wonders, my brother actually had a closet in his room. A closet, in addition to a cabinet with drawers beneath his bed. A real closet, in addition to a row of cabinets above his bed. With so much space for his personal use, Raimo would live a favored existence amongst us all, I could see. And not just oodles of more space for him to roam. No, Raimo even had enough space to plant a full-size study desk beside his bed, with two whole feet of space between the two. And—my brother even had his personal exit!

Now, I shall describe for you our bathroom. In truth, this bathroom looked like it could only have been built for a race of constant dieters. Given the dimensions of the bathroom, it must have been. I have always wondered about the girth of the person, or persons, who designed it. This bathroom was almost too tiny for even Tiny Tim to have ever tried to sneak through on his way to find the ready-at-hand tulip patch. Please forgive me if I have paid an insult to your favorite flower. I do fully realize that most people do not harbor a patch of tulips inside of their bathroom. And with the near-total absence of outdoor light in our former bathroom (a handful of cosmic rays slid in under the door) I contest the notion that tulips could have survived for much more than one week in it.

To some folks, cultivating tulips inside a bathroom with sufficient sunlight may not seem like a bad idea, since the natural fragrance of these flowers should slightly help to mask the distinctly unpleasant odor that rises from the toilet after they attend to business in the morning. Myself, I would count on a high-powered ceiling fan, which we had not, to draw the odor out—rather than rely on Tiny Tim's favorite flower. Even a small open window, too small for your neighborhood burglar to crawl through, is better in eliminating unwanted smells than having your very own tulip patch in your bathroom.

Which reminds me. Our bathroom had no window. Not even a very small window about the same size that freaked-out passengers who are stuck below deck on an ocean liner which is about to sink are said to look through as they peer out of such on the face of a postcard. A postcard is not big. And even with the aid of a magnifying glass I have never noticed any frightened passengers staring out of the portholes of a ship on the face of such.

No window. Boo-hoo-hoo. No window until one awaited day that father eventually found the time to cut through the white paint and thin aluminum hull of our trailer and put a window no larger than a ripe, juicy, full-grown watermelon into our bathroom, so that we could all finally see the splendor of the great outdoors while taking a shower standing in the small bathtub, each in turn of course. But, with a window so tiny, it shall suffice for me to say that our bathroom was still a dark, forbidding place, even during the daylight hours when the light switch was not flicked on.

A sink and toilet of the same stingy proportions as the bathtub barely fit into the remaining space not taken by the tub. Squeezed in by design these essentials of a bathroom were. Yet again, who am I to complain now? The toilet seat fit my rear end without difficulty. But this worn seat, a veteran of the smelly scene, was barely large enough for any adult to sit on.

And all in our family soon found, each on his or her first sit on the poop-loop, that the walls surrounding the toilet were so tight about it that one had to be mindful of these walls, and, in accordance, lower one's elbows to avoid scraping or bruising them in contact with the partitions while wiping one's butt with tissue in such a narrow confine as this.

Beside' the risk of minor injury while cleaning one's posterior in such a dreadfully tiny space—working with toilet paper is delicate work. At least, it was for myself as a kid. A careless slip had a dramatic effect on the natural color of one's five fingers.

As we all know, I am not a captious complainer. Though, I *do very much* prefer to keep all of my fingers their natural color. I do not like to witness my fingers stained to look like dark chocolate. I am no racist by anyone's standard, either. It is just that my fingers are naturally pink. I like to keep them that way. I did when I was a kid and still do now. So you all see, my obsessive preference for my natural pigmentation is really only a matter of preference. You do understand, don't you? To deflect attention from my own obsession for clean, pink skin, let me ask you this. What would we all do without a bar of soap and running water in our bathrooms? See there. I gotcha!

Chapter Thirty-six

BEING A BOY, I had to get out-of-doors to explore my new habitat in detail at the first opportunity. Despite the shortcoming of our trailer with regard to space, the open countryside that surrounded our trailer park promised for myself, as I looked at it, an existence that was nothing like the lackluster life of a city slicker stuck within the confine of an apartment. No. Nothing like it. My new environment swore adventure. And to my untamed instinct the Boden Brothers' manufacturing plant was a good starting point in my quest for such.

I did not discover the whereabouts of the many treasures waiting for me to claim them from the large open garbage bin. But I know who did. Let me introduce you to Randy Dutton. Randy was about to begin grade four then, come September. Like myself, Randy would commence the new school year at Columbia Elementary. I knew from what Randy had told me, that the school lay on a large tract of land, very near to the bank of the mighty Columbia River.

I had not yet seen the building that would be my school. From Randy, I knew only that the school stood less than a crow's mile to the northwest of the Court.

Randy lived along with his mother, Hulen, at the far east end of the park. His mom, Randy said, worked in the trailer park's grocery store, which sat in a paved square; the store was just a block from our door. The park store was visible from our front window. A typical country store it was, owned by Mary Grant and her husband, Ronald.

Later, Mother would obtain a cashier's job in this store, as would Helen.

I had already been to the Grants' store several times, and I liked it for all the tasty treats a body could find there. Excepting my eczema, since I was a regular kid in a medical respect, it may surprise you all to learn that where my sweet-seeking youthful taste buds were concerned, my favorite filling was not a chocolate bar or a frozen confection. You may also have noticed that I did not use the word *food* in the preceding sentence. I said filling.

This is obviously not the kind of filling one obtains while lying flat on one's back in a dentist's recliner—that isn't food, only food is food. And this filling was meant to leave my hungry and aching belly appeased. Fruit pie is tasty food, and filling food. Num-num. To be specific, I liked cherry pie. Apple pie too. But because of its tart taste, cherry pie was my favorite.

In the last thirty-five years since I first walked into Mary and Ronald Grants' store, my preference hasn't changed one iota. Cherry pie is still my favorite even though apple pie ranks a close second, and therefore, deserves honorable mention.

I'd soon learn that the park store would consistently have both varieties. Wrapped in a richly colored, square aluminum pouch, a package not much larger than a handheld radio, I couldn't wait to sink my teeth into one of these delicious pies each time I'd bought one. And, one pie cost only a quarter. You know, I liked these pies so much, that I'd even purchase one for mother on her birthday, I just can't recall which flavor now. But mother's favorite always was apple pie.

I remember Mary Grant was somewhere in her fifties, five feet in stature like mother. Mary had fire-red hair, cut fairly short above the shoulder, the same style as mother's. And like mother, Mary was not overweight in proportion to her size. Mary Grant was a good businesswoman, and probably because of this it was Mary who worked in, and ran, the Grants' store.

White on top, Mary's husband Ronald looked older than Mary. Ronald Grant was not the hard-nosed business sort which you might expect to run a trailer park. Ronald Grant, who was father's height, was quite an easygoing fellow and perhaps for this reason more than any other kept himself out of the store his wife ran, he choosing to oversee the hired help that looked after the maintenance of the trailer park. From what I saw, both Mary and Ronald were not hard to get along with.

I figure that Hulen Dutton was then in her late fifties or early sixties judging by her gray hair. Hulen was a tall woman, who for several reasons reminded me of a cowboy. First. Hulen sometimes wore a straw Stetson during the summer. Aside from this indelible mark of the rugged American west to grace her head, it was her height as much as her laidback style which convinced me that Hulen Dutton would not have looked at all out of place on a white horse with a lasso gripped firmly in her hands.

Although, not always was her manner calm: I recollect that Hulen did raise her high-pitched authoritarian voice against Randy a few times when I had chanced to be within earshot. But never without some justification that she must have felt brooding within her. If my memory serves me correctly, Hulen had separated from her husband. Randy, whose father I never saw, lived in a fairly new mobile home then, with only his mother in the residence. The Duttons lived directly beside the highway that cut a swath between the trailer park and the Boden Brothers' firm.

Now, just how I'd met Randy, and how Randy became my friend, is a real mystery. I don't have any recollection of our first encounter. Perhaps I'd bumped into Randy as he was pedaling his bicycle in front of our trailer, on his way to the park store for a cool, wet, sweet treat, or a package of donuts.

Randy liked donuts a lot. Especially bismarcks. And when Randy had good company, he liked to share these in a tiny space that he had hollowed out of an impenetrable thicket of blackberry vines. (Blackberry bushes grew in patches, large and small, all over the countryside about the trailer park.) Access to Randy's open-air wilderness retreat was by way of a low opening he'd cut beneath the dense entanglement—a narrow tunnel which led upward a dozen feet or so into the steep hillside of blackberry bushes.

Here it was that Randy and I sat early one Friday evening, eating Randy's bismarcks from a package of twelve. Great fun it was too, except that Randy could have really used a couple of stools in his hideout. Of course, these might have rolled down the sloped tunnel. But not quite into my backyard because a row of trailers stood between the brambles and my place.

In lieu of stools, me and Randy sat atop a derelict piece of thin plywood that Randy had likely snatched from the Bodens' garbage bin. This, while we talked boys' talk and munched on his donuts as the evening sun looked on our activity, quite pleased that its tiring work on this day was almost done.

A few words or more about Randy's bike and other things now. Randy's low-riding bike was a pretty-aerodynamic-looking thing. Given this, his bike had the look of a motor-driven bike—a minibike—about it. And boy did Randy's bike look ever-so-cool to me, who as yet had no bike. I wouldn't until I'd buy a used one with my hard-earned money. I'll tell you all, about it soon enough. Right now, I prefer to tell you about Randy and his nose.

No. My friend Randy did not suffer from the same embarrassing inconvenience that first wrought havoc with the social life of one Rudolph, the jet set reindeer with the neon nose. No. It was just that Randy had an unwholesome habit. Randy, I'd discovered one day to my horror, liked to pick at the inside of his nose with his fingers. And it was because of this habit of his, a habit I at my enlightened age now thought gross, that our friendship would nearly end on a weekend afternoon. It was an afternoon when my friend, just prior to his departure homeward, decided to leave a half-inch-long booger, partially solid and partially not, on the edge of our kitchen porch.

Thoroughly lambaste that booger if you wish, but I shall be brief in regard to Randy's not-so-welcome gift then. I didn't appreciate Randy's act and I told Randy so. Randy then told his mother how I felt. Hulen then queried me as to why I no longer wished to play with Randy. Hulen Dutton did not think Randy's deed much of a crime. But I still did. And I told Randy's mom to make sure that Randy would leave no more mementos of this kind attached to, or about, our homestead for our clan to gaze at in wonder. Hulen must have given her son my message, because Randy did no more of the same. My mother it was who cleaned Randy's best regards off of our front porch, using her broom.

On to more important and less taxing matters. Let me go back to the waste bin at the Boden Bros.' factory, just so that we can rediscover what I found amidst their trash that would instantly bring a smile to the face of any poor lad. I must give Randy Dutton his due here because, as I implied before, it was Randy who led me to the treasure trove at Boden. Credit, even though I know that I would have discovered their G-bin in short time, anyway: the plant itself was in plain view from the highway.

What intrigued Randy and I was the fact that some real nice odds and ends of building material were often relegated to the Bodens' trash bin, material that we boys well knew still had usable value. Not as firewood, either. Although, there was much firewood to be had for the taking.

As I muse over our many discoveries then, I shall mention first a couple of non-ligneous items I'd found in the Bodens' bin, courtesy of the American way; a system of largesse to me and my friend I remember that way as. Leftovers that these had been, it appears that such had represented only waste to the Boden Bros.' establishment.

Given what we boys would frequently find in the bin then, I at times tend to wonder, like at this moment, if some of the guys who worked at the Boden Bros.' plant back then might have intentionally discarded perfectly usable material into their mill's refuse for their own purposes, during the day. Only to return at night, or on the weekend when the factory was closed, to drive away with the deposited booty. Perhaps. Or maybe the foreman slept on the job. Or. Maybe the proprietor just did not care. I don't know. But here is what I'd found amongst the usual trash. Laminated plastic sheet, manufactured for use in surfacing counters. Not big pieces. But large enough to fit a stool seat. Or a small tabletop. Pure aluminum moldings. These strips ranged anywhere from a few feet to ten feet long.

In 1969 aluminum molding might have been inexpensive enough to throw away. For some people. Throw it away, the American way. Yet, I know that aluminum strips nowadays, when found in reasonable quantity, are worth real money. In fact, at most any junkyard in North America the staff will charge about two dollars U.S. for just one pound of pure aluminum scrap.

Back to then: I'd already hauled a nice batch of the strips home, and father had used them to fashion the frame for an awning over our front entrance. Father had been pleased with my find. And he'd encouraged myself to find more. So I'd set out on a second trip to Boden for more of these.

With the aluminum that I dragged home, father soon built an awning over our back porch; oh, I hadn't actually dragged all these metal strips home. I hadn't, because by the time that father was ready to build the second awning I had already managed to acquire a bicycle. And I was glad that, although I'd been burdened by a great many pieces of molding, I had not wound up impaling anybody with the sharp ends of these "discards". Especially glad was I, since I carried no liability insurance whenever I rode my two wheels. Inasmuch as I'd not caused an accident, I supposed that my evil eye had to have kept innocent bodies far away from my path.

In the Bodens' bin I almost always found short pieces of wood that were mainly stock some two inches wide and three-quarter-inch thick, up to four feet long. Softwood. And hardwood that looked like oak to me—nice strong stuff to make cabinet frames from.

Which is what I believe that the employees at Boden used the hardwood for.

But danger lurked in the trash bin too. One had to be careful while searching for treasure inside of it because there was the ever present odd nail driven into a block of wood, with the sharp point and most of the long shaft sticking up in the air. A careless step here could mean a rusty spike in one's foot, I knew.

Occasionally, I discovered a marketable beer bottle in the garbage, though this was seldom. More often, I found bottles that were no good for a refund. And because these bottles were always bone-dry of beer, I figured that the blue-collar chaps who toiled inside the plant probably worked so very hard that, in their desperation for moisture, they sucked out every ounce of beer.

Succinctly, on one visit to the G-bin I recall feeling heavy and uncomfortable with a full bladder. Quite badly I had to go for a leak then. Now, as I peered within the bin I noticed one small empty bottle lying amidst the waste of a manufacturing operation. I knew the non-refundable bottles by sight. And I knew that this particular bottle was no good for a return. No matter. I reached over into the bin and grabbed the bottle.

I saw no one in sight. Right to left, front to back, there wasn't a single probing pair of eyes in sight. I was perfectly sure that there was nobody in sight. After all, the factory was shut down, this bein' a Sunday evening in the beginning of August.

I wasted no more time in looking about for any possible spectators lurking in my general vicinity. I laid open my fly, and peed my sincere regards into the beer bottle. This was almost like me now goin' to a self-service gas station. Fill it up! I was able to produce enough of my best juice to fill the bottle.

Next, I set about to find myself a cap. I knew that there were always a lot of discarded caps from beer bottles lying in the dust beside the bin. I looked about, and I soon managed to locate a forlorn cap which exactly fit the amber glass bottle in my other hand. Then I made use of a small flat rock to hammer the metal cap onto the bottle. By that I mean the edge of the cap. An edge that a bottle opener had once twisted and disfigured. I made sure that I had a snug fit.

Fighting the urge to giggle, I then placed the "full" beer bottle in the middle of the Bodens' loading dock. Lest you judge my activity then, with scorn, please note that I was only trying my hardest to be as helpful as I could. While working very hard on a hot day, a man could work up a terrible sweat, I knew. A working man could die from thirst, I knew. I had a sincere respect for those pangs of thirst.

Too, I appreciated a good laugh. I called the stuff that I'd made, "Roy's Bubblee Brew". R.B.B. And, if thee many are at all wondering about my consistency of production, I shall have you all know that I still make plenty of Bubblee Brew every day, but I no longer package the nourishing liquid so nicely.

Also, if anyone happens to be wondering about the "best" and "very best" Bubblee Brew, the recipe for sure success is this. The "best" Brew is aged in a bottle of dark glass or plastic for about a month, while the "very best" Bubblee Brew should be left alone to ferment in a dark, warm place for one year. Even two years. Or more.

Should any of you have any doubt about the potency of this recipe—I can assure you all—do not worry. By any such time my recipe will pack one very, very, very powerfully putrid punch. And a final note: My recipe is not to be confused, under any circumstances, with any drinkable punch.

Chapter Thirty-seven

AUGUST OF 1969 PASSED INTO HISTORY. It is September. It bein' so, I shall tell you about my life at my new school, Columbia Elementary, now.

I had just turned all of eleven years old in the last month. I am enrolled in grade six. And my homeroom teacher is Mrs. Wells. Mrs. Wells is in the vicinity of fifty years old. She has long, curly, auburn hair, and as I will find out later, she can be both amiable and stern.

Flash forward more than three decades. Yes, I recall that my teacher was stern, all right. Mrs. Wells once seized my scalp hair in her viselike right hand and drew me clear of my chair. The reason? We students were writing a test then, and Mrs. Wells wrongly assumed that I was cheating.

I solemnly do swear that I had not been cheating. My teacher had caught me peering inside of my desk. It was an act that looked to her as being more than just a suspicious act then. And even though I was totally innocent of any wrongdoing, my teacher appeared to believe firmly in the principle—*thou shalt not peer within thine desk whilst a test is in progress*. Not only that, further—*thou shalt be considered and treated as guilty until proven otherwise*. Let me state here that I do not believe in cheating on a test. In grade six I could not have agreed more with my teacher's distaste for cheaters.

But let us not forget what I have said here. That I was entirely innocent of the crime I now was being accused of on this day. No matter. Mrs. Wells, being Mrs. Wells, would not relinquish her iron grip on my scalp hair a whit, until she realized the horrible error she'd made. Seconds before, with my scalp stinging with pain, I had protested: "I was only trying to find my pencil". (I'd said so between my clenched teeth.) After all, a hand cannot write without a pencil.

I'd known straightaway that I had a point. But my teacher's reply had been tart: "Then you should have asked for one." With those words, Mrs. Wells had finally released her powerful grip on my head. And, although our encounter had been brief, my scalp still hurt. Emotionally.

Mrs. Wells bade me to follow her to her desk, which stood, as teachers' desks usually do, at the front of the classroom. I obeyed my teacher. Mrs. Wells reached for a pencil, from amongst several that always sat in a tall cup atop her desk, and handed it to me. The pencil had already been sharpened. For this fact, and the pencil itself, I was thankful. I was thankful, too, that my "hair-raising" experience was over. I returned to my seat, and Mrs. Wells said no more.

As of the present, I still object to the unjust, rude, and rough manner my teacher had treated myself on this one day, for, as her action had expressed volumes, like Mrs. M (the scoop about poop) years before—Mrs. Wells had given me not the benefit of a doubt. She never formally apologized to me, either. And so, I still ask myself this question. Whatever happened to the age-old principle that all of us are to be judged as innocent until proven otherwise? A good question it is, because a disheveled desk in which a pencil might easily lie concealed from view, or a pencil stolen by another child from one's desk, is no excuse at all. In the view common of some folks.

Believe me, after this run-in with my teacher then, I, as a child of eleven years, understood perfectly well why it is that totally innocent people—good people—are sometimes convicted by the American-style judicial system. Convicted of a crime that they have not committed. Are convicted wrongly, then are sent to jail by cantankerous, befuddled, geriatric, nose-picking judges who likely rely on super odor-crushing activated charcoal insoles in their shoes to address the noxious stench of their feet—as these would otherwise foul the air in many a courtroom in the U.S. of A. and Canada. I figure that each magistrate who acts in this manner, and I'm referring to zilch to do with the stinky feet here, should stick his or her pinkies up his or her nose, so that he or she sneezes. This act, gross though it would be, might release from within each of such every ounce of obvious pent-up anger for the world. By dynamic expulsion. Enough!

Oh, dismally crude though her mannerisms still seem to me, I know that Mrs. Wells did not hate me. I know, because Mrs. Wells once did myself a kind act. Perhaps, in part, my teacher did the following in an effort to try to make up for what she had done to me earlier. Mayhap this, in part, was Mrs. Wells' sincere attempt to make amends. An apology of sorts. Well disguised, though.

AT COLUMBIA SCHOOL we pupils were required to take part in scholastic activities beyond the confine of our homeroom. These activities had been formulated to fit within mini-courses, called modules.

When I'd first heard the term module, I'd thought that this word sounded like terminology to be used only in conjunction with the word, lunar. That is not surprising to me now, because this was the school year of 1969 to 1970 in progress, and the astronauts of NASA, Neil Armstrong and Edward "Buzz" Aldrin, had barely finished stompin' on the surface of cratered green cheese, one-quarter of a million miles distant from our homeworld. Jumpin' around like two curious kangaroos, in our moon's wimpy gravity, they'd been.

Back to Earth now. One of these modules at my school, which on recollection were each a couple of months in duration, could, for instance, teach a kid a simple thing like how to build a kite. Preferably—the proper way. Yep, I'd picked that course. Mrs. Moonie taught it. And yes, to answer your unspoken question, Mrs. Moonie, so far as I was aware, was indeed a transplanted alien migrant who had managed to escape from lunar soil, bearing a false passport. And, armed with only this important piece of documentation 'sides the clothes that she had stolen off a visiting astronaut from Earth, apparel which she now wore, she had cleverly conned both the FBI and CIA, as well as every teacher and student at my school, into believing that she was human. Even everyone in the whole world. Except me.

Naturally, being a moon person who wished to avoid being scrutinized too closely herself, Mrs. Moonie, who probably could also have used spectacles, did not look too closely at my kite, and unwittingly she'd end up according me a better grade for the construction and subsequent performance of my kite than I deserved. Oh, I *had* manufactured, with no aid, a device that actually flew. But hey, accidents can happen to both the brightest and dumbest amongst us, right? (No comment please.) Not always being the first of those opposites, in this instance I had failed to heed "Momma" Moonie's meticulous instructions. I had attached the twine to my kite on the wrong side, *and* my line was too short.

Only a light breeze was blowin' on the dry, overcast afternoon when I and my classmates took to the school's large grass field. As Mrs. Moonie watched her other students' creative successes take to the gray, threatening sky, one after one with little effort, I soon discovered that I had to run like mad to make my kite rise toward the heavens, its skyward advance limited by the length of my twine, and the fact that my bird flew upside down.

Fortunately for me, with myself running feverishly on the ground, my kite maintained a height of a few hundred feet. And for this convincing presentation, the success of which I attributed to my desperate running rather than my poor carpentry, I received a "2" or "3" as a grade on my report card, I can't recall which. In Canada, my mark being equivalent to a B or C. Not bad, considering that I had botched my project, *and* conned my teacher.

What about the other modules I'd chosen from a selection of mini-courses? At Noel-time one module involved the Bethlehem scene of nativity. Yes. I had picked drama class as one of my choices. In keeping with the part that I played, I'd had to don a white robe and pretend to be one of the trio of wise-men-kings who had journeyed from this weird-sounding place, a name which had never caught my ear before—Orientar. The other representatives of our threesome were played by my classmates, Tony—a tall, muscular African-American boy, and a white kid called Ron.

Ron was a nice guy. A peaceable sort. Tony was a nice guy too. Usually. I say usually because Tony belonged to a pack of four, and someone from this pack once slipped a thumbtack onto the seat of my chair in Mrs. Wells' homeroom.

Of course, having suffered a run of bad luck for much of my life up until this time then—I could not expect a sudden change in my fortune. I sat atop the sharp point and got my rear end punctured.

As we all know, a thumbtack is really a small, short nail. And it will hurt a soft, tender butt, unprepared for the shock of the inoculation, to sit on one. I had no trouble identifying the guilty party by the mischievous smile on the face of each of my tormentors. In fact, armed with this evidence, I promptly reported the foursome of Tony, and Harold, who was another black boy, as well the likely culprit—a white kid whose name was Bruce, and their friend Chuck, to Mrs. Wells.

Though Chuck belonged to the pack, Chuck was not a bad kid. And Chuck had probably been nothing more than a spectator to the crime. Even so, all four of these dudes clung together like their asses had been stuck together with Zany Gloo.

Yes, I ratted on them. But you know, it was my ass that one of these fellows had gleefully chosen to rudely perforate.

In hindsight, I suppose I am fortunate in that I don't suffer from the life-threatening condition of hemophilia. Plenty angry, I'd had no choice then but to spill the whole episode to the only person who was likely to do a thing at all about this incident. Whereupon the *Funtastic Four* accosted me during phys. ed. class, on the grass field behind our school.

And it was, you know, four against one. And—such odds were very heavily stacked in favor of my elimination from ever being considered as a healthy-looking candidate for the cover of some glitzy swimsuit mag, specializing in photos of subjects with lean, tanned, unbruised faces and bodies. Ever? Well. Almost.

Never in my life have I looked like anything as massively powerful as *The Incredible Hulk*. Deep inside, I had always known that I could not, even in a rage—or in my case then—more like a chimp's tantrum, ram my fist through a steel wall, one foot thick. Neither have I ever been hideously green. I knew that I could not hope to drive my tormentors away by ripping my shirt open at the chest to flash my body color. A full spray can of skunk odor might have done the trick. Yes, I did not have any such irritable and feared weapon. And, as frightening as my poop smelt in the toilet at home every morning once I unloaded the contents of my intestinal chamber into it, the unholy odor had always failed to cling to my body after I first learned to use tissue paper as a small boy.

In fact, my lithe, smooth, untanned and untoned body neither looked nor smelled bad enough to scare anybody away. Except, unfortunately, maybe the hottest chicks.

Tony and Harold were, by far, the biggest and, by far, the strongest guys in Mrs. Wells' class. Bruce was taller than myself by a couple inches. Only Chuck was my size. I shall not despair here overly much because, this many years later I am still alive and breathin'. So, to fast-track a hopelessly long account of reality to its inevitable end, it was to turn out on this day on the field at Columbia School that I would escape corporal punishment by playing stupid, and, by assuming an air of disinterest in any entanglement which would surely have soiled my clothes with my own blood. Some people who might not like me, might argue the point—but I gainsay that I am completely stupid.

Anyhow, it seems that I was talkin' about modules when I got sidetracked. Sidetracked, like I always do in life. Drama class was never my interest as a boy. Never my bag. Stage drama was just too frooty-tooty for me. Too much make-believe with silly characters. All too much for my practical mind then. Indeed. There were no acting parts for any of my favorite crime-stopping comic book inhabitants here! So. Geology was more like it. Geology was more in the groove. I had always well remembered the beach of ocean rocks at Campbell River. I had remembered because I guess that rocks still meant something to me. Rocks still mattered. Being part of a module class studying rocks then, I was asked to take part on an excursion into the mountains. This field trip would turn out to be a one-day adventure.

Everything for me would have proceeded without a hitch. Then I forgot about my geology teacher (Mr. Jacoby) who'd insisted that each child remember to have a parent, or the child's legal guardian, fill out an authorization form allowing that child to go on the trip. In my mixed-up life I could often have used an extra guardian angel to look over me. (Besides mother, who always was an angel to me.) Just to make sure that I wouldn't have screwed-up along the line of life (I *always* did). Nor got taken advantage of by older people. My forgetfulness then, now brings me back to Mrs. Wells' attempt to make amends for her having laid hold of my scalp. My teacher's quite informal apology: Mrs. Wells used her own car to drive me home. I obtained mother's signature, allowing myself to attend Mr. Jacoby's field trip. Mrs. Wells—had apologized.

Get back to that nuisance of a field trip I must now. In one sentence: Pretty much a snooze trip. As such, this trip is not really worth me wasting your valuable time and mine, having me bore you all with details of it. Please don't anyone dare get me wrong, though. Please. Remember, I do like rocks so very much. I sincerely do. Coconut's honor. Or whatever.

The Earth is made of rock. Everywhere that we look on the land, there are rocks. And back at home, in the hay fields about the Bodens' factory, I'd quite often find on the ground where the earth had been cut into by heavy machinery, a black rock with jagged edges. What this rock was, I'd known not at the time of my first having encountered it. But wherever I had found it lying on the ground with its grayish-white, rough and hard, egg-like shell cracked open, thus allowing the light of day to shine on its black inner beauty, I'd observed that it had a fine sheen to it, which reminded me of Alaska black diamond, a stone that I happened to be familiar with because mother had a fine pair of matching earrings made of that semiprecious material.

Even though I didn't know what the common black rock was, I suspected that it was of volcanic origin. So, at home I consulted my encyclopedia. I found in its voluminous interior the answer to my question. It turned up in my book that some American Indian tribes had once used a very hard flint-like stone, which shone like black glass, to tip the shafts of their hunting arrows with. The points of these arrows were hard enough to withstand a substantial impact. And, the soft hide and flesh of a mule deer, elk, moose, or buffalo, can't be said to have been hard for this material to have penetrated through into the vital organs of these animals.

This rock, called obsidian, will, when sharpened to a point and driven by a flexed bow's lethal force, slice through bristled hide with the ease of a table knife through hot butter. I have always liked pretty stones, so it stands to reason that I like obsidian. But you knew that. Didn't you?

BACK TO SCHOOL. I sat at the back of Mrs. Wells' classroom. Next to a short, blond-haired kid by the name of Danny. I liked Danny because Danny had experienced a hard go of it, as the saying goes. A hard go of it since the time of his birth. As a newborn, Danny had required an incubator to keep him alive. Danny had been born prematurely. And though Danny's severely sloped forehead was the only telltale sign that the boy's past was not quite like anybody else's in the classroom, looking at Danny from a short distance then, anyone who had not met him might have wondered whether Danny's physical deformity was an indication of compromised mental capability. In Danny's case it wasn't. Danny was not stupid. I had found Danny to be a nice kid.

Then, there was Steve. Steve, whose surname, like Danny's and many other kids' from my distant past, I've plumb forgotten. Like Danny then, Steve was a little different from the other kids in the classroom. Steve had a peculiarity as visible as Danny's forehead. Steve would move his long neck about in a swivel-like motion, slowly, from one side to the other. It was a movement which kind of reminded me, at first, of a giraffe. Kind of, because Steve was a tall, thin kid. And as each student sat behind a desk in the classroom, the awkward-appearing twist of Steve's neck did not go unnoticed by the other kids. Some of my classmates initially thought Steve was just kidding, putting on a show. Other kids believed, when they spoke of Steve in his absence, that the boy was conducting neck exercises. It wasn't too long before Steve's classmates realized that the oscillating movement of Steve's neck was involuntary, and that Steve suffered to make the motion.

I still don't know what the cause of Steve's disorder was.

I didn't know much about Steve, except that he lived with his parents on a houseboat moored along the waterfront. Steve's home lay on the broad Columbia River, little more than a bird's fart from school as I like to put it.

In Mrs. Well's classroom there was another Steve. He was someone who was always intent on amusing himself at the expense of his classmates. Like for instance—me. The most interesting thing about this Steve was that he was not a stupid kid. Just aggressive. Like a weasel. Steve was not big for his age, either. Only my size in height and build.

It was on a warm, sunny afternoon in early spring of 1970, while we students stood as a large pack waiting in the schoolyard for the door of the school bus to open, that Steve chose to try his luck with myself. He picked a fight with me.

Or more accurately, it was a skirmish. A brief episode of violence which ended in a draw. I have to be honest about Steve here and hand him some credit. Being as he was then, the kind of kid whose instinct drives him to seek the thrill of a fight, prior to our confrontation Steve had picked up more than the odd pointer on how to fight, from his previous engagements. And of such events I am now sure that there had already been more than a few in his life then.

But I'd been no pushover. I figure that I must have convinced Steve of that because the boy never sprung himself on me again. Given the many years that have passed, I remember our scuffle only as having been a stand-up shoving and wrestling match with ample boisterous encouragement having been thrown in for either side by my classmates, who'd watched our activity with keen interest. This violence, of course, having been necessary to liven the afternoon for the spectators, and—for Steve himself who always liked excitement so much.

Fight-hungry though this Steve always was, he was as I say, not dumb. I figure Steve's mistake in picking his fights was that he never seemed to care enough about himself to be impressed by the fact that his violent behavior might well prove to be his undoing, someday.

When it came to fighting, Steve never really learned anything of true value from his past mistakes. I say that, because one year earlier Steve had tangled with a lad whose first name was Cory, in the school gymnasium, while the entire student population and every teacher of Columbia School, had watched. As we all know, I did not attend the school at that earlier time. But I'd heard of Steve's and

Cory's public grudge match as soon as I'd begun attending class at my new school.

Here's a flash recap of their fight. Oh, for a run-through on the combatants—Steve, you folks already know well enough, now let me introduce Cory to you. Cory, I knew to be a fairly behaved youngster who was very methodical in everything he did with his hands. Cory, who was roughly Steve's height and weight and therefore weighed about the same as myself, possessed a knowledge of both basic boxing and wrestling maneuvers. Cory was wiry, agile, and he was lightning-quick with his hard, bony hands. With those hands of his, coupled with his wiry triceps, Cory had the power to hit plenty hard with speed.

Not surprisingly, with such favorable credentials to back his opponent, Steve could only quickly discover that his much-hyped fight with Cory would turn out as nothing less than a monumental disaster for Steve then. Indeed. Steve's and Cory's fight, which was a classic boxing match with these boys wearing real boxing gloves and boxing trunks, would be over almost as soon as it had commenced.

Ding! That's the bell. The two fighters warily circle each other. Oh!!! There it is. Cory just struck Steve hard! A jackhammer blow! A mighty right that was that connected—square in the nose!!! The punch must be stinging Steve fairly because Steve looks panicky and, the hardwood floor of the gym is tasting his tears of mingled pain and frustration now. With Steve's eyes lookin' now like they're blurred of their fine vision by the saltiness of his tears, and with his aching nose looking like it's possibly shedding some blood, the fight is now being called to an end! Cory is being declared by the referee—as the victor!!!!

Wrap up the time reel, the fight is over.

In retrospect, prior to their public match, I guess Steve, being as disposed as he always would be to seek out for himself the thrill of a fight, even if this clear tendency of his would land him in nothing but trouble, had trod upon Cory's toes a trifle too often. And on this day when these boys slugged out their dislike for one another, Steve paid the price of public humiliation for his reckless animosity.

In summary, one can say that Cory succeeded in hammering the daylights out of Steve's nose, and appeared to have won the fight handily. Yet Cory, as good a pugilist as he was, did fail in one regard. Cory failed to hammer the tenacious spite out of Steve's enduring spirit. In this twisted sense, I suppose one can say Steve won an honorary victory because he still managed to cling onto his injured pride. Certainly, ready he would be to look for trouble on that other day with me.

HERE AT COLUMBIA SCHOOL it was that I received a grounding in industrial education. Or just shop as we kids knew it then. The industrial ed. workshop was located in the basement of my school. It was in here that I had cast a small soap dish from blue resin. Once I had taken my piece out of the plastic mold, I should have first filed, and then sanded, the bottom, which was rough. But I hadn't because I was too uncertain of my capability to perform even such a simple task well. In fact, quite fearful was I of ruining the dish then. After all, I had something to lose. The resin, catalyst, and coloring agent I'd used to cast the dish had cost me a quarter. Unfinished though the bottom was, I nonetheless carefully wrapped it up for Xmas and gave it to mother.

It was in shop that I also learned the skill of using a band saw. I had cut a six-inch circle out of a thin sheet of red Plexiglas. Thereafter I proceeded to file, sand, and use the buffing wheel on a grinder to finish the rough edge that the saw had left. Then—it was all up to Mr. Long, my shop teacher.

Mr. Long heated my project atop a hot plate that he had set on low. Carefully, Mr. Long arranged five round wooden pegs into the shape of a star, on a small wooden board into the top of which holes had been drilled. Then my teacher donned some leather work-gloves, and taking the acrylic disc off the burner, placing the disc on the pegs, he firmly pressed down in the center of the disc with a can of Comet cleaner.

The finished product, courtesy of Mr. Long's experience, had turned into a dandy candy dish. I gave this project of mine to mother too. For her birthday. Mother's present was a gift of love from me. Wonderfully pristine. This is but a memory. Memories are all that I have left now.

Chapter Thirty-eight

OH YEAH. The ultimate question. Did I have a girlfriend yet? Well. No. Not really. Not a steady girlfriend. But I did sort of have a girlfriend. Sort of yes, though she likely considered me more of a friend than anything else.

This girl was tall. Taller than myself by more than just a couple inches. And this girl was, I thought, full-bodied in all of the right places. I s'pose you all know what I mean? Oh, you don't? Well, how about if I just say that she was the ideal weight. Not fat. And not as skinny as a toothpick, either. Her hair was as dark as midnight. Thick it was, though it was always cut short above her shoulders. And this girl's face was pretty enough, I thought, and I never failed to take notice of her whenever she was close by. Her name was Vickie Hayes.

Vickie was a student in Mrs. Wells' class at school. Vickie lived in our trailer park, on the nice, newer side. She lived on a wide, well-paved street with an impressive-looking string of modern mobile homes on both sides of it. Vickie did not live in an ancient, beaten-up trailer like my family did. She lived in a newer, first-class mobile home, along with a younger brother and her parents.

Like I said, Vickie was a friend from school. She was, er, just a friend. I say that with mixtion, er, I mean conviction because, even though I well knew the pad that Vickie's parents' mobile home sat on then, I never dropped by to visit Vickie; that'll tell ya that the two of us were not good friends; the hint is that we just kind of got along like friends whenever we ran into one another. Now, in July of 1970, with school out for the summer months, I chanced to run into Vickie as she was walkin' by on the road in front of the trailer park's outdoor swimming pool. And uh, in a moment or two I shall explain to you why it was that Vickie would be present at poolside on this one sunny, hot, summer midmorning.

I had swum in the park pool on each baking summer day ever since my family and I had vacated the apartment at Thirtieth Place. In fact, had any of you happened to come by on most any day in the summer when the weather permitted it, you would have found me not only here in the pool but in the pool's deep end. Deep being the eight feet of water required to fill every full-size pool. Or, almost as likely, you could have caught me in the shallow end of the pool, because I would, as was my wont, spend a good hour or more between ample breaks traversing back and forth, underwater and above, 'tween the deep end and the shallow. Only to return to the deep.

And besides the fun of slicing through the wet like a fish—when I dove fully erect from poolside, I would search the bottom of the pool with eyes as keen as those of a hawk's—for the few pennies, nickels, dimes, quarters, etc. (never did I find quarters or coins of greater value), that folks might have devested themselves of in the chlorinated depths of blue. Whether their seeming generosity was by accident or intention did not concern me. Some adults, I knew, did throw small objects, even coins, into the pool just so that the young kids would make a splashy and amusing spectacle of racing one another in their attempts to retrieve and pocket the treasures of the depths, whilst other grown-ups, those with loose pockets in their swim trunks, probably lost currency by sheer accident.

I shall explain why Vickie was now present at poolside. This is as easy for me to explain as my eating a piece of cake. No contest even. I have the perfect alibi: the park rules forbid that anyone venture into the pool without someone in attendance who would watch over the swimmer. The reason? When alone, people have drowned even in their bathtubs at home.

Anyhow, I was now in the water. And Vickie, who had agreed to baby-sit me because of the park rules, was in her blouse and shorts at poolside. Everything was perfecto. I had not been in the drink for more than a couple of minutes with my girl companion watching over myself, when guess what? No. Vickie did not fall into the pool so that I could do the manly thing and rescue her tender tootsies from further hardship. No. Nothing that romantically picture-perfect.

Rather. Something perfectly awful happened next. What else could it be, you fine folks should ask of yourselves. This. With Vickie looking on at poolside—along comes sis. And guess what? How on Earth it was that a fairly emotionally-distant creation like my sister could ever detect my preadolescent crush on Vickie, I don't know, but detect it Helen did.

I know that Vickie had sensed something in the air too, because Vickie instantly withdrew into herself. Vickie knew that Helen was my big sister, so what gives? You know what I think? I think Vickie knew that I liked Vickie in the way that a boy likes a pretty girl.

Vickie, I saw, had sensed my unease when Helen had dropped in. Preteens are often ill at ease when an older sibling unexpectedly shows up. They are—when one of the younger ones is a boy and the other is a young girl. Somehow, Vickie knew exactly what I was thinking at the time. Somehow, Vickie correctly interpreted the *sudden change* that had come over me. Vickie knew exactly why I had, well, kind of stopped talking to her.

That was not good; although, I wanted to cool things between myself and Vickie mighty fast just then. I now call this, to you all a seemingly benign event little doubt, by an appropriate name. THE BIG CHILL. Vickie knew that I was dreadfully afraid of being made fun of by an older sibling for talking to a pretty girl at poolside, a girl who was my age. A girl who was clad only in a *light* blouse and shorts.

If Vickie had been unaware of my interest in her before my pool debacle, she sure did know it now. And she probably felt ashamed of me for being so cowardly that I did not wish the truth of my feelings toward her to come out into the open. Ashamed I was of myself. I should have done otherwise, even if it had meant that an older sibling would, as a result, make fun of me, I'd soon think afterwards. Come to think of it, maybe Vickie Hayes does kind of like me, I thought. As a girl likes a handsome boy. Maybe.

What I was sure of then, is that this had been a golden opportunity for me to meet a pretty girl who was my age, in privacy. An opportunity that had somehow slipped through my grasping fingers and gotten lost. Know what I think now? This: Perhaps I was only dreaming. Maybe there was nothing for me to lose to begin with. If Vickie did like me some then, as a girl likes a boy, perhaps she did not see myself at eleven years of age to be tall enough, and muscular enough, to be seriously considered as her future love-interest. I am knowledgeable enough in the ways of the opposite sex to know that physical bulk and raw muscles always go together as one very desirable plus-factor when it comes to the preferences of most pretty and physically beautiful girls. Too, in regard to girls as individuals, my premonition is often remarkably accurate.

Vickie Hayes may have fallen seriously in love with, and eventually married, this hunky dude at school, a fellow by the first name of Ed. I figure that could be, because I had seen Vickie's blue eyes sparkle with excitement and admiration during noon hour at school when Ed, an electric guitar in his hands, had strummed "Secret Agent Man". A guitar that Ed had been smart to have brought from home. Chicks. They always go for the big, brawny guys.

The worst part of this very sad matter then *was* that I never heard the end of the verbal jabs about Vickie, which Helen would level at me whenever the devilish mood seized my sister, for the next ten years to come. And this, by far, was the worst part.

NICE GIRLS are different from boys. I say this because, being, as they should be, members of the gentler sex, nice girls are above doing nasty things like boys do to one another. Girls in general, I figure also, are in some respects more sensible than boys. Not just because girls do not fight amongst themselves as much as boys do, but because boys can act like complete idiots in many another way, as well.

Just so that I can prove to you the validity of my belief, I offer you a very good example. I truly hope that you shall not mull long over this that I will reveal here—before you cast your lot with my side in the court of public opinion.

Here be my case. Some adolescent boys feel that they need a *blood* brother. A skinny, straw-haired, freckled kid from Alaska, by the name of Bob W., felt this way.

Did I look gullible enough to be a suckhole, or what? I still wonder. I do because, you see, Bob wanted to use a weird rite of his to initiate me into his pack of three friends then. I may be wrong on this point, but I believe that of these pals of Bob's, only one was not a younger brother of his.

Today, I happen to believe that peril often abounds where the innocence of crassness exists. In long ago yesterday I did too: the procedure for my becoming a bona fide blood brother, sounded, when I'd heard Bob describe it, like something that might have been concocted by similar age boys as we, boys who'd lived in some small remote settlement in the frontier days of Daniel Boone. Without television, boys who'd been bored nearly stiff by lack of their having had any superhuman heroes to gawk and marvel at on the boob tube. If this particular theory in bored stupidity is correct, I thought, then indeed very bored boys those boys must have been to have wished to slice their own wrists with a sharp blade.

Listening to Bob talk of the carving job he had planned for my arm (the right arm or the left arm doesn't make any difference in this bizarre undertaking, either), the slashing itself was, according to Bob, just a small inconvenience, after which each boy who took part in this ceremony would then rub the other's wrist, dripping with red blood, with his bleeding own. The gruesome act was intended, Bob said, to mark a pact. This pact required that each participant be willing to risk his own life, if necessary, in order to save the other (or others) should an emergency requiring that decision to be acted on ever arise. And, always to support one another to the max in any social situation. All this, whilst uttering profanities laced with a healthy dose of black humor.

Unfortunately for Bob's riveting bloodletting idea, which Bob went to great lengths to describe in gory detail, the sight of fresh red blood dripping from my wrist did not at all appeal to me. And for this reason I had to decline Bob's generous offer to have him slit my wrist with his switchblade, and make a mess of my perfectly good right, or left, arm. Some kids! They are so lonely and desperate to make new friends, and so very bored, that what they sometimes will do for companionship and excitement— frightens even me. And believe me, in the lazy days of summer when there is not much for most youngsters to do, many a boy of ten, eleven, even twelve, will be just too bored to act like anything other than a boy.

By the way: Bob's bloodletting rite may well have had its origin in American native-Indian custom. But whether it did, I shall not hazard a binding guess. As such, I belatedly apologize to Bob for my having to deny him a slim chance to gain credit for creativity. Myself—I have never fancied as any true talent at pretending to be novelist James F. Cooper's *The Last of the Mohicans*. Yes! That's so BLOODEEEE right! A Mohawk! And if not a Mohawk, then whomsoever it was who'd invented the blood-bonding ritual.

Chapter Thirty-nine

"SNICKELFRITZ." Our next door neighbor, Dave P., called me by this somewhat obnoxious handle. Sure, I called other people names, too (in light of this, I shan't be too hard on Dave now). One dude I called, Groovy Groove. I called him by this name because this blond-haired grown-up chap resembled in every detail a comic strip character by that name. And once, I called him that right in front of his blonde bombshell of a girlfriend. I granted the young man this much—he had excellent taste in women.

Unfortunately, Groovy did not appreciate my labeling him thus, and probably the poor fellow had no clue to why I called him that. I guessed that the man did not read Saturdays' comic section in *The Oregonian*.

The Groovy Groove in the comic strip was cool. *I* have, as you know, always wanted to be cool. I figure that, to be cool—one has to imitate other people who one believes, look cool. Or, those who are cool by the way they acquit themselves. To be truly cool, one has to do one's very best to imitate cool people. Just like a monkey does.

About Mr. P now. For the payment of a measly dime, Dave once drafted me into his employ. Dutifully I kept my evil eye trained upon his trailer while he enjoyed a daylong excursion to Seattle, with his wife and small baby boy.

This is how the preceding would become reality. The P gang left on their trip in the late morning of a Saturday. With low wages having been the norm in the 1960s, I guess Dave had figured that an eleven-year-old boy with no job experience could easily be sucked into providing maximum security for his home and belongings at a pittance. Sometimes I wonder whether I really am, er-make that *was*, terribly stupid. Ah, that Dave. He was a shrewd one.

In keeping with Dave's verbal contract of employment then, I kept watch over Dave's dig from Saturday morning into the afternoon. Then, as the long hours stretched interminably onward and twilight set in, I began to wonder whether Dave and company would return home before it was my bedtime.

As the clock struck nine in the evening, I made a decision. At this hour I decided that continuing my vigil over Dave's premises for a mere dime just was not worth me staying on the job any longer. I had been a faithful employee all day long and now it was time for Roy-the-boy to retire. And apart from the late hour, Dave had not paid me in advance. Reasoning thus, I quit my surveillance of Dave's place from our kitchen window, a job which had been for myself—literally—a pain in the ass. Aside from my sore butt from having perched on a stool throughout the day, the telling hallmark of a lengthy, top secret operation nagged me. I had a stiff neck from having stared at Dave's abode all day long.

I still sat atop the kitchen stool, this while I engaged in conversation with mother. I was no longer looking at Dave's place. I was no longer on the job. No longer was I waiting for Dave to show up. Almost an hour flew by.

Mother felt sorry for me, and she made me a peanut butter sandwich. I wolfed down the sandwich like any hungry man would've. I was about to head off to my room and prepare myself for bed. It was ten o'clock in the evening now. I went to my room. Then I heard it. I finally heard what I had waited all day long to hear. My keen jungle-trained ears caught the unmistakable sound of a car engine. Then silence. Followed by the slam of two car doors being shut simultaneously. There was a pause. Then came a knock on our kitchen door.

I still had my day clothes on, and knowing that it had to be Dave, I started on my way back to the kitchen. Mother beat me. "Roy," mother beckoned as my feet and legs took me to our front door. Our late evening visitor was Dave, all right.

"Howdy partner," said Dave, as cheerfully as a spring chicken emerging from a five-minute nap. Dave did not look tired at all. Not like myself at this late hour for a kid. Dave slid a dime into the palm of my right hand, as full payment for my guard duty. To my surprise, my neighbor made no mention of the fact that I'd departed from my post of duty early and had left his home unlooked after. I suppose that Dave knew me well enough to know that I had stayed on the job as long as any kid with a bedtime curfew of ten o'clock could have been expected. Of course, Dave didn't know about my curfew. Still, he knew that I was a good, reliable kid. Not a kid who would easily shirk my contractual responsibility.

"Thanks," I said to Dave for his dime.

"Good-night Snickelfritz," he said.

"Good-night Dave," I replied.

Dave got himself a real deal that day. Mind you, I wouldn't lift my pinkie for ten cents now. But way back in 1970, an extra ten cents in my pocket made me a small fortune richer. Ten cents then, was still a lot of money to me.

I say this not just for his money: a nice guy my usually distant pal Mr. P was.

The only thing about him which I found really annoying was that Dave frequently would lounge in a reclining chair with his bare feet stuck right in my plain view, behind his kitchen window.

This in itself would not have been upsetting to me. I only found it distasteful when I ate breakfast, lunch, or dinner at our kitchen counter. Quite so, because the thing about Dave was that he did not like to leave his two chubby feet alone in peace. No. Dave had a habit that was quite miserable for anyone to watch while that observer happened to be eating. Unknown to Dave, I soundly cursed him every time that I caught my neighbor engaged in this, to me, despicable activity. Every time that I was desperately trying to chew on a mouthful of food whilst at the same time keep myself from puking from within my gut the slimy contents of what I'd already managed, through great effort and suffering in having watched Dave, to consume.

In fact, I used to powerfully feel that there should have been a law, either Federal or State, to ban what Dave always did with his toes. Dave, you see, had a fetish for picking at the crevices betwixt his ten toes. And with my curiosity bein' what it is, I still wonder, from time to time, whether Dave ever found anything interesting wedged between those toes of his.

Now, I'm a nice guy too. Just like Dave, minus his affliction. And, I suppose that since I am a nice guy, I should hand Dave the benefit of a doubt. But seriously, I do hope that my then-neighbor Dave bathed his feet with soap and water, before he did what he did.

The senior Mexican couple who lived in a newer, spacious mobile home on the other side of our trailer had no habits of interest to me. None that I could spot from my bedroom window, anyhow. Like Dave and his young wife, our other next door neighbors were nice folks. Their last name may have been Gazzara.

"LÄTTÄ LÄTTÄ" AND "ROADRUNNER" NOW. These curiosities of the human species were not our neighbors. Yet, considering the amount of time that each of these women, mother and daughter, managed to fritter away inside the public washrooms across the street from us then, any casual observer who would have happened to come by our trailer park and who would have happened to witness the amusing antics of these elderly gals, might well have been led to believe that this mother and daughter team actually lived in the restrooms, I think.

The mother of the colorful pair, Lättä Lättä, I figure to have been in her late eighties or early nineties. Lättä Lättä, leaned more than a bit toward the chubby side then. But, despite her excess body weight, and considerable age, she appeared as fit as a fiddle.

Lättä Lättä's daughter, Roadrunner, who looked in her very late sixties or early seventies, was much leaner. This did not surprise me because Roadrunner, in action, was a veritable dynamo.

We in the family called Roadrunner, Roadrunner, because her favorite pastime was to run in and out of the washrooms. I had noticed that Roadrunner and Lättä Lättä usually carried a faded gray rag in one hand or the other, and I supposed the daughter and mom team used such to tidy the inside of each washroom with. This included both sides of the small building that consisted of the restrooms. Both sides Roadrunner and Lättä Lättä looked after. Both sides, yes. Mens' and ladies'. Every day of the week.

Roadrunner was not hired help of the Grants', nor was Lättä Lättä. And why anyone on Earth would spend every day, between meals and personal business of course, venturing in and out of restrooms was beyond the comprehension of anyone in our family, particularly me, Helen, and mother too—when mom had free time to take notice of the two women. In truth, all three of us were equally amused by watching the show that Roadrunner and Lättä Lättä put on.

To be fair as I must, Lättä Lättä wasn't nearly as odd as her daughter. Lättä Lättä wasn't as obsessed with keeping the washrooms clean then. To be fair, Lättä Lättä wasn't too odd, I think that she was mostly, just old.

Incidentally, Lättä Lättä, to satisfy your curiosity, means squat squat. In Finnish it does, because this word, lättä, describes a quantity lacking in height, thus—a squat person. I believe that my mother had coined this name of Lättä Lättä. And I am fairly sure that it was Helen, sis always having been the evil one in my mind, who'd conjured up the rather cruel name of Roadrunner to describe Lättä Lättä's daughter.

I shall not reveal in my narrative what this mother's and daughter's first names were. I can't: I don't remember more than a single first name. And the duo's last name, or names—in the event that one or both of these women were married then, I have no knowledge of now. Anonymity, I feel, is a good policy to follow when describing people who, though I strongly doubt it after so many years having passed by now, might still be alive and offended by my descriptions of them—should either mother or daughter ever happen to find this book in her possession.

As for Dave P., I am not worried about him at all. No, because audacious Dave had had the incredible nerve to call me Snickelfritz. It's my turn now. I shall make my pal Dave more careful as to who, he calls what. But—I don't want to see Dave sweat, any more than Dave himself does. Ah Dave, he always did have such a great sense of humor. Now that I think of it. And I hope Dave still does. Truly I do.

WHEN I STOP TO THINK OF IT STILL, the Boden Brothers' garbage bin was one heck of an interesting place for myself to visit and rummage through as an eleven-year-old boy. Beside' the many treasures that I discovered in the receptacle, a short fifty feet from the waste bin then, was a long row of blackberry bushes. This was of interest to myself also.

Speakin' of berries, I know that "Grizzly" Adams, old mountain coot that he was, would tell you that black bears like blackberries. He would, if he were alive today. And grizzly bears enjoy the slightly tart taste of a wild vine-ripened blackberry as well. At least, they did in Oregon until the 1890s, by which time every wise grizzly had been driven off the land. And those grizzly bears that were not driven elsewhere had met their untimely demise by lead slugs. These slugs had a rather nasty way of bringing closure to all matters of contention.

Enough about the gray bears' woes in the history of Oregon. Let us consider the blackberry itself. Wild blackberries taste about the same as domesticated blackberries. If there is such a thing as a civilized blackberry, that is. To myself, all sweet edible berries are a real treat. Each of the blackberry groves, for—there was a parallel grove of the luscious fruit on the opposite side of the Boden Bros.' factory then, should have been called, Garden Grove. And these rows, they crawled along the earth right to the highway shoulder in front of the plant. If I had been brought into this life as a bear, I would have hugged the earth here— on either side the spot was densely packed with the vines of the tasty wild blackberry.

I don't know of any folks who've sampled a fresh succulent blueberry, raspberry, or strawberry, and I'm no culinary guru on the topic of berries, and declared the taste of the fruit a trifle on the dull side. But if any have, those folks would probably favor the biting taste of the wild blackberry in comparison. When the wild blackberry is truly ripe it is delicious. At least, I have always thought so. Like the raspberry and even more so the strawberry, the blackberry, the civilized variety or not, packs a healthy dose of ascorbic acid (I believe it is likely this acid that imparts a sharp taste, but since strawberries are supposed to contain the most ascorbic acid of all berries, I can't explain why blackberries have a sharper taste—maybe mature strawberries contain more sugar than ripe blackberries—such would effectively cloak the strawberries' greater content of ascorbic acid), which we all know as vitamin C. And I am sure we know that without this precious vitamin we would all be lying still in the grave, dead of scurvy. Scurvy, the dreaded scourge of any old-time pirate or honest seaman.

The only negative side to the wild blackberry that anyone who wishes to pick the fruit will have to contend with is the challenge presented by the blackberry plant's thorns. Thorns that can easily impale or scrape one's exposed hand or arm. Or bite through one's trousers into the meat of one's legs with the same efficiency as the needle-sharp tines that grow on your grandmother's favorite rosebush. I know that the former have scored my flesh too many times in the distant past. It's why I eventually learned to treat a

337

blackberry vine with the same degree of respect I have for your grandmother's rosebush.

Here is some advice for the blackberry enthusiast. Thick leather gloves can absorb the effect of the thorns. *I* don't like leather gloves because leather is manufactured from animals, animals that have suffered when they were killed for their skins and meat. So, leather is far too cruel a material for me to wear nowadays. However, I do strongly recommend that *you* wear some kind of gloves when you are picking either blackberries or raspberries. Wild or not. Even if the loss of touch in your fingertips slows your picking down a bit, you should wear gloves.

It is a good idea to wear a thick glove on each of your hands, regardless of whether you use one hand, or both, to pick the fruit. With gloves on your hands, you may find that you crush a few more berries than you will if you do your picking without them. Yet, the protection offered by a good pair of gloves is well worth your wearing these.

My motivation to wrest the wild blackberry from the vine to home was powered by temptation. Mother made excellent pie from the blackberry. Like I said in other words, the wild blackberry provided a zing always quite refreshing, a crispness in flavor that other kinds of berries just do not possess. Excluding the civilized cherry. Cherry pie is the closest thing to blackberry pie, that I know of.

Mother also utilized the blackberries I had picked to make blackberry juice. I've read that blackberries make for excellent wine, and that means they may alternatively be turned into cider, I think. Though, I confess that I have never heard of blackberry cider. How about a frozen treat made from blackberry juice and sweetened a little with sugar? Yep. Mother made that also. In fact, mother could do some amazing things with so little then. She would make use of anything that I'd happened to find out in the field, which could be used as food. Vegetables and fruit. Not insects, no grass, and no leaves; these mother definitely did not want.

One interesting feature about the wild blackberry plant is that it does not grow well in hot, dry zones. The blackberry plant prefers cooler weather, and above all—moisture. On the outskirts of Portland, where we lived, there were wild blackberry vines scattered all over the rural landscape. You sort of knew that already. Or did you?

During the two summers that we lived in the Court, mother would sometimes join me in the Boden Bros.' blackberry patch. Just the two of us. Enjoying each other's company while we spent a pleasant morning, or afternoon, picking the wild fruit.

SNAKES ABOUNDED IN THE DARK DEPTHS of the blackberry patch where the light from above scarcely filtered through the maze of thorny vines and leaves. The particular snakes that I am about to tell you of, I later identified as two distinct variations of garter snake.

Owing to their copious numbers, garter snakes were quite a common sight in the patch. One of these variations of the garter bore the usual pair of yellow stripes; regardless of what color the stripes are, these always run from head to tail along the back of the serpent. Locally, garter snakes colored thus were known as yellow racers amongst the school kids of my age. The other variation of the garter snake less frequently spotted was the rumored-to-be more aerodynamic red racer.

Reports among the school children had it that the red racer climbed trees, whereas its yellow-striped cousin stayed low to the ground. I knew that to be partly rubbish. With my keen young eyes ever alert in the patch, I had come upon the occasional red racer slithering along the ground, but never, had I seen snakes of any kind draped about the branches of the cottonwood trees that rose majestically out of the earth as they shone their indifferent gaze on the still blackberry patch.

Although the brambles never moved, the airwaves about the Boden Bros.' plant were anything but dead—as the deafening roar of a huge electric fan impinged upon the ears of anyone who happened to be in its vicinity as it spewed fine dust into the air.

The particulates coated the blackberry patch. In summer, when we picked the blackberries off the vine, mother always found it necessary to thoroughly wash our pickings in the kitchen sink. Unusual though I thought it to be, this coating of dust was pure white, a color which caused myself some concern as to the nature of the sprayed matter, for, this dust appeared more like drywall dust than wood dust.

The mice and gray hare that called the dense undergrowth their home did not seem to notice the dust, albeit downright skittish the rabbits were. Perhaps the latter knew what the dyed-yellow rabbit's foot that hung from a short chain attached to the belt at my waist, meant. If so, I belatedly extend to all of rabbithood its credit, now long due. And if these wild rabbits inhabiting the bush and tall grass about the Bodens' plant then actually knew what my grisly souvenir meant—then they sure were a lot smarter than I ever did figure them to be.

Just so that you know and do not assume that I'd done the horrible deed myself, I shall mention here that the severed and dried rabbit's paw had been bought from a store. Unfortunately, I had purchased the item.

I will say here that, at the time I'd bought the rabbit's foot, which some folks consider an item that will bring the bearer good luck, I saw nothing wrong with what I had done. Nowadays, my philosophy has changed dramatically, a change evident in the comments I made earlier in my narrative. Nowadays, I'd almost like to chop the legs off the fellows who'd amputated so many poor rabbits then, even though these must have been rabbits that were already dead, rather than alive, when they were deprived of their forepaws. Not that the morbid practice of some callous jerk "harvesting" the legs of a rabbit after its death should make much difference to me in comparison to my view of the greater crime, but only because I now view all meat farms as immoral. Yes, you see, to me dead-meat-to-eat is immoral, regardless of what species of animal the meat is from.

Besides that, let me tell you—my luck, seldom good, never got any better with that chopped-off rabbit's foot hanging from my belt. I return to what I was talking about before by saying this. No rabbit who lived beside the Bodens' enterprise ever did seem to pay any attention to the dust.

Neither did the snakes. Although, I must say that I have never known snakes to advertise any feeling they might possess other than to aggressively display their fangs, and hiss savagely when they are cornered. On account of the considerable time I spent picking berries in the blackberry patch then, I think it fortunate for me that there were no rattlesnakes lying about. And the common garter snake was of no overriding, practical concern to me then, as this species of snake never attacked me.

The garter snakes were fairly small: on average, a foot and a half in length, and, thin in girth. And since the garter snake, unlike the venomous rattler, has no poison tooth—I paid the garter snake little respect.

I knew the nonexistent combat capability of a garter snake against a human, as did the other boys of my age. As would have these boys in my stead, the vulnerability I'd soon exploit to the fullest. I was an eleven-year-old kid. And uncivilized.

Snakes, in general, have always made the fine follicles of hair growing out of my skin, stand. It might be a blistering summer day under the sun. But whenever I spot a snake— any kind of snake—on the loose—I instinctively recoil within myself. Instantly, I will feel ice-cold with tension: in this I react as though I am reacting to impending danger.

I suppose that I respond thus because all snakes are cold-blooded. All snakes look slippery of skin. Kind of slippery in a deceitful way. In my estimation, all snakes look quite ugly. They look like the opportunistic creatures they are, which prey on smaller animals in nature's food chain. Snakes hunt, kill, and then eat. To me, all snakes are therefore despicable.

One can say that my ongoing dislike for all species of snakes mirrored itself in my behavior as a boy, my sense of revulsion toward all snakes, big or small: a sense of loathing can cause a boy to act uncharacteristically.

I had another friend. A boy whose first name was Eddy. Last name? I can't remember. Unlike my chubby friend Randy Dutton, Eddy was a skinny kid. Like myself, Eddy was in grade six. Eddy's family was poor. Eddy had a younger brother too. My friend Eddy was a good kid, who had been brought up in a farm environment. Yet, regardless of the environment in which a boy is brought up, be it on a farm or in the city, most every adolescent boy has a dark side to him. A side that his parents may never see.

I admit that my sense of revulsion toward snakes was not the only reason that I would do what I would do with Eddy on one day in the summer of 1970, and I strongly suspect that, for Eddy, the same thing was true. True, because on a warm and bright Saturday afternoon with time laying heavy on our hands, me and Eddy made fast work of a small colony of yellow racers. A dozen snakes in all. Within a matter of five minutes elapsed from the time that we'd discovered the tribe of snakes, we had stoned every yellow-striped garter snake that belonged to this particular lair, to death.

We, not the den of snakes, had been the aggressor. As our actions had told, we, not the snake, had briefly descended to the level of brutes. Long years later, I now regret my action on that day. On this day in the distant past, my revulsion toward the lowly snake had combined with my wish to draw blood. And other than my revulsion toward the snake as it is a predator, again—an ugly-looking one at that, I can offer no understandable excuse for what I did with Eddy on that afternoon. I know that a thirst to witness blood is not an excuse. I know it now. Thirty-four years later in time. Sadly enough, most boys and men have this hang-up. Especially those of us who hunt or fish for the purpose of recreation. I do not hunt now. Nor do I fish.

Notwithstanding the reputation of women as the gentler sex, I know that wilderness type women do exist, who hunt and fish like so many recreation-seeking men do.

Spilling blood for the purpose of spilling it. I believe that all of us mentioned here, all of us in the so-called human race, would do well to learn to better control our unrefined impulses. I hope that I am not alone in this realization.

As you can see, I am not proud of what I did on that long bygone Saturday afternoon. And I have tried to forget about the incident ever since I realized the folly of that other way. I can do nothing else now than salvage a small measure of grim solace for myself, knowing that what I was thirty-four years ago—I am not now.

The ground lay bright red with blood about the snake den. I looked at Eddy. Eddy looked at me. We both looked at our handiwork. Eddy seemed in a hurry to leave. He soon did, walking slowly by himself along the highway toward home.

I still wonder if Eddy ever thought about the matter further. Was the slaughter of a den of snakes just another day in the life of a farm kid? Like I said, Eddy was not a bad boy by disposition. Eddy was a good, peace-loving kid. Just like myself.

Earlier in the year of 1970, with the arrival of Easter, Eddy's parents had given their oldest son a small basket of colored eggs. These, Eddy had brought home to mother. For this gift, mother had thanked Eddy. My mind opens wider a door to the past.

Mother, always sensitive, was deeply moved by the generosity of spirit that Eddy's parents had shown toward us. I had already told mother and father about Eddy. While mother did the dishes, father listened as he ate supper in our tiny kitchen, he atop a bar stool of his making. The next morning, a Sunday, father and I went shopping with a single purchase in mind.

Father drove us to Safeway. There, I bought a basketful of colored eggs with money that father had given me for this purpose. Asking me for directions first, father then drove his red Rambler sedan, a car that he had traded his aged Volkswagen van for at a local used-car dealership, straight to Eddy's place.

Eddy's home lay on a familiar route for father, who worked, just a short distance from here, for that motor-rebuilding enterprise I mentioned before, Machinery Sales. Despite the title of this firm, which may suggest to you that father worked for this company with his neck stuck into a clean and fresh-pressed white collar, father was no salesman in their office out front. After all, father was an industrial electrician and this is the nature of the work he did for the small company.

We had already arrived at Eddy's place. Stepping out of the Rambler, I knocked on an old, weatherworn gray door from which the paint had begun to peel. A door with no window and no peephole. I noticed, too, that large slivers of wood had fallen off from each corner of the door frame.

There was sound coming from inside. I heard loud voices. The commotion drew closer to the door. The door opened with a rusty screech. The hinges need to be oiled, I thought. But that thought immediately deserted my mind as I looked into the eyes of a familiar dark-haired, middle-aged, slender woman who peered from the doorway.

I needed not to introduce myself to the lady. I already knew Eddy's mother. "Here," I said, smiling. I handed her the basket of Easter eggs.

"Oh! How lovely. A basketful of Easter candy!" Eddy's mom insisted graciously with obvious delight, though from the expression on her face I knew equally well that this lady was taken aback by my reciprocal gift.

As I spoke with Eddy's mother, I looked to either side of her, my gaze drifting well past her into the interior of the family's ground-level apartment. I noted that neither Eddy nor his younger brother nor the boys' dad were anywhere in sight within. I would have asked Eddy's mother if Eddy was home, but I well knew that father, always temperamental, was impatiently waiting. Knowing this, I hastened to explain to Eddy's mom that I had to go. "Anyway," I said, "have yourselves a happy Easter." I bade Eddy's mother farewell and jumped back into the Rambler.

I felt good. And all that I'd done was to return the generosity and warmth that Eddy's family had shown toward our clan. It was only fair. Eddy's family was poor. More so than our family. For Pete's sake, Eddy did not even own a bicycle. Neither did his brother. The boys' parents had simply been too cash-strapped to buy their boys such an expensive item. Eddy's parents were so poor that they could not afford to buy either of their sons a used bicycle which the boys could have shared. For our family, to have received a brimming basketful of eggs from such an impoverished family as Eddy's was nothing short of monumental selflessness. These words of gratitude are intended for each member of Eddy's family.

I don't know whether Eddy's mother worked outside of their home, and what type of work Eddy's father did, I no longer remember. This was a long time ago, you know. A time when the west was still the wild west. A time when almost every boy that I knew imagined that he wore a six-gun on his belt. Loaded and ready to play.

'SIDES EDDY AND RANDY DUTTON, I had a friend who I can actually call that. His name was Bill Bennett. Bill was a lad from Montana way. The home of vast blue stretches of sky. Bill was in grade seven, and he was a bit taller than myself. He was slim, even bony. Just like Eddy.

From what he had told me, I knew that Bill liked to hunt. And I never liked to listen to his accounts of him and his (dad) shooting up some poor moose, or a deer, each of which belong to magnificent species. I didn't think that shooting an animal like a helpless doe, or even an antlered buck in its prime, was any sport. I never would come to know whether Bill and his dad had hunted in Montana, during autumn, for recreation and meat equally, or mostly for fresh meat to put in their freezer for the winter months.

I knew that Bill's parents, like mine, were not rich. Even though I'd never visited Bill at his folks' place a couple of miles from home, I did know, from what Bill had said, that his family lived in another mobile home park. They lived in an old trailer, scarcely more luxurious than our own. In regard to hunting, if you'd asked me whether Bill had ever *actually* pulled the trigger *himself* when he had been out in the bush with his dad, my answer would have been, I don't know.

Except for the den of snakes Eddy and myself exterminated, I never did any hunting.

Sure-sure!

Okay-okay! One exception. This! Save for a few hundred very lonely and bloodthirsty mosquitoes I'd seen fit to vanquish during my earlier boyhood years, I never did any hunting.

Yeah right, sure-sure. Think we can't read and remember, silly?

Okeydoke—I return to Bill. Like Eddy, Bill was a decent boy. And like Eddy, Bill exemplified all that was good about America.

Bill had straight brown hair and he was dark of skin like a sun-beaten Indian of the Great Plains. I never knew if Bill was part Indian. Though Bill might well have been endowed with the blood of Cheyenne, Shoshone, or Sioux, I did not ask Bill about his blood heritage. And I did not ask him about that because I did not want Bill to feel any different than my other friends. As you will expect from my earlier comment regarding such, I have never been racist and I do not think highly of people who are.

As I say, I don't know whether Bill had Indian blood in him. What I know is that Bill's survival instinct was like that of an Indian brave. This instinct manifested itself in a little sermon Bill once gave me. We boys were at G.I. Joe's then. Bill and I were inside the building that housed the hardware department. Anyhow, Bill queried of myself as to whether I was feeling at all hungry. This was a Saturday morning. About half past ten. In answer to Bill's question I replied: "Nay". Even though my belly could have accommodated a cheese sandwich, I wasn't too terribly hungry so early in the day. However, on this midmorning Bill had already worked up a healthy appetite himself: he'd pedaled his bicycle two miles from his home territory.

Bill slid a quarter into a vending machine advertising an assortment of canned soup products. Then he made his selection. The machine spurted out a tin of soup. Now as Bill peeled open the lid on his tin, which on recollection was a beef product, Bill told me sternly: "Never," said Bill, speaking as though I were just a year-old child wrestling in his own diaper, "pick a candy bar before you head out into the bush, if you can have a tin of soup with the same amount of money. In an emergency the soup'll keep you alive longer".

Though Bill's short speech sounded a bit overcooked to me then, ceremonial if you like, Bill gave no other indication of his act. Albeit, true to his spoken words, my friend had chosen soup. Soup! Yes, soup—when he could have gotten for himself a fabulous chewy bar of Oh Henry! This power pack of sultry, hunger-piercing chocolate, liberally jollified with delicious peanuts—Bill had given up. Unbelievable.

And yet, debatable though his belief was, Bill's decision showed his woodsman's will to survive. Any candy bar packed with peanuts will contain a lot of protein. A small tin of beef stew does also. The innate difference between these foods is that the candy bar will provide both energy for quick release and peanut-sourced protein to lend staying power. Enough about soup and candy bars.

Chapter Forty

MORE ABOUT BIKES AND THE BOYS WHO RODE 'EM. Like Bill himself, the cool, streamlined machine he rode was tough: Bill's bicycle had seen much use. Bill's bike had been built in the same style as Randy Dutton's two wheels. The racy appearance of the boys' bikes was no fluke; despite their small wheels these bikes could move. Neither bike was a ten-speed, either. In fact, both bikes were gearless. In Bill's case, the fact that his bike was without gears did not deter my friend from pedaling like hell, literally pushing the faded, medium-blue, tubular frame he sat astride into rocket-like acceleration.

Since the latter half of the 1960s when it first appeared on the scene, this style of bike, built to resemble a minibike, has proven so popular amongst preadolescent boys that it is now as common as American apple pie. Whenever Bill came by our trailer park, he came on his bike. And often, Bill would challenge me to race him on my two wheels. Oh, I forgot to tell you the account of my acquisition of an easier and faster means of locomotion than my legs were capable of providing me.

My means of transport, though arguably just as fast as Bill's, was on sight nowhere near as streamlined. The perfect word that I shall use to describe Bill's bike then is—sleek. My bike, you see, was just an ordinary fifteen-year-old bicycle, originally purchased from Montgomery Ward. Hawthorne, read the label beneath the handlebar. My bike had been designed to be a classic bicycle for adults.

My bike, unlike Bill's or Randy's, was, in fact, a bicycle that had been built to carry an adult rider. My bike was not a kid's bike.

My bicycle was black. And I'd picked it up for an asking price equivalent to its age. Merely fifteen dollars. Still, in 1969 this had been a lot of money for myself to dish out for a used set of wheels. But I had wanted to ride a bike badly—ever since my first bike, back in San Diego, had been sold prior to our move north. I'd bought the Hawthorne from an elderly chap who lived on the opposite side of our trailer park's swimming pool.

The sale happened this way. I had scouted the community bulletin board at the park store and come upon the ad for the bike. Being just a raw boy then, once I saw something that I had an overpowering desire to own, an item not beyond the scope of my limited monetary worth, I was not one to procrastinate in my decision-making. I'd decided on the spot that I wished to own a pair of wheels once again.

Lacking a writing instrument and paper, I'd memorized the phone number displayed in the bulletin. And once I was back at home I had immediately delivered the important news about the ad on the wall at the grocery store to my brother, I requesting his assistance. As this was a Saturday, a time when Raimo was not busily engaged in any activity of importance to himself, he decided to accompany me to the residence where the bicycle was being offered for sale, just to make sure that I would not be taken advantage of. When money, even a small amount of money like fifteen dollars, is involved, most older siblings like to make sure that a prospective purchase for younger kin is worth the asking price. A fair deal is the only good deal. Raimo knew that only a decent bike, a used one at that, was worth fifteen dollars. Even a three-speed as mentioned in the advertisement. I phoned the number I'd seen in the bike ad, and we then left home to see the bike for ourselves.

The owner of the bike, an old gent, was busy pulling weeds out of his flowerbed when Raimo and I showed up. "Good-day." the man said as he looked up from his task to address us. He continued almost in the same breath. "The bike is right out here." He led us to a storage shed beside his mobile home. Propped up against the back of his shed was the bike. The man had doubtless placed it there to keep the tires out of the strong afternoon sunlight. Raimo set to inspecting the bicycle.

As I looked on, Raimo asked the man about the number of gears. A needless question, I thought. Raimo and I already knew the answer. Knowing Raimo, I knew that he was just trying to be talkative. "It's a three-speed," the old man said even as Raimo was turning the right side handle, the gear handle, to confirm what he was hearing the man tell him. "This bike has got plenty enough oomph for the city commute," the man stated, looking at me doubtfully. "Whose the bike fer anyway?" The man's Georgia drawl was unmistakable.

"Him," said my brother, nodding at me. The old fellow then addressed myself, who had until now remained quiet.

It had been easier for myself to let Raimo, who was, after all, a salesman by his chosen summertime occupation, do all the talking. "Is this yer very first bike lad?" The old man probed my face.

I considered the question as I responded slowly. "Yeah," I replied. The fact that it was my second bicycle in life that I was looking to own made no difference to me. Nor did Raimo seem to notice my omission of past ownership.

I was trying my best to look cool, and I didn't like the man's use of the word "lad". To me, a grown man of eleven, that one word implied that I was still a child. As I mulled over the point my blue eyes narrowed as I looked at the man, I trying hard to squint like Clint Eastwood did some years earlier when his gunslinging movie character was about to kill somebody evil in the 1964 epic western, *A Fistful Of Dollars*.

My focus was halfway between the old man and the bike when my brother turned to me. "Well," he said, "it seems to be in pretty good shape. What do you think?"

Raimo asked me as if I still possessed a mind of my own. Of course I wanted the bike. At that moment I felt just as the famous fictional English P.I. Sherlock Holmes must have whenever Holmes took a break from his complex investigations at crime scenes long enough to remark on the lack of perception that his best friend Dr. Watson had displayed. Intellectually, Watson never was in Holmes' lofty league. My right hand was already digging inside my pants' front right pocket for a ten-dollar bill.

I slowly dragged out the ten-spot. Next, I carefully pulled out a five. I'm not acquainted with the newer U.S. bills, but a Canadian or other foreigner should always be sure to be much careful with old American money. Why? Because the backs of U.S. banknotes from the past are all green. To a foreigner, even a transplanted migrant from neighboring Canada, the back of an old U.S. ten-dollar bill will look pretty much the same as a five-spot. On the backside all old U.S. paper currency looks like play money.

Now hold on. I know that to a good number of Americans my remark may sound disrespectful and be viewed as inflammatory but, believe me, I am only making an observation with no intent of offending the American public. Besides, the people of our two nations travel a two-way street. I imagine that Americans who've visited Canada view the always colorful Canadian bills in the same manner. But you know, at least American travelers all know about our long-established tradition of multicolored bills and therefore never have to worry about the possibility that they had gone instantly colorblind when they'd visited Canada. And so, in conclusion, yes I'm afraid that old American money has a green ass, and it's certain to stay that way. Green. Just like Martians.

I handed the pair of bills to the old man. And I make a note of it here—his aged face was not green. Neither were his clothes. "Great," the old fellow chirped, he clutching his money and beaming at me as lively as a budgie happily taken with antidepressant medication. "You did jest git yerself yer very own bike, son. And a mighty fine bike it is too." So said the talkative man with finality in his tone. His rasping voice had done nothing to hide his true southern accent.

"Thanks. I hope that you have a nice day," I heard myself say.

Having noted his bulging waistline, I wondered if the happy geezer liked peanut butter sandwiches as much as I did. Eating too many peanut butter sandwiches, commonly mixed with jam, will make anyone fat, I knew. This old jovial guy had probably eaten his fill of them. Probably. But somehow, I kind of doubted that he would have understood or appreciated my interest to know all things in life. That included the nagging question I had in mind. And even without him becoming wise as to the purpose of my question, were I to grill him on the subject of peanuts, I probably could not get him to reveal just what it is that he eats every day which will make a stomach bulge as much as his does, I thought.

In fact, I was almost certain that I was right about the old man and the connection that his ample waistline had with peanut butter, or, maybe, with just plain roasted peanuts, straight from the shell. With him bein' a southerner from Georgia, where I knew that peanuts have long been grown in abundance, I knew that he had probably eaten quite a few as a boy. Peanuts that he had plucked right off the bush. Lucky duck.

I knew that in the northern climes of Canada there were no peanut plantations. Here, all that any boy lost deep in the woods, miles from home, had to suck on were the shoots of dandelions. These contain a white nourishing liquid, like your Uncle Tom's cow wallowing in the pasture, back at home. Dandelions, and in season, wild berries. About dandelions though: I would have gladly betcha that Huck Finn knew all about dandelions. I truly would have. But I knew that Huck Finn only lived in the pages of a well-read book.

GOOD BOOKS CAN GENERATE GOOD DEEDS. And one good deed tends to produce another.

I have, by nature, always been big in generosity. Even my detractors, and there are at least a few of them around in this world of ours, will readily admit this much.

During the summers of 1969 and 1970 in Portland, my brother worked at yet another sporting goods store. This establishment was called Save-More. It was situated on Lombard Street, which was a long five-mile commute each way for Raimo. Because the distance posed some hardship for Raimo, who had sold his scooter back in San Diego, and thus, who now had no transportation of timely convenience (with the possible exception of the city bus) at his disposal, I did the decent thing. In return for my brother having helped me to purchase a bicycle with my own money, I volunteered my bike into his service for the summer months. Hey, I figured, what are brothers for? Right?

With my bike parked beneath his ass, Raimo, I figured, could make the weekday commute to work, and return home in relative comfort, without suffering a torn ligament in trying to outrun any one of the several malicious dogs that lived along his route, shadowing his passage.

For Raimo, I was positive that having a bicycle to ride sure beat, by light-years, walking the five long miles to work in the morning, and then, having to retrace his steps to mother's counter for a square meal in the evening.

As for this favor of mine Raimo felt indebted and in turn rewarded me with a swell present for my eleventh birthday and would for my twelfth. On my eleventh birthday I'd received from Raimo a quiver with four target arrows in it. For my twelfth, well, that would be later.

Concerning the usefulness of the arrows, though. My novice's attempt at carving a short bow for myself then, from a cedar tree limb, failed miserably. My handmade bow just had no suppleness to it. My bow just did not wish to bend. Even though I tugged on my bowstring with all my youthful might, it did not. In dismay, I thought this: Next time, will somebody please reward me with a store-sold bow? One that actually works?

As you recall Heini's stool back in sunny San Diego— you may find it hard to suppress a wide grin. But don't you dare try to stop that grin. Please. Everyone well knows that constructive do-it-yourself projects, both large and small— are not for me. I still wonder why Raimo never hopped on the city bus to get his butt to work. Maybe the service *was* too irregular, for his timetable.

While Raimo had use of my bike during summers then, Helen had bought her own. Helen's bike was of the same classic style as mine, though unlike my bike Helen's bicycle was spanking new. And it was the same color as mine.

I realized that black may not be every lady's favorite color, but despite the color Helen's bike was obviously very much a ladies' bike because it was missing the horizontal bar leading from directly beneath the seat to the vertical frame beneath the handlebar.

To pay for her new wheels, for a while Helen had baby-sat a little cutie who had black curly locks, a toddler who we called, "Gom-dee-gom".

Everyone in our family called this little girl that, because every time that Gom-dee-gom had visited us in our trailer, whilst in my sister's care she'd uttered only a single word. "Gom." I took it that that word, (is it actually a word?) is native Hawaiian for food. Gom-dee-gom must have always been hungry, because I'd heard the little lass repeat that word so often.

Gom-dee-gom's father was native Hawaiian, and I never knew his name. And the tiny tot's mother was a blonde-haired lady in her late twenties or early thirties, by the name of Judy. I never talked to either of Gom's parents, even though Judy and her husband lived in a trailer just three or four spaces from our own. Please do not ask me about Gom's real first name. I don't recall that. And Helen, who does remember the name of the little girl she looked after, would not ever tell me because even now sis does not like the idea of me writing a book about our family and our past associations with other folks, no matter how remote in time those connections be, to divulge to humanity what Helen deems the equivalent of State secrets. Helen's personal secrets included. To my sister all these secrets be of monumental and historic import. My-oh-my! What vanity exists on this small planet.

KNOWING HELEN, I know that sis would certainly pull every bit of hair stuck to her head, out in clumps, were I to reveal to you—Helen's darkest secret. Which I shall do without delay. And my reason for perpetrating this terrible act is that I wish to discover what Helen shall look like bereft of her fine head of hair. Yes! I clap my hands together in joyful anticipation. My sister will soon become bald. Helen will soon look like Yul Brynner of yesterdays long past. *Am I evil or what? No. Banish you all must this thought.* Instead—what all must concentrate their mental energy on is that long-gone day in San Diego when Helen had slipped the transparent tape onto my head's lush carpet.

Here then, is Helen's most cherished secret. Helen's secret, yes. One-hundred percent. These be three unpublished novels which sis wrote in Portland. I know not the titles of the other works, but I do recall that one of Helen's early works was dubbed, "Sharon Brook and the Secret of the Hidden Lagoon". You know, over three decades later I still wonder what, on Earth, could be so valuably secret about some unpolluted and generally unheard of desolate, stagnant swamp which few tourist's eyes have ever seen—infested, no doubt, with a couple lonely catfish, or their like. And besides that, home to hordes of hungry, malarious mosquitoes. Oh well. I certainly am not going to lose any sleep over my sister's insistence to safeguard a secret of such lowly importance as this. Like I always say: who cares?

After her stint at baby-sitting, with mother's help Helen had landed a job as a cashier at the Grants' grocery store. A summer job, which sis had now quit to become an assistant at a Portland veterinary clinic. Helen's duties here in the latter, Raimo had already described in this way: "S.D.P.S." Get it? I knew that you would!

Although Raimo's description was in this particular case accurate in large measure then, I must confess that Raimo also had, on occasion, been less than kind in his opinions of what other folks did for a living in order to survive. In 1969, Helen, who had a vision of becoming a veterinarian herself but would later change her mind to become a nurse, did not seem too perturbed by Raimo's unflattering characterization of her line of employment.

Chapter Forty-one

HALLOWEEN OF 1969 in the trailer court was boring. Nothing exciting happened. Sure, me and Helen had gone trick-or-treating. And, as I say, it was by my high standard of measure an *uneventful* affair. Dismally so. End of story. Okay-okay. I hear your unspoken thought protests. I shall continue then. Satisfied?

But truly, uneventful Halloween was because, well, I didn't seize the opportunity to try my hand at movin' any eligible lady off. (And, as you must instantly surmise from that statement based on my colorful past in Campbell River, an eligible lady could also have been—a married lady. Yes, in C.R. the only reason I'd stooped so low as to entertain the thought of stealing some other fellow's wife is because I used to believe [I still do, you know] in fairness for all.)

Anyhow, my thinking went like this. He's had his turn—so it's my turn. My turn to try my hand at movin' any eligible lady off for the purpose of matrimony.

But not on my bicycle. Now that I owned one. Nor on my back. Only in my mind. What did you expect? I was older and less boastful now. Heh-heh. I know what you're thinking again: a confessed ladynapper like myself never fully recovers from this terrible affliction. Roy: no comment. Okay-okay. Guilty. Back to Halloween of '69.

Actually, to tell the terrible truth, there was a part of our Halloween in the trailer park that was bone-chillingly exciting for one soul then, but it took place in the daylight hours shortly before Old Hallow's Eve. And by our

357

Halloween, I really mean my Halloween as well as sis's and mother's, *and* my friend Bill Bennett's.

The most exciting part of our Halloween, happened thus. Bill was visiting me in our yard. We boys were sitting on the front porch as we made talk. The chat ended.

For, there had been a heavy thump behind us. A thump that had emanated from inside the trailer, in the direction of the kitchen window. Of course, Bill and I looked up into the window to ascertain the cause of the noise. And when our two pairs of eyes met the window glass, we beheld between the swaying curtains—a face. Not just any face did we see. No—a face it was which instantly sent major shakes rolling through Bill's lean frame, and should have through mine— there in the kitchen window, clearly framed between the parted curtains, was the seeming mask of evil itself.

Guess who? Who-who-who—who-who-who? Who else could it be but my sister? With a light-brown, lady's nylon stocking pulled down tight over her face, grinning, as befits her nature, in devilish glee. Did I say that we boys were sitting? Well, we had been. By now Bill and I had jumped up.

I noticed that Bill looked like he was fighting the urge to flee to his bike, which was leaning against our fence post. Bill looked plenty scared. As for myself, I'd jumped for an altogether different reason than the sheer terror my friend was in the throes of. I wasn't even the slightest bit scared. No.

I had been only momentarily startled. Startled, because you good people have absolutely no definable conception of just how revolting Helen can look with a see-through sock pulled over her face. Man-oh-man!

As a kid, I frequently thought that my sister looked bad enough without the sock to bolden the often-mean features of her face. Especially when sis, like many teenage girls of her age then will do, put on excessive makeup. Nevertheless, the stocking definitely added another dimension of evil to Helen's countenance. Halloween or not, it always did.

And Bill? After the first few seconds of his fright Bill's shock must have worn off. My friend looked more relaxed now as he doubtless had realized that he'd been duped. It was now a perfect time for mother to get in the act too, by trying her luck in the pageant of facial misfits. Yet, even with the same nylon mask over her face I thought that mother didn't look half as bad as sis had. I am obliged to say that, because I always was MY mommy's little boy.

ALL OF YOU FUN FOLKS already know something of my sister Helen. By this time, you all know that Helen was capable of being not only a ringleader in a gang of two desperadoes, her and me, but that sis was perfectly capable of being mischievous toward me as well. Remember my bad-hair day? Helen's mean streak was a fact of life that I had become accustomed to long since.

Further, please chew on this: For my having (as most always) been a good boy, father had rewarded me with a model airplane kit. A kit that had cost father twenty-nine cents. The wings and foot-long frame of this toy were made of balsa wood, which is incredibly light. This unique property of balsa is exactly why the material is so well suited for building model aircraft with. My plane had a thin plastic propeller to keep the weight of the plane down. The propeller was driven by a fairly wide elastic band that needed to be wound by hand.

Now, on one gray, rainless Saturday midmorning in early November, I happened to be playing with my plane on the road in front of our trailer, while my sister sat looking on from our front porch. That Helen's mind was on the prowl I could easily tell: I noticed that Helen had a familiar evil-eyed look about her on this morning. It was a look which I knew I had to be wary of because it had always spelt trouble for me.

Events unfolded thus. I had wound my airplane, and, as I threw the craft into the sky, unnoticed by myself— Helen silently blasted off from her sit on the porch. And she sprinted after my prized plane like a hunting cheetah speeding in pursuit of a gazelle. Seeing is believing. Running hard, sis caught up with my plane in its mid-flight and snatched it from out of the air, with one hand.

Looking on as I stood in the street, far back of the scene, I was horror-struck. I was in no mood to have my airplane, my very personal property, stolen from right in front of my eyes. Nor was I in a mood to have my play interrupted. I tore off after Helen and quickly overtook her. Without pausing to scream out the fury in me, I grabbed sis roughly by the back of her long, blonde locks. I then yanked downward on her hair. As hard as I could. Not surprisingly, Helen screamed in pain and spun about on the instant to fight me—and in so doing she dropped my plane on the pavement.

Being the reasonable fellow I have always been, on this day I mostly just wanted to make sure that I got my cherished toy back in one piece. I had no intention of starting World War III. Mostly. Surely, you all do understand, don't you? Well then. Preamble over. Unburdened of guilt, I now feel free to state the simple truth of how I felt on this day. I was really peeved. So I faced my sister with all of the pent-up ferocity of a caged wolverine that has just been released to freedom. Truly, an Indian devil I was, this being the term that some indigenous people of North America use in referring to the wolverine. Luckily for both of us, sis was sane enough to know that she was to blame for the whole incident, and she wisely chose to back off from a fight with me.

I learned two valuable lessons on that day: One is that, sometimes, engaging in decisive physical action begets peace; second, it is just as important to remember that eternal vigilance is key in the matter of security.

OTHER than what I have already mentioned and therefore won't repeat, not a heck of a lot that is worth me telling you folks about would happen in my life between Halloween of 1969 and the beginning of the summer of 1970. At school, I always played my violin in a small band. Too, our group had yet to perform before the students and teachers in our school's auditorium at Christmastime. In hindsight, a boring affair that was.

What else was new? Oh yeah. There was one major difference in our family life now. A major, major difference. There were only four of us cooped up like jailed sardines in our fabulous trailer now. Raimo was gone with the wind of opportunity; he'd been accepted into the University of British Columbia med school in Vancouver. Three hundred miles to the north, in familiar territory he was. With his three-year-long stint of premedical studies over, Raimo had already begun his four long years in the study of human disease and medicine.

I'd had mixed feelings about my brother's absence. I'd missed him at first, but after a relatively short transition period of a few months I had grown to appreciate the healthy fact that I had much more freedom about home now without Raimo sternly looking on and ready, always ready, to deal out corporal punishment to me at his whim.

I valued my freedom immensely and I always felt like Raimo's personal whipping-bag when he was around. Nothing new in that.

Raimo would visit us every couple of months when a long weekend presented him with the opportunity to make the two-way trip between Vancouver and Portland by Greyhound bus; with frequent stops a journey of about eight hours in each direction. In Vancouver, Raimo occupied a basement suite in a small house that belonged to a nice lady. I didn't know much else about the eight or nine months that my brother was spending in Vancouver, attending school.

It was a Friday evening in mid spring, with the sun getting ready to retire after another day of duty warming the globe, that Raimo returned. As chance wanted it, only me and Helen were home. Mother and father were out on this Friday evening; as usual on Friday evenings they would bank and afterwards shop for the next week's groceries at Safeway.

There was a knock on our kitchen door. Our screen door. With the weather being warm now, the exterior door lay wide open. Despite the fact that the outer door lay open there was no cause for alarm, because we in the family always kept our screen doors, our secondary defense against intruders, shut at the front and back of our home. Shut by way of a sturdy steel hook, attached at either end in an unyielding frame—as all wise folks should do, even if they have not much of value that anyone, or his dog, might wish to steal.

At the knock on our door I looked up from our kitchen counter where I was sitting on a bar stool, reading the newspaper. Helen was in the kitchen as well. Doing nothing except minding her own business—a change from the usual. It did not altogether surprise me. Every family pest needs some downtime, now and then, just to recoup energy. Beyond the screen, on the porch, caught in the late evening light stood Raimo. "Hi," my brother greeted me. As I'd recognized him I'd gotten up from my seat to undo the hook locking our screen door. I greeted Raimo as he came inside. "Where is everybody?" So inquired my brother even though he well knew where mother and father were. But I explained mother's and father's whereabouts as Helen joined in our conversation.

My surprised joy on seeing Raimo again was very short-lived: a mere five minutes later he asked me if I wished for him to hand me a licking. This, when I had paused to contradict his opinion on some now long-forgotten topic. From the look of him then, I'd have sworn he was dead-serious. With Raimo, I thought, was it ever an act? If it was that day, it was a mighty convincing piece of acting.

No, I didn't, and don't, think it was an act. I cannot, as I say, recall what the topic of discussion then, was. But knowing Raimo like he was then, his umbrage had arisen, probably, over some trivial thing like the spelling of a word. Perhaps the spelling of a city street in Vancouver. Probably.

Yep. Raimo was back home, all right. It was again time for me to tread extra carefully.

AS SCHOOL ENDED and the summer of 1970 commenced, I began once more to think about the amazing abundance of blackberry vines so close at hand. And by mid-July, with summer in full swing, I seriously began to wonder whether other folks might be willing to part with a little pocket change for an opportunity to savor the sweet, biting quality of the vines' sun-ripened fruit.

To answer this question I set about to find out. I told mother about my new idea. And since I lacked a commercial basket in which to place my berries, I asked mother for a bowl. I knew that mother had only soup bowls of ceramic in her kitchen cupboard. She gave me one. I thanked mother, and picked up a pair of white, cotton, garden gloves from our storage shed out back. The gloves I stuffed into the rear pocket of my trousers. I tapped on our kitchen window, spoke a few words, and waved good-bye to mother. Through the thin glass window I'd spoken loud enough that mother had heard.

Mother smiled at me and nodded, returning to her chores in the kitchen. (I had just informed mother that I would be absent for a while, my time to be taken up by a morning of berry picking at Boden.) And so, I left on my mission to make money. And I hoped, lots of it.

Arriving on site after a short pleasant walk under the youthful radiance of the early morning sun, I did the usual thing before I set to work. Habits, good and bad, are hard to ignore. I simply had to check out the garbage bin to see if anything that might be of value to myself or father had been discarded by the employees of Boden. But no. There were absolutely no items of interest exposed to a quick glance within the open bin on this morning.

Seeing nothing within the bin to take home, I walked around to the other side of the Boden Bros.' plant, to where I knew the blackberries that grew on the thorny vines—

were the plumpest and juiciest. I pulled my gloves out and donned them. I began my work.

The fruit that hung from the prickly blackberry vines was in prime condition. Thanks to abundant sunshine of recent days, these berries were not laden with too much water. No. Agreeably plump and ripe by their midnight color these blackberries now were. Ready they were to be picked and eaten.

With no scarcity of fruit on the vines, I had not spent a long time in the blackberry patch beneath the sharp gaze of the morning sun, certainly no more than ten minutes, before my small soup bowl was brimming with blackberries. Satisfied that my bowl was full, too full for me to attempt to add any more fruit to the dish, I crossed the highway back to our trailer park and home.

In our yard I washed the white dust that had been spread on my berries by the Bodens' factory fan off of my take with clean cold water from our garden hose. I showed mother my berries, telling her that I would be away for a while yet, on official business. A man's business. Mother smiled. Mother knew how important I felt as a boy about to become a salesman. She needn't worry, I told mother. I would be home soon.

With my bowlful of blackberries now thoroughly washed, I then left home, tracing my earlier steps, back toward the Boden Bros.' plant. But I did not cross the highway between the factory and our trailer park. Instead, I stayed within the boundary of the trailer court. I proceeded to walk up to the steps of my first potential buyer. I knocked on the door of a small fifth-wheel.

A teenage girl, blonde of hair and freckled of face, answered the door. Behind her were two small boys. I read, or rather—guessed, the situation on the spot. The girl, who kept her hair long as most girls do, looked only a couple of years my senior. She did not appear old enough to be the mother of the boys. So, I figured that the girl was either an older sister of this pair of boys, or, she was a hired baby-sitter.

On second thought now, perhaps I should refer to her possible job then, in a *less* offensive tone. A more neutral tone. Yes, I shall. Possibly, this teenage girl was a sitter of children. In other words, this girl was possibly a child-sitter—no boy likes to be insulted. Aye, take it from me because I was once a boy too. In his mind, every boy is a man, you know. No matter how small he may be.

I performed a swift mental calculation. "Child-sitters," I knew, did not earn a lot of money. So, I figured that if the girl was indeed a child-sitter, she likely would be willing to part with no more of her own money than a twenty-five cent piece with G.W. stamped on it. Hmm. I wonder whether George ever got a perm, I thought. No matter. A quarter. Hmm. If even that, considering that I expected, as a condition which would allow me to complete the sale, any potential purchaser of my wonderfully wild berries to give my bowl back. Or rather, make that mother's bowl. But, if this girl was a sibling of the young boys or—even a distant cousin, what then? In this case, she might be looking after the boys for free, not earning a single cent for herself.

Make no mistake. I was puzzled as to what the girl was. Puzzled, and my natural hesitation was showing. But since I was standing in front of her, I felt obligated to try my sales pitch on the lass anyway. After all, it had taken all my nerve to get my butt to this crucial wannabe salesman's make-it-or-break point. It took all my courage to fight off my habitual shyness now (like it always did with other things). Yes, I was determined to not leave empty-handed, if I could make some money instead.

"Would you like to buy some wild blackberries for a quarter?" I asked the teenager, meekly. I'd tried my damnedest to sound as smooth of voice as a professional salesman's, even though I was clad in my trademark old and faded blue jeans with large patches on both knees.

Looking pensive, the girl replied: "I don't know if I have a quarter." This answer did nothing to comfort me. And yet, despite the girl's statement I could see the obvious. She appeared eager to buy my dishful of berries. I was now beginning to believe that the girl was in a dire financial strait. I was starting to feel sorry for her. Yes, sorry. The thought even occurred to me, as the nanoseconds sped by, that perhaps I should give her my berries for free. It did—truly. But my fortress of stubbornness was not to be so easily crushed. My nagging doubt was still alive and well. Every good salesman should know a sob story when he hears one. I held on for a few more crucial nanoseconds. "I'll see if I can find a quarter," said the girl. She turned around at the doorway and disappeared inside the trailer.

She soon returned with a shiny twenty-five cent piece. "Here you go." She placed the quarter into the palm of my hand.

I felt a little less sorry for her now. "My mother wants me to bring her bowl back though," I said.

"Sure," said the girl. Now that I had a done deal, I gave the girl the bowlful of wild blackberries that I had just sold her. She emptied these into another bowl. Her bowl. The girl gave back mother's bowl. And with mother's bowl plus my money in hand, I thanked the girl as I left. Just like any professional salesman would have. And—I did not forget to smile.

I was glad inside. I swear that even all the skin on my body felt glad. So warm and fuzzy with excitement I felt. And proud—I had just completed the sale of a bowlful of berries that I had picked. Sold the black gold to my first customer. On my very first attempt as a worldly salesman. I could feel my star rising in the world. I felt important. I could hardly wait to tell mother about my overwhelming success. This, I knew, was just my first big sale of the summer. Greater things lay ahead for me.

I returned home and told mother the good news. "That's wonderful," mother said, beaming at me. But unknown to me at the time of my joy, my feeling of greater success in the offing was terribly premature—because I sold only this one bowlful of wild blackberries in the summer of 1970, even though I'd knocked on the door of every mobile home and travel trailer in our park. I had not bothered to count each occupied pad I'd visited, though I figure that I must have visited a couple hundred homes. Yes, my luck was all in the beginning. Now I know why folks call initial success, beginner's luck.

SO CLOSE to the plenitude of snakes, small rodents and birds, was one occupant who lived next to the blackberry patch that the wild creatures knew as their home. On the same side of the patch, not within it, on the same side as the trash bin, there lived in a large old dilapidated house a senior fellow who I called, "Sam". I called him Sam because I didn't know his real name; I never would. But exactly for what reason I called him thus, I don't know. At the time, maybe the old fellow just looked to me like his first name was, or should have been, Sam. Or, just as likely, perhaps I named him thus because my brother had now begun to call me Sam. Why? Well, I suppose that Sam is as good a name as any when a caller wishes to impart flavor to a conversation. Like Joe Blow, Sam has its root in the slang later common to hillbilly America. Sam, as the abbreviation of Samuel, has kind of a rustic flavor to it. I like the name.

Anyhow, Sam lived alone, and he lived the life of a man who shunned the public eye. I can say that Sam lived a very solitary existence. He lived the lonely life of a true hermit.

Mother knew Sam too: he was an occasional customer of mother's at the Grants' store. Mother knew Sam better than I; I only knew him by sight—I never talked to the reclusive old man.

Here for you is the true story that mother recounted to me later. One summer day, Sam strolled into the Grants' store. On this occasion Sam would not linger in the park store for long. As I understand from what mother told me, nor was it ever his habit to do so. On this early afternoon Sam was on a looky-loo mission. The old fellow was looking at the collection of headwear hanging from the revolving hat rack. At the time, Sam happened to be the only customer in the store. Now, while Sam was intently engaged in perusing the collection of hats, mother, who had time on her hands, was watching Sam with interest from behind the counter at the front of the store.

This be the meat of mother's story. After carefully scrutinizing every hat hung from the rack, Sam decided to try on one which he seemed to have taken a liking to. Removing the antiquated gray flop that he always wore, Sam set a light-colored hat he'd removed from the rack prior to that, onto the aged remnants of white hair still left on his crown. With one hand, Sam balanced the hat so that it would sit true with the top of his face. And that quickly Sam made up his mind. He removed the merchandise and set the hat back on the rack.

Being a hermit, Sam was a quiet sort as befits a hermit— Mother said that he never talked much at all. Yet even though Sam was quiet, he was courteous enough to say "Good-day." to mother before he departed from the store's premises, empty-handed on this day.

After Sam had left the store, mother, being somewhat curious, decided to have a look at the one hat that Sam had displayed real interest in and tried on his head. Mother took the hat back off the rack, and turned it over. And there before her eyes, said mother, lay a greasy ring of black soot about the headband. Ample evidence that Sam used firewood to heat his home, and, he never, or, almost never, took a bath.

Yes, both of those reasons were surely the cause of Sam's less than hygienic head. And *if* Sam ever cleansed the exterior of his body, he did so not more than once each year. Or thereabouts.

Hermits are an eccentric breed. Sam may have believed in the same kind of thing that another old man I once heard of, believed in. I figure it is quite unlikely that this other old feller even owned a television set. I figure so, because this particular old man refused to believe that the American astronauts who had made the lunar landings possible, ever had touched down on the burly ball of green cheese, that bald world one-quarter of a million miles away in space. And the old coot was a striped, true, red, white and blue American himself. Patriotic, he sure was.

Yes, despite his allegiance to the U.S. of A., the old man, in fact, vehemently swore that the crowning glory of America's achievements in space, the momentous moonshot of 1969 by Neil Armstrong and fellow astronauts Edward Aldrin and Michael Collins—all three very brave men—and Neil and Buzz (I mean Ed who is Buzz)—who many of us TV fans can remember bouncing gleefully about the sandy boulder-strewn lunar landscape like kids on an earthly outing, was pure fabrication. It was all, he said, a creation of Hollywood. It was all an event that never took place. According to him—it was all just a bold lie.

Which makes me wonder. If the geriatric genius had no TV set, nor had access to view a friend's boob tube, how did he find out about the event in the first place? Ah! By junkers, I've got it now! He must have known how to read the fine print in the newspaper. A newspaper in which he placed little or none of his trust. It is amazing what old age can do to a person's mind. I hope that I never get really old so that I don't become senile. I'd much rather drink from the fountain of youth and stay young and vigorously healthy until it is time for me to kick the bucket.

DURING THE ALMOST TWO YEARS that our family lived in Portland, we ventured out together on only three occasions to the countryside, near and far. Trip number one: From the bank of the wide Columbia River, at a site that lay not many miles downstream from the parking lot of my schoolyard, we once crossed the channel to an uncharted island (just kidding) midstream in the Columbia. The name of this isle was Lemon Island.

We spent a nice, bright Saturday afternoon on the sandy shore of this oasis of nature within the city of Portland. Oh, we couldn't have made the crossing without my brother's shallop, of course. Oh, and on this particular day in late July it had been a trifle windy to be sunbathing, but at least the moderate wind had allowed us to sail back across the water and—had let us be back at home in time for dinner then.

Trip number two: There was, and still is, the mighty ravine which I aver is one of the prettier highwayside spots in the Pacific Northwest. I speak of Columbia River Gorge Nat'l Scenic Area, home of Multnomah Falls. While in Portland, I visited this picturesque waterfall, seen from I-84, twice: once on a family excursion and once when we sixth-graders were coming back into town from Mr. Jacoby's rock-hunting field trip.

The unspoiled grandeur of Multnomah Falls is breathtaking to behold. From beside the highway a steep dark trail shrouded in the thick verdure of conifers in their natural state snakes up the mountainside. A delightful scene is the backdrop of the falls itself. This—a magnificent cascade of cool pristine water that tumbles in an unstoppable torrent from high up into a shallow pool at the foot of the falls.

Trip number three: By far the lengthiest outing we'd embarked upon during our residency in Portland was a 160-mile-long round bound to Astoria, on the panoramic Oregon coast. During that quiet summer weekend we had stayed in town long enough to take in the scenery as well as a quick fries.

Well, maybe it hadn't been so quick. Maybe, because chance had led us to a small restaurant where the waitress, who probably was the proprietor too because she'd been the only one around, had accidently dropped the first batch of fries on the floor. Maybe—since she'd seen that we'd seen the spill—she had felt compelled to prepare a second batch of spuds for us. And I'm pretty darned sure that if she owned a cat or dog then, her animal got fed a real treat on that day. What did you say? Cats don't like oily, deep-fried vegetables that have lain about on the floor? Well, how about dogs?

CHAPTER FORTY-TWO

FATHER HAD DECIDED ON A MOVE AGAIN. And for our family the eventual return to Canada was imminent now. Unlike many of our previous moves—where our future was never cast in stone, we all knew that this move to another country would be permanent. It was getting to be near the end of August, 1970. Little more than a week ago, I had turned twelve years of age. For my birthday, Helen had given me a book chronicling the life of a man who I spoke of before. Grizzly Adams. From my brother, I had received that book on marine life I mentioned in the stuff I wrote about Namu the killer whale.

Not having much to do, as this time in the latter half of August was still my summer vacation, I just did whatever I could think of to occupy my spare time. I played alone about our small yard, and I climbed the large old cottonwood tree behind father's small, self-made aluminum storage shed, a shed which stood to the left of our trailer and my brother's bedroom. I had always climbed the cottonwood because the thick growth of branches on the lone spruce tree that grew at the front of our pad had prevented me from climbing that tree. It was from the cottonwood, sitting high above ground on a massive branch, completely hidden within the blind of green leaves, that I viewed our homesite from a tree for the last time. The arrangements for our journey north had already been made. Father had seen to that.

It was early morning on the day of August 22, 1970 that a tow rig from Doug's Towing of Port Moody, British Columbia, pulled in front of our humble trailer.

The interior of our little mobile home was congested— almost everything we owned was now inside our trailer. Including a couple of half-full, fifty-gallon oil drums that sat upright in the kitchen. Almost everything, excluding Raimo's boat, which had been secured by rope to the roof of our Rambler. And excluding the Rambler itself.

The tow rig linked up to our trailer. The driver of the truck, a squat man in his mid-fifties who bore a heavy Newfoundland accent, proceeded to check our trailer's tires for adequate air pressure. He checked the signal lights at the back of the trailer also. Everything was shipshape. Everything was in working order. As I looked around at the scene it seemed as though time almost stood still. I checked my wristwatch. The two hands that marked time told me it was exactly one-quarter before eight o'clock on this bright Saturday morning. The park store would open later.

Despite the early hour, and the fact that it was a weekend morning, the neighborhood had turned out to watch our departure. Our neighbors were there to wave farewell to us. Most of them knew that we were leaving America. A land that had been our home for almost five years. A land where my parents had worked and we kids had gone to school.

The truck driver cranked his engine and the heavy, powerful rig instantly roared into life. Then the driver pulled forward. As our trailer turned a corner, our family got into the Rambler. Father drove, following close behind our traveling home as it made its way around another corner and onto the highway, bound for the north.

Two hours of steady driving later, along I-5, the truck driver pulled his rig before a service station in Chehalis, Washington to check his vehicle's brakes and take on fuel. I badly needed to pee, so the stop was a welcome respite to hit the washroom running. Soon we were back on the road toward Canada. Some one and three-quarter hours later we breezed through Seattle. And by three o'clock in the afternoon we came up to the international border crossing at Blaine, Wash. Father now drove very slowly.

Just a short distance away, on the other side of this familiar invisible line, was British Columbia. And Canada. I looked back along the way that our family of five had come. Back along the long road that we had traveled. I looked back at the land called the United States of America. America, the eminent superpower of the world. And—as I looked, I traveled again not only the physical road—I traveled through time as well. Within my mind and its memories. Memories. Some glad. Some sad. As father drove the Rambler onward, we crossed the line to the Canadian border post.

The waiting customs officer, an old man, conferred briefly with father. Father then got out of the Rambler and opened the locked kitchen door of our trailer, as the tow driver looked on from his cab, through his passenger door's mirror. I was watching the situation closely and there is little which escaped my attention.

With the trailer door open, the old man visually inspected what he could of the interior from ground level; he chose to not venture in. Not that he could easily have made his way inside because the oil drums which blocked much of his vision, barred his entry. With him being near retirement age then, doubtless, he did not wish to strain himself by attempting to hop over the oil tins.

The old man turned back to father. "Okay," he said. "You're free to go!" Then, as he was leaving, he turned back in his tracks and retorted: "And this time—stay in Canada!" That said, the cynical old fogy smiled at us not a bit.

We followed the tow driver into the small community of White Rock, and from there into the equally little town of Langley. Then, from Langley onward to Murrayville.

Back in 1970, Murrayville was little more than a village between Langley and Aldergrove, but closer to Aldergrove which is three miles east along the Fraser Highway. The tow driver made a right hand turn off the Fraser and pulled our home on wheels into a mobile home park I'd been told was owned by a man whose last name was, or pronounced as, Yonker. His work all but over, the truck driver uncoupled his load as he, with father assisting, leveled the trailer on our new homesite.

Along the roadway the late afternoon sun shone its bright light, failing to penetrate the dark surroundings of tall evergreen trees which lay in their natural state everywhere in the park. Lots of trees for me to climb, I thought. Unknown to myself, I was a lot older now than I had been just a few short days since, and I never would bother to climb any of the trees that grew in my new environment.

A very recent rain had left the pavement and earth wet. The earth soaking wet. I noticed, too, that the air was moist and cool. Being almost late August, the seasonal change was just around the corner. I would soon face the beginning of another school year. Then winter. A Canadian winter.

And, as I stood in our driveway, in my well-worn and patched blue jeans, a twelve-year-old boy awaiting autumn and my slow ascent toward manhood, I smiled, for the time being, secure in the knowledge that I was back in the best place I could be. Home. Home, no matter where on Earth it is.

CHAPTER FORTY-THREE

INTO THE FUTURE

THIS BOOK, as you all know, has unveiled my extraordinary adventures from birth to the brink of puberty. As you bear with me in my narrative, I shall wave aside my self-imposed age constraint for a spell: there is one account in my family's history that falls well beyond my earlier years. An incident this is that I simply cannot resist telling you about.

In 1973 to 1974 I'd attended a secondary school called King George, in the metropolitan hub of Vancouver's West End. Now, whenever I happen to know what I am talking about, I am a stickler for detail. And in order to avoid any confusion that could arise in the minds of my reading public, I, because I chance to know what I am speaking of here, would like to clarify the following. The King George School is in Vancouver, Canada. And Vancouver, just like every Canadian city, town, or village, is home to the hockey stick and many poor, frozen Eskimo dudes. This city is definitely not Vancouver, Washington, U.S.A.

The West End of my Vancouver is a 1.5-mile-long stretch of development principally comprised of concrete high-rise buildings, nestled between Stanley Park and downtown. Time frame—the end of July, 1973. Summer break. I would enter grade ten in September.

Changes had taken place in our family. One change was that Helen had removed herself from the familial nest in

Murrayville in February of 1971. Sis had gone to live with a girlfriend's family, following a serious spat with dad. This altercation had arisen from the usual kind of tension that will exist between many a stay-out-late-and-party daughter, and her go-to-sleep-early-and-snore father. In Helen's case, it had taken only one very late night-early morning party and a decent-looking boyfriend of sis's who father had not much liked. Oh it wasn't really that father hadn't much liked him, because, with father having been unemployed then, father would not have much liked anybody.

Climax. Helen had split to ride on her adopted family's wings so that she could finish high school; sis had known that she could attend whatever social functions she wished in the after hours, rather than engage father, who'd been as cranky as a wolverine, by fisticuffs. Following Helen's departure, the four survivors in our family had headed into Vancouver with our trailer in tow. We'd set up shop in Vancouver, in another small mobile home-and-trailer park. From here, we had moved about town until we, at last, wound up for the third time in the West End (minus the trailer which father had had moved to a rented property in Richmond after we'd left the big-city trailer park). This in a span of just two and one-half years after we'd vacated the trailer park in Murrayville.

Father had found work since we had left Murrayville, work in father's customary line of work. But father, being father, had always felt stressed-out in his job as an electrician. So he had quit his job. He had then taken up the management and caretaking duties in a West End high-rise, with mother to help him. While father took care of the outdoor maintenance of the property as his primary chore, aside from collecting renters' checks mother kept the interior of the building looking shipshape. As I implied, me and Raimo were living with our parents. Raimo had completed his last year of medical school just a short while ago.

So far as I know, the building in which we lived on the ground floor then, still stands today. It sits at 1355 Harwood

Street, overlooking English Bay. A small high-rise called The New Marquis. At least, that was the name of the place in 1974, when father and mother would leave the employ of the couple who owned the property, Mr. and Mrs. Prescott.

Enough of this torture. Bare facts, for the sake of facts, are boring the heck out of me. Here goes my real story. July of 1973 now. One day, father had decided to save the Prescotts who were nice people to work for, some money. Specifically, this was the cost of hiring a professional pest-exterminator to evict an unruly bunch of wasps from their earthen home in the back garden. And now, more than a few words of wisdom. In my hard life I have learned the hard way that predictable results will ensue when two equally intractable and equally aggressive foes lock horns in their desire to be boss over land they share and each claim. Should the expected confrontation not end in a draw, the result is always sure to leave the loser of the fight with a bad taste in the mouth.

In the case of men who fight, one or both are likely to be minus a few front teeth. My father, in most things, easily fit the description of the word, stubborn. And like father, homeless-to-be wasps can also be mighty stubborn. And wasps, as you probably have learned from my encounter with them in Campbell River, can get exceedingly peeved when someone attempts to dislodge them from their home. It is understandable. I would too, if someone kicked me in the ass and then threw me out of my home. Or tried to. One need not be an expert in matters of the mind to understand the psychology of a wasp.

Neither does one need to immerse his, or her, mind in the musty annals of science literature to appreciate a wasp's instinct for survival of its community. When attacked, any wasp will, without fail, protect its home turf and its revered queen. To a wasp, always its much adored queen.

On this warm July day I first became aware that something was terribly amiss with father when I heard a commotion in the lobby. I was in my room at the time, a room I shared with Raimo. This is a one-bedroom suite, and my parents slept in the living room, the kitchen between us. This suite is the only suite on the ground floor of The New Marquis. When the building was built, this suite was doubtless intended to be the manager's residence. Anyhow, when I heard noise coming from the lobby, I rushed out of my room to witness an incredible spectacle when I opened the door of our apartment.

The instant I poked my head into the lobby is, in my mind, still a blur of action frozen. Time itself stood still for me that very moment. Well, almost, b-e-c-a-u-s-e as I stared into the lobby—I stared in disbelief. Profound disbelief. Yes, for, there in the center of the plush red carpet, jumpin' about and doin' as clumsy a rendition of a Mohican war dance as I've ever seen—was father.

To you all I know that my disclosure is hard to believe. But I swear that that be the truth. The absolute truth. And— nothing but the truth. And not only that, folks. Get this. My dad was garbed only in his undershorts. His undershorts, which, in his frenzy looked alive with an electric charge. I confess that dad was attired in real nice shorts too: large red hearts on a white background.

Being then, as I said it was, the end of July, I knew that it was not Valentine's Day. And in any case, by way of his appearance I knew that father was not redeclaring his marriage vow of eternal love for mother. Besides that last observation of mine, I figured that it would have been kind of late in father's life to begin now. Particularly with such fanfare.

Fortunately for my sake I am not completely dense when I appear to be in shock. Since I well knew that father had never showed any indication of harboring a secret desire to flash his undershorts in public, I quickly construed from the high decibel of noise father was creating in the lobby (noise loud enough to drown out a Led Zeppelin rock concert) and from his frantic movements on the carpet, plus the sight of his managerial navy-blue dress slacks pulled below his knees, plus the extreme discomfort showing on father's grizzled leather-tough face, that father's underpants were alive with passion. The angry passion of at least a dozen pissed-off wasps who were quite busily engaged within father's underwear—stingin' his foul ass.

As for mother now. I must tell you folks about mother in father's time of need. You all see, mother did witness this incident just as I did, yet mother seemed too preoccupied with the thought of her self-preservation then to attempt to offer father any immediate succor by hovering in father's path, as his legs beat the carpet, carrying him from one end of the lobby—to the other. Nay, mother had no intention of drawing father's tormentors away from him by offering herself as a sacrifice. Not that mother could have done a thing to help father, anyway. No, because there was just no way that mother could have gotten father to stand still—even had she possessed a lasso, and had she succeeded in roping father with it.

As the incident turned out for father, he ended up having his rear end punctured so many times by the angry wasp fraternity that he must have felt his behind had nearly been stung right off him. I know that many folks who read this book will say that father had long had this punishment for his various ill deeds in life comin' to him. I could not agree more with these folks. Having watched father prance about on the carpet, I learned something about father that day: I'd never known father was capable of capturing within his tortured movements the gyration of the hips that defines the twist—as had been so ably demonstrated by father at super speed.

(Can you all remember this early 1960s custom-made, silky-smooth swirl of the hips which Elvis brought along with him when he'd appeared on *The Ed Sullivan Show*? Note: I guess that Ed wasn't too impressed by Elvis's act then, because, with his swirling routine Elvis apparently got himself removed from Ed's good grace and his show. And Ed wouldn't allow Elvis to return to his show. Ever.)

I do believe that father would not have been much amused had I ever secured the nerve to tell him that, on this day in '73 he did the best impersonation of the King of

R & R in speeded-up action that I had ever witnessed. (But Elvis always kept his fancy pants on.) Elvis, who father, like Ed, was never a fan of.

During the furor in the lobby, father had doubtless failed to take notice of a young lady renter who had entered the building via the front entrance. A woman who had paused for an instant, with her mouth agape, to stare at the comical spectacle father had been busily creating. I am sure that lady, who I never did come to know, had not believed her eyes before she'd seen her way well clear of father as she'd beat a hasty departure to the elevator; the look of disbelief had been etched into her face so powerfully that she could not even have thought to laugh or smile at the sight of father, a man who she doubtless had thought to have taken leave of his senses—and his professional's managerial dignity—in having exposed his colorful underwear in a public place.

As for me—in all of my life I had never before this incident witnessed my father being as energetic as he showed me that he could be—on this one summer day when a colony of agitated wasps made a mockery of him.

WHENEVER I CHANCE TO THINK OF MY CHILDHOOD, I instinctively conjure to mind the assuring image of a very powerful, nay—invincible, protector, who would never fail to shield me against the many pitfalls in life. I speak of Excalibur the sword, the sword of legend who the youthful arm of Arthur did wrench free from the stubborn stone. As the magician Merlin so well knew—the awesome power of Excalibur could only be drawn upon in the service of a righteous cause by one pure of heart. It is fitting then, that for so long as Arthur would live only he would ever hold the sword of myth and destiny in hand.

I think, too, of *Puff the Magic Dragon*, who I never had a chance to meet. Except in my dreams. In particular, I think of one line in this famous song about a mythical dragon and the little boy who imagines him. It is a very sad lament. Too sad. With all my will I cannot quite let go of the past to utter the words. In my heart, I can only utter the truth that Puff and the other fantasies of my own early years have vanished quietly into the mist. And the mist itself—has escaped into time.

I am now much older in years. And in wisdom, I hope. Soon, my curly brown locks will begin their slow but steady fading descent toward gray. My blue eyes shall lose their luster. I will become an old man. A wizened old man of the sea, with an unshakable, penetrating gaze. An old man, all alone. Except for his memories. Unfathomable to most. A solitary figure, and some souls might well aver, a man likely to be mysterious to the very end of his days. An old man lost irretrievably in time, like the *Titanic*. Aye, for, I have seen many things in my life, not all of which I understand. And some things—I suppose that I really do not want to understand. The memories of countless yesterdays will live on within me. To haunt me.

I wait for now. Then at last, when the soft, dry caress of a utopian summer is gone from the land and the autumn winds begin to blow in earnest, dragging storm clouds from the northern horizon, I shall head out into the eye of the advancing storm as I stand alone at the bow of my ghost ship—*The Flying Dutchman*. But I shall not ride the deep-blue waves of the sea. No. I will ride the winds of time. And I shall bide my time there for eternity if need be. I know that there is no tomorrow without today. No matter. I am patient. I know that there is still time left for me to dream.

AFTER OUR RETURN TO CANADA, Helen eventually realized her true goal in life and became a registered nurse. She is married and has a son and daughter. With my parents' support and financial backing, Raimo was handed an ideal opportunity and went on to fulfill his dream in medicine. A married man with a grown son and daughter. And I? What did I become?

In our family, the remnant of it, I remain the holdout in regard to the institution of marriage. The last one. The lonely one. Every day my lungs breathe of life I am reminded of such, just as I am always conscious of a past that I can never hope to escape while the spark of life still burns within me. And why would I want to? The past—lives within me. In my heart I am still a fighter. But more than that—I am Timewalker. Timewalker forever.

CHAPTER FORTY-FOUR

I Still Watch *I Dream of Jeannie*
Just As I Did When I Was A Kid

PERHAPS THE HARDEST LESSON I have learned in my life is that I am no James Bond. In refined looks, capability, and the manner in which I comport myself, no. Nor do I have a craving for danger. Excitement yes—danger no. You may add the following to my list of depressing failures too. You well may, because my accumulated experiences over the years do not amount to much. Not in the matter of love. Certainly, not for a man in love with the beauty of beautiful women. Unlike James, I have no experience in the fine art of lovemaking. Nor do I have a flashy set of wheels, armed, from floor to dashboard, with the very latest in techno gadgets. Being a hopelessly honest man, I cannot do less than concede my greed here. Money, as you all know because I said so earlier, means nothing to me. Or—almost nothing. However, a car is not like money. A car is transportation. And although I am a self-declared walking man who has sometimes been known to boast that I have no need for a car and do not even desire one, choosing instead to rely on my two legs (since I am so very much into healthy living), I do think about pretty ladies every day, and naturally, a nice sports car to chauffeur them all around in.

Well, not quite. I am looking for one lady. Yes—that's right. You all heard me. I require just one (very nice) lady. One lady, plus just one very nice sports car.

And—please believe all of you, me. It really galls myself to finally be forced to admit that I shall require four inflated wheels and a motor, after all. That stubborn independent streak of mine just doesn't seem to want to let go of me, and make my transition toward the Modern Age easy! But who, if anyone, am I fooling with that charade of mine? I desire a car. Yet, because I like style to surround me—no mere go-cart will do. Therefore, with myself having made my need to lay hold of a nice sports car perfectly clear, at last, to myself—and everybody else, I now feel free to tell you all that nothing less than a dandy, spanking new, jet-propelled racing machine, will do. Quite spiffy—just like the Batmobile.

And like the BM, it must be black on the exterior. Yes, any car just like the BM is a nice car. But, let me be reasonable to myself—if you all shall let me. I can hardly be expected to push and pull a prime bikini babe home, all the way from the beach to my cozy hilltop lair, in a cramped shopping cart powered by my slim frame. Further, I doubt that my lovely date would be suitably impressed were I to do so, or, for that matter, were I to even make the attempt to do so. And what about my kidnapped (my-oh-my, did I say kidnapped?) love's objection, if any should exist?

Realistically, I cannot be expected to win her heart by tying her down with rope in my shopping cart, where she would sit, cooped up for a good couple of hours like a defeathered chicken, uncomfortable and humiliated beyond words. Yes, I think that you all shall agree with myself when I say that I should be ashamed of myself for even painting with words which convey my disgust openly, such a terrible scenario as I just have. Yes, shame on me. My ways of thought are so very crude. Forgive me, will you? Please? Me and thee must know that this is my caveman mentality speaking, that is to blame.

Being very, um, wise as I truly am, I would be much wiser to take the highroad in soliciting my first date with a girl, in this lonely life of mine. I happen to believe that a magnificent strategy is required here. I may instead carry a hand-painted sign on my back. A sign strapped to me with heavy chains. If I choose to adopt this bold plan, the sign will read this:

WIFE WANTED—34-30-34.

Or simply this: NEED WIFE—APPLY ON SITE.

I believe that this plan is a good plan. This plan is unlike my first impulse to go about capturing a wife with that miserable shopping cart, which would prove to be a laborious undertaking for me. My second strategy is better than my first brainstorm, too, because it would be less likely to get the cops excited and—in hot pursuit on my trail. Kidnapping—or in my case—wifenapping, is a serious criminal offense even in pacifist Canada. If one is caught. Heh-heh.

And if the lack of a wife drives me toward desperation and the better, wiser half of my brain deserts me, we must all look on the bright side of this matter. For my ingenuity in having captured a wife at last, a feat ably demonstrated by my success—however fleeting a success it may be, the judge, be the judge man or woman, should later be highly amused by my having displayed ribald showmanship, and thus, he or she should extend to me the benefit of a lenient sentence. If I'm caught. Heh-heh. The judge might even feel a tad grateful toward me given the fact that my wifenapping operation had been carried out with a shopping cart, which surely can not have caused a serious adverse ecological impact, that vile impact tailpipe emissions from most motor vehicles produce.

I figure that for my crime I would get only ten years behind bars. Or thereabouts. Not bad, I say. I look at the obvious benefit of my lengthy incarceration. Sheltered, I would be at last, under maximum security in the nearest zoo. Safe and sound. With chimps as companions. My only companions. How wonderfully dreadful! Oh well, I have always had a hankering for ripe bananas. And in my new confine I can be sure that I would receive plenty of them. Uh, plus occasional room service at no cost to myself. Perhaps I should be convinced that this is a rare opportunity, one I simply cannot afford to pass up. Perhaps, as I continue to weigh my predicament, it really is much too good an opportunity for me to ignore.

Personal to Santa Claus

Dear Santa,

Please bring Roy, the very good boy, a sweet, sensitive blonde, brunette, or redhead toy. Roy loves toys so very much. A lovely swimsuit model, sincere and understanding, would be especially nice. So says Roy. But um. What else have you, Santa?

P.S. Written by your pal Roy—the perfectly lovable boy. Oh yes, Roy almost forgot. Roy deserves this wonderful toy because-because-because today Roy did all of the good things that every very good boy should do. For example! Roy tied his own shoes, brushed his own teeth, and um, Roy even washed behind both of his own ears. And um. Roy did not do any bad things today. And um. Roy forgot to do any bad things yesterday. Right now, Roy is getting sleepy telling Santa all about the good things that Roy did. So. It is time for Roy's daily nap. Good-bye dear Santa. Ookee-tookee-tookee-lookee-lookee-tookee-ookee.

From Roy.
The well-behaved boy.
(Being a very good boy is so tiring for Roy.)

Sensible Is My Name In Love,
But, Will Boy Meet Girl?

DISARMED OF MY CHILDHOOD NAIVETÉ at Campbell River, when, as my readers shall recall now, I had threatened to scoot off with another man's wife at the tender age of seven on Halloween night, I have, as you all know, at last come to my senses. No two-hundred pound lady primate for me this time around. Seriously, with adulthood and manhood I now realize the grim reality I face: I am very shy around attractive younger ladies; hiding my interest in such ladies is not at all easy; although, because I am a fair bit older than any of the gals who arouse my sexual interest, I, owing to a tongue-paralyzing fear of my being turned down for a date, somehow manage to do just that. Somehow.

In the past, I have truly been at my wit's end whenever I have been in the company of feminine beauty. And I have tried every technique I could think of, at these times, to avoid the direct gaze of every living picture of womanly beauty at her best. Whenever I be confronted by Venus, I seem to possess the undesirable habit of staring, when I am indoors, at what else but the ceiling of whatever building it is I happen to be in. And believe me—I can stare straight ahead for a long time. Just like a stork.

Too, I have tried to disguise my inner desire by my having shown a high level of intelligence in the selection of objects that I'd pretended to find terribly interesting. These objects are stuck to the surface of almost every handy ceiling. Yes my friends, what, on Earth, would I ever do without lighting fixtures?

In very old buildings, and there are not too many of those around in my town these days, I can even be expected to stare upward at exposed and corroding plumbing pipes, which will, to any curious onlooker, appear for some inexplicable reason to have attracted my undivided attention. I tend to do this when I am alone in the company of a pretty girl. Not always. But usually.

In regard to my utter fascination with ceilings, I muse thus. Perhaps, if I am lucky, the lady may even be fooled into believing that I am exercising my masculine neck, an exercise I demonstrate by straining my neck as far towards the ceiling as I can make it go. And—to lend credibility to my ruse, the young lady will see for herself that the blood vessels showing from my neck and head stand out visibly, as though they are about to pop from the severity of my exertion.

True to my purpose, I have tried the obvious escape as well. I have tried looking at the floor as if to see what might lie there. In a seemingly bold move, I have sat in a dentist's chair and stared at the feet of a pretty dental hygienist, as though I had been admiring her choice in shoes—in my attempt to evade that beautiful, radiant smile, tinged with, as each second has passed us by to the next, the swiftly built curiosity and amusement she must have felt about my highly unusual antics.

Being truly no fool in most things, I do realize that the strange behavior on my part must betray my heart of hearts. But realistically, what else can I do?

And consider this. When I attempt to engage in a meaningful dialogue under these circumstances, I, in fact, am able to speak clearly enough. Unfortunately, I tend to nervously swallow from time to time. So then, in order to disguise (I hope) my nervousness, I pretend to have the common cold. To successfully complete this act, requires that I draw mucous inwards from my nose—into my throat. In my doing thus, I figure that the object of my secret affection should not, by rights, be able to guess that my swallowing is related to sexual tension. And since she and I are alone (alone, because the dentist, who is a busy fellow, has more than one patient to attend to, and that—elsewhere) and, since she is in such close proximity to myself, that I harbor a strong romantic desire to elope with her.

Wisely, I never pretend to be afflicted by anything as potentially deadly as the flu, because if I were to do so, the object of my secret passion would, in all likelihood, wish to beat a hasty retreat from the room. As concerns my use of the word *object*, I must stress that this word is to be considered in a plural sense by my readers: there is no one special lady in my life who I exhibit the awkward behavior in front of.

Back we all are in the room now. Whilst my charade that I suffer from the common cold is going on, my hands perspire as though I had just run a marathon at Mach 1. The only things missing from this captivating drama are the exhausted appearance and heavily strained panting of a long-distance runner.

In my adult life, whenever I have chanced to meet a pretty woman and ventured to look directly into her eyes, I have, at these times, been keenly conscious of the split microseconds that pass us by whenever my gaze dwells but a moment too long on her misty, longing eyes, as they look into my own. And this mistake of mine, if it is to be judged as such, has usually only served to compound my initial nervousness.

There is another slight problem. Once I encounter a beautiful woman, I find that it becomes difficult for me to joke. This, despite the fact that I am, at most times, at least half-full of funny business (humor is a salve for a wounded mind). Yes, before a beautiful woman my train of thought— directly reflected by my unsmiling neutral demeanor, in spite of my concentrated effort to resist, becomes noticeably serious, as though I had on all these different occasions involving different women, recognized in each case my true love, the love of my adult life. And always, it is as though nothing else in the world matters in the instant of our meeting, when we lock into one another's eyes.

I make no joke here. The failure on my part is but one more impediment that bars myself from gaining ground in the pre-dating game. On the one hand I desire, as do all sane men, an attractive lady. Yet, I feel that I manage to shoot myself in the foot each time I am confronted by physical beauty.

Having been single for all of my adult life, is enough proof to me that all beautiful women are easily able to penetrate the titanium shield which encircles my mind. And what they, no doubt, see beyond this protective barrier is a dismally bashful, love-sick puppy of a man. Unattractive to them. So, the questions for me, are these. Be I a hopeless case that no good-looking woman will ever have any desire to have a serious, lifelong relationship with? Be I nothing more to such a woman than a sorry bundle of frayed nerves, strapped within a man's body? Be I a bundle of psyched-out conduits without a shred of manhood intact?

If I be those things, then perhaps I am too emotional a man to be accepted by Venus in all her splendid beauty.

Too often I have wondered how I might *best* allay the keen intuition of Venus so that my emotion toward her will remain undetected by her. Mightily so this is, for, when I am in the sole company of Venus, it is, as all of you now know, almost impossible for me to stop staring at the ceiling. Or floor. In either case, a dead giveaway the staring is. And in the rare moments when I do look at her, I feel that my eyes always betray me and reveal to her, to every Venus, absolute confirmation of her suspicion in regard to my amorous mindset.

My eyes are such public fools. They will always reveal my attraction toward a lady's undeniable charms. Attracted I am to Venus. But am I in love when I behold her? If I am, then I truly must be a terrible human being. A terrible man. What kind of man be I, if I be this kind of man that I love all attractive women for their beauty on the outside? Without looking deep within them? Be I this kind of man? Or, be I a man with a conscience? Whatever I be—I be. But, I believe that I be both of these things.

And what course should I adopt then, knowing myself as well as I do? I believe the following course the right one for me. This course will mean that I shall make myself available to the world of women. Though I shall not stare wistfully at them all. I shall simply wait until I, through stubborn waiting, at last manage to stumble upon the right lady for me. And for me, knowing who the right lady is, may not be as big of a problem as it could be. I shall simply wait for some very hot chick to show up someday as I am standing in line at my local supermarket, ready to pay the cashier for my groceries. I shall not protest when I am seized by her and dragged by my hand from the store. I shall not protest when she takes the initiative in an attempt to, at last, crack—and shatter—my cool wannabe-cool exterior.

I shall wait for her to plant her mouth over my lips like a suction cup. And kiss me silly. Kiss me, and thereby liberate me from my self-imposed dungeon of habitual shyness as she breathes the force of life from within her, into my soul. Do I ask for too much? I only ask to be loved.

Should Venus fail to rescue me from my shackles, I will need to embark on a journey to find her. Otherwise—I may never know what it is like to be kissed by a pretty woman. Kissed by her, the special vibrant light of my life whom I have long sought to discover. Kissed by her. An act of softness from the heart of Venus, which should instill me with the courage to kiss her in return. Of course, I could opt to wear dark sunglasses when I visit the dental clinic the next time.

OBLIVIOUS TO MY INNER EXISTENCE, the other major roadblock, besides my crippling shyness with pretty ladies, that I certainly face in life which will, if unchanged, likely continue to bar me from ever finding a great lady is that I am hopelessly incompetent in regard to just about every serious task I have ever set my hand to in life. Uh-huh, for this reason I fear that I shall remain forever shunned by the outside world. A world that is heedless of my deeper self. Groan, a life of perpetual solitude likely awaits me.

Let me give you a shining example of my incompetence at work. Fresh out of high school, I'd suffer to work for a few short months in the dusty confine of a cabinet-making shop. I was eventually handed the simple task of drilling a lot of holes into my projects. Now, as it turned out at the end of the day, one side of my worktable was riddled with holes. I had bored these holes, in fact—several hundred of them, so deep that the top of the table was in dreadful danger of collapse. Needless for me to say—my boss—was not pleased. Nor was he at all amused. I shall not mention what happened to me after my screw-up. However, you may be interested to know that my employer went out of business, not too long thereafter. I still wonder whether that was my fault.

I believe that with this one incident I've just mentioned—you all will have a very accurate idea of how incompetent I can be. And the way I see it—lovemaking is no different than making a cabinet. In love, I am afraid that if I should somehow manage to defeat the odds for success—and I do screw-up—I may not get a second chance, to try and smooth over any initial mistakes which I certainly can be counted on to make at the outset of a courtship. I guess that I am just one very unlovable and lonely fellow.

Incompetent at everything in life, I foresee that I shall likely continue to suffer tremendous setbacks in my ongoing attempt to find feminine love in this rotten life of mine. In my desperation to find my first kiss, I fear that I have just one last, forlorn hope of so doing. I fear that I have no choice left. No choice, except to sell my soul by bending the rules of moral conduct. I am speaking of the very darkest combination of all possible evils. Seduction and trickery. I realize that I must stoop to anything to solicit that all-important first kiss.

Without further torturing my readers' curiosity, here then is my much-thought-about plan. First—I shall proceed under guise of dark sunglasses, a fisherman's bonnet, a raincoat, and rubber hip-waders to the nearest unsuspecting pharmacy. This odd attire may attract attention. Particularly if my visit to the pharmacy should happen to fall upon an overcast day with no threat of precipitation in the forecast.

But no one need fear for me. I have no disabling fear that anyone I know, or anyone who may know me without my knowing them, shall recognize me. Garbed as I'll be in disguise, I will look exactly like a fisherman of the seven seas when I enter the store. Without, of course, the salty smell of fish stuck to my wearables.

And, once I am within the premises, I will hang about in the beauty products' aisle whilst I peruse the selection of lipstick. Then, once I have made my choice from amongst the sizable selection of lip color on display behind the cosmetics' counter, I will reach out with my gloved hand (yes, I shall be wearing men's black dress gloves too—made of vinyl because I never wear products made of animal hide) and take hold of some red, or even pink, lipstick. The brand does not matter to me, either.

I shall then proceed to the nearest checkout. Here I will pretend to be immensely interested in the color of the tile floor. While I am staring at the floor, I shall pay for the lipstick. I shall not glance at the cashier even once.

With the first half of my covert mission accomplished, I will walk home, making absolutely sure that I am not being followed by any curious onlookers who may have witnessed my suspicious garb and behavior whilst I was in the store.

At home, I will remove my fisherman's outfit, my gloves, and my sunglasses. Then I will carefully apply the tube of lipstick not to my lips—but to each of my cheeks. While I attend to my cheeks I shall try to be very careful. I do not wish to use up all the lip product in this one tube at once. Deliberately, I will paint the figure of a woman's full lips on my cheeks. I will do a superb job of it, for, my artwork must appear convincing. That done, I will pause only long enough to change all my clothes, putting on a fine suit of teal, with slacks to match. These, to accompany a clean, white, well-pressed dress shirt.

READY FOR ACTION, I shall make haste toward my ultimate destination. This being wherever pretty, young ladies are known to congregate. Even a grocery store will do. Remember that I am shy around ladies now. Thus, I have never entered the premises of a nightclub in all of my adult life. Aye, during business hours.

My lack of experience in that regard can be easily understood by most any civilized culture, because, up here in the oft frozen wasteland of Canada we Canadians have little else to do during the harsh winter months but build igloos.

And in the fleeting summers we sometimes watch as polar bears devour our most unpopular politicians—who are let loose on the desolate, windswept tundra beforehand—to run for their lives, clad only in their undershorts. But don't all of you good folks beyond Canada worry. Our viewing activity is in no way indecent because all the unwilling participants are men.

I return to the matter of gaining my first kiss from a truly attractive lady. I am sorry that I became a bit sidetracked because of the igloos, polar bears, and politicians. With my special secret plan in mind now, the only thing which I do know for sure, is that whatever public place I decide to travel to in search of my special girl, I shall make sure I spend as much of my time there as I possibly can. Will I succeed in finding my true love in such place? I'm not sure. However, I have developed a theory governing the gravitation of girls to boys, a theory which may work to my advantage.

My theory (even though it is not actually my theory in the sense that other men have known of it long before I thought of it), if valid—rules thus: single women gravitate, as the moon does toward the Earth, to handsome men who are, or appear to be, married.

Since I wear no ring of any kind on my fingers, all women must, of course, construe that I am not married. This, I reason, is not a bad thing. In fact, once I divulge my complete plan to you all, I hope that every reader shall agree with myself, and deem that the odds of my finding success, appear almost equal to the odds of married men who have. Yes, because the way that I see it, with no identifying symbol of any woman's claim of ownership visible on my fingers, I should be seen by all reasonable-minded, attractive, single women, as perfectly eligible, marriageable material. Psychologically free, I, of any disruptive defects of the mind brought about by long, torturous years of listening to a nagging wife.

And further to my advantage in this game of securing a date, I believe that every eligible lady in my chosen place of meeting them, including any who may then be watching from the high-resolution security cameras above me, will immediately deduce, once every lady sees that both sides of my face are adorned with fresh red, or pink, kiss marks, the strong likelihood that I cannot be a total dud. Why else, each lady should ask of herself, would this romantic insignia of unbridled affection be stuck to his cheeks? Someone, some lucky girl, somewhere, must find him, each peach will reason, incredibly attractive.

I sincerely hope that my audacious ploy works like a charm, so that all respectable women will feel the pressing urge to initiate a meaningful conversation with so-well-kissed a man as I will appear to be. And therefore, they will reason—so popular a man. I have nothing to lose except my independence and virginity. Should all else fail and I have need to utilize the lipstick method of finding courtship, I shall let you, my staunch readers, know exactly how my little experiment turns out someday, in my next book. But I caution all of you, not to expect too much of me. No one should be too optimistic about my chances of finding true love in life. Also, bearing in mind the way matters usually have a way of going in my life—I may need to name that next book thus: Timewalker Sucks.

Is the life of a man to be judged by his speed—or by the barrel of a gun that harbors no greed?

NO FAST BANANA!

I USED TO DRIVE a pony, which I would always leave parked at curbside on the street where I live. One day, I discovered a proposition pinned beneath one windshield wiper. The proposal was from an escort agency looking to hire new, fertile blood. Evidently, somebody living within peeping distance of my vehicle must have thought me hard up for cash. Anyhow, the notice swiftly wound up in my vehicle's trash basket.

I wasn't insulted at all. I wasn't, because, at least I learned something heartwarming: some female out there must have had her woman's eyes trained upon me, and liked what she saw, enough to afterwards let me know of her scrutiny. I'll take the not-so-subtle surveillance of my fanny as a genuine compliment. To myself, this is positive proof that secret admirers exist in the most inconspicuous places. In my neighborhood. Even for me. Yet, this incident occurred a long while back. Very sadly, as of the present, the total membership in my secret admirer fan club remains at zero. Boo-hoo.

I REPEAT THAT I AM NO JAMES BOND

NEITHER AM I TV's secret agent man, who was always cool and competent. I hark back to my childhood dreamworld for an instant. A dreamworld where I had stiff competition like *him*, to measure myself against. And invariably, from one day to another, even as I grew a little taller and stronger with each day that slowly passed, I nonetheless came up too short for my liking whenever I compared myself to that intrepid, capable man, who was just one more hero amongst the many that filled my boy's mind.

In my self-comparison to secret agent man, I felt that I would never be able to favorably compare myself to him, because, amongst many reasons, for one—secret agent man like his counterpart, James, never suffered the ignominy of having a stream of toilet paper trail from his pants whenever he'd left home to go to some public place. But had he, and had he done what I almost did on that early morning so long ago when the dog that barked behind me saved me from public disgrace, I am sure that despite the dark sunglasses he always wore, which usually lent a tone of seriousness and mystery to the man, those shades of his would not have helped our wannabe-mysterious man the least in his attempt to be perceived in the public's eyes as a truly cool man.

This is because—for any cool man—image is everything. Well, not necessarily to himself always, but always to the discriminating tastes of the public. To be cool—one must look cool. Every wannabe-cool man must know this sage advice: all of the very hottest chicks dig the very coolest-looking guys.

My definition of looking cool has no double meaning, either. To me, a cool-looking character is just that. It is not some poor Eskimo dude at the North Pole, sitting inside his icy igloo, frantically rubbing his frostbitten hands together before a small blaze in an effort to unfreeze them, whilst his teeth are busy chattering, up and down and sideways, from Arctic cold.

Nor do I have in mind the guys who spend their entire working lives in the controlled environment of any frigid meat-packing plant. And other guys that I don't mean come, unlike myself, each—complete with a stable work history just like the never-failing Maytag fix-up man, though I am not sure whether that guy services broken-down fridges.

By my definition of a cool man, I don't mean any of Santa's many little helpers, either. Helpers who probably work so hard that they never get the chill, up at the North Pole. Even if there is a power outage, causing Santa's electrically powered battery of baseboard heaters to switch off, which'll make his workshop as cold as the Abominable Snowman's cave. Being overweight by more than just a few pounds, Santa himself doesn't strike me as looking at all like a cool dude should look. Especially with that long, fluffy, white beard of his, and with that jolly red-and-white suit always covering his pudgy body whenever he makes a public appearance.

Ever since I turned six years of age, I have felt that the more cool a man can look, will work to his benefit. To any man, simply looking cool should, by rights, ensure more dates with ravishing women, although I admit that, at the age of six I didn't exactly think of girls who were my age, as being women. Cool. A Joe Cool kind of cool. This, I am convinced, is what every eligible sane man must strive for.

Yes, every unattached man should immediately forget about his career, promising or not, and disown his longtime aspiration to possess oodles of money. He should forget about every accomplishment of his life. Real or imagined. He should just concentrate his hardest on looking cool. The recipe which shall lead to his happiness in life is really that simple. Looking cool is all that single men like myself need to do. And never—should we let any soul see us when we're grimy. Take it from me. I am convinced that if all unattached men do as I've instructed here, everything else in life shall automatically fall into its proper place for them. And if I follow my own advice, it will for me too.

Of course, that philosophy of mine doesn't really go any distance towards explaining why it is that I have never been married. Nor engaged to be married. Nor, for that matter, have I ever in the long, winding course of my life—had a girlfriend. I don't mean a girlfriend who is just a friend, either.

I shall explain myself now. The answer to those very perplexing questions is in Albert Einstein's most advanced formula. Whatever that is. I, like anyone who ever played hooky (oops!) from school at some convenient time and consequently never got anywhere in life by so doing (even the stupidest will eventually learn from an old mistake), have immense confidence in Albert's mathematical wizardry. Yes, I know that Albert's formula, which must be as brilliant as Albert was, will finally allow me to silence my critics by providing to all ladies of good character, a believable explanation as to my abstinence from the dating circuit. However, with the weather in my mind being so very cloudy at this moment, I think that I shall need to postpone my very interesting explanation until some other time. I don't know when would be a good time, either.

Perhaps you all, being ladies of virtue, might be satisfied with a less detailed explanation than any that would be afforded us by Albert's intellectual's understanding. Yes? *Bien.* Because, this is my excuse as to why I am still single today, at the age of forty-six. You see, dating circuits are not for me because, I am only one man and, I can never hope to date every willing, attractive single lady alive on Earth. Whew.

Apart from that excellent reason, in terms of circuitry, let me say that my body contains no hardware which is mechanically driven. Unlike a used car nearing the end of its life—I am totally dependent. Er-make that dependable. In fact, the only similarity between me and a badly rusted bucket of bolts on tires is that we both evolved into being in the last century. Oh. We share something else. I, like an inanimate piece of corroded metal, am even-tempered. Nowadays I am so, always.

RETURN that terrible recurring fear which lurks in the deepest depths of my soul. A fear hidden from sight beneath the smooth surface of my skin. I can and shall face this fear, for, I am a man. Being a man, I can do no less. My fear, I realize, is a fear of reality. It is a sense of foreboding that warns me. Uncanny, some people would consider it. Indeed, and truly ominous this unwelcome feeling of mine is.

To myself, as unsettling this feeling is, as a rapidly advancing gray storm cloud moving upon me from an otherwise azure sky to encircle me would be. It is a feeling I cannot easily shake, this, my presentiment of an approaching menace, is. My premonition tells me that I shall probably die as an unwanted, unloved recluse. And these days, my inner sense is rarely wrong about anything. So, why should it be wrong to this regard?

Yes, given my inadequacies and hopeless fears, I may never know what it is like to be kissed by a pretty woman. I may never know what it is like to stroke such a lady's eyebrows with my lips. Nor may I know what it is like to touch noses with her. And from the depths of my lungs, breathe sweet air ever so gently into her ears—and to softly whisper lullabies into them. Nor may I know what it be like to take this very special lady into my arms with more sensitivity than any man who has ever walked on the surface of Earth could possibly muster.

I believe that I could sit for hours on end with her warm head in my lap, stroking her lips, face, and hair gently with my lips. And running my fingers through her hair. Or curling these precious filaments of my lover, of feminine beauty at her finest, into gracious little twists with my fingers.

With fine scissors, I would cut off a tuft of my brown locks and ask Venus to do the same with her own for me. I would then join the two follicle friends by tying them together at the center, like a bow on each of Santa's Christmas gifts. So that they embrace each other. And support one another. And keep one another good company. I would then ask my love to keep our mutual and very private bow for the remainder of her life.

Too, if I were away and she were lonely or distraught, I would wish that she take our bow of union and touch it to her cheek, so she would be reminded that all will be well when I return.

I am a man of pure heart. Emotional intelligence is the very essence of what I am. And I seek the very highest level of emotional intimacy in a woman. Without this emotional bond there can be nothing for me. I am really this simple a man. I am a man of feelings—more in tune with a woman's needs than any other man could ever hope to be. Assuredly, for, on this earth there is no man who is more sensitive than I. And kind, so very gentle of heart. I am Timewalker. One man. Only one. And my emotion surfaces from deep within my heart. An emotion so wonderful it shines like the light of an angel.

I truly can feel the musical chorus in a woman's heart when it speaks to me. So well I know what emotion is in her heart. I know, because I am emotion, as pristine in its purity as the form of a perfect crystal. And this may very well be my Achilles' heel.

A beautiful woman's love, when it is unconditional and therefore pristine in its wondrous beauty, has its own special and tantalizingly potent way of unraveling a man. Its own way of unclothing a man so completely that he is left to contemplate reality only in his birthday suit. Regardless of his dignity, a man's clothes take their leave of him almost as though each piece of his apparel has a heart, and thus, a will of its own.

No man blessed with bodily health and proper mind can for long resist this powerful impulse. Even the most decent and respected of men obey the natural force of gravitation toward beauty, their base animal instincts moved by a force so very powerful that it will never fail to draw lowly man closer and closer to the woman he loves. *This* is the primate need of man speaking. It stands beside the need to hold one's love close. This *other* need—the need to cuddle and protect. King Kong experienced the full intensity of *these* desires when he held actress Fay Wray in the palm of his giant hand in the 1933 motion picture classic named after him. Though he was but an ape, I am sure that Kong had felt a mighty big tug at his heart as he fell before Fay's spell of raw physical beauty—so aptly captured on film in the fragility of her tiny form.

Unfortunately, I am nowhere near the size of Kong, so I could hardly hope to cradle a woman in my hand. Nonetheless, the boundary between primeval ape and modern man is not distinguishable in the matter of love. Men love women for being everything that men are not. Physically and psychologically—women are different. The desire to hold and protect the vulnerable female form is inherent in every decent man, just as it is in his hairy-chested cousin, the great ape.

And should any man of glowing health elect to play the part of a fool and attempt, at first, to resist the supercharged, invisible force of sexual love, based—so much—on a woman's appearance, with his puny will, the superhuman effort he will expend in so doing will only serve to exhaust him. Like a salmon about to spawn, he is then ready to be sucked in through a vortex of passion, of quivering lips and hot, sweaty bodies.

For a man, there is no antidote to free him of this affliction. He is bound to his own want. Like a slave, he is literally bound stark naked and vulnerable to a woman's charms and desires. She, in turn, will be drawn in the same way to the man she loves.

No one must ever doubt it. The more beautiful that a woman is—the more captivating she will be to a man. Men always judge women by their external beauty first. In fact, men love to celebrate and immortalize a woman's external beauty. Whilst they often overlook her inner beauty. Men always subscribe to the foremost because they wish to believe that a beautiful countenance cannot hide a less than endearing soul. A man will look into a woman's eyes and decide, then and there, what she is.

But are a woman's eyes, the most distinguished features of her face, truly the windows of her soul? Eyes which, to a man, speak of the world otherwise hidden from his sight, within her. Some men say so. Other men may quietly think so.

And what do I think? I think this. If I must decide on a woman's inner beauty, I sincerely doubt that her external features, no matter how beautiful she may be, necessarily mirror her soul. With my eyes I have seen plenty of evidence to point toward the conclusion that women who possess great beauty on the outside, are not always pure of heart. In my admittedly limited experience with women as human beings, I have found that many attractive women, in fact, are nowhere near as attractive on the inside as they are on the outside. I don't know why this is so often the case. I only know that it is.

Perhaps beauty that is skin-deep results in there being less of a need for the individual to develop her inner self. Being physically beautiful, such a woman can in her years of comparative youth never know what it is to be ugly, perhaps alone and unloved. Not until she is old and frail can she know this. And then, when the full realization of what she has slowly lost with time hits home repeatedly with ceaseless, merciless force, she will yearn in her heart for yesterdays of long ago.

But, in the meantime, until she be old, wrinkled of face and body, the power over man lies with her. It lies with every beautiful woman. And her power is truly great. Just as I said before, with this power she can undo a man's clothing, using his own will. To simple man, her power is like the heat of fire when it has ample oxygen to burn. Burn a man, it does. It sears a man with its intensity as it cuts through him like a blowtorch through a single sheet of paper. It is the power of passion with no limit.

And when a man unravels due to the emotion of true love he feels welling up within him—this is not to be mistaken for weakness. Even so, should a woman return my love, her love, like the intoxicating fragrance of the sweetest flower, could, I fear, transform my legs into jelly.

Worry not: caught in this delicate situation, a woman's purposeful stare will invite even a shy man, such as I be. Though, before I shed my clothes for her, I must search for and find both genuine love and respect in her gentle eyes. In her heart, how a woman feels about me in every way is most important to myself, and I am ultrasensitive to what she wants. Yet, if she does not respect me fully—then the hurt will linger in me.

I digress. Did I not mention that I am a good listener? I will listen to whatever she might wish to tell me. There would be no secrets between us. None at all.

As I am a hopeless romantic, the following would be a foregone conclusion, because this is the only way that I know. I would speak directly to a woman's heart. I would speak directly to her soul. To that end, should I muster the courage as I must, I would carry her in my arms from the ocean's surf, and play idly with her toes, like a true romantic man should do. Taking her bare wet feet in my hands as we lie upon a sandy shore, I would press each of her ten toes gingerly into my chest so that our communion would be complete. So that we would be as one.

And, each of her toes I would treat with equal emotion—I happen to believe that each of her toes has a personality all its own. I would treat them all with equal love and tenderness, as though they were all little children. And I would beautify her many toes, and the tips of her fingers, with red nail-polish. Apply, too, I would, deep glossy rouge to the subtle inviting smile resting on her full lips of desire.

I would overlook no minor detail to make sure that she is, and stays, happy. I would think of everything. And our lips would meet time and again as I and my love embrace one another. Then at last, when the sun's radiance would take its leave of the sky and night would steal its way in, the lesser warmth in the cooling air would mean little to us as we would hold each other tightly—with only the shared heat of our bodies to keep us warm throughout the long darkness. Thus we would do until the brightest stars no longer shone their twinkling light down on us. Come morning, our world of happiness would turn its face to a new day. A new reality. A new beginning in time. The sadness and loneliness in my heart would be alleviated.

I do not wish to accept the possibility that forever I may be alone. That forever, the rest of my life, I shall have no one to love. Undaunted still, the blue flame of romance burns undying in me, seeking the love of a woman. Love that only a woman can give me.

And lest there be any doubt about it amongst my readers, I search only for the love of one woman. Not that of a multitude of women. Yes, I am monogamous, and some say of me, too loyal, as though loyalty were somehow a fault. I heed not these voices. Should I ever find this lady love of mine, I will expect her to be as well.

As every man should know, a woman needs to be made to feel that she is truly loved. She needs to be nurtured with kindness and sensitivity. That I would do—I wish not only for a lady to be my lover—but my best friend. And, she must be a friend who will pledge to remain true to me until I am no more. Then, only then, can I feel comfortable enough to surrender my soul to her embrace. And if she truly loves me, she will think kindly of me, always. Thereby, allowing both of us to feel unencumbered enough to confide in one another. Always.

For my part, this lady needs to know that I will stand beside her even as we advance into old age, as a man who deeply loves a woman should do. I shall, if I find her, care for her in both sickness and health—no matter what. This lady needs to know that, in the depths of my heart, her growing age will never conceal her inner beauty from me. As I imagine her to be, the softness of her heart is so beautiful. And in her tender heart she will come to know that my love is real and lasting. Not merely spoken.

I make mention of the last, because I do not think much of any man who will leave his wife for a younger woman merely on the basis of creeping age. I strongly feel that if a man, of his free will, marries a woman—he should do so for life. In return, a woman should observe the same rule of allegiance, of untarnished fidelity to one man only.

Now, despite what I say here I know that sometimes, for whatever reason, the love between two people can die. In response to that I can only repeat the point I have made, that I am prepared to love this lady with all my heart; hopefully, she would love me as well. And yet, because I am kind and understanding, I would never attempt to stop her, should she ever decide in her heart to leave me.

It is my belief that every kind woman has a little girl hidden deep within her. And I, better than any man that I know, understand this little girl. This little girl who lives in every kind woman's heart is, to me, like a soft mass of jelly. Full of emotion. Ready to be loved. All one has to do is love her without end. Love, so that her heart does not weep for lack of love. And, so that she may feel fuzzy all over herself as she smiles. For so long as we both live, I would do my utmost to shield her vulnerability from all manner of harm. Yet, I be not possessive, only protective.

As everyone must guess, this is a very special lady I search for. Oh, I know what you must be thinking. What man can pretend to understand how a woman truly feels? I don't pretend. I just can. Always I can. And I can because I speak the language of emotion better than any man I know. Emotion is, and always will be, the universal language of all womanhood. And the rare man. Emotion is the language of love.

Even though that upbeat stream of thought has but scarcely left my mind, I again commence to wonder whether I shall find my special lady in time. Thus does my mind drift to the sentiment I have claimed. The possibility that I shall be alone until I die. If this is not to be, I will say that this very special lady will need to be a lady driven by the loving pulse of my heart and the warm, inviting touch of my lips, rather than a lady attracted by the thickness of my wallet. My wallet, in which I am sure that any lady who would look for money, would be sorely disappointed.

In one regard, perhaps I be a fool. I say so because I have already fallen deeply in love with my mystery lady. Without my having ever seen her. I don't know who she is. Nor do I have any notion where on this planet, if she be here, that it is I should look to find her. And if she is not here, I have no idea where in our universe, or—in that of another, my path should lead.

I shall not desist in my ongoing effort to find her. I will—not—stop. I shall not, even if I must scour every nook and cranny on this planet and, on that of others, ten times over. Yet I tell myself that such effort must be needless. My ladylove has got to be here on this planet—somewhere.

BEING NO SOCIALITE, I have little hope that she will find me—the robe of habitual solitude that encircles my soul hides the heat of the flame within me. A blaze of passion that is invisible, unspent, and as pristine as the clearest mountain lake. Intractable from the task ahead, I yet again acknowledge the possibility that despite my best efforts to become a married man, I may yet fail in my quest. And I know that if she cannot find me, and I cannot find her, then half of my soul will slowly want to wither in me and disappear from existence altogether. Even as I resist this impulse with my other, stronger, half.

I am keenly cognizant human life is short. I know that in enough time the flame of passion in my heart will die, as I will die. Die, in spite of my stronger-half's will to keep living; though, at that distant point in my life I may not know for what reason exactly, it is that I should continue to live.

Even now as I write, my resolve, which should never wander to ask, is asking. My optimistic half consoles the pessimist in me. The pessimist tells me that I am living in a night with no end. One long night of loneliness and pain. Alone I am. In self-imposed exile. Within my own world. Is that what I want? At the very least, is there no one in all of this world, to give me one kiss? Just one paltry kiss. It need be only one kiss. I need but one.

But this question of whether there is or isn't won't, I know, make any difference in the end, anyway. In the end, when the daylight fades from my weary eyes, the force of life replaced by eternal night. I tell myself that, knowing that it is true. In the end I will die, surely. I will slide, either willing or unwilling, into that vast, uncharted, eternal abyss known as death. Uncharted I say, because no one that I know of has ever returned from the dead, once his or her corporeal presence has ceased to exist.

And what will I become before and after that? Before, when the youthful vitality finally seeps out of my muscles as I grow, with increasing old age, steadily weaker by the day? And then after. Will I at last be, in the final chapter of my existence here on earth amongst the still living— though dead, nothing more than a decaying old log? I put to myself this question as though I know not the answer. A rotting old log, half-sunken within the ground, with a company of eager toadstools sprouting into the air, on top of me. Oblivious I, to the green carpet of forest moss that will seek to cover me from head to toe as soon as I exhale my final earthly breath.

And will the toadstools lay their claim to me before my embattled exterior becomes home to a hundred-thousand centipedes, all toiling, all tunneling, as though to hasten my spirit on its way through the black earth beneath them? Through earth that was once my body.

This, while above me, delicate, sticky spider webs crawl upward toward the luxurious umbrella of branches offered by yellow cedar trees as they look down upon me, and into this dark place where the sunlight can but feebly penetrate the almost unbroken canopy of green branches above my place of rest.

And will this connection between earth and sky attract the occasional blue jay, who would be but a chance visitor scurrying about for an insect or two? Or perhaps a furry squirrel, who would stop to breathe the frosty greeting of late autumn in the windless air while scouring the forest floor for acorns? And would the squirrel, being but a squirrel, after all, have any respect for my home? For I, who am but a slow, lingering breath away from the absolute end? Or would my bushy-tailed visitor defecate on what I've become while it gnaws on an acorn?

I know that in time the rotting old log I once was will disappear entirely, my moist reddish-brown skin having long since been eaten away by the centipedes, the toadstools, the moss, and the encroachment of time and elements. A familiar musty smell will rise into the cold air to meet the senses of those who must venture close, those who leave the beaten path to find this forbidding place and the beauty that lies here everywhere. Of my former self, there will be no trace.

And the challenged mortal souls of man, should they rest their gaze on my home for long, will contemplate the change that each season, in turn, will bring to the forest. Then, inevitably then, as if to speed this process of change along the first small snowflakes will begin to fall upon my unmarked grave. Pure, crystalline, frozen water. It is these first flakes of snow that will foretell the coming of the lean winter months ahead, when the silent forest, like me, sleeps beneath a mantle of white. And rotted old logs, like old men, have nothing more to say.

BUT I KNOW that dismal earthen scenario will never be. And the worms and other meal bugs—all parasitic scavengers, shall not, if I am granted my final wish, ever be lucky enough to have their heathen way with me: my long-standing wish is that the fire of the furnace be ignited to consume my mortal remains. If I am granted that one wish, I will not know of it then, as the hungry flames lick greedily at the shell of flesh and bone that was my body, and gradually devour that which represented me.

May the fire of the furnace burn as bright as the fire of my will did in life, so that I need not contemplate the other fate I speak of. That other end is unstylishly macabre, rude, and unspeakably uncivilized for my high standard in body-disposal etiquette.

Ideally, had I my druthers, I would opt for a yet more aesthetically pleasing form of dispatch. What I have in mind is nothing less than a *Star Trek* matter-transport beam, set on a course of disintegration with maximal spread throughout space. This beam of energy would break apart the molecular bonds that make any body, a whole body. Ultimate technology. In the service of a final purpose. A kinder fate, where one could vanish to peaceful nonexistence with the same informality one came into being. For me, this end would be the very kindest end. An end where a man's soul, caught within the radiant beam of high-octane energy flowing freely through his body and— in an instant scattering his remains far and wide, would be freed without final insult.

Freed at last, to the farthest reaches of this cold, heartless universe of matter and energy, space and time. To a final resting place beyond the most distant stars known. To a fitting end. For this holder of the journeyed pen, guaranteeing that my tired half need never waken from sleep to know misery again. To know love. And then pain. Never again to know profound sadness as I have known joy. My wish. Given the option, I would have it this way. This way, because it is—my way.

Beyond those reflections of feeling in me, it is a somber thought for this writer to have to bear another. This is that, in just a short one hundred years in a universe of time, time—which I believe has no end, this laborious account of mine may be but vaguely remembered, if it is remembered at all, as the childhood odyssey of a boy who once lived. A boy who slowly grew into a man. Both of them long gone and scattered to dust.

Epilogue

IN ENDING THIS ACCOUNT I have this to say. My view of the universe and life presents as follows. Now, not everyone will agree with this view, a view that is a bleak reflection of our surroundings. So be it, but this is my view. Regardless of our age, we are all children, in a sense. Some of us wiser than others. And, as we would be seen from another galaxy far away—should any sustain advanced civilization on them, we happen to live on a tiny, obscure planet, a world orbiting a small star in one galaxy. One quite ordinary galaxy—amongst billions almost like it. What exactly is the meaning of all this, if, there be any meaning?

What is the meaning of life itself? I have grappled with this question ever since I was old enough to think independently, and I've carefully weighed it. And I have, at last, come to the conclusion that there is no underlying meaning to life. No meaning, because there is no meaning to the universe. We exist. It exists. That is all.

As I consider that answer, I frown. I frown because I wish that the answer to life were as emotionally satisfying as the lyrics of one very famous song said. Most everyone shall recall having heard this musical masterpiece, for, it is none other than Bob Dylan's timeless classic, "Blowin' in the Wind".

In the weary half of my heart, the ghosts of my past are beckoning to me. Calling out to me to come home at last. To give in. And come home. "Forlorn one," they beseech me endlessly. "Come home now," they say. When my heart

413

speaks thus—I know that my heart speaks of its sorrow. In my mind, I know home is but a sad dream. Not real. Only a slowly fading vision of countless, long-ago yesterdays. Home, my true home, is a place I can never return to. Even could I—why would I? I could not. The innumerable hurts of distant yesterdays are forever seared into my mind.

My friends, in my attempt to explain to you all just how I feel now, I must echo the sentiment I expressed as a four-year-old boy, sitting in meditation on my family's front porch at Lanark Street. Forty-two years ago. My friends, I wish for you all the very best in life. I have nothing more to say.

"FINAL DAY"

At the end of the final day
All is swept forever away
Like the tiny grains of a sandcastle
Before the waves of the sea

—the author

While half of the world lies in peaceful slumber, a solitary writer writes on from the depths of his heart, as a full moon keeps watch over his silent, lonely vigil.

Yours forever,

Timewalker forever

Roy's Honest Confession:

First, I reluctantly confess that I pulled your stiff legs some with my slightly exaggerated account of my father's jiggin'-and-jumpin' frenzy in a public place, which I so mirthfully described for you in this book. Yes folks, that's right! Blame Roy! In truth, even though this incident (the stinging itself) did occur, father had then beat a very hasty retreat into the confine of our apartment suite rather than drum about in the lobby of The New Marquis while his ass was gettin' severely stung by the angry wasp brotherhood. So, I cannot recollect a lady renter who witnessed father's antics. Blame Roy. And know this. Father's undershorts were exactly as I described them. And—sorry, I forgot—before he'd felt the wasps' anger father had been wearin' more than his underpants, and the slacks that he rolled down in the ensuing melee. Please accept my sincere and fervent apology if I gave you a "bum" impression.

Going further back in time now, second, I have never ejected a stream of urine into an empty beer bottle, and then proceeded to dress the product for a thirsty, working man's consumption. Blame Roy.

Third, I have never once hung about to do mortal battle with any man in the hope of seizing his full-grown gorilla-size wife, on account of his unwillingness to hand me his wallet. Nor have I ever too-too-too seriously thought of confiscating some other fellow's wife, for any reason. I'm a nice boy. Sort of.

Fourth. Besides those stirring revelations, not once had I ever left for school dragging toilet tissue, discolored or otherwise, on the ground behind me. What? I HEAR you! What a lofty load of kooky crap! I heartily agree. But, c'mon. By now, the healthy red glow of excitement deposited on your cheeks by my toilet tissue tale, etc., must have receded a trifle. So! MY ADVICE: lie wide awake, on the tender tips of your toes—'cause there is bound to be more of Roy's finest B.S. to come—in the far, far, far future. Relax!

Other Insignificant Bogus Claims

Listen up my friends, because here's

Item 1. Fish are just fish. At no time in my young life did I ponder the question of whether fish go to school, go to school because we humans must. No true fisherman thinks about such nonsense.

2. Concerning googol. I don't know exactly how many sheets of paper I used up in my stubborn attempt to corner googol. Please forgive me.

In addition, my comment that I would not eat or speak is a creation. Any hunter knows he must eat. And every boy must speak. Oh! I almost forgot. Raimo had no preference for the comic strip *Archie*. Nevermind. I do know *Tarzan* was a favorite of his. By far it was.

A-L-S-O: Consider those angry wasps whose hive I'd demolished. An arrogant, nasty act, was it not? Anyhow. Those fellows pierced my tender flesh with their sharp incisors but a mere three or four times! Ha ha!

3. The rubber dinghy that belonged to the neighbors' kids from the car wash beside us, in Campbell River. Actually, it's very probable sis did not yank the plug on the inflatable boat, with the intention of permanently resigning it to the salty underwater realm. And if she did not (note that my memory has badly faded from my coconut), this would naturally explain the reappearance of the dinghy a mile up the beach, high and dry.

You see, in such case, the powerful to-and-fro motion of the ocean waves will have pushed aside some of the large, heavy stones sis and I delightedly, with the enthusiasm of the children we were then, had piled on the raft until it had sunk to the shallow bottom of the briny nearshore, leaving the outbound high tide to later completely free the air bag and draw the floating rubber, still full of air, out to sea. Subsequently, the next morning's inbound low tide would have been the cause of the dinghy's grounding on the farther shore. Blast it! Do you always insist upon a logical explanation for everything? No comment!

A-N-D. The parking lot where our neighbor had his fearsome fit—was—on reconsideration, notably less than *a score of feet above the low-water mark*—the height differential that I gave you.

Curse the brainless breakwater. The "massive three-foot-thick" logs that formed it were of various thicknesses; most were two feet in diameter, or less. Fancy that.

4. Blackbeard's Grave. The precise monetary gain I'd discovered in the grass surrounding Lavers' trash bin is unclear to me. However, I will say that it was significantly less than two dollars and forty-nine cents, the amount I stated. As for the empty M.J.B. coffee tin I used to store my wealth, the tin father had modified to become a stash can, I believe father gave myself this tin during our tenure in the Portland Mobile Home and Trailer Court. Father's alterations to the tin were as I described.

What about the "rusting giant wreck" of a ship visible a couple of miles down the shoreline? You mean that sunken flunky? Little more than a bird's cuss from our neighborhood that was. Not one inch more.

5. Tiger the cat, and the busted lamp. There was no light bulb in a shade, I broke, much less a lamp shattered into fourteen shards. There was a cat, though, and his name was Tiger. And he'd had his rear end stuck right in my nose! So. Did I swear then? Um. I dunno. I do know that I did not accidently bite my tongue. With the exception of Raimo who did not attend the nighttime gathering, he having chosen to stay in his bed then, this incident, except for that described here, is true.

6. How old was Helen when she'd received the red trike from our parents for Christmas? Six? No. I think she was three months shy of it. And from what I wrote, you might have guessed that I'm not sure as to when, exactly, it was that our parents had purchased the secluded property near Hedley? It may have been as early as '57, but the likelihood, I feel, is that it was in '58. And I now believe our family maintained its residence in the little cabin father had built, twice. If I'm correct, in the interim we lived at Lanark Street, the house on Lanark having been bought prior to our second exodus from Hedley. I know that we spent one Christmas in our wilderness abode, counter to my narrative—perhaps two. To the best of my knowledge we left Hedley for Vancouver in early spring of 1960, just as I said. As concerns our time in Hedley, modern living it was not, though we eventually hooked up to the convenience of electricity; prior to that and after it we may have had here a battery-powered radio, like the poor castaways on *Gilligan's Island* reruns. No TV? I'm not s-u-r-e, but for a good long while certainly no electro-juice with which to operate it.

7. A man long since forgotten by his country. A dead man with no known first name, only a last. A man of mystery. Peterskoff. The surname may actually have been spelled differently, perhaps Petreskoff, Peterskov or Petreskov. I don't know because all known government-held records were, as best I can gather, systematically destroyed (by which side—capitalist or communist—I don't know) in either the Russian Revolution of 1917 or in the civil war era that gripped and shook the country from 1918-'21. Insofar as the Kellosalmi family of that time goes, it appears that not all of my father's siblings were still living in the family's home in Kotka when my dad was a stone-dropping five-year-old growing up. The two older boys—young men then, were living elsewhere.

8. I believe father's 1957 Buick sedan may have been sold or abandoned ("father's pride and joy"?) in Montreal right before our family boarded the big boat to cross the big pond. Yes, I am skeptical that this car mysteriously reappeared on our lawn at Lanark Street after our return from Finland, though I could be very wrong. I am equally doubtful of my stated age for that car given that it was, as mentioned, weathered and badly rusted. And the flight from Finland to Vancouver didn't happen without a couple of stops, to refuel.

Lanark Street. What about it? Well, before Lanark there was life on Adanac Street in that very same city by the sea. Not for me, though. I was born later and you knew that. Was it at Lanark I learned to walk? I believe so, and I believe I may have gained that necessary capability sooner than the approximately nineteen months of age my narrative suggests that my first steps were taken.

9. Regarding my account of events from page 89 to 94. In likelihood, the Vancouver bank where I had briefly become isolated from mother by the revolving door was located closer to our neighborhood, rather than in downtown. As well, this incident and what I depicted as having followed it (mother's disclosure to me, of human mortality by aging), may not have occurred in turn, nor do I know the true order these events occurred in time. Add to this, the fact ridged potato chips were not available until later times. But. I do remember myself as a three-year-old boy, munching on potato chips that had been, as I said, slightly burnt along the edges, while I had sat with mother, facing an old man on a city bus. As for the old man's nose, I do not recollect his nose was at all crooked. But. And but but but.

10. Hiccup. Me again. Seems we didn't move directly from Lanark Street to the Elm in "sunny" Richmond, after all. Nope. I believe that my parents sold our house on Lanark in '63 after which we spent months at two local motels, the

Deluxe Motel, and the Lucky Strike. We spent Xmas of '63 in the Lucky Strike. Pirate's honor!

11. The beginning of my first grade in school. Never did I seriously consider jumping out of the half-open window of a moving school bus in a desperate, last-minute attempt to evade the restrictive atmosphere of a classroom. Too bad.

Having made it safely to school, not once did I wonder whether my desk there was meant to hold bubble gum. Not once did I wonder whether a pencil sharpener is powered by a bunch of eager, hungry termites, either. In either case, I wasn't that stupid. Too bad.

12. Now, the railway tracks. Honestly, I can't remember whether there was a rail line in my neighborhood. Though, there was an electrical transmission line snaking through the neighborhood, and near my school Samuel Brighouse, a roadside ditch beneath this line, to lead me toward home. Ah home! Back to mommy and delicious donuts! Back to TV cartoons! And back to toys! Back to my own soft, wonderfully comfortable bed, for my daily nap. Yawn.

13. Let me clear one thing up. Subject? My fairly private territory as given earlier. My bed.

Perhaps contrary to your impression of me (if so, it was planted in your bean by my highly selective taste in a bedmate), I am not a bit against sharing my berth with my to-be-chosen (who is she, where is she?) ladylove. Yes. I know. What donkey drivel I be made of! I'm perfectly horrible, *aren't* I?

14. Earplugs. In the immediate aftermath of a stone fight with the X boy, it certainly did not dawn on me that earplugs would have been a nice gift for myself to have received from Santa, for Noel. Drat no! I've always liked toys, not earplugs.

15. The name pronounced Lolly (actual Finnish spelling is Lalli) is real, but the rest of Santa's known elves possessed more-Finnish-sounding names that do not even remotely resemble those I invented in this book. Pity.

16. I'm incredibly moronic at times. You know that. W-h-a-t? You don't? Really? Well, try this for breakfast! I'm so dumb that, once, in my childhood innocence it was, I almost did wonder whether a sometimes difficult-to-understand thing like a girl's bean might suddenly blow apart from a simple cause such as overwhelming embarrassment. A serious internal matter for any girl to be abashed it be, a dilemma which, rightly, should be life-threatening. Yes, I almost did wonder this. A-L-M-O-S-T. But not Q-U-I-T-E.

17. Fresh breath time. Mr. James Bond. I never wondered whether he used mouthwash to prevent his breath from developing an unpleasant odor. That's right. Never. Consequently, the question of what brand of such he might have used, never crossed my mind. Plus. I never strove to imitate his walk. Not even for girls. I had more-important things to worry about. The end. No! Wait! Did James wear a hairpiece, or sport dentures? No. Did he ever use skunk spray on crooks? Of course not. He was James Bond—two eggs plus number seven!

But—if no one took me to the cinema, where did I, as a seven-year-old, view J.B. movies? Answer: I didn't, not until years later, on TV.

Scary stuff on the tube these days. Do I recollect that we had a TV in Campbell River? Maybe we did but I never got a chance to watch cartoons—if we did.

Will an ostrich in Africa bury its head in the sand when a hungry lion is about to make a meal of the bird? Answer: No.

Back to, um, school. In Campbell River I'd attended another primary school, for a short month (I think it was), before I'd enrolled at Cedar Elementary. I just can't remember the name of that other institution. Heck! It was grade one still. Who cares? Savvy that? Suck on this! My fierce fight with googol occurred in that motel I mentioned, whatever its name was. While we lived in the motel I attended the "nameless" school.

18. San Diego. 3850 Demus Street. I wasn't half as pathetic as you think. I wasn't, because-because-because I was just not so farty a kid as I first led you to believe. Really! I wasn't. And. I wasn't half as awful as you fear, either. With father's handmade slingshot, j-u-s-t once-upon-a-time it was, I plastered the area to one side of my neighbors' window with my berries, not the entire side wall of their house. Quit blaming me! Will you?

The cat that Raimo briefly animated to F.O. status with his air gun. That cat might've belonged to the folks across the street; they had a cat but it may not have been gray, rather, it could've been black with a white chest.

The nonexistent air conditioner. I believe we may have had one and if we did, to save money, we never used it. Mumble bumble!

Ooo-ooo. What about the banana tree? I now suspect that that it was not. But at least it was a tree. Ooo-ooo-ooo.

Dollars no, but sand dollars at La Jolla's beachfront? I do-do-do not think so now; sand dollars *are* found on sandy marine beaches *but* La Jolla is rock. Don't worry. I did find a sand dollar on one of the beautiful sun-drenched beaches in the San Diego area; don't ask me which one 'cause I'd have to guess. It's been a long time.

Our camping trip in August of '67. The elevation of the lake with the dead fish and cow dung on the beach. I forget. But—I'm still thinking and I'm starting to think that was a lake on a plateau overlooking the desert, not as high in altitude as I first remembered.

19. Mrs. Miller's spelling bee. Who knows what was happening in my mind at the time? I do. And I don't recall any wild imaginings involving a gun-toting confrontation, a duel or telepathic messaging. Reason? I was too busy trying to ensure my survival, by performance, in the spelling contest then. The same can be said for Mrs. Posterick's spelling bee two years previous.

20. The other J.B. Jerry Bursack. His surname may actually be spelled a bit differently: the last letter could be an h instead of a k.

Our relic trailer in Portland, Ore. On s-e-r-i-o-u-s afterthought, we had at least one very small bathroom window, maybe even two, in our bathroom before father got busy with his tools. Father may have merely enlarged a possible preexisting second window. No window? Unlikely. Bubble that.

About the conversation involving the old man who sold his bike to me. This contains fiction as supplementation, but the bulk of this chat did take place.

The fight-hungry Steve who attended Columbia Elementary. Was it a "mighty right" from Cory that toppled Steve's claim to boxing glory? Dunno that. Maybe it was a mighty left, instead.

The real wild-west days. When was the last surviving grizzly bear sighted in the State of Oregon? Take a guess. That'll do.

Update: April 3, 2013: And—by the way, I am no longer defenseless when it comes to simple do-it-yourself projects—I've learned something in the last seven years!

21. Toes with personalities. C'mon!

This book is based on this writer's recollection which is not infallible: some events may have occurred sooner or later than I depicted.

Update: April 3, 2013: The author is still single, and, as always, avidly looking to capture a woman's heart. Could it be *yours*?

P.S. But please don't expect him to show up on your doorstep as a panting travel-beat pedestrian, because he now steers a beautiful car. Not just his legs. Okay-okay. The car is NOT quite the Batmobile, but the only other thing still missing is the beautiful girl. Oh! One other thing. Remember—he's terribly timid. Still. So, remember to use kid gloves when you kiss him!